Recentering the World

Recentering the World recovers a richly contextual, detailed history of Western-imposed legal structures in China, as well as engagements with international law by Chinese officials, jurists, and citizens. Beginning in the Late Qing era, it shows how international law functioned as a channel for power relations, techniques of economic domination, and novel forms of resistance. The book also radically diversifies traditionally Eurocentric accounts of modern international law's origins, demonstrating how, by the mid twentieth century, Chinese jurists had made major contributions to international organizations and the United Nations system, the international judiciary, the laws of armed conflict, and more. Drawing on extensive archival research, this book is a valuable guide to China's often conflicted role in international law, its reception and contention of concepts of sovereignty, property, obligation, and autonomy, and its gradual move from the "periphery" to a shared spot at the "center" of global legal order.

Ryan Martínez Mitchell is an assistant professor at the Faculty of Law of the Chinese University of Hong Kong. He holds a JD from Harvard Law School and a PhD in Law from Yale University. His scholarship on China and international law has appeared in a number of leading scholarly journals.

Law in Context

Since 1970, the Law in Context series has been at the forefront of a movement to broaden the study of law. The series is a vehicle for the publication of innovative monographs and texts that treat law and legal phenomena critically in their cultural, social, political, technological, environmental and economic contexts. A contextual approach involves treating legal subjects broadly, using materials from other humanities and social sciences, and from any other discipline that helps to explain the operation in practice of the particular legal field or legal phenomena under investigation. It is intended that this orientation is at once more stimulating and more revealing than the bare exposition of legal rules. The series includes original research monographs, coursebooks and textbooks that foreground contextual approaches and methods. The series includes and welcomes books on the study of law in all its contexts, including domestic legal systems, European and international law, transnational and global legal processes, and comparative law.

Books in the Series

Acosta: *The National versus the Foreigner in South America: 200 Years of Migration and Citizenship Law*
Ali: *Modern Challenges to Islamic Law*
Alyagon Darr: *Plausible Crime Stories: The Legal History of Sexual Offences in Mandate Palestine*
Anderson, Schum & Twining: *Analysis of Evidence, 2nd Edition*
Ashworth: *Sentencing and Criminal Justice, 6th Edition*
Barton & Douglas: *Law and Parenthood*
Baxi, McCrudden & Paliwala: *Law's Ethical, Global and Theoretical Contexts: Essays in Honour of William Twining*
Beecher-Monas: *Evaluating Scientific Evidence: An Interdisciplinary Framework for Intellectual Due Process*
Bell: *French Legal Cultures*

Bercusson: *European Labour Law, 2nd Edition*
Birkinshaw: *European Public Law*
Birkinshaw: *Freedom of Information: The Law, the Practice and the Ideal, 4th Edition*
Blick: *Electrified Democracy: The Internet and the United Kingdom Parliament in History*
Broderick & Ferri: *International and European Disability Law and Policy: Text, Cases and Materials*
Brownsword & Goodwin: *Law and the Technologies of the Twenty-First Century: Text and Materials*
Cane & Goudkamp: *Atiyah's Accidents, Compensation and the Law, 9th Edition*
Clarke: *Principles of Property Law*
Clarke & Kohler: *Property Law: Commentary and Materials*
Collins: *The Law of Contract, 4th Edition*
Collins, Ewing & McColgan: *Labour Law, 2nd Edition*
Cowan: *Housing Law and Policy*
Cranston: *Commercial Law from the Nineteenth Century: Law as Backcloth*
Cranston: *Legal Foundations of the Welfare State*
Darian-Smith: *Laws and Societies in Global Contexts: Contemporary Approaches*
Dauvergne: *Making People Illegal: What Globalisation Means for Immigration and Law*
David: *Kinship, Law and Politics: An Anatomy of Belonging*
Davies: *Perspectives on Labour Law, 2nd Edition*
Dembour: *Who Believes in Human Rights?: Reflections on the European Convention*
de Sousa Santos: *Toward a New Legal Common Sense: Law, Globalization, and Emancipation*
Diduck: *Law's Families*
Dupret: *Positive Law from the Muslim World*
Emon: *Jurisdictional Exceptionalisms: Islamic Law, International Law, and Parental Child Abduction*
Estella: *Legal Foundations of EU Economic Governance*
Fortin: *Children's Rights and the Developing Law, 3rd Edition*
Garnsey: *The Justice of Visual Art: Creative State-Building in Times of Political Transition*
Garton, Probert & Bean: *Moffat's Trusts Law: Text and Materials, 7th Edition*
Ghai & Woodman: *Practising Self-Government: A Comparative Study of Autonomous Regions*
Glover-Thomas: *Reconstructing Mental Health Law and Policy*
Gobert & Punch: *Rethinking Corporate Crime*
Goldman: *Globalisation and the Western Legal Tradition: Recurring Patterns of Law and Authority*
Haack: *Evidence Matters: Science, Proof, and Truth in the Law*
Harlow & Rawlings: *Law and Administration, 4th Edition*
Harris: *An Introduction to Law, 8th Edition*
Harris, Campbell & Halson: *Remedies in Contract and Tort, 2nd Edition*
Harvey: *Seeking Asylum in the UK: Problems and Prospects*
Herring: *Law and the Relational Self*
Hervey & McHale: *European Union Health Law: Themes and Implications*
Hervey & McHale: *Health Law and the European Union*

Holder & Lee: *Environmental Protection, Law and Policy: Text and Materials, 2nd Edition*
Jackson & Summers: *The Internationalisation of Criminal Evidence: Beyond the Common Law and Civil Law Traditions*
Kostakopoulou: *The Future Governance of Citizenship*
Kreiczer-Levy *Destabilized Property: Property Law in the Sharing Economy*
Kubal: *Immigration and Refugee Law in Russia: Socio-Legal Perspectives*
Lewis: *Choice and the Legal Order: Rising above Politics*
Likosky: *Law, Infrastructure and Human Rights*
Likosky: *Transnational Legal Processes: Globalisation and Power Disparities*
Lixinski: *Legalized Identities*
Loughnan: *Self, Others and the State: Relations of Criminal Responsibility*
Lunney: *A History of Australian Tort Law 1901–1945: England's Obedient Servant?*
Maughan & Webb: *Lawyering Skills and the Legal Process, 2nd Edition*
McGaughey: *Principles of Enterprise Law*
McGlynn: *Families and the European Union: Law, Politics and Pluralism*
Mertens: *A Philosophical Introduction to Human Rights*
Moffat: *Trusts Law: Text and Materials*
Monti: *EC Competition Law*
Morgan: *Contract Law Minimalism: A Formalist Restatement of Commercial Contract Law*
Morgan & Yeung: *An Introduction to Law and Regulation: Text and Materials*
Nash: *British Islam and English Law: A Classical Pluralist Perspective*
Nicola & Davies: *EU Law Stories: Contextual and Critical Histories of European Jurisprudence*
Norrie: *Crime, Reason and History: A Critical Introduction to Criminal Law, 3rd Edition*
O'Dair: *Legal Ethics: Text and Materials*
Oliver: *Common Values and the Public–Private Divide*
Oliver & Drewry: *The Law and Parliament*
Palmer & Roberts: *Dispute Processes: ADR and the Primary Forms of Decision-Making, 1st Edition*
Palmer & Roberts: *Dispute Processes: ADR and the Primary Forms of Decision-Making, 3rd Edition*
Picciotto: *International Business Taxation*
Probert: *The Changing Legal Regulation of Cohabitation, 1600–2010: From Fornicators to Family, 1600–2010*
Radi: *Rules and Practices of International Investment Law and Arbitration*
Reed: *Internet Law: Text and Materials*
Richardson: *Law, Process and Custody*
Roberts & Palmer: *Dispute Processes: ADR and the Primary Forms of Decision-Making, 2nd Edition*
Rowbottom: *Democracy Distorted: Wealth, Influence and Democratic Politics*
Sauter: *Public Services in EU Law*
Scott & Black: *Cranston's Consumers and the Law*
Seneviratne: *Ombudsmen: Public Services and Administrative Justice*

Seppänen: *Ideological Conflict and the Rule of Law in Contemporary China: Useful Paradoxes*
Siems: *Comparative Law, 3rd Edition*
Stapleton: *Product Liability*
Stewart: *Gender, Law and Justice in a Global Market*
Tamanaha: *Law as a Means to an End: Threat to the Rule of Law*
Tuori: *Properties of Law: Modern Law and After*
Turpin & Tomkins: *British Government and the Constitution: Text and Materials, 7th Edition*
Twining: *General Jurisprudence: Understanding Law from a Global Perspective*
Twining: *Globalisation and Legal Theory*
Twining: *Human Rights, Southern Voices: Francis Deng, Abdullahi An-Na'im, Yash Ghai and Upendra Baxi*
Twining: *Jurist in Context: A Memoir*
Twining: *Karl Llewellyn and the Realist Movement, 2nd Edition*
Twining: *Rethinking Evidence: Exploratory Essays, 2nd Edition*
Twining & Miers: *How to Do Things with Rules, 5th Edition*
Wan: *Film and Constitutional Controversy*
Ward: *A Critical Introduction to European Law, 3rd Edition*
Ward: *Law, Text, Terror*
Ward: *Shakespeare and Legal Imagination*
Wells & Quick: *Lacey, Wells and Quick: Reconstructing Criminal Law: Text and Materials, 4th Edition*
Zander: *Cases and Materials on the English Legal System, 10th Edition*
Zander: *The Law-Making Process, 6th Edition*

International Journal of Law in Context: A Global Forum for Interdisciplinary Legal Studies

The *International Journal of Law in Context* is the companion journal to the Law in Context book series and provides a forum for interdisciplinary legal studies and offers intellectual space for ground-breaking critical research. It publishes contextual work about law and its relationship with other disciplines including but not limited to science, literature, humanities, philosophy, sociology, psychology, ethics, history and geography. More information about the journal and how to submit an article can be found at http://journals.cambridge.org/ijc

Recentering the World

China and the Transformation of International Law

RYAN MARTÍNEZ MITCHELL
The Chinese University of Hong Kong

CAMBRIDGE
UNIVERSITY PRESS

CAMBRIDGE
UNIVERSITY PRESS

Shaftesbury Road, Cambridge CB2 8BS, United Kingdom

One Liberty Plaza, 20th Floor, New York, NY 10006, USA

477 Williamstown Road, Port Melbourne, VIC 3207, Australia

314–321, 3rd Floor, Plot 3, Splendor Forum, Jasola District Centre, New Delhi – 110025, India

103 Penang Road, #05–06/07, Visioncrest Commercial, Singapore 238467

Cambridge University Press is part of Cambridge University Press & Assessment, a department of the University of Cambridge.

We share the University's mission to contribute to society through the pursuit of education, learning and research at the highest international levels of excellence.

www.cambridge.org
Information on this title: www.cambridge.org/9781108498968

DOI: 10.1017/9781108690157

First published 2023

A catalogue record for this publication is available from the British Library.

ISBN 978-1-108-49896-8 Hardback

人君中天下而立，则正身以为四方之标准 ... 若就君德论，则德到这处，极至而无以加。

The lord of men centers the world around him and rectifies himself to provide a standard for all four directions . . . As for the ruler's virtue, this signifies that when virtue has reached this stage it is at its utmost, and nothing can be added.

Chen Chun 陳淳, *North Stream's Glossary of Scholarly Terms* 北溪字義, c. 1217

巴西议员在会曾有言日: 今知天下果无公理 ... 请俟第三次会诸君再视巴西是否强国、 弱国、 大国、 小国。臣闻其说, 心窃壮之。

The Brazilian delegate said at one point: "Now I realize that there is after all no just principle under Heaven . . . Please wait until the Third Hague Conference, gentlemen, and see whether Brazil is a strong country or a weak one, a large country or a small one." As I listened to his comments, I privately felt a sense of grand resolve.

Lu Zhengxiang 陸徵祥, Memorial to the Qing Court regarding the Second Hague Conference of 1907, January 16, 1908

依國際組織以求世界永久和平，可說是中華民國國民一致的外交原則。

The pursuit of perpetual peace in the world by means of an international organization can be considered the foreign policy that is the consensus of the whole Chinese citizenry.

Zhou Gengsheng 周鯁生, "Xianfa Zhong de Waijiao Yuanze 憲法中的外交原則" [Principles of Diplomacy in the Constitution], *Zhongyang Ribao* 中央日报, December 28, 1946

Contents

Acknowledgments

This book was the product of several years of research and writing, during the course of which I received various forms of support and assistance. For their supervision of the original PhD thesis in which this account originated, I would like to thank Paul Kahn, Tony Kronman, and David Grewal. For extensive earlier guidance on related topics, I would like to thank William Alford. For valuable comments and feedback on sections of the manuscript, I would like to thank Jeffrey Wasserstrom, Samuli Seppänen, and anonymous reviewers of the *Asian Journal of International Law*, in which a version of Chapter 5 was previously published, as well as the journal *Humanity: An International Journal of Human Rights, Humanitarianism, and Development*, in which an article featuring discussions closely related to Chapter 9 and the Conclusion is forthcoming. For their helpful research assistance at various stages, I would like to thank Huang Xinyu, Wang Yiqiao, Lucas Brang, Luca Bonadiman, and Wang Qian (Frances). I thank Du Weihua, Tang Qihua, Egas Bender de Moniz Bandeira, and David Porter for timely responses to factual queries. I would also like to thank the Research Grants Council of Hong Kong and its reviewers for their support of my Early Career Scheme project on "The Development and Influence of Chinese Theories of Sovereignty" (Project 2191202, Reference No. 24603119), which provided a foundation for this book's completion. Lastly, I would like to thank all of the members of my family, particularly my father, James Lee Mitchell, who departed as this book neared completion, and my daughter Xingyuan, who arrived *ex caelo*.

Archives and Databases Consulted

Archives of China's Imperial Maritime Customs
British Cabinet Papers (CAB)
British Foreign Affairs Office Archives (FO)
Chou Ban Yi Wu Shi Mo (via Shu Tong Wen Guji Shujuku) (CBYWSM)
Dacheng Guzhi Dui
Foreign Relations of the United States Series (FRUS)
Guoshiguan (GSG)
Hongse Wenxian Archive
Japanese Foreign Ministry Archives
Kuomintang Party Archives
League of Nations Archive (LON)
Ming Shi (via Shu Tong Wen Guji Shujuku)
Neige Daku Dang'an
PCIJ/ICJ Judgment Database
Qing Dynasty Imperial Examinations Collection (via Shu Tong Wen Guji Shujuku)
Qing Shi Lu (via Shu Tong Wen Guji Shujuku) (QSL)
Quanguo Baokan Suoyin (CNBKSY)
UN Documents Archive (UNDOC)
Waijiao Bumen Dang'an (WJDA)
Wellington Koo Archives
Wilson Center Digital Archive
Yuan Shikai Quanji Shujuku (YSQS)
Zhongguo Lishi Wenxian Zongku

Treaties, Agreements, and Legislation

Cases

Convention on the Rights of the Child (CRC), November 20, 1989, United Nations, Treaty Series, vol. 1577, p. 3. 282

The Pious Fund of the Californias, United States v. *Mexico*, Award (1902) IX RIAA 1, ICGJ 409 (PCA 1902). 255

The SS "Wimbledon," United Kingdom and others v. *Germany*, Judgment (1923) PCIJ Series A no 1. 148, 265

Status of Eastern Carelia, Advisory opinion, PCIJ Series B no 5. 265

Questions Relating to Settlers of German Origin in Poland, Advisory Opinion, (1923) PCIJ Series B no 6. 265

Denunciation of the Treaty of November 2nd 1865 between China and Belgium, Belgium v. *China*, Order (1927) PCIJ Series A no 8. 267

Radio Corporation of America v. *the National Government of the Republic of China*. Award of the Tribunal of April 13, 1935. PCA Case no. 1934-01. 172, 271

Corfu Channel, United Kingdom v. *Albania*, Order, Compensation Due from Albania to the United Kingdom: Appointment of Expert (1949) ICJ Rep 237. 200, 267, 268

Separate Opinion of Vice-President Wellington Koo, *Barcelona Traction, Light and Power Company, Limited (Belgium* v. *Spain)*, Judgment of July 24, 1964 on Preliminary Objections, ICJ Reports 1964, pp. 51–64. 279

Dissenting Opinion of Vice-President Wellington Koo, *South West Africa (Liberia* v. *South Africa; Ethiopia* v. *South Africa)*, Second Phase, Judgment of July 18, 1966, ICJ Reports 1966, pp. 216–238. 279

Barcelona Traction, Light and Power Company, Limited (New Application: 1962) (Belgium v. *Spain)*, Second Phase, Judgment of February 5, 1970, ICJ Reports 1970, p. 3. 279

Nuclear Tests Case (Australia v. *France)*, Judgment of December 20, 1974. ICJ Reports 1974, p. 253. 285

Military and Paramilitary Activities in and against Nicaragua (Nicaragua v. *United States of America)*, Judgement of November 26, 1984. ICJ Reports 1984, p. 392. 285

Introduction

"In the Nineteenth Century, There Was No International Law"

This book seeks to clarify the process by which international law ideas became objects of both reception and contention by officials, diplomats, jurists, and intellectuals in Chinese society. It also explores how this reception history intertwined, often in ways now obscure or forgotten, with changes to the international law profession at the global level. An additional aim will be to challenge certain prevalent notions about the history of international law in general.

Such notions include: 1) that the late nineteenth- to mid twentieth-century turn to increasingly formal international legal organization, legislation, and institution-building was a kind of natural, path-dependent evolution of the European law of nations as it existed at the beginning of that period; (2) that "peripheral" states were only indirectly connected to the development of legal norms during this era of transformations; and (3) that China and other non-Western states' emphasis upon articulating their own "sovereign" rights during and after decolonization has represented a rejection of international law as such, rather than a reappropriation.[1] In reality, as Georges Abi-Saab wrote of the latter process, it was precisely bound up with the "transformation of very large parts of the globe, mostly in Africa and Asia, from *objects* to *subjects* of international law."[2]

A conceptual history of international legal order as conceived in and in relation to China, like the one undertaken in this book, must place the family of concepts and arguments it comprises into their own discursive, social, and also material contexts.[3] From the beginning, the story of China's reception of international law was also the story of the Chinese state's and society's own incorporation into new, rapidly transforming global power structures. China was very much still at the heart of its own conceptual world order when, in 1776, the Qianlong emperor ordered officials to ensure that merchants pay back delinquent debts to the Western foreigners at Canton because "as these *yi* traders ventured over so many seas to get here in search of profit, we must treat them fairly and send their ships back laden with goods: only thus would we comport with China's great stately propriety" (*fang de zhonghua da ti* 方得中華大體).[4]

At just the same time in Britain, the first readers of Adam Smith's *The Wealth of Nations* were encountering his view that China had, "even long before [Marco Polo's] time, acquired that full complement of riches which the nature of its laws and institutions permits it to acquire." For Smith, despite the wealth, population, and order so long admired by European intellectuals, China's failure to realize the benefit of liberal foreign trade had long left it "stationary"; with the result that "the greater part of Europe being in an improving state… China seems to be standing still."[5] This premise, with its close linkage between civilizational progress and the continuous outward expansion of economic relations, would in coming decades grow ever more influential. By the mid nineteenth century, as Qianlong's successors sought to stem mounting foreign encroachments with continued offers of magnanimity from the imperial center, the notion had fully coalesced among British and other foreign merchants that China needed to be "opened" and its economy more fully integrated into the global network of European-centered trade.

From the First Opium War of 1839–1842, that project of opening was well entrenched. As the preamble to the 1982 Constitution of the People's Republic of China would later put it, "After 1840, feudal China was gradually turned into a semi-colonial and semi-feudal country."[6] Much of China's subsequent law and politics has been premised on this notion that the country's "modern" history began at this point, and in direct response to Western economic imperialism. Certainly, at this point, China was indeed gradually incorporated as a "periphery" into systemically unequal economic relations, backed by direct and indirect forms of coercion that reinforced foreign capitals' dominance in productivity, trading agency, and financial capacity.[7]

At the same time, modern Chinese legal and political thought emerged in a polity whose market was, in many ways, at the very forefront rather than the periphery of global capitalist expansion. While constructed as the quintessential "backward" state actor, it was also treated as a workshop for the latest projects of avant-garde governance, from cooperative institution-building to (imposed) multilateral projects of free trade promotion and the "opening" of local markets. Both frontier and experimental laboratory, there are few subject/objects of international law that could better exemplify a "simultaneity of the non-simultaneous" (*Gleichzeitigkeit der Ungleichzeitigen*) in legal history than did China from the mid nineteenth to mid twentieth centuries.[8]

This book builds upon growing scholarly attention to both the histor(ies) of international law[9] and China's specific legal interactions and experiences.[10] As noted, international law did not come to China as some kind of ready-made universal rulebook – despite the occasional pretensions to this effect by Western officials and, on occasion, even their Chinese interlocutors. Instead, the global professional community that would elucidate and seek to codify this "gentle civilizer of nations" in its modern form was itself first taking shape precisely during the mid to late nineteenth-century period when Western global capitalist expansion finally penetrated China's theretofore largely "closed" political and economic space. The rapid imposition of regulatory structures in areas ranging from war to navigation to diplomacy is best understood against this context. Rather than unbidden flashes of moral genius in the minds of men who happened to be elite jurists of expanding commercial empires, the new ideas of global order were very much "the scholarly manifestation of a partisan political project, the civilizing mission."[11]

That notion, of international legal order as a "civilizing" project, was applied to China just as much as to more notionally "savage" zones; indeed, in some respects, China's supposed "half-civilized" status made it a more important target for "civilizing" legal innovations. Its vast existing and even vaster potential market, as noted previously, also served as a continuous draw for new international agreements and legal regimes of varying degrees of formality intended to ensure that civilization, trade, and Christianity could flourish in tandem on soil once secluded by isolationist policies. It is seldom appreciated the degree to which many of the most dominant and influential voices in Western international law during the period under consideration, including nineteenth-century figures such as Johann Caspar Bluntschli and Fyodor Fyodorovich Martens but also more recent heroes of the "invisible college," constructed ideas as to international law's content and potential in part via an Orientalizing gaze for which China – as the most significant state to be "almost" fit for membership in the club of the civilized – had a special status, giving rise to elaborate new justifications for domination. As we will see, from their very earliest encounters with such notions and their advocates, many Chinese interlocutors were well aware of the role of international legal argument in the procurement of Western geopolitical/commercial interests.

A special concern for international legal history in general is the question of "how to write the history of international law in a way that does not simply subsume the non-European periphery into an essentially European narrative of progress."[12] This book seeks to make the voices of Chinese interlocutors with international legal order in the period under consideration more fully available to today's readers, in part to underscore the profound contingency of international legal order as it has subsequently developed.[13] It is indeed the case that "the limits of our imagination are [the] product of a history that may have gone another way."[14] The failed or stymied projects of reform examined in this book, as much as those that succeeded, may illuminate aspects of international law that remain relevant to its current function and structure. This is the case even if, as we will see to be the case, China today more often stands for the status quo of international rules and institutions than for any effort toward their radical revision.

Synopsis

One aspect of general international legal history that this book helps explore is the function of *spatial appropriation* as a driving force in international law's development over time.[15] Not only cynical agents of expanding empires, but also many "progressive" international jurists in the West, and even avowed pacifists, saw the extension of this legal order to ever more new spaces, including China, other Asian states, and the vast African interior, as something akin to a manifest destiny for their field. The quintessential experience of international law as an "object," to employ Abi-Saab's dichotomy, was for a state to be rendered an "empty" space available for the application of imposed regulatory regimes. This was precisely China's experience after the coerced opening of its ports to foreign traders by the Treaty of Nanjing and in other bilateral "unequal treaties," but much more so in the aftermath of the multilateral 1860 Convention of Beijing. From then on, many new ideas concerning the rights and personality of states, freedom of trade, global governance, the use of force, and territorial integrity, among others, were tested in a region where outright conquest was usually less profitable than indirect domination.[16]

Finally, a key narrative presented throughout the book will be how Western-derived international legal structures and ideas came to operate as a new politico-legal grammar for public discourse across, and among, East Asian states and peoples. Although local and foreign intellectuals at times found (and, some argued, exaggerated) intriguing parallels between features of the ancient Chinese state system prior to unification and the international law of the West, few seriously denied that the latter was in most respects experienced as an imposed, unfamiliar order. That nonfamiliarity was generative of new ways of describing not only interstate relations, but also the internal character of states. Most fatefully of all, by the turn of the twentieth century, the concept of "sovereignty," newly associated with the ancient two-character phrase *zhuquan* 主權, had already become something like the foundational norm of public law, domestic and international, throughout East Asia. This notion's modern content was in large part transmitted as part of a larger lexicon of public law notions, and shaped by diplomatic and commercial interactions, especially through the medium of a Meiji Japan aspiring to regional hegemony.

Reflecting this inextricable connection between modern China's international legal history and the notion of sovereignty, this book also builds on, and in some cases challenges, recent studies of the "genealogy of sovereignty in China,"[17] illustrating that modern sovereignty discourse has always been very closely tied to notions about an underlying world order, and often initiatives to reform that order. The role of these diverse origins in the early development of modern Chinese notions of sovereignty and world order will be a particular focus of the early part of this book's narrative. Importantly, throughout the period covered by the first of this book's first three chapters, it was not "sovereignty," but rather the Chinese concept of *guoti* 國體 – loosely translatable depending on context as "state form" or "stateliness" – that served as the dominant metric for evaluating legal interactions. Only gradually did *guojia zhuquan*/state sovereignty come to serve as a "basic concept"/*Grundbegriff* of legal and political discourse.

Meanwhile, as we will also see, *guoti* itself was interpeted in different ways by different actors, and as early as the 1850s was invoked by some officials in the name of territorial control or autonomy over economic policy, rather than solely by reference to imperial *auctoritas*. While even much modern scholarship in East Asia tends to remember the Chinese side of early encounters with the West as stubbornly insistent upon "an egocentric and universalistic world image with a strong sense of superiority [i.e.,] Sinocentrism,"[18] close attention to the discourse of "stateliness" reveals a far more dynamic and self-aware praxis of engagement. Relatedly, Chinese international lawyers have often seen in this modern field family resemblances to various ancient ideas and practices among the warring states of China's preunification era. As one of the profession's most important twentieth-century figures, Wang Tieya, suggested in his 1990 course at the Hague Academy of International Law, there was in that formative period of China's culture already something like a "quasi-international law," or at least perhaps a "rudimentary international law . . . analogu[ous] to that of the Greek cities" of the ancient Mediterranean.[19]

China's nineteenth-century Manchu rulers, too, brought to bear in their relations with the West a different set of conceptual categories that, at times, facilitated a pursuit of "equal" relations – perhaps in a more genuine sense than did Western treaty practices using formal equality to mask informal control. For later generations of officials, diplomats, and eventually lawyers, as well, it was to be the inherent *equality* of sovereign states that was often treated as sovereignty's essential feature, though this notional equality was also closely linked with territorial control. For a state already embedded in a dense fabric of legal relations, "reclaiming sovereignty" most often meant learning to put law to use, not rejecting it. Already by the 1850s, erstwhile Qing efforts to "unilaterally apply . . . norms based on its own world image"[20] to the encroaching West were giving way to far more nuanced strategies mixing compromise, self-assertion, and emulation. Western legal regulation, however, took on ever more universalist aspirations as it changed from a framework of more or less coercive bilateral dealings to a truly world-spanning imperial code.

A body of law that China first encountered as a system of imposed norms and alien "projects" gradually, over roughly a century, became space for the projects of its own people.[21] Some young intellectuals of the Qing Dynasty's last years, for example, already argued that "in the 19th century, there was only power, no public [international] law" (*zhi you qiang er wu gongfa* 祇有強而無公法).[22] Given that Western states "preserve[d our] territorial integrity only in name, while in reality laying claim to their own interests," such observers suggested that, from their standpoint, the real history of international law – a discourse "that only exists among equals" – had yet to begin.[23]

Being primarily a work of conceptual history, this book does not purport to provide a comprehensive overview of the many elements of international law doctrine that it discusses. Nor is this mainly a study of diplomatic history, international relations, or political economy, a sociological study of China's international law profession, or a biographical study of individual figures in the field, although it necessarily includes discussions related to all of these subjects. Its topic is, more modestly, an account of certain historically situated ways of thinking about the world, the state, and law. The ensuing analysis of international law's conceptual history in, and in relation to, China will proceed via engagement with both primary and secondary sources. Naturally, the many existing excellent studies of China's social and diplomatic as well as legal history from the Late Qing through modern eras have greatly contributed to the analysis herein.[24]

Meanwhile, combining these sources with the close reading of archival documents that have never previously been translated and, in some cases, not yet utilized in any Chinese or foreign historical study, has helped to illuminate previously underemphasized aspects of Chinese encounters with international law and its ideas. In some cases, these consulted sources comprise records that have only been made available in recent years. Foreign ministry archives from the mid nineteenth century through the mid twentieth century, private correspondence and memoirs of diplomats and other officials, and databases of scholarly and popular publications have proved invaluable sources for evaluating changing ideas about international law. So too, of course, are doctrinal international law writings, both those articulated from the Western "center" and those from writers in its vast "periphery." At no point during the period under examination, or since, has "international law" been a monolithic discourse lacking for alternative voices and vocabularies.

The nine chapters of this book focus on Chinese engagements with international law in the period between 1850 and China's World Trade Organization (WTO) accession in 2001. Already by roughly the midpoint of that long span, amid the fateful experiences of the Paris Peace Conference and "May Fourth Movement" of 1919, both Western international law and ideas of sovereignty as the constitutive legal status of statehood had been thoroughly internalized in China. As of the first decades of the twentieth century, global legal ordering had become a field in which Chinese jurists, diplomats, and politicians, as well as those of many other once "peripheral" states and peoples, could articulate and pursue their own projects, rather than only being the objects of those initiated in the West. China's own domestic polity, meanwhile, had itself long since been inextricably embedded in a web of transnational relationships and structures, views about which and the possibilities for their revision would shift across a number of regimes, and a radically changing world situation.

The nineteenth-century "family of nations" as well as the post-1919, post-1945, and post-1989 frameworks of international law have been ways of mentally ordering the world as well as authority structures based on shifting centers of wealth and power. The Great Qing *gurun*, which was coercively incorporated into the law of nations as a key object of administration, eventually turned into the Chinese republic that cofounded the modern international legal order in 1945, and whose state socialist successor is ever more deeply intertwined – or even synonymous – with it today, sharing a place at the summit of institutions such as the United Nations Security Council and at the core of regulatory systems like the WTO. Across that span of time, generations of publicly engaged individuals sought out ways to reform the vast array of rules and power networks in which they found themselves and their polity thoroughly imbricated, though they also often endorsed many of its essential features and, ultimately, contributed in many ways to entrenching its current status quo. In all of these senses, for readers anywhere in the world today, the history of ideas regarding China and international law is a matter of "self-knowledge."[25]

Part I

Preserving Stateliness, 1850–1894

1

Universal Prosperity

In early January 1850, a boat carrying the renowned but officially disgraced 66-year-old official Lin Zexu moored on the Xiang River by the city of Changsha, as Lin made his way home to Fujian accompanied by his three sons, his late wife's coffin, and a large quantity of books. While passing through Hunan, Lin sought out a local scholar in his late thirties named Zuo Zongtang, who had been recommended to him as a serious thinker on policy matters. On board the vessel, Lin and Zuo talked long into the evening about the problems afflicting the Qing Empire, of which the most important involved "bureaucracy, finance, and maritime defense." As Zuo would later recount, they went over "countless" documents together, discussing in particular affairs related to Xinjiang, where Lin had formerly been exiled. One day, he thought, that far-off region could be made as politically secure and economically productive as the Yangzi River Delta.[1]

After being dismissed in 1840 from his high-level position as the viceroy of Liangguang for his role in helping to "provoke" the First Opium War, Lin had spent several years working in exile in the region of Ili, near what is now China's border with Kazakhstan. There followed several years of service in Ili and elsewhere, most recently Yunnan, where his wife passed away in 1847. Lin was now returning to his native Fuzhou to retire. Once home, however, he hardly had time to settle before learning of the death of Emperor Daoguang, who had raised Lin to his former esteemed rank and then laid the blame on him after full-scale war broke out with Britain. Following Daoguang's death, his nineteen-year-old son and successor, the Manchu prince Iju, ordered Lin Zexu out of retirement to help face a new crisis – the growing, religiously tinged uprising against Qing rule centered in Guangxi that would soon transform into the Taiping Rebellion.[2]

Several officials remonstrated to the new emperor that Lin's health was weak and that he likely could not bear the strains of returning to active service, but Iju angrily rejected these views, especially because they came from officials who had, after Lin's removal, reversed course to sign the conciliatory 1842 Treaty of Nanjing that opened new ports for British trade, provided reparations for the opium that Lin had destroyed, and handed over Hong Kong as a "supply depot." In a scathing imperial order issued soon after taking the throne, Iju demoted the Manchu high officials Mujangga and Kiyeng, who had both influenced his late father's appeasement policies. The Lin affair provided some useful ammunition: Mujangga had "sought to prevent the use of talent" out of jealousy for his own influence, and "tried to confuse Me with false reports." Kiyeng, meanwhile, was to be punished most of all for his decade-long course of conciliation, in particular, during his tenure as viceroy at Guangzhou, where he had gone on to sign treaties with France and the United States on terms similar to those of the Treaty of Nanjing. Both officials, Iju charged, had abused his father's favor and "usurped imperial authority" (*qie quan* 竊權).[3] Such behavior would now be banned, Iju declared. In reality, however, his decade-long rule was to be marked by even worse defeats and, eventually, a near-total submission to Western commercial and legal structures. By then, Iju's official reign name, in Chinese *Xianfeng* and in Manchu *Gubci Elgiyengge* – both meaning "Universal Prosperity" – would seem deeply ironic.

As it turned out, the reports of Lin's frail health were apparently accurate after all, as he died en route to his new post, never to take up the task of suppressing the new rebel movement. British colonial officials in Hong Kong expressed some regret at the death of their erstwhile opponent, whose tough approach might now have been helpful in suppressing the "banditti" and "desperadoes" who threatened local trade as well as state authority.[4] They were displeased, as well, with the demotion of Kiyeng: Future concessions might have been more easily procured had he stayed in office in Canton.[5] Also of concern was competition from foreign rivals including France and (particularly) Russia, who were already seeking to emulate British success in China. And, perhaps most importantly, the British mercantile community both locally and back home was vocal that the status quo remained insufficient. Full access to China's vast interior market would have to come sooner or later. Perhaps, many British merchants and politicians came to feel, the key to commercial progress was to establish direct, European-style diplomatic and legal relations with the Throne, preferably but not necessarily by noncoercive means.[6]

Law among States?

When Kiyeng was brought to task by his new emperor over concessions like paying reparations for the opium destroyed by his predecessor at Guangzhou, opening up ports, approval of extraterritorial jurisdiction, or de facto legalization of missionary activities, he could draw upon the words of the late Emperor Daoguang for his defense. These moves, he said, had all been but ways to "set aside minor details and focus on grand policy matters" – for example, allowing consular jurisdiction would help Qing officials avoid adjudicating "foreign nuisances."[7] Kiyeng maintained that he had faithfully followed the orders he (like Lin before him) had received from Iju's father:

At the very start of the tensions with Britain in the early 1830s, and periodically since then, Daoguang had ordered his officials to "first of all avoid harm to stateliness [*guoti*], and secondly avoid provoking hostilities."[8] When Lin promoted assertive defiance of British demands, and Kiyeng promoted conciliation, both cited stateliness as the basis for their policies.

The term translated here as "stateliness" (*guoti* 國體) was as vital to late Qing political cosmology as it was capacious and, at times, ambiguous.[9] Literally referring to the "form" (*ti* 體) (which itself could mean "body," "structure," "system," "essence," or "propriety," *inter alia*) of the "state" (*guo* 國), this ancient term was already in use by the time of imperial China's unification under the Qin Dynasty.[10] At times, it was used to refer to "the state as a whole,"[11] or, synecdochically, to high-ranking ministers, laws and institutions, or other core elements of the polity and its inherent order.[12] The term's most common concrete applications in Ming- and Qing-era texts were in the context of impeachments against corrupt or misbehaving imperial officials who had harmed the "form of the state" by improper conduct or overstepping their powers.[13]

Often, *guoti*'s most important dimension was an overriding sense of "state dignity," rather than a set of specific formal norms identified identically among those using the term. This had parallels in the West. Clifford Geertz, for example, writes that the Western concept of "the state" had united the three "etymological themes" of estate, statecraft, and "stateliness," of which the last conveyed "pomp, in the sense of splendour, display, dignity, [and] presence."[14] Commenting on this complex of symbols, Martin Loughlin has argued,

> [S]ince the quality of *stateliness* is inherent in the idea of kingship, the presence of majesty itself operates as an ordering force. Only under modern conditions, in which the charismatic facets of political leadership are gradually superseded by the emergence of an impersonal conception of rulership, could the concept of the state be detached from the splendour and display of majesty [and] express the idea of the *public realm*.[15]

In the Chinese context, at least, *guoti*/stateliness/state form certainly conveyed some notions of a transpersonal public realm even while still firmly bound together with the imperial majesty – as we will soon see in its 1850s invocations. Of course, Han Chinese political cosmology had, since the pre-unification era, treated the rule of a legitimate emperor as notionally universal, applying at least in principle to "all under Heaven." At various times, Chinese dynasties had indeed been forced to acknowledge more equal relations with foreign states, but they then tended to later reassert their nonpareil status. The Manchu Qing rulers, however, combined an (eventual) embrace of this "Han" discourse with alternative notions of political ideology and great deal of *Realpolitik* in managing their sprawling empire.[16]

Although they had initially expressed reserve regarding *guoti* and other Chinese political terms, the empire's new Manchu rulers began to make frequent use of it by the time of Prince Iju's long-reigning great-grandfather, Qianlong. Indeed, Qianlong did much to extend the term *guoti*'s application to the realm of "foreign relations" – specifically invoking it to assess whether certain forms of interaction with both hostile and friendly rulers outside Qing control were compatible with the Qing Empire's own idiosyncratic moral and political structure, that is, the *abkai gurun i doro* (Ma.)/*tianchao tizhi* (Ch.) or "order of the Celestial Dynasty."[17] As such, the term *guoti* and the Manchu concept *gurun i doro*, the "proper order of the state (or dynasty)," with which it came to be associated, were treated as distinct from, though linked with, the idealized Chinese political ontology comprising degrees of status radiating out from the Son of Heaven.[18]

These concepts matter to the history of China and international law because it was in these terms, not those of either state sovereignty *or* true universal rule, that the topic was first approached. In line with the element of pragmatism in Qing rule, neither Kiyeng nor Emperor Daoguang seem to have considered the former's conciliatory approach to interactions with the West as compromising Qing stateliness. Rather, these were ways to help "pacify, bridle and rein"[19] warlike foreigners while maintaining state dignity and order. Requests truly incompatible with the "proper order of the state," such as for diplomatic stations in Beijing or a regularized exchange of permanent emissaries, could be outright denied. In other situations, though, a bit of tactical finessing could be employed. The exchange of letters between US president John Tyler and Daoguang surrounding the Treaty of Wangxia in 1844, for example, was stage-managed by Kiyeng as a game of trilingual code-switching between English, Chinese, and Manchu, with terms subtly shifting between versions in order to avoid offending either side's sensibilities.[20]

The *Daicing Gurun* (Great Qing State), too, would not sound ontologically different from the *Ho Juweng Gurun* (the United States) or, for example, the *Coohiyan Gurun* (Korea); the Chinese version's *Zhonghua*, by comparison, reasserts the Sinocentric world order.[21] In the Ming era, it had been exceptionally rare for any official imperial text to refer to China alongside any other counterpart as two equivalent "states."[22] Yet, a Qing-era translation of a Manchu imperial message could easily refer to a treaty with the United States as "benefitting the people of both states" (*juwe gurun i ursebe ishunde tusangga* [Ma.]; *li liang guo zhi renmin* 利兩國之人民 [Ch.]). There were, in any case, already Qing precedents for such usage. The relationship with Russia, especially, had long been construed on terms of relative equivalency, facilitated by vast distances. The 1689 Treaty of Nerchinsk that resolved border issues, for example, while composed in Latin by Jesuit intermediaries, was also produced in two unofficial translations in Manchu and Russian. The former, like the later nineteenth-century agreements with Western states, had already referred to the contracting parties as *juwe gurun* ("both states"; *utrum imperium* [La.]; обоих государств [Ru.]).[23]

The basic notion of an interstate legal agreement[24] that establishes the framework for trade and passage of persons across delimited territorial boundaries was, thus, not in itself unfamiliar. At issue was whether the specific provisions to be determined were incompatible either with the dynasty's interests or with the ambiguous but all-important value: *guoti*. As per the views of officials like Kiyeng that had promoted friendly relations, if the Western side cared only about their greed for tangible profits (as Qing officials at this point invariably thought to be the case) and the Qing side insisted only on the most essential principles of stateliness (though they may disagree about what exactly that essence consisted of), then peaceful coexistence might prevail. There would be no need, in that case, for extensive investigation of the other side's aims, ideology, or rules and customs. Accordingly, before the 1860s, there would be only one attempt by a Qing official to inquire into the Western idea of a "law of nations," and it was not by one of the officials "friendly" to foreign powers, rather very much the reverse.

Sovereignty and Property

In July 1839, shortly before being disgraced with blame for the First Opium War, Lin Zexu had ordered one of the first ever translations into Chinese of a Western text of international law, a handful of pages from Emer de Vattel's *Droit des Gens*.[25] Neither the passages from Vattel (which he is not known to have ever directly cited) nor Lin's earlier letter to Queen Victoria that admonished her over the opium trade had any clearly discernable impact on the conflict. Indeed, although some of Lin's actions may have been influenced by his access to the Vattel text,[26] by the point that he had requested the translations, he had already destroyed opium cargoes and restricted British trade. With further escalations on both sides, a de facto state of war began by late September.

The translated sections of Vattel's *Droit des Gens* (in the 1834 English edition by Joseph Chitty), amounted to no more than a few pages of text. Yet these were enough to convey clearly that the power to exclude foreign trade was indeed explicitly part of a state's inherent authority: "the lord of the territory may, whenever he think proper, forbid its being entered."[27] Aside from confirming that foreign traders' contraband could be confiscated and was indeed subject to the laws of a host country, there were specific references, as well, that noted without condemnation the long-standing Chinese and Japanese practices of restricting commercial access to foreigners.[28]

More difficult to parse was the conceptual basis for that power, and its supposed limits. As one of the most important foundational concepts of Vattel's text,[29] "sovereignty" is invoked dozens of times throughout the work.

As it happened, the brief translated sections that Lin commissioned even included an outright definition of this alien term:

> The sovereignty is the right to command in the whole country; and the laws are not simply confined to regulating the conduct of the citizens towards each other, but also determine what is to be observed by all order of people throughout the whole extent of the state. In virtue of this submission, foreigners who commit faults are to be punished according to the laws of the country.[30]

In the 1839 Chinese translation overseen by Lin's assistant Yuan Dehui and the American missionary doctor Peter Parker, however, this sentence was transformed:

> 国家抚有天下，治理亿兆，而律例亦不止此。自法制一定，普天之下莫不遵守，故外国有犯者，即各按各犯事国中律例治罪。

> The state occupies and controls [its part of?] the world (*Tianxia*), governing and ordering the innumerable [people], but the laws are not limited to this alone. Upon the legal order's promulgation, all throughout the world must obey it, and if foreigners violate it, each will be punished based on the laws of the state where they have done so.[31]

In this first major encounter of Chinese interlocutors with ideas of "sovereignty," then, the term was simply ignored. However, what is so interesting about this ill-fated translation encounter is how unimportant conceptual differences were to the practicalities of the matter at hand. For Vattel's actual concrete point in the translated passage is indeed adequately conveyed: Even if China were to be treated as just a state like any other, rather than a notionally universal moral/political authority presiding over all *Tianxia*, it could restrict its borders and trade at will. "Every state has . . . a right to prohibit the entrance of foreign merchandizes," another passage reads, "and the nations that are affected by such prohibition have no right to complain of it, as if they had been refused an office of humanity. Their complaints would be ridiculous."[32]

The actual problem, ironically, had to do not with Chinese universalism and Western particularism, but the reverse. For in taking actions such as destroying the opium shipments, Lin may have exercised a theoretically valid authority of a state to enforce its own laws domestically, yet he had *also* infringed rights in property legally attributed to a foreign state and its citizens. *That* division, between rights of sovereignty and rights of property – the latter being seen as in theory universally enforceable – was a key feature of Vattel's text that was lost in translation. Particularly important was the idea that "the *empire* and the *domain*, or *property*, are not inseparable in their own nature, even in a sovereign state."[33] Vattel's French terms *empire* and *domaine*, and their close English equivalents in Joseph Chitty's 1834 translation, are used as stand-ins for the Roman law terms *imperium* and *dominium*. This conceptual binary would increasingly shape the Western international legal order introduced to China from 1842 onward.

Already for Jean Bodin in 1576, "sovereignty" could be directly equated with *imperium* (aka "empire"), and thus distinguished from the realm of property relations, including those comprising the so-called public domain.[34] In the two centuries between Bodin and Vattel, the conceptual distinction had grown increasingly clear to the effect that, while states may stand alongside each other as sovereigns, equally politically supreme within their own territories, they were also uniformly *limited* vis-à-vis property rights. Over those, states exercised not empire, but instead merely jurisdiction, as well as what was called *dominium eminens*: eminent domain. In that realm, which comprised both real and moveable property and other such forms of wealth, a state could only be first among equals: If it seized property for some compelling reason of public interest, for example, it ought to do so in a just manner and provide fair compensation.[35]

Moreover, foreign states and citizens could acquire property rights in each other's territories, creating obligations for the sovereign on that basis.[36] The precise contours of the *dominium* concept were still rather hazy in the mid nineteenth century, whether as a matter of international law or broader public law doctrine. However, what tended to unite the different invocations of the notion was that "whether understood as a public or private power, its [ultimate] source was always the right and freedom of the individual."[37]

If validly acquired, then, *dominium*/property rights in opium should be protected just like any others. That was certainly the view of Lin Zexu's counterpart on the British side in the dealings leading to the First Opium War, Charles Eliot, who despite personal distaste for the opium trade, "consider[ed] himself bound to protect, not only British persons, but British property."[38] During the British parliamentary debates associated with the war, the premise of defending property rights played a highly significant role, as did Vattel's text in Chitty's 1834 translation, which included extensive additions and comments reflecting (and justifying) recent British colonial and imperial practices.[39] Some pro-war voices tried to invoke Vattel's arguments and Chitty's emendations regarding acquired property rights and duties of sociability to counter the former's other, inconvenient, assertions about the rights of sovereigns to restrict trade. Meanwhile, others in the war party adopted a different approach, arguing that membership in the community of international law should be limited, its protections "interpreted as applying only to such commercial states as recognize the general principles of public or international law."[40] Gradually, as Western property interests in China grew under the regimes established by the Treaty of Nanjing and its successive follow-up agreements, the latter view would gain sway.

The sections of Chitty's Vattel that Lin had translated did very little to elucidate this deeper conceptual dynamic at work. Instead, they suggested a world order of equal sovereigns that (albeit in tension with traditional Han

Chinese universalist political discourse) was actually easily assimilated to the Qing willingness to describe their polity as a *guo/gurun* alongside semi-peers held at arm's length. After Lin was dismissed by Daoguang, he entrusted his collected translations to the reformist Hunanese scholar Wei Yuan, who would include them as part of an influential geographical anthology titled *Illustrated Treatise on the Seafaring States*. The Vattel translation, however, was apparently not seen by Wei as important enough to feature in the initial publication in 1844, though it was then included in expanded editions of 1847 and 1853. Regardless, these parts of the work drew relatively little attention compared with its much more copious material on world geography, aspects of European political history, and military/naval affairs, among others.[41] By the time Lin died in late 1850, his erstwhile attempt at engaging with the Western law of nations had made few clearly discernible intellectual waves.

Trade, God, and Law

Lin's early ersatz translation project aside, the law of nations would first come to China as part of a web of other foreign ideas spanning the realms of economics, politics, and theology. Ideas from all of these fields were invoked in pedagogical projects aimed at transforming China. Particularly influential during the earliest stage of China's "opening up" between the 1830s and 1850s was the Lutheran missionary and sinologist Karl Gützlaff. Born to a tailor's family in Pomerania in 1803, in his early teens, Gützlaff obtained official support for his future schooling by audaciously presenting Prussian King Friedrich Wilhelm III with a laudatory poem. A few years later, he underwent a Pietist conversion experience and embarked on a missionary career. Arriving in Java in 1827 on behalf of the Dutch Missionary Society, Gützlaff soon left its bureaucratically organized service and shifted his growing ambitions to China. A biographer has suggested that "hope of social mobility, an appetite for adventure, the ideal of the romantic hero, as well as the desire to bring the gospel to the heathen" motivated Gützlaff to pursue a missionary life and to choose for his target the vast, inaccessible Qing realm.[42]

In pursuit of these aims, he had already by the early 1830s engaged in daring efforts alongside fellow missionaries and merchants based in Canton and Macau, including major opium-smuggling firms, to gain access to China's interior for purposes of both trade and proselytization. While interpreting for opium merchants, Gützlaff began translating a new edition of the Bible in Chinese and also worked to produce and disseminate Chinese-language material on Western topics. Such "intellectual artillery" would, some in the Western trading community hoped, help awaken the Chinese to the truths of Christianity and free trade, allowing "barbarism [to] vanish before civilization" in China just as in other zones of European expansion.[43]

At no prior point in history could a roving Westerner with Romantic ideas about transforming China have played a role quite like that of Gützlaff in the 1830s. In 1838, for example, he published pieces in his Chinese-language *East and West Monthly Journal* that introduced Western political systems to readers in Canton. In such works, Gützlaff was among the very first to attempt to convey in Chinese European notions of political liberalism, which he usually translated as "the principle of self-rule" (*zizhu zhi li* 自主之理) and of national autonomy, which he at times translated as *zi cao qi quan* 自操其權 – perhaps best loosely rendered as "wielding state authority autonomously." In attempting to convey the role of parliament in Britain's political system, he combined these terms, describing it as holding the *zizhu zhi quan* 自主之權 – that is, "state authority of self-rule."[44] This passage, from the year before Lin's Vattel translation, was perhaps the first ever attempt to convey Western ideas of "sovereignty" into Chinese, though they were not presented in a systematic or coherent fashion.[45] Gützlaff's goal was, in any case, not to spread ideas of sovereignty but rather of liberal political economy and Protestant Christianity. The character *zhu* 主, conveying in Chinese lordship, ownership, and rule (rather like the Latin *dominus* and its various derivations as forms of *dominium*), appeared frequently in his texts, most often attributed to God and "free" peoples.

Describing liberal government as allowing great personal freedom combined with legal restrictions on the powers of monarchs and officials, he suggested that the wealth and power of Britain and, to a lesser extent, other Western states, was owed directly to this powerful ideology and its religious foundations.[46] Such discussions were interspersed with brief essays and reports on the benefits of trade, recent political and economic news, and historico-religious material. In his writings on such topics, Gützlaff at times adopted the narrative trope of a fictional dialogue among Chinese scholars supposedly fascinated by Western culture and ideas. In reality, his conversion efforts, both in matters of religion and political economy, proved far less effective than he had evidently expected.[47] Far more successful were his books on China in the West.[48] By the end of the 1830s, moreover, Gützlaff would serve as an interpreter for the British during the First Opium War and then as Chinese Secretary for the British administration in Hong Kong.

Gützlaff died of illness at age the age of forty-eight in August 1851, a bit less than a year after Lin Zexu. He had at that point already trained various local converts and Western officials and missionaries. Four years earlier, for example, he had baptized a thirty-year-old former fabric merchant from Dongguan named Wang Yuanshen, who had arrived in Hong Kong in dire straits after his business's collapse due to the recent opening of Chinese ports to English textiles. From then, Wang would become one of the most trusted and faithful aides to Gützlaff and to the several Lutheran brethren the latter invited from the Berlin Missionary Society. In a history of Christian missionary activity in China written decades later, Wang would recall his good fortune at having encountered the "true," Protestant faith at a time when it was still utterly unfamiliar to most of his countrymen.[49] The long-lived Wang would pass his devout Lutheran beliefs on to his son as well as to a grandson, Wang Chonghui, who, as we will see in later chapters, was to become perhaps China's most important and influential twentieth-century international lawyer.

An important new associate of Gützlaff's toward the very end of his life was the American Presbyterian missionary William Alexander Parsons Martin. Martin was an Indiana native, born to a family of frontier missionaries and raised with the aid of a former slave housemaid who remained in his Virginia-born mother's service despite residing in a free state.[50] In later life he recalled that his "interest in China was first awakened in 1839 by the boom of British cannon battering down her outer walls."[51] Though only thirteen at that time, he would have already been contemplating destinations for missionary service, like his father and his brothers.

A decade later, on the orders of the Presbyterian Mission Board, Martin first arrived in Hong Kong on April 10, 1850, his twenty-third birthday, and immediately set out to conquer its then still-rugged Victoria Peak via an arduous hike.[52] Over the years to come, he would become the most important nineteenth-century figure in the introduction of international law texts to China. Like Gützlaff before him, Martin would also throughout his life endorse the agenda of "opening" China to Christianity, free trade principles, and liberal politics. Though he arrived in China a decade too late to have anything to do with the First Opium War, Martin would long espouse the view that Britain had indeed had cause for a "just war" in the 1830s based upon the Qing refusal to establish formal diplomatic relations or liberalize trade.[53] These ideas were, as we have seen, technically un-Vattelian. However, they closely reflected the zeitgeist in 1850s British-ruled Hong Kong.

"China Need Not Handle That"

For Qing intellectuals, Lin Zexu's reputation as a prophet of "national security" was further cemented soon after his death by events in the far west, today's Xinjiang. During and after his exile there, Lin's call to develop the "Western Regions" had been in part motivated by fears of Russian incursions that might resemble those of the British in China's south.[54] As early as 1851, another "foreign disturbance" indeed emerged in connection with Russian demands for increased trade access (along with extraterritorial consular jurisdiction) to match the privileges that had been obtained by Western states since the end of the First Opium War.

By the mid nineteenth century, various political actors in the Russian Empire were dissatisfied with the territorial and diplomatic status quo that had been maintained with the Qing since 1689. A particular focus was the vast region of the Amur River, spanning much of Outer Manchuria. As early as

1843, for example, the Russian admiral and explorer Ivan Kruzenshtern had advised that "[China] has already agreed to retreat from many of its ancient rules relating to trade with European powers, [and so] it will of course concede to its powerful close neighbor the right of free navigation along the Amur, so necessary to Russian trade."[55] Projects for the commercial and military development of Siberia, as well as the acquisition of new fertile and strategically important territory, facilitated the political rise of Nikolai Nikolaevich Muraviev – later to be ennobled as "Count Amursky" – who set himself the task of promoting Russian expansion in the region after his appointment as Governor-General of East Siberia in 1847. In both Manchuria and Xinjiang, Russian officials were by the beginning of Xianfeng's reign actively seeking to exert influence and to assert a very different relationship between the two empires.

At the Qing court, Russian requests for the same benefits granted to Britain and others were met with equanimity. Xianfeng instructed his representatives that there was "some benefit and no harm" in approving Russia's requests for trade access, establishing consulates, and extraterritorial jurisdiction in two of its three requested zones in Xinjiang. Thus, the resulting 1851 Treaty of Kulja extended these privileges to Russia in Ili and Chuguchak, but not Kashgar. In the name of preserving China's "long-term peace" with Russia, such compromises were fully permissible, and compatible with "both *guoti* and border defense."[56] The Qing pragmatism as to claims of universal political rule was very much on display in Xianfeng's instructions. In a turn of phrase that Ming rulers would have found outrageous, for example, he referred to Russian extraterritorial consular jurisdiction with the straightforward description: "China need not handle that" (*Zhongguo bu guan* 中國不管).[57] A similar willingness to accept ontological parity for pragmatic purposes was on display a few months later when, in response to reports of Russian administrative reorganization in Siberia, Xianfeng told his officials: "these are all internal matters of that state; they have nothing to do with China" (*jun xi yi guo nei zhi shi; yu Zhongguo wu gan* 均係伊國內之事。與中國無干).[58]

Though there is no known evidence to suggest that Xianfeng or his advisors would have encountered Lin's commissioned translation of Vattel, these postures were indeed consistent with a more or less orthodox "Vattelian" view of intersovereign relations. China's Western interlocutors, meanwhile, were beginning to innovate new legal forms, or rediscover old ones ripe for profitable transplantation (in the case of consular jurisdiction), and applying these ideas to the Qing territorial space that was newly opening up as a field for power and trade.[59] The pattern of an unregulated "private" expansion of European settlers in non-Western spaces being followed by public power and formal legal structures had globally intensified since the turn of the nineteenth century, from the North American West to India, Burma, Australia, and New Zealand, among others.

Private settlement was also a significant element of Russia's new expansion into the geopolitically and commercially enticing space of Outer Manchuria. Throughout the early 1850s, Muraviev continued to seek to convince St. Petersburg to permit a more aggressive line in the expansion of Russian influence over the Amur region. The Qing acquiescence to most demands in the Treaty of Kulja greatly aided him in making his case, and by 1854 he had received approval to begin negotiations for the opening up of the Amur River and also, if possible, the acquisition of some of the territories already being staked out by Russian settlers.[60]

While these envisioned Amur negotiations would not begin in earnest for several more years, another set of important transnational developments was occurring in Shanghai. Shanghai's trade had grown immensely since its opening up to foreign commerce following the 1840s treaties, and this trend continued during the Taiping rebellion and other disturbances in the Yangzi River Delta region. When in 1853 the city was occupied by an insurgent group, disrupting revenue collection, this provided the impetus for a plan developed among Western consuls to create a new framework for collecting customs revenues. Under titular Qing authority but de facto management as a primarily British-run bureaucracy, the Maritime Customs Service (MCS) was an idiosyncratic, hybridized venture.[61] At the same time, with its functions of tax collection, inspection, and later policing and infrastructure, the MCS also embodied a new logic of international organization being applied on the frontiers of Western commercial expansion.[62]

Central to the establishment of the new transnational organization in 1854 were the British Consul in Shanghai, Rutherford Alcock, and the Vice-Consul, Thomas Wade (who had been yet another disciple of Gützlaff's). The latter was appointed to the Shanghai Customs House along with counterparts from the United States and France, and would serve as the de facto first director of the MCS. Although it had been founded merely as a matter of expediency during a period of interregnum in Shanghai, with customs revenues going uncollected, Qing officials proved willing to accept the arrangement for the remainder of the 1850s on a localized basis. Later on, it would be extended to all of China's open ports and waters, with authority by the early twentieth century encompassing, *inter alia*, "domestic customs administration, postal administration, harbour and waterway management, weather reporting, and anti-smuggling operations."[63] From its modest and entirely localized beginnings, the MCS would eventually become the cornerstone not only of Qing trade, but of the empire's entire fiscal state.[64]

The transnational interactions of 1853–1854 in Xinjiang and Shanghai were very different, but both showed how Xianfeng, despite early vehemence about appeasement, was willing to take a cooperative stance to Western initiatives. By this point, however, Western commercial ambitions in China demanded a full institutionalization of Qing legal obligations in place of any discretionary imperial favor. Two more of Gützlaff's diplomat-sinologist protégés played significant roles in the process by which this was carried out. One was Wade's successor at the MCS, Horatio Nelson Lay. The other was Harry Parkes, a relative of Gützlaff's British wife. In 1856, when Parkes was serving as the acting British Consul in Canton, he and the then-Governor of Hong Kong, John Bowring, helped to transform a minor fracas over the seizure and inspection of a Chinese-manned but British-flagged vessel in Guangzhou, the sailing ship *Arrow*, into a pretext for conflict. This "insult to the flag" was used by Lord Palmerston – foreign secretary during the First Opium War and prime minister from February 1855 – and others to secure support for coercing Qing authorities to make new concessions as well as to make good on old ones, such as Canton's full opening as a treaty port, that still remained unfulfilled.[65]

Reconstituting Extra-European Spaces

In 1856, the Regius Professor of Civil Law and former Drummond Professor of Political Economy at Oxford, Travers Twiss, referred to the current situation of the Far East in his first influential treatise on the law of nations. Relying on the standard distinction between a "natural" and a "voluntary" (or "positive") law of nations, Twiss wrote that European states' coercive dealings with China "as contrasted with their intercourse with one another" showed how natural law rules could be applied in relation "to a less cultivated state of mankind." On the other hand, "non-intercourse with Japan … may be regarded as a recognition of the principle … that independent nations are not compellable to enter into society with one another or to hold intercourse of any kind."[66]

Twiss' attempt to distinguish the Qing and Japanese cases was difficult to square with the ongoing process by which both states were being coerced to open their doors. There was a franker acknowledgment of this dynamic in another influential treatise of the previous year, the posthumous sixth edition of American diplomat-jurist Henry Wheaton's *Elements of International Law*. While serving as US minister to Prussia in the early 1840s, Wheaton had argued in favor of US action to begin opening up China's markets and also supported Russian aims to create a free navigation regime on the Amur River. In the sixth edition edited by William Beach Lawrence, the latter added passages extolling progress in "the march of free trade" and in the commercial promise associated with the recent opening of China and Japan, as well as the useful regime of extraterritorial jurisdiction that supported it.[67]

Vattelian ideas about the "voluntary" character of diplomatic and commercial intercourse were swiftly losing their relevance as a matter of doctrine as well as in geopolitical practice. Undoubtedly the greatest transformative factor in this shift and in its practical implications for the Qing Empire was the 1853–1856 Crimean War, where Russian expansion into Ottoman territory was checked by a coalition led by Britain and France. The ensuing Congress and Treaty of Paris of March 30, 1856 set the stage not only for a major reshuffling of the intra-European balance of power and international legal order – particularly via the formal "admission" of the Ottomans as a formally equal sovereign state – but also greatly reinforced both Russian and Anglo-French motives for further expansion into Qing space. In the former's case, acquisition of the Amur zone could help to make up for grave recent losses elsewhere. For the latter, meanwhile, the forms of global legislation innovated at Paris might find useful new applications.

The Treaty of Paris has long been regarded by international lawyers as a milestone in the advancement of modern "positivist" conceptions of international law, that is, as a body of rules legislated by treaty and custom among a community of states – though, as we have seen, a crucial aspect of "positivity," its voluntary character, was increasingly restricted to Europeans.[68] The treaty also saw the deployment of an explicit formula that asserted the existence of a "public law of Europe" (*droit publique de l'Europe*), developed since 1815, to which states could accede as if signing up to a systematic body of rules similar to a legal code.[69] In "joining" this public law system in 1856, the Ottoman Sultan effectively restructured the legal order of his empire, not only by confirming preexisting rules and institutions, but also accepting newly imposed ones.[70]

The 1856 Treaty functioned much like a transnational constitution guaranteeing, *inter alia*, the "neutralization" of the Black Sea, freedom of navigation and commerce there and in the Danube River, the de facto autonomy of the Christian principalities over which the Sultan was now to exercise mere "suzerainty," and other such commitments favorable to Anglo-French interests. The economically and strategically vital Danube River was not only to be "internationalized," but, following a model first applied to the Rhine in 1815, was also to have created for it a dedicated international organization, the "Danube Commission," to administrate, regulate, and police the waterway.[71] The signatory powers of the treaty would also be able to station forces at the river's mouth. Meanwhile, Britain, France, and Austria signed a separate agreement among themselves pledging to guarantee "the independence and integrity of the Ottoman Empire."[72] Some international lawyers would later describe the 1856 Treaty of Paris as the first time a non-European power was admitted to join the post-Vienna European Concert. It would be more accurate to say that it marked the creation by European lawyers of a sui generis public law regime for a vast "external" realm, with agency and benefits flowing to the West.

Much the same approach was soon to be adopted with respect to the Qing space. The British policy was to be spearheaded by Lord Palmerston's "High Commissioner and Plenipotentiary in China and the Far East," the Earl of Elgin, personal name James Bruce. From 1857, Elgin took the leading role in what would often be misleadingly called the "Second Opium War." The seizure of the British-flagged *Arrow* vessel had provided a (shaky) basis for military reprisal against the Qing state, though this was delayed by the outbreak of the Indian Rebellion of 1857 – violent suppression of which would mark the end of Company rule and beginning of direct colonial administration. By the end of the year, Elgin shifted focus to China and his forces captured Canton, sending its Viceroy Ye Mingchen to Calcutta as a prisoner of war. Meanwhile, the last Mughal emperor, Bahadur Shah Zafar, was being put on trial in Delhi for, *inter alia*, "Assuming the sovereignty of Hindostan" and "Causing and being accessory to the murder of the Christians."[73] Though under distinct circumstances and with different implications, the beginning of the British Raj in 1857 was as monumental a transformation as the reconstitution of the Ottoman Empire via treaty that had been carried out the previous year. Next up was China.

Reprising their cooperation in the recent conflict with Russia, Napoleon III's France entered the war soon after Britain upon the pretext of an "exemplary reprisal" over a Catholic missionary that had been executed by authorities in Guangxi for illegal proselytization. Meanwhile, though the United States and Russia resisted British entreaties to join the conflict, they shared common interests in further opening of Qing space, joining ensuing negotiations. As had been the case for the Crimean War allies with respect to the Ottoman realm, there was a set of shared goals and aims widely recognized among Western states active in China, though different aspects might be emphasized by this or that power, or individual commentator.

One notable effort to sum up shared goals of the West was articulated in 1857 by William Martin, who since arriving in China in 1850 had relocated to Ningbo in the Yangzi Delta region. In a letter to the former US minister to China, Caleb Cushing, Martin argued that the United States should recognize the Taiping rebel movement as a sovereign state. The borders of the Qing realm that foreigners had heretofore recognized, he thought, mattered little – racial differences between groups, like Han and Manchu, were far more important. Seeing the Taiping movement as an instantiation of global patterns of religious and civilizational progress, Martin drew on an American frontier analogy to help convey his bold proposal: "It was not the waters of the Rio Grande, that divided Texas from Mexico … but the impossibility of Anglo-American Protestants … being one with Spanish Catholics."[74] Just as "Protestant" Texas had become a more enlightened polity after breaking off from Mexico, or Christian Greece from the Muslim Turks, so, Martin thought, might the Han Taiping rebels if given foreign support, firepower, and autonomy.[75]

At least for the time being, he argued, it would be best to recognize two legitimate Chinese regimes – that of the Qing in the regions that they still held sway over, and that of the Nanjing-based Taipings over the center and south: "Divide and conquer," he avowed with a clear nod to British policy in India since the beginnings of the Company Raj, "is the stratagem to be employed in storming the citadels of oriental exclusiveness."[76] Western traders and missionaries might be able to more quickly gain access to the entirety of China's interior, and the command of its vital waterways, via parallel diplomatic offensives: "Of the Tartars [Manchus], we might demand the navigation of the Seghalien, and access to Peking; while with the Taipings we might treat for the navigation of the Yangtzekiang [Yangzi River], and the opening of Nanking." The thirty–one-year-old Martin appended to these suggestions a brief list of demands upon the Qing emperor that, he thought, should serve as the core of future American policy:

(1) "Freedom of religious opinion, and religious worship throughout the realm."
(2) "Freedom to citizens of nations having treaties of amity and commerce with China, to pass and repass through his dominions, at will, without distinction of place."
(3) That "The emperor shall install a department of Foreign affairs, who can meet the ambassador of foreign countries."
(4) That "The emperor shall open the Yangtzse, and its affluents (or rather all the navigable rivers in his dominions) to steam navigation."
(5) "And finally, that he shall become a subscriber to the laws of nations."[77]

"That He Shall Become a Subscriber to the Laws of Nations"

Multilateral pressure and mounting military losses led Xianfeng to seek a rapid end to the conflict. First, his envoy responded to new entreaties from Nikolai Muraviev by agreeing in the May 28, 1858 Treaty of Aigun to a "joint administration" of the Amur River Delta region and its full opening up to Russian trade activity. Then, on June 1, Xianfeng sent orders to two specially appointed representatives, the officials Guiliang and Huashana, the former a seventy–three-year-old Manchu grand secretary and the latter a fifty–two-year-old Mongol former court historiographer: They could "take appropriate measures to respond to the foreigners' [various] demands, provided they do not harm *guoti*."[78] Given the military advantage of the foreign forces, particularly their naval supremacy, Xianfeng now felt that Kiyeng had perhaps been correct in arguing for conciliation. Somewhat desperately, he called the elder official out of disgrace to join the negotiations at Tianjin. Perhaps this familiar and well-liked face could pacify the rampaging foreigners.[79]

That plan backfired, with dark consequences for Kiyeng himself. Serving as an interpreter for the British side, Gützlaff's former student Horatio Nelson Lay produced some of the memorials that Kiyeng had submitted to the throne from Canton years earlier justifying his approach to "bridling and reining" the foreigners. Lay vituperatively depicted such terms (along with customary references to the savagery of aggressive foreign groups, et al.) as signs of duplicity. These aggressive denunciations of Kiyeng, perhaps calculated to intimidate the other Qing negotiators into granting further concessions, forced the seventy-one-year-old Manchu to withdraw from the proceedings. A severely displeased Xianfeng then sent him a silk cord with which to strangle himself for the affront of "returning to the capital without permission."[80]

In the ensuing negotiations during which Huashana and Guiliang represented the Qing side, each of the foreign powers presented slightly different demands, and the Russian and American sides generally sought to maintain status as neutral mediators rather than belligerents. Nonetheless, the basic shared aims were clear: All four foreign empires hoped for increased trade access, particularly to inland China, the opening of new "treaty ports" where foreign merchants could trade their commodities, reduced tariffs, an official protected status for Christian missionaries and their converts, and a permanent diplomatic presence in Beijing (to facilitate future "equal" negotiations).[81] Given the circumstances, it was understood that the court would accede to many key demands. The exception upon which the emperor insisted, though, was for "provisions concerning ritual" (*chufei li xiang gan ge kuan wai* 除非禮相干各款外),[82] aka the matters of "stateliness" upon which no compromise could be allowed. The British insistence upon stationing a permanent envoy in Beijing was obviously such an issue. Ironically, before his imperially ordered suicide, Kiyeng had also pursued more or less the exact same course of action, seeking, for example, to have the Russians intervene on the Qing behalf to advise retraction of the diplomatic representation request so incompatible with Qing *guoti*.[83]

Xianfeng's envoys found themselves intimidated by Lay into signing the Treaties of Tianjin, which included the opening of Tianjin and several other ports; free navigation and trade on the Yangzi River; freedom of religion for Christians; allowing Chinese subjects to freely travel abroad on Western ships; the establishment of extraterritorial jurisdiction; the elimination of the character *Yi* 夷 (invariably translated into English as "barbarian," and earlier a bête noire of Gützlaff, among others)[84] to refer to Europeans along with other non-Qing subjects; excusing the kowtow for foreigners at imperial audiences; and introducing a unified customs regime.[85] All of these concessions Emperor Xianfeng hoped to avoid, but could, perhaps, reconcile with *guoti*. The same was true of the three slightly different provisions on tolerance of Christianity included as Article 8 in each of the French, Russian, and British treaties. Here, in fact, the Qing side committed explicitly to recognizing that Christianity was not incompatible with *guoti* (in the French text, "l'établissement de l'ordre et de la concorde parmi les hommes").[86] It is significant that "*order*" (*l'ordre* [Fr.]; порядок [Ru.]) was here translated for internal consumption as *guoti*, showing how Qing ideas of "stateliness" merged with state form and structure.

The other significant appearance of *guoti* in the actual (nonbinding Chinese version of) the text of the 1858 Treaties of Tianjin, however, went more to the heart of Xianfeng's concerns. In Article 3 of the treaty with Britain, it was stipulated that British diplomats could reside permanently or occasionally at

Beijing and would "not be called upon to perform any ceremony derogatory to him as representing the Sovereign of an independent nation, on a footing of equality with that of China.[87] In the Chinese version, likely drafted by Gützlaff's student Lay, the corresponding text is literally: "Great Britain is a self-ruling/autonomous country, and is equal with China [英國自主之邦與中國平等]. The plenipotentiary representatives of Great Britain shall not encounter any ritual that conflicts with [British] stateliness (*guoti*) when paying respects to the Great Qing Emperor."[88] Under the most-favored-nation (MFN) clause included in the other treaties, moreover, the same rights claimed would likely be claimed by the other three powers.[89]

While the negotiations were still underway, however, another member of the imperial clan expressed a different view as to what matters touched most directly upon the Qing *guoti*. This was Xianfeng's half-brother, Prince Gong, personal name Yixin, with whom he had been brought up in the palace. On June 23, after a preliminary treaty with the United States had been signed, but before the more comprehensive British treaty, Prince Gong submitted a memorial warning that "no clause [demanded by the foreigners] is as critical as the one regarding opening up the Yangzi River for trade."[90] Rather than focusing on trying to get the foreigners to abandon their plans for diplomatic incursions into the emperor's sacred space, Prince Gong's more pressing concern was to avoid providing them a means to dominate China's waterways.

The vision that filled Prince Gong with dread, though, was a stirring goal for some Western officials and sinologists. As Martin had put it to Cushing the previous year, "it will not be long before our ships are frequenting all ports from Siberia to Cohin-china [sic]; and our steamers stemming the current of all those mighty rivers."[91] In 1858, Martin himself had the opportunity to promote these aims as the interpreter for Cushing's successor as minister to China, William B. Reed, during the negotiations at Tianjin.[92] That the resulting agreement reflected almost all of the goals he had articulated the previous year (except for promoting Taiping secession à la Texas) was, of course, not due to his own influence. The new order imposed at Tianjin was in key respects just an imposition on the Qing emperor of norms applied to the Ottomans at Paris two years earlier. With different methods but similar implications for traders and missionaries, Paris 1856, Delhi 1857, and Tianjin 1858 all looked like "steps on the chain of providence" for Martin, as for Gützlaff's other spiritual successors.[93]

Confrontations over Stateliness

"The real task of bourgeois society," wrote Marx in an 1858 letter to Engels, "is the creation, at least in outline, of a world market, and of a type of production resting on this basis. As the world is round, this task [now] seems to have been brought to a conclusion with the colonization of California and Australia and the inclusion of China and Japan."[94] As it happened, the Qing emperor now seemingly held much the same view about the inevitability of submitting to the Western commercial system, though not to the diplomatic demands that, for him, were of far more fundamental importance.

After Tianjin, Xianfeng dispatched his envoys Guiliang and Huashana to Shanghai where they would, alongside the regional viceroy He Guiqing, take part in the "Shanghai Tariff Conference" with foreign consuls as a gap-filling follow-up to Article 26 of the British Treaty of Tianjin regarding the setting of tariff rates. However, Xianfeng sought to use the talks as a chance to either annul the Treaty of Tianjin altogether or at least eliminate what he still saw as the worst affront to imperial *guoti*: the stationing of diplomats in Beijing.[95] Before his envoys left Beijing to join He at Shanghai, Xianfeng came to favor (and perhaps himself devised) a so-called internally determined approach (*nei ding banfa* 内定辦法), sometimes referred to by later historians as "the secret plan of 1858," which he thought might serve as the *coup de grâce* in the coming negotiations.[96]

This internally determined approach comprised a remarkable proposal to waive all tariffs upon all Western trade in exchange for the foreign powers abandoning their request to be received as equals in the capital and (per Prince Gong's urging) to internationalize the Yangzi.[97] For the emperor, not only "tariff autonomy" (a term not then in use), but even the very right to have tariffs at all could be sacrificed, if needed in order to preserve stateliness. Had Xianfeng's internally determined approach been followed, it would have created the largest customs-free market in the world. Based on his estimation that the morally unedified foreigners were motivated chiefly by greed for profits, he insisted that they would view the elimination of all duties as an act of great "benevolence" and as worth exchanging for their insolent diplomatic demands, so incompatible with the Qing order. However, he encountered unexpected resistance even after explicitly ordering his negotiator He Guiqing not to "usurp authority."[98]

Already early in the negotiations, He Guiqing had submitted a memorial to the court noting that "the two clauses [of the Treaty of Tianjin] that cause the most outrage are the diplomatic stations in the capital and the opening of the river. Yet . . . the foreigners seek to take advantage of us in many [other] ways [as well], even seeking to transport goods between our own domestic ports for sale."[99] He later went so far as to argue, in direct contravention of the emperor, that "at this time, to accomplish the foremost aim of preserving *guoti*, the key matter is to take back our economic authority [*liquan* 利权]."[100] In repeated memorials, He argued for the importance of the ability to set tariffs for China's autonomy, its national prestige, and its ability to conduct such important affairs as suppressing rebellions.[101] Engaging in a risky course of insubordination, he also managed to convince fellow officials of the dangers of Xianfeng's approach.[102] His fellow representatives to the Tariff Conference, Huashana and Guiliang, themselves became convinced that China's customs must remain in place to preserve China's power and, as they remarked, "to esteem *guoti*."[103] In particular, the funding for regional military units – vital for confronting the Taiping rebels – was dependent upon customs revenue. Like Prince Gong but in contradiction to Xianfeng, these officials ascribed "stateliness" and "state form" less to the imperial person than to Qing finances, administrative institutions, and territory.

Remarkably, the emperor's representatives never even informed their Western interlocutors of the offer that their ruler had made. He Guiqing instead negotiated for set tariff rates that would now be officially collected (as had already become unofficial practice since 1854) by the foreign-run MCS under titular Qing authority.[104] All along, the other officials had sought to persuade Xianfeng to abandon his proposal, including by appealing to his sense of dignity by arguing that "Western foreigners pay [customs] tax in place of tribute, and if this tax were exempted, it would further promote their habit of despising the Celestial Empire."[105] However, Xianfeng still considered the matter of financial administration to be far removed from the essence of the state's structure or dignity, and open for extensive flexibility and compromise. As to the demand for permanent diplomatic representation, he continued to exhort his officials to "rescue" the unacceptable situation: If they failed to do so, "not only will you be unable to face Me; how will you face the Empire?"[106]

After the failure of his representatives to deliver on his desired policies, Xianfeng ordered a quixotic military resistance that featured one victory in June 1859 at the Taku Forts by Tianjin, though defeat at the same strategic point the next year decided the outcome of the conflict. In the face of invasion, the emperor retreated to Manchuria in 1860, leaving Prince Gong behind to negotiate the war's end and the new terms of relations with the West.[107] In October 1860, British-led forces stormed Beijing and committed the now-infamous sacking of the Summer Palace, claimed to be a reprisal for mistreatment of Western prisoners but also, in Elgin's words, "a blow to [the emperor's] pride as well as his feelings."[108]

Although notions of what would later be called "international criminal law" had an indefinite presence in law of war doctrine at the time, the paradigm of criminality suffuses Elgin's explanation for his decisions. His choice to punish the emperor rather than lower-level officials was based in part on what he viewed as the former's "responsibility" for violations of the 1858 Treaty and mistreatment of prisoners, and in part on prudential and economic considerations. To punish other officials for specific acts, such as the truce-breaking attacks by the Mongol general Sengge Rinchen, would for Elgin have meant "throwing the responsibility for the acts of Government . . . on individuals," which "resembles too closely the Chinese mode of conducting war."[109] Meanwhile, imposing heavier reparations costs on the Qing would have interfered with the need to "appropriate [only] such a portion of the Customs Revenue, as will still leave to [China] a sufficient interest in that Revenue, to induce it to allow the natives to continue to trade with foreigners."[110] By contrast, injuries to imperial "feelings" and "prestige" were very much to be desired, in part for reasons having to do with securing economic rights:

> [T]he Emperor's affectation of superiority is not in itself of much consequence to other sovereigns, but it has an unfavourable bearing as regards the validity of the treaty rights which they obtain from him on behalf of their subjects, because it imparts to them in some sort the character of concessions made of pure grace by a suzerain to vassals and enjoyed therefore under some not very definable conditions of fealty.[111]

To deliberately injure China's *guoti* in the sense of diminishing the prestige of the imperial office was, therefore, a calculated effort justified by rational economic interests as well as Britain's own concerns over dignity and "stateliness." In negotiating an end to hostilities, Prince Gong clearly understood himself to be unable to secure any significant concessions, including preventing the opening of the Yangzi River that he had viewed with such trepidation two years earlier. The only consolation was that the Convention of Beijing served mainly to reinforce the commitments of the Treaties of Tianjin rather than add major new obligations. However, Xianfeng's anathema, full formal equality in diplomacy, was very much included.

In order to deal with the new postwar reality, Prince Gong petitioned to create a new office to handle diplomatic matters with the West.[112] To be sure, Xianfeng by this point recognized the need to accept the imposed change of circumstances. However, his initial reaction to the memorial suggested a continued stubborn failure to grasp the full scope of the situation. While approving Prince Gong's proposal, he also, as was his imperial prerogative, personally decided on a name for the new bureau: "The Office in Charge of Affairs Relating to Commerce with the Various Nations."[113] For the emperor, it seemed, foreign affairs and the incursions of Western states were still essentially matters restricted to the realm of trade, not to any larger political or legal world order in which his empire was embedded.

Prince Gong responded by requesting in another memorial that the word "trade" (*tong shang* 通商) be removed, ostensibly to avoid the "suspicion that I and other ministers will only conduct trade, but not handle [other] affairs."[114] Whatever the emperor's original intentions, he again approved his brother's request, and the "Zongli Yamen" was established. This office would gradually begin China's engagement with the ideas and practices of international law.[115] Xianfeng, though, would not live to see it. In August 1861 the thirty-year-old Iju passed away suddenly, ostensibly of illness, at his palace in Jehol. Following his death, although he had left orders for his five-year-old successor to be supervised by eight regents from his entourage, this group was suppressed in a rapid coup by Prince Gong, allied with Xianfeng's widows Cixi and Ci'an and their clans.[116] The titular reign of the young Tongzhi emperor would proceed under the coregents' authority and also, for the first time ever, with a foreign diplomatic community ensconced in the capital and foreign gunboats enjoying free rein over China's internal waters.

Conclusion

Qing officials and intellectuals viewed the imposition of the Western international legal order through the lens of their own lexicon of public law concepts, which were more nuanced than the traditional Han Chinese rhetoric of a universal mandate of Heaven would suggest. Though Qing authority had never been construed in the terms of "inner" and "outer" sovereignty as developed in the West since the thought of Jean Bodin,[117] this did not preclude roughly equivalent relations between one great *gurun* and others, especially those too distant to be targets or threats in land-based conquest. Neither universal rule nor state sovereignty, but rather the relational value of *guoti* – foreign deference as to the key points of China's "stateliness," with varying views as to what exactly they comprised – was the standard determining how such relations should be handled.

For centuries before the mid nineteenth–century turn, China had already been tied to processes of capitalist protoglobalization through flows of silver and commodities such as silk, ceramics, tea, and cotton.[118] Its relationship with Western states and their merchants had subsequently changed dramatically in the post-Napoleonic era of rising free market ideology, intra-European peace, and liberal empire, especially after the end of the British East India Company's monopoly on the China trade in 1833.[119] But, while both the First Opium War and the religious/economic/legal proselytization efforts of Karl Gützlaff and likeminded emissaries were harbingers of later changes, it was not until the late 1850s that China's place in world order was comprehensively transformed; in place of a *catena* of commercial/jurisdictional relationships, there was now a united front of "the West" and the imposition of a multilateral legislative/regulatory regime. In the brief span between 1856 and 1860, the rules of the "European system," encoded in the so-called public law of Europe, were effectively globalized over the course of the Ottoman adhesion, formal annexation of India, opening of Japan, and imposed reconstitution of the Qing. Economic, geopolitical, and legal expansion proceeded in tandem into these vast non-Western spaces.

In the classical self-understanding of the international law profession, these events were generally treated as isolated peripheral elements of an era when the *droit publique de l'Europe* progressively evolved into *droit publique international*; a process of gradual universalization.[120] Many later historians of the field have however noted the ways that newly globalized doctrines of multilateral diplomacy, internationalized regulatory spaces, and liberalized trade favored Western interests at the expense of those of their interlocutors in "outside" zones of expansion.[121] One influential view of this shift toward transitive legislation of non-European spaces has seen in it the displacement of a “natural law” with a “positivist” conception of the law of nations.[122] That supposed shift away from natural law has, however, sometimes been seen as exaggerated.[123] For the ultra-conservative twentieth-century jurist Carl Schmitt, for example, the “common land appropriations” by European powers through the nineteenth century were still largely continuous with prior eras in which shared ideas of private *dominium* ensured that “[despite] territorial change[s], the international economic order . . . retained all the . . . safeguards that it needed to function.”[124]

That description of the period’s legal-economic expansionism as a collective project has been shared by critical observers who (unlike Schmitt) saw it as illegitimate and unjust. As Karl Marx phrased it during just this period, “[t]he tendency to create the world market is directly given in the concept of capital itself. Every limit appears as a barrier to be overcome.”[125] From the Qing perspective, certainly, the newly imposed structures of international law and political economy came to China in 1860 as a package and in the form of a collective Western project. They also prompted new and at times prescient, if inconsistent, invocations of the value of *guoti*. While Xianfeng offered tariff-free trade in the name of preserving the sacredness of the imperial space and his imperial person, for some of his key officials loss of economic authority/ *liquan*, or vulnerability to territorial incursions, seemed still more important elements of “stateliness.” Though China in 1860 could not avoid concessions on any of these grounds, each would inform subsequent, sometimes conflicting aims that colored the reception of Western international law.

2

Synarchy

On August 20, 1862, the new US minister to China, former Massachusetts congressman Anson Burlingame, first met with Prince Gong and officials of the Zongli Yamen. While the American Civil War raged, just a month before the Emancipation Proclamation and as the German *émigré* jurist Francis Lieber was beginning to work on codifying the laws of war, Burlingame represented President Lincoln's administration in declaring the aim of more equal cooperation with the postcoup Qing government. One early manifestation of this approach was supporting the translation of a major work on international law into Chinese.

William Martin had begun such a translation independently, and based on advice from Burlingame's predecessor, had abandoned his original choice, Vattel's *Droit des Gens*, in favor of the more up-to-date *Elements of International Law* by Wheaton.[1] Wheaton's work, in a contemporary posthumous edited and updated 1855 edition, was one of the most comprehensive and influential treatises on international law then available in English. Indeed, one section dealing with diplomatic legations had by 1862 already been translated for Zongli Yamen officials by the deputy chief of the Maritime Customs Service (MCS), Robert Hart. By the September of the following year, Martin was able, with Burlingame's help, to gain an audience with Prince Gong, where he received official approval to complete the translation and was given the aid of four learned court scholars to help finalize the text.[2]

Prince Gong was initially suspicious of Martin's motivations, but eventually decided that he simply "sought to make a name for himself in China like [sixteenth-century Jesuit] Matteo Ricci." The importance of international law had also become obvious over the course of the Arrow War. The translation that resulted from Martin and his team's efforts, titled "The Public Law of the Myriad States" (*Wanguo Gongfa* 萬國公法), remains famous today as the first full work on international law to appear in Chinese and the first to be widely disseminated in East Asia. Although the text was often cryptic and hard to follow in its introduction of countless neologisms, certain of the introduced concepts and terms had quite a lasting impact.

Among the most lasting of the text's innovations were adaptations of traditional terms to convey new concepts. These included the use of *gongfa*

公法, literally "public law" with an overtone of justice, orthodoxy, and propriety, to translate "international law." Compared with the translation of Vattel's *Droit des Gens* as *Geguo Lüli* – translatable as "The Law Code of All States" – the use of *gongfa* clearly represents an attempt to imbue international law with associations from a word with traditional implications of legitimate order. Another, similarly important innovation was the translation of the term "sovereignty" into Chinese as *zhuquan* 主權,[3] alongside continued uses of Karl Gützlaff's earlier version, *zizhu zhi quan* 自主之權.

In fact, *zhuquan* too was already a fairly common and quite venerable term, in use since the preimperial era. Literally meaning the "authority of rule," it first referred to rulers of the preunification Warring States, and later to the emperor. Its most frequent uses by the Qing era were in contexts of official corruption or insubordination – that is, "usurping the ruler's authority" (*shan zhuquan* 擅主權), appearing various times in this sense in the official *History of the Ming*.[4] Another use that would have been especially significant for the court literati aiding Martin included references in the classic seventh-century BCE *Guanzi* treatise on statecraft, which warns: "When the treasury is depleted, the ruler's authority wanes" (*zang jie ze zhuquan shuai* 藏竭則主權衰).[5] There could hardly be a more fitting warning for the post-1860 age in which the Qing Court was dragged into the newly world-spanning systems of both global law and markets, while seeking to reassert its status as the most prestigious entity within the space of its vast *gurun*.

The intellectual dimension of that global incorporation, meanwhile, would center on transmitting concepts of state debts and obligations – in other words, compelling recognition of foreign and private *dominium* rights – rather than ideas of "sovereign" rights or power.

Ruling Completely

The new reign era of Xianfeng's five-year-old successor was titled *Tongzhi* in Chinese, which could potentially be translated as "Ruling Together." The influential twentieth-century American historian of China John King Fairbank considered this title as highly significant. He even proposed his own Hellenistic neologism, "synarchy," as a kind of philosophical translation of it. For Fairbank, the idea of synarchy, or joint rule, incorporated phenomena such as the Qing state's pragmatic acceptance of the MCS as a de facto internationalized trusteeship of China's customs and other fiscal administration, the "joint management" of legal cases arising in connection with consular jurisdiction, and other such forms of transnational governance. Looked at on a broader historical scale, Fairbank thought, it could also be applied to practices such as the Manchus' reliance on a vast Han Chinese official class to run the Empire. This willingness to forgo exclusive control over policy could seem a laudable alternative to sovereigntist autarky.[6]

That there was any genuine intent by the post-Xianfeng leadership to extol transnational cooperation with this reign title is quite doubtful, though. Indeed, the Manchu version, *Yooningga Dasan*, is better read as meaning "complete governance" or "ruling completely."[7] Not for the first time, subtle differences in the Chinese and Manchu versions of the imperial reign title suggested messages being tailored to different audiences. In the latter case, *Yooningga Dasan* suggested a commitment both to finally defeat China's rebel movements and to restore control over the full Qing space, and very likely also subtly implied the aim of *reclaiming* administrative authority over matters such as trade and border policy – far from embracing Western appropriations of the same. As Stephen R. Halsey has recently demonstrated, "the threat of European imperialism after 1850 inaugurated the most innovative period of state-making in China since the early seventeenth century," in many ways laying the foundation for China's eventual rise (or "return") to Great Power status in later generations.[8]

Indeed, very early in the Tongzhi reign era, officials were already calling for "self-strengthening" (*ziqiang* 自強) and, relatedly, returning to the theme of "economic authority," or *liquan*, that He Guiqing and other officials had called attention to during the Arrow War. As one official memorialized to the postcoup regent council in 1862, "Christianity is now filling the empire, foreign chiefs reside in the capital, the foreigners know everything about China's real situation, and, even when they cannot take [an aspect of] *liquan* now, they will wait and do so later."[9] Such concerns heavily influenced the new regime's willingness to engage in more intensive treaty relations, as well as to adopt foreign diplomats' suggestions for measures such as establishing rail and telegraph networks throughout China; all could, they worried, be used as means of further dominating China's economic authority by predicating its exercise upon an ever more foreign-dominated infrastructure.[10]

Even if Qing officials were wary of such dependence, Fairbank's idea of "synarchy" valorizing it was nonetheless indeed relevant to the Qing state of the time – as a key premise motivating their Western interlocutors, if not themselves. This disposition to merge the interests of the Qing and the (Anglo-American) West was shared by Martin and Burlingame, but also and perhaps most of all by Robert Hart, who took over the position as inspector general of the MCS in 1863, replacing Karl Gützlaff's protégé Horatio Nelson Lay after a contretemps in which Lay had attempted to raise a European naval force formally in Qing service but in practice under his own exclusive control. As Hart criticized afterward, such a move would have been totally incompatible with China's "sovereignty," and could never have been accepted. His own view, which he brought into his tenure as inspector general after succeeding Lay, was that "independent China, in her own dominions, has the right and power, in virtue of her sovereignty[,] to do everything she has not promised not to do."[11]

By contrast, some Western consuls, seeking to use their powers to advance the commercial and social interests of their own communities in China, took the opposing view: "China cannot do anything that foreign Governments have not said she may do."[12] The dispute in 1864 that Hart summarized with these clearly phrased alternatives, however, was not about the Qing state's autonomy as such but rather *his own* ability as MCS inspector general to enforce customs duties against foreign merchants despite the extraterritorial jurisdiction system in place. It was not really Qing autonomy, but rather the authority of the MCS as an "internationalized" trustee of Qing authority when weighed against a separate treaty-based power (i.e., extraterritorial jurisdiction) that had been granted to Western states' consuls, that Hart was defending here.

Burlingame, too, defended Qing "sovereignty" with respect to this question. In June 1864, he wrote to US consuls that: "the Chinese government has the right, as an incident of its unyielded sovereignty, to enforce its own revenue laws" – referring to enforcement by the MCS.[13] The principle being defended was that the MCS, though a *sui generis* public law creation most closely resembling the river organizations of the Rhine and Danube, could nonetheless exert full jurisdiction over foreigners in customs matters. With its role as a foreign-run, titular Qing agency established via transnational practice and agreements, the MCS was a kind of constitutionalized commingling of the economic interests of Western states with those of the Qing Empire.

The general political economy of the Qing polity had been transformed since 1860, not only by the forced opening of new treaty ports and adoption of public law norms favorable to Western capitalist expansion, but also through the new phenomenon of state debt. Already during the 1850s Western diplomats and Qing local officials had pursued the idea of partial foreign financing of the Qing war against the Taiping rebels. In the wake of the Arrow War, the cash-strapped imperial court soon began a program of large-scale borrowing. Between 1861 and 1868, it took out more than 3 million USD worth of loans from foreign providers, denominated in silver taels and, in large part, guaranteed by the revenues of the MCS.[14] The latter would soon go on to become the defining feature of the Late Qing fiscal state – a loan default being rendered notionally impossible as collection was in the hands of a transnational agency.[15]

If "sovereignty" was introduced to China via the international law reception beginning with Martin's *Wanguo Gongfa*, it was only as a heavily asterisked version of the concept. Indeed, this is quite apparent in the way the term is presented in the translated text itself. There has not to date been any study of the *Wanguo Gongfa* translation process sufficiently detailed to assess exactly how *zhuquan* came to be associated with "sovereignty." Martin and his team indeed coined some new terms that sounded "strange or un-Chinese" at the time, such as *quanli* 權利 for "rights."[16] However, that was definitely not true of the venerable and familiar but now recontextualized term *zhuquan*.

Meanwhile, this was only one of a "cluster of terms related to 'sovereignty' and 'independence' [including] … *zizhu zhi quan* 自主之权, *zili* 自立, [and] *zizhu* 自主."[17] As we saw earlier, "*zizhu zhi quan*" (literally "authority of self-rule") had been Karl Gützlaff's attempt to render the notion of "sovereignty" in his 1830s publications on liberalism. His successor Martin, sharing many of his views and aims, was certainly responsible for the many invocations of this alien-sounding neologism in *Wanguo Gongfa*. This may in turn suggest that *zhuquan*, as a preexisting familiar term with classical (and hardly liberal) connotations, was actually included in the text based on a suggestion by Prince Gong's scholars. If so, its specific function in the translation would perhaps have been felt as reaffirming some traditional Chinese notions of state power, in contrast to the many aspects of the text that challenged them.[18]

Whether or not that was the case, it is safe to say that the *Wanguo Gongfa* translation of 1864 did not present an especially coherent description of "sovereignty" as it was used in Western international law discourse. In part, that was due to the ambiguity of the concept itself in its original context. On the one hand, Wheaton could provide the relatively clear definition that a "sovereign State is generally defined to be any nation or people, whatever may be the form of its internal constitution, which governs itself independently of foreign powers."[19] On the other hand, the question as to what constitutes a "state," able to possess sovereign attributes, was itself quite opaque. In Wheaton's section "Definition of a State," there is the basic definition drawn from Cicero that a state is a "society of men, united together for the purpose of promoting their mutual safety and advantage by their combined strength."[20] This, however, then has to be qualified to exclude four non-state types of "societies of men": corporations, robber and pirate bands, "wandering savages" and, finally, a "nation" that had not yet established an organized polity.[21]

Each of these categories raised its own problems of a lack of corresponding terms in the Chinese political lexicon. Above all, though, the fourth category, that of a "nation" without a "state," was the hardest to convey. Martin's translation settles for stating that: "sometimes a group of people of the same kind [*tongzhong renmin* 同種人民] united for mutual protection still do not form a single State. For multiple kinds of people may submit to the same ruler [*tong fu yi jun* 同服一君]; that is the case in the three States of Austria, Prussia, and Turkey."[22] Perhaps despairing of accomplishing in a single go the full introduction of European-style nationalism into China (though, as Gützlaff had been, he was certainly sympathetic to this goal), Martin did not dwell at length on trying to explain the idea of the nation as opposed to the state.

Another especially difficult section, consisting of content heavily muddying the presentation of "sovereignty" in both the original and the translated text, is Wheaton's discussion of "semi-sovereign states," including in this category protectorates and vassal states of European powers and the Ottoman Empire, as well as Native Americans in the United States.[23] For Wheaton's category of "tributary and vassal states," *Wanguo Gongfa* has "the sovereignty retained by *Jingong* and *Fanshu* states" (*jingong fanshu suo cun zhuquan* 進貢藩屬所存主權) thus employing terms long used for polities standing in relations of ritual submission to the Chinese emperor, including at various times Korea, Vietnam, Japan, and Ryūkyū, among others. The actual examples in Wheaton's text, however, are quite different, as the section discusses mostly the position of the Barbary States in relation to the Ottoman Empire and of Native American tribes, specifically the Cherokee, in relation to the United States. Martin's text truncates the Ottoman section and focuses on the latter example, even including parts of the US Supreme Court's judgments in the cases *Cherokee Nations* v. *Georgia* (1831) and *Worcester* v. *Georgia* (1832).[24]

To identify the Cherokee and other Native American groups, Martin makes use of the term "Red Miao," the same phrase used by the Qing to describe a number of the most recalcitrant non-Han inhabitants of the southern frontier regions in and around Yunnan.[25] As presented by Martin, Chief Justice John Marshall's ruling that "America's Red Miao" stood in the position of "a ward to his guardian" vis-à-vis the United States might have seemed comprehensible for Qing officials used to the rhetoric of benevolent imperial care and instruction for China's Miao. However, more difficult to convey was the doctrine that "[a] weak power does not surrender its independence and right to self-government ... by association with a stronger and taking its protection," and that thus while *some* "American Red Miao" were under direct rule by the US government, others kept a hazily defined status of limited or "half-rulership" (*banzhu* 半主).[26] References to various intermediate degrees of "semisovereignty" and dependency undermined any effort to present sovereignty as an identifiable status attached to a set of consistent rights.

Sovereignty and Obligation

Interestingly, when it came to the crucial matter of public debt, Martin's *Wanguo Gongfa* text did not rely on the newfangled terminology of sovereignty. Instead, it made use of the term *guoti*, which had been so important during the recent Qing debates of the Arrow War when it came to defining the essential features state authority and diplomatic propriety. That was also the sense in which it was now employed to convey the inescapable character of debt obligations between "sovereign" states, even after changes of government. Wheaton's original passage on public debts explains that:

> As to public debts ... a mere change in the form of government, or in the person of the ruler, does not affect their obligation. The essential form of the State, that which constitutes it an independent community, remains the same; its accidental form only is changed.[27]

Meanwhile, the translated passage by Martin and his cotranslators reads, literally:

> As for State debts . . . despite a change in the monarch / ruler, or a change in the State law (*guofa* 國法), there will not be any effect on such accounts. For this State still is independent, and so its *guoti* is still present. What has changed is [the State's] *impression* but not its [essential] *form* (*suo bianzhe qi ji, fei qi ti ye* 所變者其跡，非其體也).[28]

For any debt attributable to *guoti* as "the essential form of the state," debts could not be escaped even given a change of ruler or dynasty. For Westerners making large silver loans to China during the 1860s, this was an important principle to inculcate in the Qing leadership.

Another, closely related instance in which Martin and his team also had recourse to *guoti* was in dealing with the issue of when, and how, valid treaties can expire or lose their efficacy. Wheaton gives four conditions in which this can occur, including war between the contracting states, the end of one state's existence, fulfillment or expiration of the treaty, and transformation of the "internal constitution of government" of a state – this last, however, affecting only "*personal*" and not "*real*" treaties. The latter would "[still] bind the contracting parties independently of any changes in the sovereignty, or in the rulers of the State."[29] The legal principle of *rebus sic stantibus* – "changed circumstances" potentially permitting derogation of treaty obligations – was thus presented in Wheaton's text as a limited exception granting only *relative* autonomy to states, but not acting as a bar to their treaty-based obligations.

Treaties could still bind a state even after a "change in sovereignty," Wheaton asserted. Martin's translation, once again, turns to *guoti* to convey the idea of an essential state personality: "some treaties pertain to *guoti*, while some pertain [only] to the person of the monarch/ruler. Those which pertain to *guoti*, even if there is a change of dynasty, still must be adhered to and cannot be abandoned."[30] The distinction between *real* and *personal* obligations is thus here rendered as those pertaining to *guoti* 國體 versus *junshen* 君身 – that is, "state form/stateliness" versus the "person of the ruler."

Another, related set of Western public law terms that could not be easily rendered in Chinese dealt with *territorial* sovereignty, usually discussed in international law texts by reference to the Roman legal terms *imperium* and *dominium*.[31] These notions, which had been especially important to Jean Bodin's development of the distinction between internal and external state sovereignty in the sixteenth century, are explained by Wheaton as entailing that a state's authority over the property of its citizens, including land, is "*absolute*, so far as it excludes that [authority] of other nations; but, in respect to the members of the State, it is *paramount* only."[32] In other words, as Bodin had helped to establish, in Western public law, the ruler of the state could not arbitrarily seize private property, nor dispose of state property as if it were his own possession. In the subsequent history of Western public law, this had developed into the binary distinction between *imperium* as the power to compel personal obedience of subjects to sovereign authority and *dominium* as the power over property (including real property). Only the former power was originally unlimited, while the latter was, as Wheaton said, only "paramount" in the sense of a reserve of so-called eminent domain (*dominium eminens*): valid private property rights and title could not be disregarded even by an absolute sovereign.[33]

As with the duty to fulfill debts and treaty obligations, the duty to recognize property rights was presented in mainstream international law texts as inherent to sovereign status. Martin's translation faced difficulty conveying the idea of an authority over territory only paramount vis-à-vis claims by foreign states, however, and so *dominium* was simply rendered as the opaque "authority to possess and control things" (*zhang wu zhi quan* 掌物之權).[34] As with the other aspects of sovereignty presented in *Wanguo Gongfa*, the nature and extent of territorial sovereignty was not clearly defined. However, the basic premise of a right to exclude foreign territorial intrusions – except when waived under extant treaty obligations – was easily inferred. Based on the discourses of sovereignty and international legal status reflected in both the Wheaton translation and in the communications of Western diplomats, China's rulers could expect to exert *imperium* over all Qing subjects, including rebels like the Taipings, and at least *dominium eminens* over imperial assets and territory – though both powers were in practice now limited by treaty obligations, debts, and private legal claims based on property ownership.

Although the appropriation of the old term *zhuquan* to convey the new Western term "sovereignty" did not catch on among Qing officials in the 1860s, some of them did clearly come to appreciate the "two-sided" nature of state power as generally depicted in *Wanguo Gongfa*. As long as external obligations to the Western community of states were maintained, stable imperial rule in China's own territory could, perhaps, be successfully reestablished. Prospects of this kind received a major boost in 1864 with the final defeat of the Taiping Rebellion in a military campaign led by influential Han Chinese officials including Zeng Guofan, Zuo Zongtang (who had been in imperial service against the Taipings since shortly after his meeting with Lin Zexu in 1850), and Li Hongzhang. These officials would amass vast influence during and after their victory (with substantial Western assistance) over the Taiping rebels, and were central to the new policy of "self-strengthening" (*ziqiang* 自強) initiated after 1860. Involving initiatives in military modernization and pursuit of technical capabilities, the self-strengthening policies would, for a time, seem adequate to put China on the path to recapturing its *imperium*.

Territory and Community

The idea of an international legal power to exclude territorial incursions was invoked by the Zongli Yamen three years into its existence, soon after the publication of *Wanguo Gongfa*. This occurred in response to an incident involving the Prussian capture of Danish ships in waters near Tianjin during the Second Schleswig War of 1864. For the officials of Prince Gong's new ministry, such hostile action by one foreign power against another in China's waters was "in truth a violation of China's authority" (*shi you ai yu zhongguo zhi quan* 實有礙於中國之權).[35] Mixing such allusions to the new language of legal rights with more familiar discourse of stately dignity, the Zongli Yamen officials emphasized that "to capture a ship in Chinese waters is to show contempt of China."[36] Zongli Yamen officials successfully protested that Prussia was improperly "wresting away China's authority" (*duo zhongguo zhi quan* 奪中國之權) with its move, prompting a reversal of course by the Prussian side, as well as an apology and small amount of restitution.[37] The first treaty between the German *Zollverein* states and the Qing Empire, which put the former on par with the large European empires in pursuit of commerce in China, had been ratified a few months earlier;[38] preserving this status quo was, of course, in Prussia's interest.

The Prussian affair of 1864 helped to convince Prince Gong and other leading officials of the potential utility of international law texts. Dozens of copies of *Wanguo Gongfa* were then printed and distributed to Qing officials in the various treaty ports.[39] However, the incident remained anomalous. Most other 1860s diplomatic disputes were handled by the Qing side on the basis of compromise and negotiation, with minimal references to foreign legal norms. A dispute over incursions by Russian timber harvesters in the territory of traditional Qing tributary state Joseon (Korea), for example, could have raised difficult questions about the latter's exact international legal status. However, in practice Li Hongzhang was able to satisfy the Korean request for assistance by means of bilateral negotiations with the Russian side, allowing the Qing state to continue "properly using our greatness to nurture the small" (*bu shi zhongguo yi da zi xiao zhi li* 不失中國以大字小之體).[40]

Other contentious matters arising in the 1860s turned on similar negotiations. One significant dispute emerged with France over attacks by locals in Guizhou against French Catholic missionaries – the same issue that had provided France a pretext to join the Arrow War. The French chargé d'affaires specifically invoked his own country's *guoti* to demand capital punishment for the presiding official, Tian Xingshu, who had allegedly permitted the anti-Catholic outbreak and the execution of several missionaries.[41] Prince Gong responded by saying that Chinese law and the treaties with France required removing Tian, but not executing him. Further supporting this position, the Zongli Yamen invoked China's *guoti* as not permitting such punishments to a high-ranking official based on foreign demands.[42] This French attempt to enforce obligations on China by using the "native" concept of *guoti* demonstrated how the formalistic rules of treaty law might, at times, serve Qing interests better than vaguer standards drawn from its own conceptual lexicon: Certainly, no European state of the time would have amicably allowed itself to be commanded by a peer to execute one of its regional governors.

In the end, Tian Xingshu was exiled to Xinjiang, much as Lin Zexu had been two decades earlier as punishment for his own confrontational line against the West. Once there, however, he was soon enlisted to serve under the new viceroy to the far western Shaanxi-Gansu region, Zuo Zongtang, who had been sent to quell rebellions by local Muslim groups.[43] The effort to pacify the Qing Empire's restive Muslim-populated western regions, including Xinjiang, would occupy Zuo for much of the following decade. In 1866, Zuo prepared to launch his military operation in the west via a novel form of large-scale financing, in the amount of 1.25 million silver taels, guaranteed against the maritime customs receipts of several treaty ports secured by the MCS.[44] This large sum, with collection fully in the hands of the MCS and deposits going to HSBC, marked a major new stage in the "internationalization" of China's fiscal state. The Qing government was giving up more financial *dominium* in order to preserve political *imperium*.

General recognition of the need to maintain diplomatic and economic cooperation with the West while reasserting "complete governance" over the Qing realm promoted greater influence for the Zongli Yamen. It also facilitated the latter's establishment of the Tongwenguan, or Translators' College, which initially prepared students to act as English interpreters before later expanding into other languages as well as a general study of Western academic subjects. Another move to draw closer with the "international community" of the West was the new practice of dispatching diplomatic missions abroad. An initial mission to Europe by a staid Manchu official in 1866 left little impact at home or abroad. The following year, though, a more ambitious, if idiosyncratic, mission was undertaken. The leading American diplomat in China, Anson Burlingame, was appointed by the Qing Court after the conclusion of his diplomatic service to the US government to serve as head of a special delegation to visit the United States and Europe.

The choice of a foreigner to lead such a mission gave rise to much surprised comment within foreign diplomatic circles in China. It was, in fact, a move that would allow China's delegation to engage with the norms of Western diplomacy without justifying the assumption that China itself had adopted such norms permanently going forward.[45] To greet a foreign leader with a mere bow, for example, might risk implying to Western diplomats that they too should be able to treat the Qing emperor with no greater deference. It was thus necessary, Burlingame's instructions held, to clarify to his interlocutors that his mission was adopting "the etiquette of the Far West, which is different from China's state system." This caveat would serve as an insurance policy against engagement being invoked later on as precedent, pragmatically accepting Western diplomatic forms without "altering China's *guoti*."[46] Zeng Guofan had supported this approach by pointing out how, during Kangxi's reign, the emperor had chosen to deal with the Russians "according to the ritual of a peer/rival state [*diguo zhi li dai zhi* 敵國之禮待之][, while] he dealt with Korea by contrast as a tributary vassal state, and thus in a very different manner." The new decision to treat the West "as if peers in matters of form" was thus "following Kangxi's illustrious example."[47] Or so it was still possible to pretend, if only just.

Profit and Progress

Upon Anson Burlingame's return to the United States at the head of the Qing delegation, he was greeted with, among other high-profile events, a celebratory banquet in New York City. Making an opening speech before a gathering of local political and business leaders associated with New York's Republican Party establishment, Burlingame described the emergence of a new China that now welcomed Western religion and trade, and thus deserved a conciliatory attitude. Among those associated with the elite gathering were jurists important to the rapidly transforming field of international law, including David Dudley Field, a prominent New York lawyer, political figure, and top American authority on transnational commercial law, and Francis Lieber, then a Columbia University law professor famous for his military code.[48] Others included sitting New York governor Reuben Fenton, presidential candidate Samuel Tilden, previous governor and future US secretary of state Hamilton Fish, Theodore Roosevelt, Sr. (father of the future US president), and various impresarios of the burgeoning China trade.[49]

In his remarks, Burlingame declared that China had to be regarded as an impressive "nation" in terms of its size, antiquity, "homogeneity," and sophisticated culture, and also that a more equal meeting of the minds between the West and China would both be possible and, most importantly, highly profitable. China's new openness, manifested in his own role as its delegate, embodied for Burlingame an impressed fascination with all the Western world order had to offer:

> She tells you that she is willing to trade with you, to buy of you, to sell to you, to help you strike off the shackles from trade. (Applause.) She invites your merchants, she invites your missionaries. She tells the latter to plant the shining cross on every hill and in every valley. (Applause.) For she is hospitable to fair argument. I say she tells you she is willing to strike off the shackles of trade. She offers you almost free trade to-day. (Cheers.) Holding the great staples of the earth–tea and silk–she charges you scarcely any tariff on the exports you send out in exchange for them. (Applause.)[50]

Of course, the "almost free trade" that Burlingame extolled was the result of the treaty terms exacted a decade earlier amidst the Arrow War. However, the ensuing years of peace and growing profits (for some) had seemingly demonstrated the folly of those Western diplomats and politicians who portrayed China as a "barbarian" state to be "exclude[d] from the council halls of the nations." Burlingame instead advocated a more equal course of dealing, "Giv[ing] to those treaties which were made under the pressure of war . . . a generous and Christian construction."[51] In almost sensuous terms, Burlingame depicted how China:

> [F]eels the spark from the electric telegraph falling hot upon her everywhere; [and] rouses herself, not in anger, but for argument . . . She finds that she must come into relations with this civilization that is pressing up around her, and feeling that, she does not wait but comes out to you and extends to you her hand.[52]

Burlingame's China was one aroused by Western trade, religion, technology, and law. Indeed, as he told his well-heeled audience, "she comes [to you] with your own international laws . . . she tells you that she is willing to come into relations according to it, that she is willing to abide by its provisions."[53] Overall, his comments demonstrate the alignment of the mid nineteenth-century conciliatory position toward China with then-burgeoning ideas about both international law and the spread of free trade. Already in the late 1850s, Palmerston's Arrow War had been criticized by some liberals in Britain as not just aggressive, but also an ultimately self-defeating impediment to free commerce (though the prowar party had invoked the same ideals).[54] Now, China's "opening" could once again be portrayed in the register of an ultimately friendly process of mutual accommodation and profit. The Chinese market still seemed to represent enormous short-term potential. As Burlingame noted, foreign trade between 1862 and 1867 had "risen from $82,000,000 to $300,000,000," an impressive increase that was, however, "but a tithe of the enormous trade that will take place with China when she gets into full fellowship with the rest of the world."[55] This commercial potential suggested that if foreigners would "let [China] have her independence; let her develop herself in her own time . . . [then] she will initiate a movement which will be felt in every workshop of the civilized world."[56] In return for its consumption of finished imports, meanwhile, China would send back "our tea, our silk, [and] our free labor."[57]

Soon after, David Dudley Field presented a toast on "International Law, Preserving Peace in both Hemispheres."[58] Field was at this point already leading efforts to codify both domestic law and legal procedure – indeed, the first major codification of the American rules of civil procedure, which came to greatly influence subsequent development across the common law world, came to be known as the "Field Code" – and also the rules of private international law.[59] He would go on to cofound the Association for the Reform and Codification of the Law of Nations (the ancestor of today's International Law Association) four years later.[60] Simultaneously, Field also served as the president of the American Free-Trade League, calling for a rejection of protectionist policies and a more globally integrated US economy.[61]

In his remarks, Field tied the recent inclusion of China in the international legal system to the latter's embodiment of universal rules of political economy.

He argued that "there never has been presented a better opportunity for a reform of the international code than that which this oriental mission now presents ... [for e]ach new member of the brotherhood of States brings a contribution to its precepts."[62] These are strikingly cosmopolitan-sounding comments. However, the contribution Field referred to was not one stemming from China's *own* culture or politics, but rather a sort of positive externality from economic integration with the West. Echoing Burlingame, Field called for "a just and equal compact between sovereign nations" as the basis for ties between the United States and China, and linked this notion with an economic/diplomatic relationship in which "neither ... desires an advantage over the other, but both of them seek the freest intercourse of persons, the most liberal exchange of products, constant reciprocation of good offices, and perpetual peace."[63] To develop relations on such a free-trade basis would be to reveal the higher truth of international law whose "tendency is ever towards melioration."[64]

If viewed through the lens of Hayden White's theoretical typology of historical narratives, Burlingame and Field's "emplotment" of the narrative of China's entrance into international legal relations embodied a highly "Comedic" worldview,[65] founded upon the all-harmonizing power of trade. The ancient polity China, once transformed, could ironically serve as the ultimate example of the commercial genius underlying modern (American) progress: "That great empire which we now welcome into the community of nations, will help us, we trust, to still further meliorations."[66] This mood of "melioration" was also very much on display in the major blackletter law consequence of the mission: the signing of a new bilateral treaty in 1868.[67]

This agreement, henceforth known as the "Burlingame Treaty," was one of the few nineteenth-century treaties that conferred important rights on the Qing state and its subjects, including the ability to appoint consuls in American cities, freedom of emigration of Chinese to the United States, freedom of religion of Chinese subjects in the United States, access to public education institutions, and other such *mutual* obligations.[68] Indeed, the Chinese text of this treaty was dominated by a term hardly seen in any previous: *yiti* 一體, meaning "in common" or (in this context) "reciprocal," and, by implication, "equal."[69] Another important element of this treaty was its clarification in the English text that "in making concessions to the citizens or subjects of Foreign powers [in Qing territory] ... for purposes of trade, [the Qing emperor] has by no means relinquished his right of eminent domain or dominion over the said lands and waters."[70] The corresponding Chinese text, however, referred not to *dominium eminens* but instead to the emperor's retaining a vague "administrative authority over land and sea territory" [*guanxia difang shuimian zhi quan* 管轄地方水面之權].[71]

Deeper Qing inclusion into the Western "international community" came just as the latter was being transformed by accelerating trends of economic globalization and Anglo-American cooperation. The seminal *Alabama* arbitration between the United States and the United Kingdom, in particular, would help to inaugurate a new age of voluntary dispute resolution between Western countries as well as the further juridification of interstate relations. For free-trade enthusiasts like Burlingame and Field, legal and commercial integration with China would automatically benefit all of those concerned – both China's rulers and Western states, great business concerns like those represented at the 1868 banquet, and also the everyday man and woman, who would do better because "Free-Trade means cheap food, cheap clothes, cheap house rent, cheap fuel."[72] As the tool for delivering these rational goods, Field thought, international law (especially once codified) would embody the "the world's collective will."[73]

An alternative approach among leading pioneers of international law, however, focused more on differentiation and hierarchy. Such views (which Burlingame had alluded to critically) were now frequently associated with the invocation of a "standard of civilization" as the notional basis for membership in the international community.[74] The more "civilization"-minded international lawyers of the mid nineteenth century saw commercial/religious penetration of foreign realms less as profitable cooperation than as pedagogical instruction. Legal historians have noted the way ideas of civilization functioned as a proxy for race or religion,[75] and also lacked clear criteria except, perhaps, whatever would most favor the expansion of Western European racial capitalism.[76] On the other hand, members of the international law profession like Field who focused explicitly upon commerce per se seemed actually to favor somewhat more equal ties, at least as long as the Qing were opening their markets. By contrast, the jurists most concerned with "civilization" were less willing to envision the potential equality of non-Western polities.

Among the figures who did the most to promote the idea of "civilization" as the basis for international legal rights and personality was the Swiss-born jurist Johann Caspar Bluntschli. His writings, and those of his close colleagues, fully demonstrate the paradoxes of an ostensibly universal international legal history that relied upon inventing a particular subject – "Western civilization" – as the heroic protagonist of a grand narrative of cosmopolitan progress.[77] Rather than focusing on inherently melioratory powers of trade and cooperation, Bluntschli stressed the "organic" emergence of legal forms from particular human societies as advocated by the German historical school of Savigny with its focus on notionally chthonic Germanic legal norms.[78] Applying this lens to international law, Bluntschli was one of those responsible for an emerging romanticized conception of the international lawyer as the "conscience of the civilized world."[79]

Very often, China and Japan served for Bluntschli as a useful foil for the notion of full racial equality, precisely because they were "*Culturvölker*," or cultured peoples, whose cultures were nonetheless distinct from (and in his view inferior to) that of the West. Assimilating cultural proclivities to differences in race and pigmentation, Bluntschli classed the "light yellow" China and Japan as comprising the second-highest category of civilization, above the darker and notionally more savage peoples elsewhere but clearly below the white race, which comprised the particularly "historical peoples[, who] determine the history of the world."[80] While firmly committed to these (hardly uncommon) ideas of racial hierarchy, meanwhile, Bluntschli also sought to engage with materials on foreign civilizations when they were available to him, if generally only in order to confirm his preconceived schema. On various occasions, Bluntschli examined in detail translated Confucian philosophical texts, praising the "fine state philosophy"[81] that they represented, but nonetheless portraying them, and East Asian peoples as a whole, as having failed to develop beyond "despotic" government and as lacking in "popular freedom" (*Volksfreiheit*).[82] Though seeing as laudable the Chinese ideal of *ren* 仁, or "humaneness," (rendered as *Humänitätsprinzip* or *Menschlichkeit*), for Bluntschli, China's "humane empire" fell far short of that of the Christian West.[83] Practices such as extraterritorial jurisdiction could be justified based on motives of civilizational pedagogy to promising pupils.

Lieber, a friend and collaborator to both Field and Bluntschli, had views somewhere between the comedy of all-harmonizing trade and the Romantic saga of heroic Western culture. Echoing the ideas expressed at the New York banquet that he had attended, Lieber saw China as potentially joining the "commonwealth of nations" – the translation of "Our" *Law of Nations* by Wheaton being an important step in this direction.[84] At the same time, the leading nations of France, Britain, Germany, and the United States would "draw the chariot of civilization," while newcomers to the system followed in their wake. This could be seen in how "a citizen of the American Republic has entered our city, at the head of a Chinese embassy . . . for the avowed purpose of attaching China to that Union of Nations."[85] The commercial preconditions for that "attachment" are suggested in an 1869 booklet that attacked American protectionists' claim that restrictions on trade could at times promote "national independence." That "fallacy," he wrote, "mistak[es] Chinese seclusion and exclusion for civilized and dignified independence."[86]

In much the same vein, the following year, the Belgian lawyer-diplomat Gustave Rolin-Jaequemyns wrote an enthusiastic review of Lieber's defense of free trade in the *Revue de Droit International*, adding the remark that "America is closing off its shores just as China is opening its own!"[87] Though in agreement with the condemnation of protectionism articulated in Lieber's pamphlet, Rolin-Jaequemyns argued that it had not gone far enough. For "it does not suffice to simply demonstrate that a protective tariff, however moderate, is not a good . . . it is necessary, we think, to see in it a positive evil."[88] China had, of course, by this point turned over control of most of its own tariffs to the MCS. For the many international lawyers that saw free trade/ *libre-échange* as an immanent principle underwriting the project of international law,[89] such steps were part of the march of economic and civilizational progress, just like the internationalization of the Yangzi, extraterritorial consular jurisdiction, or the imposition of diplomatic etiquette.[90]

These were the men that were founding the modern profession of international law. Bluntschli, in particular, proved a formative influence with his book *Das moderne Völkerrecht der zivilisierten Staaten, als Rechtsbuch dargestellt*;[91] and via his role in the September 1873 founding of the *Institut de Droit International* in Ghent. He cofounded the institute alongside ten others including Rolin-Jaequemyns, the Swiss cofounder of the Red Cross, Gustave Moynier, David Dudley Field (whose own international law association was founded the following month, with overlapping members), James Lorimer of Scotland, Carlos Calvo of Argentina, and Tobias Michael Carel Asser of Holland.[92] From the start, the institute tended toward Bluntschli's emphasis on "civilizational" consciousness, rather than sunny faith in the ameliorating powers of commerce per se. It was an epic and heroic worldview that "projected a vertical hierarchy where from the totality of humanity a part emerged – the civilized part – to rule over the rest."[93]

Renewed Studies

One of the flaws in Western jurists' visions of the commercial and civilizational instruction of China was the ongoing dearth of Chinese actually eager to pursue such learning. The "self-strengthening" platform adopted under anti-Taiping heroes Zeng, Zuo, and Li did not aim at wholesale adoption of Western legal, diplomatic, or commercial forms. In each of these areas, new efforts were sporadic and at times meant only as tactical concessions. Indeed, even as Burlingame proceeded on his meliatory mission abroad, Zongli Yamen officials continued to warn that Western economic agreements would increasingly strip China of its *liquan* and *shiquan* – economic and policy authority.[94] In search of ways to deal with this concern, the seeds of later, more comprehensive transformations in political economy were also being sown.

There now emerged the idea of using domestic investor capital to stimulate growth as well as technological/military development. One key proponent of such moves was Yung Wing (aka Rong Hong), a Cantonese Christian who had gone to the United States at a young age and graduated from Yale College in 1854. His 1860s proposal of joint-stock financing for a Chinese-owned-and-run steamship company was implemented in 1872 by Li Hongzhang as a state–private joint venture.[95] The China Merchants' Steamship Company, directed by the young official Sheng Xuanhuai with private funding, was both the first Chinese-owned steam transport firm and the earliest domestic joint-stock company. More such initiatives ensued, with Sheng continuing to play a leading role, extending into the areas of telegraphs, textiles, banking, and mining.[96] Like other aspects of "self-strengthening," this economic component would play an important part in reversing some of the loss of Qing state power, and of "stateliness" in diplomatic and legal interactions. Yet as in military matters, these efforts to promote Beijing's *liquan* would eventually be largely overwhelmed by more foreign encroachments. It is important to note, as well, that the Qing Court's pursuit of *liquan* was not constructed in terms of a legalized economic sovereignty or a "permanent sovereignty over natural resources," as would be theorized by twentieth-century anticolonial movements and theorists. Like *guoti* itself, it was a relational value, depending heavily on geopolitical context and shifting power dynamics.

If 1868 had been a major turning point in Qing relations with the West, holding out the prospect of membership in a more tightly knit but for the time being conciliatory legal/commercial community with the West, it also marked a shift for a man continually seeking to put himself at the center of such developments, William Martin. Based upon his useful *Wanguo Gongfa* translation and his good relations with Burlingame, Martin had been invited by Zongli Yamen officials in 1867 to take up a position at the Tongwenguan as its first "Chair of International Law and Political Economy."[97] The job came with a comfortable salary. In the face of skepticism from his Presbyterian Mission Board supervisors, who warned him against seeking "secularizing employments from a love of lucre," Martin protested that the position would allow him to exert influence over Qing officials and students. Meanwhile, on a personal financial level, it would provide "some accession of means just at a time when our older boys are entering college and our younger boys might be sent home for education... meet[ing] our exigency for which charity has made no provision."[98]

As it turned out, not only did his new position allow him to fund expensive educations at Yale for two sons, the latter helped provide some useful connections for his career in China. Before taking up his appointment at the Tongwenguan, Martin took a long leave of absence coinciding with the Burlingame Mission, part of which he spent seeking out contacts among international jurists interested in China's opening-up. His biographer Ralph Covell suggests that after leaving China in July 1868, Martin spent most of his time on the US East Coast, and "may have studied law informally at Yale under the direction of Theodore Woolsey."[99] Upon his return to China in 1869, Martin achieved another coup, as he was offered not only the chair he had deferred two years earlier, but also the role of "president" of the Tongwenguan itself, under a reorganization plan initiated by Prince Gong to expand the institution and its influence, from a mere translators' college into a quasistate academy.[100]

In his new role at the head of the revamped institution, Martin made sure to keep international jurists informed of China's – and his own – progress. In 1871, he sent a letter to Francis Lieber, extolling the latter's work and raising the idea of translating it into Chinese as a follow-up to his translation of Wheaton the previous decade.[101] This proposal, along with the expansion of the Tongwenguan itself, was noted with approval the next year by the Gustave Rolin-Jaequemyns and the other jurists of the *Institut de Droit International*, who hoped that such efforts might help to "complete the already-begun initiation of the Chinese into our Occidental civilization."[102]

In 1873, Martin then published in the institute's journal his own brief account of "the present and future of international higher education in Peking,"[103] presented as part of a personal letter to Rolin-Jaequemyns. Although in the latter's words it was "difficult" to print parts of the letter containing "too much personal flattery addressed to the *Revue* and its directors,"[104] the sections published did serve to explain the aims of the Tongwenguan and to emphasize that disseminating international law knowledge would be among its core tasks. As Martin wrote, he would instruct Qing students as well as officials that "it is due to the influence of this Universal Code [i.e., international law] that their country can be relatively safe from foreign invasion."[105] There was at this point still not any dedicated study of international law at the Tongwenguan, but Martin described his intent to begin such instruction with ten students in the following year. To pursue this course, though, he would need more international law materials. Martin's initial plan of translating Lieber's work had been dropped by this point – one wonders if this was in part because Lieber had died in October of 1872, and thus could no longer serve as a useful networking contact with elite jurists. In any case, his new intention was to begin by translating the 1871 textbook by the international law scholar and president of Yale College, Theodore Dwight Woolsey (with whom Martin had connections based on his sons' studies at Yale), for this was "written expressly with students in mind" and would thus be easier to teach with.[106]

Excess flattery notwithstanding, the editors noted Martin's plans with approval, as well as his promise to submit more material on China's progress in international law in the coming years. In addition, they expressed hope that he would "soon" send them an article on the "international customs that prevailed among the independent and semi-independent states of ancient China." Ultimately, however, Martin would not publish an essay on this topic in the *Revue* until nine years later,[107] by which time China's nascent reputation as a star pupil of international law and civilization was almost entirely discredited in the eyes of European jurists, in favor of its neighbor, Japan. The first signs of that shift, which would be fateful for the future of the East Asian region and of the world, were already on display by the beginning of the 1870s.

Ontological Challenges from China's "Closest State"

The year 1868 had been a major turning point in yet another sense: It was the year in which the Meiji Restoration refounded the imperial Japanese state. Having experienced many of the same foreign pressures as the Qing over previous decades, the Tokugawa Shogunate as well as the leaders of its major samurai domains had oscillated between conciliation and confrontation. By the mid 1860s, the domains of Chōshū and Satsuma, which had each already pursued direct negotiations and limited military engagements with Western powers, as well as modernization efforts intended to begin closing the gap with the West, led the toppling of the Shogunate. From the very beginning, the new regime in Japan embraced Western public law terms and concepts in a way that even the most ardent Qing reformers had not yet dared to advocate.

In particular, the Meiji government had focused on the concept of sovereignty. Although even into the mid 1870s Qing officials were not yet using the term *zhuquan* in connection with public law, the term was by that point fully adopted in Japan. Martin's *Wanguo Gongfa* had been read in Japan from 1865, and its various references to *zhuquan* (in Japanese pronounced *shuken*) quickly brought this new/old term into political relevance in a way that they had not in China. In 1868, the same year that the Meiji government was founded, there were two new separate translations of Wheaton's *Elements of International Law*, one by Tsutsumi Koshiji based on Martin's text,[108] and another by the scholar Uryū Mitora, translating directly from English into Japanese.[109] In these works, Wheaton's "sovereignty" is sometimes rendered with Martin's terms, and sometimes with similar alternatives. A particularly cogent attempt at conveying the concept, meanwhile, appears in Uryū's translation of a passage discussing John Austin and Jeremy Bentham's positivist approaches to international law, where sovereignty is rendered *dokuitsu saijō no ken* 独一最上の権 ("the unique and supreme [state] authority").[110]

The same year, the very first East Asian books on international law not directly based on Martin's text were also produced in Japan. These came from the first Japanese intellectuals to study international law in Europe, Nishi Amane and Tsuda Mamichi.[111] Both had been chosen by the Tokugawa government to study Western politics, law, and economics in the Netherlands. While there between 1863 and 1868, they researched these subjects under the Dutch political economist Simon Vissering, publishing multiple books upon their return.[112] Tsuda's book developed on the basis of Vissering's lectures, *The State Law of the Far West*, is often considered the first major Japanese work on Western political and legal topics.[113] Significantly, Tsuda employs the term *shuken/zhuquan* for "sovereignty," but he gives it an interpretation that is distinct from that in Martin's *Wanguo Gongfa* and that in part constitutes a return to the two-character combination's traditional imperial associations. For Tsuda, "*shuken* is the *ruler's* authority. All of the country's people submitting to this authority are considered subjects."[114]

For the concept of the state's autonomy vis-à-vis other states, meanwhile, Tsuda makes use of *jiritsu jiji no ken* 自立自治の権 ("authority of independence and self-governance").[115] While Martin's confusing presentation of *zhuquan* had left it in a vague relationship with other terms such as *zizhu* (and terms such as *banzhu*/"half-sovereignty," etc.), Tsuda provided it with a conceptually clearer definition based on state authorities' plenary *imperium* over their subjects. Similar precision also characterized Tsuda's contributions to domestic law, particularly the Meiji legal code introduced in 1870. Such efforts at legislative modernization in Japan were quickly drawing favorable attention in the West, and comparisons with the pace of Qing reforms.[116]

The first "modern" Sino-Japanese diplomatic encounters demonstrated this gap in the reception of and attitudes toward Western law. In mid 1870, the energetic twenty-year-old Japanese nobleman and deputy foreign minister Yanagiwara Sakimitsu had arrived in China alongside the ethnic Chinese interpreter Tei Einei to initiate negotiation of a Qing–Meiji treaty. Eventually managing to meet with Li Hongzhang and Zeng Guofang in Tianjin, Yanagiwara made the case for formal treaty relations between the two states. Seeing the opportunity to build up ties with another state outside of the web of Western multilateral obligations (and coercion). Li and Zeng soon helped to overcome objections by conservative officials who opposed equal relations with a state traditionally classed, like Korea or Vietnam, as a vassal/tributary.[117]

Upon departing China, Yanagiwara had left behind his own unauthorized draft treaty based on previous examples signed with Western states. This became the basis for revision efforts in which Li and Zeng, as well as Li's aides Ying Baoshi and Chen Qin, built on the draft as an opportunity to assert new rights for China in its foreign relations. Among the most important examples was the exclusion of most-favored nation provisions, which had been used by several states to claim extraterritorial and other rights initially granted only to a single power. Consular jurisdiction could also be made a mutual arrangement, rather than a unilateral grant. And interior travel by Japanese throughout China could be restricted, as was the case in Japan's own treaties with the West. This potential to "break new ground" (*bie kai sheng mian* 別開生面) with Japan was welcome at a time when relations with the West had taken a negative turn; the mid 1870 "Tianjin Massacre" of twenty-one foreigners and around forty Chinese Christians by locals in the area had been seized upon by Britain to abandon already-negotiated improvements to China's tariff flexibility and the revision of most-favored nation arrangements.[118]

When Yanagiwara returned the following year as an aide to his country's official envoy Date Munenari, a former head of the Uwajima Domain, they thus encountered a Qing side that had unexpectedly prepared its own list of demands.[119] Along with Chinese–Japanese translator Tei Einei and the international law scholar Tsuda Mamichi, Date and Yanagiwara negotiated mainly with Li Hongzhang on treaty terms. The official Japanese draft treaty, composed by Tsuda, sought to put Japan in the same position as Western states in their relations to the Qing (it was directly based on the Qing treaty with Prussia of 1861). However, in the end, the Japanese side accepted several of the Qing terms, including the lack of most-favored nation status.[120]

Undergirding the talks was the more fundamental question as to what sort of international relations should exist between the peoples of East Asia under the new conditions of compelled opening to Western diplomacy and trade. As one of the protagonists in this debate, Yanagiwara was particularly explicit regarding the implications of a turn to Western-style treaty relations. In a letter he passed to the Zongli Yamen during the negotiations of autumn 1871, he advised that China, in its relations with Japan, should follow "the great way of all people under Heaven" (*tianxia ren zhi da dao* 天下人之大道) – referring to Western international law. Though using language redolent of the ancient Sinocentric world order, Yanagiwara's point here was precisely the opposite: That only a full embrace of Western norms between independent states would be an acceptable basis for Sino-Japanese relations. In support of this, he notes that:

> When Westerners make demands on us, if we reject them we must do so based on existing norms or precedents of other states. We can only pursue uniformity, not develop idiosyncratic approaches. When norms are broken, it attracts avarice [from the West].[121]

In this case, the "idiosyncratic approach" that Yanagiwara argued would prove risky for Japan and China was to establish formal relations not based upon Western international law. That, however, was just what an edict in the name of the young Tongzhi emperor had recently proposed: That there was "no need to follow the old forms of the Far Western states [*taixi ge guo jiutao* 泰西各國舊套] when establishing a treaty of friendship and commerce,"[122] given that Japan was "a state with the same culture/letters" (*tongwen zhi guo* 同文之國).[123]

The Japanese envoy's reply now subtly emphasized that even a treaty such as the Qing side had proposed must be "signed based upon the sovereignty of the two states."[124] Yanagiwara's insistent references to *zhuquan/shuken* in his dealings with the Qing in the early 1870s reflected his side's core demand: Clear assertion of a perfect formal legal equality between Japan and China. The Meiji government, with its ambitious plans of modernization and reorganization, saw this new language as key to legitimating its status domestically and abroad. By contrast, the Qing response was characterized by consistent turns back to old terms and concepts, including the emphasis upon *guoti* /stateliness, rather than sovereignty. Indeed, this applied even to the "reform"-minded officials who advocated accepting some Japanese proposals. Li Hongzhang, for example, had argued that it was wise to deal magnanimously with "the country closest to China" (*Zhongguo zui jin zhi bang* 中國最近之邦), but also that it would be necessary to "carefully examine each provision of any treaty . . . first avoiding any impediments to *guoti* and second avoiding disturbances to merchants and citizens."[125]

When the Sino-Japanese Treaty of Amity and Commerce was signed on September 13, 1871 by Date Munenari and Li Hongzhang in Tianjin, it did not include the unilateral consular jurisdiction rights for Japan that Tsuda had incorporated into his Prussian-based draft, and its consular jurisdiction provisions were highly detailed in ways that, overall, promoted notions of comity and mutuality.[126] Overall, this new agreement was still more "equal" than the "equal treaty" with the United States that had followed Burlingame's mission: It established that both sides enjoyed extraterritorial jurisdiction over their nationals in each other's territory, that tariff rates would be set by negotiation, and that Japan would not derive most-favoured nation benefits.[127]

In Article 3, meanwhile, this agreement did contain the explicit guarantee that "each country's internal governance is to be reserved to its own independent authority." However, there were some significant differences between the Chinese and Japanese texts. The Japanese refers to each state's "*jishu no ken* 自主の權" or right/authority of self-rule: That is, sovereignty as expressed in Gützlaff formulation *zizhu zhi quan* 自主之權.[128] Meanwhile, the Chinese version avoids novel terminology and instead the relevant section reads, literally: "each state's matters of governance should be reserved for its own self-rule" (*qi zhengshi ying ting jiguo zizhu* 其政事應聽己國自主), with no reference to any formal *quan*/authority/right.[129]

This slight difference in wording was indicative of broader agendas intersecting with the relative power, motivations, and ideologies of the two states. Article 6 makes this evident, as it holds that "in future official communications . . . China will use the Chinese language, and Japan will use Japanese writing with a Chinese translation or will use only Chinese, as it prefers."[130] This provision was, of course, the exact reverse of the various provisions on language preference included in China's treaties with Western powers.[131] Despite this minor victory, it was clear that Meiji Japan posed a unique problem for Qing officials' efforts to achieve secure foreign relations while maintaining stateliness. At times it seemed as if Japanese leaders, too, were making use of the newly learned lexicon of international law in order to claim an authority to transform China.

Conclusion

In the period after 1860, the Late Qing polity operated as a formally recognized "sovereign" in the Eurocentric state order, subject to two parallel limits that had been effectively incorporated into the state's constitutional structure since the Convention of Beijing. First was the increasingly clear distinction between the *imperium* of state authority over Qing subjects and the notional *dominium eminens* over territory and property. While the latter was now restricted by entrenched treaty rights held by foreign states and their citizens in China, from extraterritorial consular jurisdiction to the "lease" of territories, the former was still notionally plenary. Indeed, the project of regaining control over rebel zones, both the Taiping rebel space and Muslim regions of Qing Central Asia, among others, took shape as an effort to recapture rightful control over the Qing realm's full territory – on the basis of already-indispensable *Western* financing.

The internationalization of the Qing public accounts through tariff-backed loans proceeded apace with the establishment of other "synarchic" institutions and practices. Consular jurisdiction, MCS-managed tariff collection and loan repayment, and Western-built logistics and communications infrastructure further tied the Qing *gurun* to the West's commercial flows and legal norms. Rather than outright conquest, Western elite diplomats, jurists, and capitalists envisioned the operation of heterogeneous legal-regulatory zones within a system of globally interconnected economic relations and Eurocentric cultural pedagogy. International law was treated by some of these early advocates of globalization as a leading force in the extension of "capitalism as civilization,"[132] and by others as something more like an emergent phenomenon.

Slightly less than a century was to separate Burlingame's musings before New York's business and political elite over "the spark from the electric telegraph falling hot upon [China]" and Marshall McLuhan's reflection that "[t]oday, after more than a century of electronic technology, we have extended our central nervous system itself in a global embrace, abolishing both space and time as far as our planet is concerned."[133] In a sense, positivist international law was simply one more technology alongside steam, rail, and electricity to be used in this (selective) abolition of unwanted barriers in space and time. Many politicians, merchants, diplomats, and leading jurists such as the founders of the *Institut de Droit International* were inspired by "synarchic" innovations in the Qing realm furthering human progress and free trade. These narratives coexisted, however, with a Qing officialdom still focused on balancing its stateliness and spatial order against inevitable concessions to the West. Though the notion of a legally construed *zhuquan* as a bulwark against foreign regulatory projects had not yet fully taken hold even among the Qing policy-making elite, it was soon to begin doing so – in large part, as the dealings of 1871 presaged, through the influence of "the country closest to China."

3

Vast Imperium

By the early 1870s, officials in the Meiji government had for years discussed possible ways for Japan to start proactively using international law to assert parity with the West. The newly appointed Meiji foreign minister in late 1871, Soejima Taneomi, advocated a more expansionist posture vis-à-vis Korea in particular.[1] Korean unwillingness to diplomatically engage with Meiji Japan was cognizable as an affront against an equal sovereign under Western (post-Vattelian) doctrines that would justify reprisal. Along with official invocations, notions of state "sovereignty" now increasingly permeated the public consciousness in Meiji society. Indeed, by 1873, a Japanese–English dictionary could simply list *shuken* as the first and primary translation for the word "sovereignty."[2] In China, meanwhile, the term as it had appeared in *Wanguo Gonggfa* was still in neither widespread nor official use with this significance.

It was also at this time that "international law" first received the Chinese character translation by which it is still referred to today throughout East Asia: The term *kokusai hō* 國際法 was coined by the scholar Mitsukuri Rinsho in the title of his 1873 translation of Woolsey's *Introduction to the Study of International Law*.[3] Mitsukuri's book title, which is most literally translated as "interstate law, i.e. the public law of the world," very clearly emphasized the "state-to-state" character of legal relations – just the point that Japan was now seeking to assert, so far unsuccessfully, vis-à-vis the Qing. The terminological innovation *kokusaihō* reiterates Yanagiwara's emphasis on "the respective sovereignty" of China and Japan as the basis for relations in his 1871 letter. If the Qing could often still fit their new multilateral treaties into old frameworks of stateliness, treating "the public law of all states" as a kind of general code of etiquette supplementing case-by-case diplomacy, this was far harder to reconcile with Meiji insistence on an explicitly "interstate law." In particular, this mounting clash of ideas emerged with respect to territories where Qing claims could be contested by expanding foreign empires.

A Region Transformed

Yanagiwara had returned to China in 1872 during a subsequent round of negotiations, reflecting dissatisfaction in Meiji official circles with the recently signed treaty. While there, he became aware of newspaper reports regarding the deaths at the hands of local indigenous groups on the island of Formosa (Taiwan) of fifty-four shipwrecked sailors from the Kingdom of Ryūkyū/ Liuqiu.[4] This development was, as Yanagiwara established in discussions with the British consul at Shanghai, precisely the sort of incident that Western states often used as a legal basis for military reprisals.[5] Though many officials still doubted the wisdom of sending an expedition against Korea, they could perhaps back one against the "natives" of Formosa.

Ryūkyūan leaders had for centuries maintained an ambiguous status as a "tributary" state both to successive Chinese dynasties and, since the seventeenth century, to the Satsuma Domain of feudal Japan. This provided a potential basis for a Meiji claim that "its" subjects had been killed on Formosa. In close cooperation with the newly arrived French-American military adviser to the Meiji government, Charles Le Gendre, Soejima and other officials began planning their response to the incident, which increasingly turned on the notion that "savage" territories could be annexed in a legitimate fashion in order to be "civilized."[6]

Soejima went to China in early 1873 to negotiate with the Qing over the handling of the incident. His visit, and the broader incident, happened to coincide with and prompt the resolution of another major diplomatic crisis over *guoti*. This was the set of dealings referred to as the "audience question," which centered on China's obligations under the Convention of Beijing to let foreign diplomats meet with the emperor.[7] The timely death of Xianfeng in 1861 had postponed such audiences. Yet, in 1872, his successor Tongzhi had turned fifteen years old and had gotten married. It was no longer possible to deny visitation on the basis of minority. Although it seemed clear visits would have to be allowed, there were still unresolved questions that Qing officials saw as implicating stateliness. In particular, would foreign envoys make the traditional *ketou* 磕頭 (aka kowtow) genuflection to the emperor? Prince Gong sent a memorandum to the foreign diplomats on this point, arguing that "in whatever concerns the dignity of the state, each side must take care that it does no injustice to the other."[8] This was also a matter of "popular feeling," as a meeting with the emperor without proper etiquette would be "in the opinion of every Chinese … derogatory to the dignity of his government."[9] Each of these references to "dignity of the state" reflects internal discussions about preserving Qing *guoti*.[10]

The US minister to China wrote that "the arguments of the Chinese ministers are unreasonable and … unworthy of serious consideration," although he acknowledged that "to them … this question is very grave,"[11] implicating not just the specific matter of genuflection but also the possible ramifications of "throwing open [the] doors to the palace" for foreign intercourse at the highest level.[12] A month after Prince Gong's memorandum, the Chinese side was still seeking to insist on points of ceremonial order. Another memorandum was conveyed to the assembled foreign ministers on April 29, this time setting out numbered stipulations in the form of a draft international agreement, focused explicitly on *guoti*. Article 1 read: "The etiquette of China differing from that of foreign countries, nothing is to be insisted on derogatory to the dignity of either side." This drew immediate protests from the Western diplomats who regarded it as an unacceptable attempt to make the kowtow a prerequisite of any imperial audiences.

While these negotiations were occurring in Beijing, Soejima and Li Hongzhang had been engaged in intensive debates in Tianjin over the Taiwan issue as well as Sino-Japanese relations more generally. Soejima's demands for compensation related to Taiwan were met with heated resistance by Li, but the most immediate result was that the treaty of 1871 was now finally ratified in order to establish a basis for further negotiations. After Soejima proceeded to Beijing in the spring of 1873, he was, as Japan's foreign minister and an ambassador plenipotentiary, technically the highest-ranking diplomatic official from a foreign state then in China. His presence thus immediately affected the possible resolution of the audience question, and also presented an opportunity for Japan to more fully assert its very newly won and fragile recognition as a formally equal power. Seojima's adviser Le Gendre wrote that it would be necessary to triangulate matters such that "foreign representatives would have no excuse for refusing to acknowledge us as one of their number" and also to ensure for Japan "a deliberative voice in the great foreign-Chinese questions."[13] Japan's aim of parity with Western states would be, for decades to come, made concrete in large part via its changing relations with the Qing.[14]

These various debates were resolved in part through the intervention of Li Hongzhang, who in May submitted a memorial endorsing a "compromise" over the audience question that, in reality, constituted a major concession to the Western demands – the kowtow might be abandoned in favor of some other suitable ceremony. Li noted that audiences were obviously meaningful for the Westerners.[15] Meanwhile, "our dynasty has set rituals for dealing with vassal states [*shuguo* 屬國], but we have no set rituals for dealing with peer states [*yuguo* 與國]."[16] Given this, it would be preferable to "show our magnanimity" by giving way on "small details" (*kuan qi xiaojie* 寬其小節).[17] By this point, Xianfeng was no doubt turning over in his grave. Nonetheless, the policy was adopted and two audiences were held in mid June: First of Soejima alone, in light of his higher diplomatic rank as a full ambassador, and then the Western envoys.[18] The concession on audiences made ripples abroad in diplomatic and legal circles, and would later be noted with approval in the *Revue* as a particularly promising sign of "progress" in China's opening up to international law among "equal sovereigns."[19] A sketch made at the time by the pioneering British photographer in China Thomas Child shows the Western delegates lined up, Prince Gong at their side, addressing the young monarch as a unified foreign bloc.

Although Soejima had achieved a major symbolic victory with the resolution of the audience question, his specific demands for compensation with regards to Formosa were rebuffed based on the premise that the natives were "uncultivated vassals" (*shengfan* 生番), to whom the Qing administration "did not reach."[20] Though from the Qing perspective this did not imply that the island itself was not Qing territory, it was sufficient in the eyes of the aggressive faction in the Meiji government to justify a military expedition against the offending "savages." The subsequent course of dealings involved Yanagiwara, who continued to pursue the Taiwan issue with the Zongli Yamen over the following year, and continued to seek to raise more general questions regarding the Qing status in the region. At one point, he compared Taiwan with Cambodia and Tonkin as areas that, because they were not sufficiently "protected" by the Qing, had already been all but abandoned to the West.[21] Japanese forces landed in Taiwan in May, and their operations, ultimately aimed at annexation, would continue through November.

Negotiations in Beijing also continued through the fall of 1874, as representation of the Japanese side was taken over by the high-ranking statesman Ōkubo Toshimichi 大久保利通, recently returned from the Japanese "Iwakura Mission" of statesman and scholars visiting the West to study a wide range of policy and administrative matters.[22] While in Europe, Ōkubo had been most impressed by Otto von Bismarck's Prussia, as a state combining technological and military superiority – displayed in its dazzling defeat of France in 1871 – with a high degree of order and hierarchy. As Bismarck reportedly said to the envoys, Prussia, like Japan, had once been "poor and weak," but had now become great in part through military self-assertion. He advised them to emulate this feat rather than focus solely on diplomacy and international law.[23]

From *Wangtu* to *Terra Nullius*

The most striking moment in the Qing–Meiji course of dealing, and the most significant for the conceptual history of "sovereignty" in China and throughout East Asia, came with an 1874 communiqué submitted to the Zongli Yamen by Ōkubo Toshimichi in support of Japan's rights to send an expedition to Taiwan – and indeed to lay to claim to it – supported by a brief but densely footnoted memorandum on international legal authorities in support of the Japanese position.[24] If any single moment marks the turning point at which *zhuquan/shuken* 主權 became the de facto conceptual crux of international law in East Asia, it would be this one.

In the space of only about three pages, the term *zhuquan/shuken* 主權 was mentioned five times. Moreover, it was now not being used generically to refer to undefined qualities of state "independence" or "self-rule," but rather as the signifier for a specific *legal claim to formal, exclusive rights to the possession of, and all authority over the administration of, a specific spatial zone*: the island of

Formosa. This was sovereignty as exclusive title to territory: What mid nineteenth-century jurists still often referred to as a state's "dominion" or *dominium (eminens)*, preserving old implications of a term otherwise increasingly used for private property ownership.

It would not be possible to use Gützlaff/Martin's erstwhile variant translations of "sovereignty" such as *zizhu zhi quan* 自主之權 (literally "authority of self-rule") for this claim, because at issue now was specifically *acquisition* of title and all attendant political, diplomatic, and economic rights.[25] In other words, the Japanese policy was now to treat Taiwan as a *terra nullius* over which existing Japanese state sovereignty could be *extended* – the very first time this status had been applied to Qing-claimed territory by a foreign power. In support of this argument were marshalled citations from several leading legal authorities. These were, in order: Emer de Vattel, Georg Friedrich von Martens, August Wilhelm Heffter, and Johann Caspar Bluntschli.[26]

In keeping with the Sino-Japanese treaty ratified the previous year, the 1874 Ōkubo Memorandum to the Zongli Yamen was written in Classical Chinese. Yet the ideas it contained were, without exception, drawn from prominent texts of Western international law. In the very first line of the memorandum, Vattel was cited for §208 of his *Droit des Gens*, holding that "the law of nations will not recognize the property or sovereignty of a nation except over empty lands where it has effectively and genuinely occupied them or formed in them an establishment or of which it will make actual use."[27] The Ōkubo Memorandum version, notably, combines Vattel's *propriété et souveraineté* (property and sovereignty) into the single word *zhuquan* 主權.[28]

Georg Friedrich von Martens and August Wilhelm Heffter are cited for related points, regarding the specific requirements of effective occupation, including the latter's observation that "occupation over persons" requires either that they submit voluntarily or "under the domination of a conqueror."[29] Ōkubo then cites Bluntschli, first for paragraph §278 of his *Das moderne Völkerrecht der civilisirten Staaten als Rechtsbuch dargestellt*, which described the legal rights that can be attached to "stateless" territories (*statenlosem Land*; *wu shu zhi di* 無屬之地).[30] Other states could gain *zhuquan* 主權 (*Gebietshoheit*) over this land if they subject it to occupation (*Besitznahme*; *zhanju* 佔據). Meanwhile, if some state makes a claim to the control of a certain territory, but has failed to effectively make use of it, then mere displays of will do not suffice to claim sovereignty (in Bluntschli: *Statsherrschaft*). There is also no obstacle to another state "ordering and civilizing" the stateless land and its people (*zu ordnen und zu civilisiren*; *jiaohua qi min, chuangzao qi zheng* 教化其民，創造其政).[31]

There are many firsts in this diplomatic memorandum. Never before had public international law been invoked in such detail and in reference to a specified set of authorities in any interaction between East Asian states. Never before had an important legal question in Greater China turned upon acquisition of sovereignty over an "uncivilized" and "stateless" territory – though gradations of civilization had certainly been applied to territorial acquisitions by European states elsewhere in Asia, for example, the British acquisition of the North and South islands of New Zealand by treaty and "discovery," respectively, or the claims to Australia on similar grounds.[32] But only the new Meiji characterization of Taiwan as "stateless" brought the concept of a *lack of sovereignty* into direct relation with soil long treated as *wangtu* 王土 – "royal land" – that is, land subject to the moral-political authority of various Chinese dynasties.

In the end, the Japanese mission in Taiwan failed in part due to a high death rate stemming from local diseases and other practical difficulties of colonization, and in part due to Western opposition to annexation. The Qing offer of compensation, made at British and American encouragement, was taken by Japan as implying acceptance of sovereignty over Ryūkyū, although the Qing side continued to dispute this claim. Meanwhile, some Qing officials now argued that other recently acquired European international law concepts, such as the norm of maintaining the "balance of power," should be invoked to counter Meiji expansion efforts.[33]

Another Vacuum at the Center

As these shifts were occurring in China's external situation, it seemed that the position of the "sovereign" in the sense of the ruler was also being redefined. After the receptions of Yanagiwara and the Western ambassadors in June 1874, there soon followed more requests for audiences with the Tongzhi emperor, some of which were granted. Very soon afterward, though, Tongzhi died suddenly, officially of smallpox though possibly from a sexually transmitted disease or perhaps even poisoning.[34] His cousin Zaitian, Cixi's four-year-old nephew, was now chosen to replace him via a highly unusual retroactive adoption process. China would go without a directly governing emperor for another thirteen years.

The discourse of *zhuquan*/sovereignty only now started to become noticeable in Qing official and intellectual circles, in this period immediately after both the Ōkubo Memorandum and the death of the Tongzhi emperor – and thus the loss (for the second time in fifteen years) of the actual *zhu* or "ruler" to whom such authority would be notionally attributed, as it was to the figure of the Meiji emperor in the Japanese context. This terminological shift occurred first in a set of international law works, the first new translations into Chinese since *Wanguo Gongfa*, that translators at the Zongli Yamen published with Martin's editorial support. The first of these, a translation of Karl von Martens' *Guide Diplomatique* (fifth edition, 1866), did not refer to *zhuquan* – though it did contain eleven uses of *guoti*, mainly as a stand-in for the original text's "national dignity" rather than its much broader range of original meanings.[35] Subsequently, by the following year *zhuquan* was used over a dozen times in Martin's long-promised translation of Woolsey's

Introduction to the Study of International Law (1871) (*Gongfa Bianlan*, 1877), which appeared four years after Mitsukuri's translation in Japan.

This adoption of the Western-influenced "Japanese" usage of *zhuquan* as sovereignty (especially as encompassing territorial sovereignty/*Gebietshoheit*) was then confirmed in the 1880 Tongwenguan translation of Bluntschli's *Das moderne Völkerrecht der civilisierten Staaten als Rechtsbuch dargestellt* (1868).[36] This was, of course, one of the texts that Ōkubo had cited six years earlier in his arguments that the Qing failure to "civilize" Taiwan had provided Japan with a right to do so in its stead and thus attain *zhuquan* over the territory. The full Chinese version of Bluntschli's work contains more than forty uses of the term *zhuquan*, and is considerably more exact and consistent in its explanations than *Wanguo Gongfa* had been. Rather than the latter, the 1874 Ōkubo Memorandum and the 1880 translation of Bluntschli's text should probably be seen as the real starting point for the modern Chinese discourse of *zhuquan*.

The translation of Bluntschli's §62–94, on the "international legal characteristics of states" (including *Souveränität*), contained some of the most significant of these references, and undoubtedly helped to shape future understandings of the term. The contents of the section reinforce this idea that sovereignty is the defining feature of the state's existence, beginning from §62 that compares the state to "a person with both rights and subjectivity" (*you ren* ... *you quanli* ... *you zhujian* 猶人 ...有權利 ... 有主見), for whom individuals are like organs or limbs.[37] In what follows, §64 defines sovereignty as "the capability for independence and lack of reliance on other states [as well as] the ability not to receive orders from other states." Other paragraphs in this section explain more key features of the concept, such as that sovereign authority "emerges from the people" (*chu yu min* 出於民) and that it can be limited by international law, but not (legitimately) by other states unilaterally. Perhaps most strikingly for Late Qing readers, §63 states that "whoever *actually* governs the state and wields state authority should be regarded for diplomatic purposes as state ruler" (*guozhu* 國主; originally "head of state, organ of the state will and State representative").[38] These are suggestive ideas for a Qing polity in the middle of what would ultimately be almost three decades without a directly ruling emperor.

Meanwhile, the idea of stateliness was also being reconstituted. Bluntschli's text explains a concept of "state dignity" (*Statsehre*), which the Chinese text translates conveniently as *guoti*, and clarifies that injury or insult (*Verletzung*; *ru* 辱) to this dignity is a proper basis for reprisals (*Genugtuung*; *zhuijiu er xing taosuo* 追究而行討索).[39] Yet this legalistic *guoti* lacked any of the robust set of substantive rights or features attributed to *zhuquan*: Only the latter constituted a right to territorial ownership and control, and was synonymous with legitimate state authority. From the late 1870s, the Qing Court's attention shifted to consolidating territorial control of the great *gurun*'s vulnerable fringes, from Taiwan to Xinjiang, and Manchuria to Southeast Asia.

Indeed, even the naming of Prince Zaitian's new imperial era seems to have embodied the aim of consolidating Qing rule over contested frontiers. Though the Chinese characters of the reign-name Guangxu 光緒 signified "brilliant (or glorious) succession," a very different message was projected by the Manchu language version: *Badarangga Doro*. This signified something close to "expansive imperium,"[40] but could also be rendered as "vast order" or, we might even say in context, "extending sovereignty."[41] The very reign name of the new child emperor thus appears to have been chosen to reflect the Qing elite's aspirations to take their place among the world's great powers while consolidating control over their ancestral territory and subjects – to the maximal extent established by Qianlong's eighteenth-century campaigns.

Qing Envoys Abroad

In the first year of the *Badarangga Doro* era, another diplomatic crisis emerged when the British diplomat Augustus Raymond Margary was killed, along with members of his staff, by locals in Yunnan near the border with Myanmar. Subsequent negotiations over compensation between Thomas Wade and Li Hongzhang extended until August 1876, when the Chefoo Convention (*Yantai Tiaoyue* 煙台條約) was signed and gave to Britain, along with 200,000 silver taels, some significant new concessions, including the opening of four new treaty ports, ensuring the prohibition of taxes on foreign goods (except opium) at all open ports, and establishing specific rules for consular jurisdiction, including the stipulation that a local official of the plaintiff's nationality would "merely attend . . . to watch the proceedings in the interests of justice," but not to take part in adjudication. Meanwhile, the law to be applied would be only that of the defendant's nationality. Wade ensured that both versions of the text specified the meaning of the treaty term *huitong* 會同, or "joint handling" of legal cases, to include these provisions.[42]

Aside from these extensive new imposed rules, there were also provisions establishing obligations for the Qing in respect of diplomatic matters. An additional article to the treaty gave Britain the right to dispatch another "mission of exploration," this time to Tibet, and made it incumbent upon the Qing to inform the imperial *Amban* and ensure all requisite permissions.[43] Meanwhile, a set of more general provisions dealt with diplomatic affairs in a comprehensive sense, requiring that the Qing compose an "imperial letter" of apology and dispatch this directly to England via a diplomatic mission (in addition to posting it publicly around the country).[44] This mission of apology was in fact an ideal way to achieve another long-standing British aim, which was the posting of a Chinese resident envoy in London, thus further "equalizing" relations – not that there had been anything equal about the negotiation process at Yantai.

In response to the demand for a diplomatic mission, the Qing Court sent the senior official Guo Songtao, who left for England in late 1875 alongside a few other delegates.[45] Guo's subsequent records of his travels in Britain and France offer a window into the views of Western law and politics of open-minded officials in the reformist circles based around Prince Gong and the Zongli Yamen in the 1870s.[46] So too did those of Xue Fucheng, who like other self-strengthening officials first came to prominence during the Taiping War alongside Zeng Guofan. In early 1875, Xue had written a memorial outlining his policy suggestions for the new Guangxu reign era, in response to a call for views issued by the two dowager empresses. Xue's memorial included advocacy of civil service exam reforms to focus on modern policy issues, creating a modernized navy, and also understanding and promulgating knowledge of international law in order to more capably handle relations with the West.[47] Xue specifically argued that officials should avoid either violating treaty commitments (*weiyue* 違約) or abandoning China's stateliness (*shi titong* 失體統) and thus inviting more aggressive incursions.[48]

Xue's views are especially significant because, after widespread acclaim for and official endorsement of his memorial, he became a close advisor to Li Hongzhang and participated directly in the negotiations over the Margary Incident, as well as subsequent diplomatic crises. After Guo's return from Europe, Xue would himself also serve as a leading Qing diplomat. His program of 1875 demonstrates the (limited) extent to which international law had penetrated elite discourse on matters of state, and served as a contrast with the ever-progressing Meiji project of achieving full recognition as a member of the Western international legal community.

Guo left China in December 1875 and remained abroad until early May 1879. While in London, he met on several occasions with prominent international lawyers.[49] After discussing international law at length with Travers Twiss, for example, Guo noted down that "the two books of Grotius are true classics; they are on everyone's lips," and that Adam Smith's "study of financial management [*licai xuewen* 理財學問] is the most renowned in England."[50]

From his previous focus on political economy, Twiss had now become a leading voice in international law, and was both a member of the *Institut de Droit International* and vice-president of Field's International Law Association (ILA). His major opus on the subject had also recently been updated in a new edition. Like Bluntschli, Lieber, Field, and others, Twiss was a passionate advocate of the mutually reinforcing nature of international law and free commerce as engines of progress.[51] Shortly after his 1878 conversation with Twiss, Guo was invited to join the annual meeting of the ILA. Although he did not travel to Frankfurt to attend, he arranged for attendance by his young colleague Ma Jianzhong, a young French-speaking scholar from a Chinese Catholic family who had been sent by the Zongli Yamen to study political economy and international law at the *École Libre des Sciences Politiques* in Paris.[52] Guo also sent ILA members a note in which he expressed enthusiasm for learning about international law, but also ambivalence given that "China is not in a position to adopt the Law of Nations at once," though he was "very desirous of attaining a knowledge of this science, in the hope that it will be beneficial to my country."[53]

At the same meeting, the Japanese consul Ueno Kagenori expressed more unreservedly enthusiastic views on the ILA and its subject matter.[54] Following the statements from each of these two "most important" Asian countries, David Dudley Field took the stage and raised the issue of extraterritorial consular jurisdiction – explaining that it might still be necessary to ensure the rights of foreign merchants and others in China, but that steps should be taken to improve the system and make it less of an imposition. Much the same view would be expressed in a meeting of Field's group the following year, in a discussion where Twiss was an interested participant.[55]

Though Guo praised both the ILA and Field himself for their "justice and solemnity," the oppressive aspects of Western international order were also very apparent to him. He noted, for example, that Westerners used the term "'half-civilized" (*hafu seweilaiyiside*) to refer to countries that they excluded from full membership of their community, particularly China, Turkey, and Persia.[56] Another passage in his diaries from the following year, as Guo was on board ship for his return journey to China, makes Guo's critique of colonial militarism quite clear:

> Whenever the Westerners open up ports, they are at first very modest. Then, their power and influence grow by the day, and the regulations and prohibitions put in place may oppress [some of the local populace]. This gives rise to mutual enmity and to attempts to expel [the foreigners]. Thereupon, one step is all that is needed to overtake the country and expand their territory by hundreds of miles. And so when they set up their ports, they need not *initially* rely primarily upon military force . . . [and yet] today, the territory remaining to be conquered [by the West] is only Asia and Africa, and no more. Meanwhile Japan is the only [non-Western] state that understands these methods. The rest are all befuddled . . . alas.[57]

Formalizing Civilizational Boundaries

Throughout the 1870s, the leading American advocate of free trade and legal codification, David Dudley Field, continued to argue for a clearer legal status for Asian polities. To this end, he initiated efforts to have the *Institut de Droit International* develop a clear doctrine regarding China's place in international law. At the institute's 1874 meeting at Geneva, Field first directly raised the question of "the possibility of applying the European international law to Oriental nations." His views were then summarized in a *Revue* article the following year, along with a questionnaire intended to solicit broader input on the topic.[58] Field noted, *inter alia*, that international law had been invoked in the interactions between China and Japan during their recent dispute over the island of Formosa and was also aware that works on international law had been translated and studied in Japan and in China, specifically mentioning *Wanguo Gongfa*.[59] Earlier that year, moreover, Field himself had made a visit to East Asia, including stops in Singapore, Hong Kong, Canton, Shanghai, and Yokohama, as part of a trip around the world.[60] On his journey, he had observed the functioning of local mixed courts and, in particular, heard a litany of criticisms from Westerners as to the state of Chinese justice, which contributed to his belief that some form of extraterritorial jurisdiction was indeed justified there.[61]

At the same time, however, Field also strongly advised against formalizing "civilization" as a hierarchical category that justified differential treatment of various states; should one really consider "that a nation . . . which possessed a cultivated literature and perfected arts, while our ancestors were still dressing themselves in animal skins . . . is non-civilized?"[62] In light of such considerations, Field argued, against the grain of his milieu, that "the perspective of civilization is *not* the one upon which the application of international law in China should depend . . . [and] a more liberal rule than that which has been applied to date may be adopted by Christendom."[63]

The greatest problem with consular jurisdiction for Field was not that it was "unequal" or overrode native sovereignty, but rather that it might actually deter the flow of global capital. Along these lines he reported a complaint made by the khedive of Egypt that, before the recent introduction of professional mixed tribunals, he had had trouble attracting investments because contract disputes would have to go before (potentially biased or inexpert) consular officials. A more professionalized extraterritoriality system, rather than its abolition, would seem to address such concerns. Indeed, Field ultimately advocated global adoption in non-Western lands, China in particular, of a system close to the Egyptian mixed tribunals, with an appellate chamber composed of six European judges and four natives.[64] Such a solution could last "until a more complete assimilation of judicial institutions between Occidental and Oriental nations."[65]

This approach to the problem, acknowledging the need to better respect the sovereignty of (some) non-Western peoples but without fully eliminating the "necessary" involvement of European judges, was endorsed by others at the institute's 1879 meeting in Brussels, notably Travers Twiss.[66] At the same meeting, Joseph Hornung, a leading Swiss judge, statesman, and professor at the University of Geneva, more strongly condemned the "self-interested" European approach to such matters, which had "forced open China's ports" and exerted rule over Egypt "solely in the interests of European creditors."[67] Despite his strong language, though, Hornung too did not seek a complete abolition of consular jurisdiction, but rather its reform to be more equitable and inclusive, as per Field's suggestions. He also noted with approval the way that European states had forced the Ottoman Empire to give autonomy to its subjugated peoples at the recent 1878 Berlin Congress, and argued that such intervention should be extended further – albeit only in the interests of subject peoples, indeed, even those oppressed by Christian rulers.[68]

The advocates of relatively accommodationist ideas toward China during the 1870s, like Field or Hornung, faced increasingly stiff opposition. One particularly negative reaction was that of the German consul at Shanghai, Friedrich Richard Krauel, who submitted his thoughts in an 1877 article in the *Revue*. It was impossible to treat the Chinese as equal members of the compact between civilized nations, he wrote, because "good faith, which presides among us in the relations between belligerents, is totally unknown in China."[69] More significant in shaping global juristic opinion, though, were interventions by Friedrich Fromhold von Martens (aka Fyodor Fyodorovich Martens), the Estonian-Russian international lawyer who would, by the end of the century, be esteemed the "Chief Justice of Christendom" among other titles of acclaim.[70] One of Martens' earliest influential works on international law was his 1873 doctoral thesis on "The Office of Consul and Consular Jurisdiction in the East,"[71] which put the concept of civilization at the center of a defense of extraterritorial consular jurisdiction. He had studied with Bluntschli, sharing the latter's interest in civilizational hierarchies, but had yet stronger views about shared religion and race as the true basis of the "legal consciousness" (*Rechtsbewußtsein*) of international law, which was absent among "heathen" (*heidnischen*) states.[72]

In 1873, Martens was mainly applying this exclusionary logic to Russia's then-primary geopolitical foil, the Ottoman Empire, which he argued could not be treated as an equal in international law given the (supposedly) xenophobic and intolerant character of Islam.[73] He was less overtly negative regarding the status of non-Muslim lands, including China and Japan. By the end of the 1870s, though, Martens' focus would shift, and he emerged as an advocate of the view that China was an outsider and potential enemy of the community of civilized nations. Martens' arguments along these lines developed largely as interventions into the ongoing major dispute between Russia and China over the border zone to which Lin Zexu had been exiled decades earlier, the area that is today called the Ili Kazakh Autonomous Prefecture of Xinjiang.[74]

The interests justifying Russia's incursion were based on the presence of the two consulates that had been opened via the Treaty of Kuldja in 1851. After local uprisings against Qing rule, Russia had seized territory but stated that it would withdraw its forces once "order" was restored. It then, however, refused to do so after Qing forces had effectively eliminated local resistance by 1877. An attempt to resolve the dispute in 1879 by the Manchu official Chonghou resulted in the Treaty of Livadia, in which Ili itself was nominally returned but whose terms actually constituted a vast concession to Russia, which was soon disavowed by the Qing Court.[75]

The Qing side then sought to renegotiate the treaty, while Russia insisted on its validity. A firm Qing position and Moscow's wariness amidst Great Game maneuverings with Britain resulted in the Treaty of St. Petersburg of 1880, whereby the Russian-occupied territory in Xinjiang was returned to effective Qing rule: a rare example of a diplomatic victory for China. Amidst this disagreement, Martens, by now a prominent scholar at St. Petersburg, published a book important for his burgeoning career on *The Conflict between Russia and China: Its Origins, Its Development, and Its Universal Importance.*[76] He begins with an invocation of Russia's two centuries of "friendly" relations with China, adding with studied incredulity "[h]ave some not gone so far as to claim that there is an affinity of race between the Russians and the Chinese and that the same blood runs through their veins (sic)!"[77] Shortly afterward, he turns to the notion of civilizational difference to call for a unity among Western states, which had "a solidarity of interests ... consisting in the obligation to be always ... the representatives of a civilization superior to that of China."[78] Any "blow that China delivers against Russia," then, was actually "directed against all of the civilized nations": A Chinese triumph against Russia would result in the "general expulsion of the *foreign devils* from the Chinese territory ... [and put] in peril the immense capital that the civilized nations import into the Middle Empire."[79]

For Martens, after 1880, a clash of civilizations, with China as the new antagonist to the West (replacing the Ottomans), was immanent to the logic of legal progress. His former teacher Bluntschli, meanwhile, did not join in his pupil's efforts to further cement civilizational boundary lines for international law, but neither did he strenuously oppose them. In Bluntschli's posthumously published diary, he records a visit on June 21, 1881 (the last year of his life), by W. A. P. Martin and his wife.[80] "He brought me a book bound in a curious Chinese cover with the title 'Bluntschli's International Law,'" the legal scholar writes with evident satisfaction, "my *Völkerrecht*, well-printed in the Chinese language and script."[81] The following month, on July 22, the last entry in Bluntschli's diary records a visit to his home by a Qing diplomat. This visitor, who Romanized his name as "Kinginthai," was the Qing legation secretary in Berlin, Gengyintai.[82] In Bluntschli's record, Gengyintai is:

> [A] very agreeable and clever young man, and tall, with braided coal-black hair ... [who] comes from the inner city of Peking ... where, it seems, the elites of the ruling race live. He is Mongol and belongs to the party that wishes to bring China forward with the use of European culture.[83]

Along with similar visits at the time by a Japanese scholar, these were signs to Bluntschli that men of the Orient were, perhaps, after all ready to learn the rules of civilization that had come to be associated with his own life and work. A few months after these visits, the *Institut de Droit International* held a meeting at Wiesbaden in which it formally addressed the question Field had originally raised in 1874, of "the application of European international law to

Oriental nations." This matter had been discussed in its pages since the mid 1860s, and was due for some conclusions.[84] It was now being considered specifically in reference to an *avant-projet* formulated by Martens, which strongly reaffirmed in principle the need for extraterritorial jurisdiction in non-Christian lands, though calling for it to be better organized and feature more cooperation among Western states.[85]

The strongest critique of consular jurisdiction again came from Joseph Hornung, who was unable to attend at Wiesbaden, but sent notes with his views, criticizing the "deplorable *per se* infraction of sovereignty" that the practice constituted against the states subjected to it.[86] There is no indication that W. A. P. Martin was invited to take part in the meeting, nor that Bluntschli, despite his interesting recent guests, personally indicated any views at all as to China's legal status or rights (though both may have contributed comments off the record). On September 13, 1881, however, Martin had delivered a speech before Orientalists in Berlin on "Traces of International Law in Ancient China."[87] Hornung, whom Martin had visited in Geneva, urged him to translate this speech, which "fills a lacuna in the history of international law," and publish it in the *Revue*, which he did in issue 14 the following year.[88] Here, at last, was the piece on ancient Chinese interstate relations that he had promised almost a decade earlier. In a postscript to the piece, Hornung notes, undoubtedly to Martens' severe displeasure, that "China [had] forced Russia to retreat in the recent matter of Kulja," and that it was entirely possible "China and the United States would one day be the two most powerful countries in the world."[89]

Although Martin and others might view China as being essentially pacifist in nature, Hornung wrote, Westerners should still reflect that "it could one day have a conqueror at its head," and, as the center of a larger Buddhist civilization, would form a third of humanity that might very well "dominate the world." Despite such dark reflections, Hornung's takeaway from all of this was just the opposite of Martens' view: The need to ensure that "this new power rising in Asia puts its increasing force in the service of civilization and law" meant that it was all the more crucial to eschew unfair treatment and "gain the ancient empire of China for our culture."[90] Prior to the publication of issue 14 of the *Revue*, Martin was himself elected as an *associé* of the *Institut de Droit International* during its annual meeting held at Turin in September 1882.[91] With this, he accomplished something like the arbitrage of Chinese and Western networks that Prince Gong and others had from the beginning suspected to be his aim. Along with his earlier flattering contacts with the institute, it seems likely that Martin's networking with Hornung and Bluntschli (who passed away before the 1882 meeting), along with the interest in "*la Question d'Orient*," brought him enough esteem to be invited into the group despite lacking formal legal training.

At the same meeting at which Martin was elected, the institute also voted into effect Martens' *avant-projet*, strongly reaffirming extraterritorial consular jurisdiction while adding a mild admonition that it should be exercised with the best interests of the natives in mind.[92] Indeed, the majority of institute members was not even willing to endorse Field's proposed transition to an Egypt-style mixed-tribunal system, which James Lorimer soon after called a mere "experiment."[93] Twiss, too, would endorse the view that "Europeans are ... *de facto* an *extra-territorial community*,"[94] deserving of special rights. In Shanghai, the mixed court that had been established in 1864 for Chinese and diplomatically nonrepresented foreigners involved in "minor criminal matters and civil suits" coexisted with more powerful institutions such as the British Supreme Court for China, among others, and was never to be granted appellate jurisdiction of the sort that the Egyptian tribunal exercised.[95]

After the dilution of Field's 1874 initiative, the *Institut de Droit International* would never again collectively take on a leading role in considering the overhaul of consular jurisdiction in China. The default position regarding the extent of non-Western states' sovereignty was now close to that soon after expressed by Lorimer, when he argued that recognition of the Ottoman Empire as a supposed equal in 1856 had been but "a cruel and empty comedy," while the proper approach was the "principle of recognition according to value (*quantum valeant*)," by which states would be qualitatively ranked and their rights determined accordingly by – who else? – Western jurists.[96]

"Une Sorte de Guerre de Mots"

When former US president Ulysses S. Grant arrived in China in 1879 as part of his postpresidency trip around the world, he was fêted by Qing officials like no previous visitor. The prestige of the occasion allowed for the smooth papering over of possible areas of tension, such as the recent trend of violent attacks on Chinese immigrant laborers in the US West Coast. Grant engaged in particularly wide-ranging conversations with Prince Gong and Li Hongzhang, and the former endeavored to have him arbitrate the disputes over Ryūkyū/Liuqiu, which had radically escalated with the latter's recent official annexation by Japan. The record of Grant's journey indicates that Prince Gong was familiar with the recent example – so important to the development of international law adjudication in general – of the 1871 *Alabama* arbitration between Great Britain and the United States, and sought a local solution along the same lines.[97]

Grant demurred over the idea of presiding over a Sino-Japanese arbitration after the mold of the *Alabama* decision, but did try to feel out potential solutions to the dispute.[98] While in Japan, Grant then raised the issue with leading officials, and even with the Meiji emperor himself. His overall conclusion, however, seems to have been endorsing a Japanese proposal to divide Ryūkyūan territory between China and Japan. This was an option that the Qing side considered, despite ultimately rejecting it.[99] Despite being willing to ascribe a mere "semi-dependence" to Ryūkyū, the Qing Court's internal documents regarding the dispute continued to focus heavily on the language of traditional *guoti* rather than the new vocabulary of public law. Prince Gong, in particular, emphasized how "Ryūkyū has long been affiliated to China and Japan's elimination of this kingdom and its ancestral dynasty, without cause, is beyond all decency and reason."[100] Although Japanese claims regarding *zhuquan* had by now brought this term to the attention of Qing officials, they still did not address the concept in their own internal high-level discussions. Instead, regional order was still to be understood in terms of relationships among polities and political actors – making varying degrees of "independence," or more precisely *zizhu* 自主/"self-rule" a more relevant concept.[101]

Qing diplomatic communications of the period show both the capacious and rather ambiguous nature of *zizhu*/"autonomy" as it was then understood. For example, a 1879 note from Guo Songtao's successor in London, Zeng Guofan's son Zeng Jize, uses the phrase *zizhu zhi quan* to refer to both the legal status possessed by Brazil after its independence from Portugal *and* to that of the country's former slaves after the recent abolition of slavery.[102] The following year, Zeng describes how Romania had transformed from a "half-sovereign vassal state [*shuguo banzhu zhi bang* 屬國半主之邦]" into an "autonomous state [*zizhu zhi bang* 自主之邦]."[103]

The concept of "autonomy," specifically in its highly elastic interpretations during the period of the late nineteenth-century rush for colonies, played an important role in Chinese encounters with public law. In the 1880s, it was especially central to the conflict with France over Vietnam, which had been gestating since the 1874 Treaty of Saigon in which the French had recognized "the sovereignty of the king of Annam and his complete independence from any foreign power."[104] At the same time, the Red River connecting the Mekong Delta with Yunnan had been internationalized and opened to foreign maritime passage.[105] The French translations of Qing communications over the dispute made frequent and somewhat confused references to "souveraineté" (i.e., sovereignty) over Vietnam.[106]

However, the internal communications of the Qing Court focused not on *zhuquan* but rather on concrete aims such as preventing French dominance of the region and maintaining China's security in the Red River delta region.[107] During discussions with Foreign Minister Challemel-Lacour, Zeng even directly asked: "How does this protectorate differ from sovereignty? . . . Does France intend to protect Vietnam in the way China does . . . or do you want to establish a protectorate like that which Britain has established in Egypt?"[108] Although such questions obviously referred to practical concerns, the Ferry administration justified its aggressive policy before internal critics by saying that the affair turned on a mere "grammatical quarrel" regarding how China's relationship with Annam should be characterized.[109] French officials would later refer to the conflict with China, which erupted into open warfare (albeit not a legally declared war) as turning on "not precisely a matter of China's suzerainty, but rather of the maintenance of certain traditional ties and of a kind of vague, indeterminate situation that China seemed to want to preserve ... regarding Annam." Thus, the whole affair could be regarded as no more than "a sort of war of words [*une sorte de guerre de mots*]."[110]

As Zeng and other Qing officials emphasized, however, there were indeed concrete practical interests of the Qing state in maintaining the status quo in the region. Like Prince Gong in 1858, Zeng Jize in 1883 argued that "internationalization" of a major waterway that provided access to the Chinese interior was a concrete threat to the polity. He even expressed to Ferry that "China sees the Red River as its throat, and must have administrative authority over it."[111] Though the practice of "internationalizing" internal waterways was itself only a few decades old, the Qing desire to retain exclusive authority over a key border river was treated as *outré* by the French side: "you will still be able to use the river as before for commerce, so why persist in struggling for this 'administrative authority'?"[112]

The military conflict that ensued after the breakdown of negotiations was prosecuted by France not as a "war," but rather as a supposed set of reprisal actions by France for alleged treaty violations by China justifying the occupation of Tonkin and expelling of Chinese forces, along with other hostile moves. The government of Prime Minister Jules Ferry described itself as being in a "state of reprisal" against China, until the alleged treaty violations (including failure to evacuate forces from Tonkin after the French had been targeted by local bandit groups) were remedied and compensation provided. These moves were criticized by some observers, for example, the influential German jurist Friedrich Heinrich Geffcken, who argued in the *Revue* in 1885 that "international law knows no such bizarre state [as a state of reprisal]; it knows only *acts of reprisal* [which] authorize[] a government to avenge without formal declaration of war, by a military action, torts of which it claims to have been the object."[113]

Geffcken argued that reprisal was only justified for one state to make another "feel the injustice of its behavior and to take measures to ensure satisfaction," and only if such reprisals were properly limited and distinct from the comprehensive hostilities of declared wars.[114] Without "a flagrant injustice or denial of justice," moreover, reprisals would not be justified, even against non-Western states. This was a point of view quite unlike those of the most influential *Institut de Droit International* members, however. James Lorimer, for example, wrote in his influential 1884 work *Institutes of the Law of Nations* that China, along with Turkey and Japan, belonged "partly to the category of recognised and partly to the category of protected states."[115] With respect to such states, "interference with their internal government ... is so often called for on grounds of humanity, [that] they are constantly relapsing into the position of protected states."[116]

During these years, Geffcken, as editor of successive editions of August Wilhelm Heffter's *Das europäische Volkerrecht der Gegenwart*, continued to refer to the notion of "half-sovereignty" as "an extremely vague concept, close to an oxymoron."[117] But the contradictory aspects of the term seemed not to bother most members of the international law profession. As Lorimer put it, "having only half a loaf of bread is better than having none at all."[118] In Martens' view, however, it would be better not to extend even that half-loaf. In his highly influential *Traité de Droit International* of 1883 he pointedly did away with the category of "half-civilized" and instead simply lists China, along with Japan, Persia, and Turkey, among the "noncivilized" peoples who cannot be considered subjects of international law.[119] Martens' treatise, coinciding with an eventual Qing defeat at sea against France and abandonment of pretensions to influence over Vietnam, did much to cement a new consensus on its subordinate status.

The early 1880s "war of words" regarding the amorphousness of autonomy and "protection" helped prompt the 1884 Qing decision to incorporate Xinjiang as an official province. Advocating haste in realizing this shift, the Zongli Yamen noted that Russia might very well see China's war with France as an opportune time for new incursions.[120] The transformation of Xinjiang into a province was carried out by a merger with Gansu; along with this shift, meanwhile, came the intensification of a "civilizing project" intended to transform local Muslim populations into more homogenized Qing subjects.[121] Meanwhile, Taiwan was formally made into its own province the following year, having been treated for centuries as a constituent part of Fujian.

At the culmination of the Sino-French War, the 1885 Treaty of Hué confirmed most French aims, ensuring that China would, from now on, recognize the "autonomy" of their former tributary and that powers of intervention and "protection" would belong solely to France. International jurists did not engage in any major protests of the escalations of European imperial expansion in East Asia. Writing in the *Revue*, W. A. P. Martin noted that China was bitter over having "lost its cause," but had luckily "gone too far [in adopting international law] to now retreat." Without bothering to argue for China's side of the conflict, or that French actions in Vietnam were improper, he instead focused on his own achievements in translation – including a new 1883 edition of the *Institut de Droit International*'s *Oxford Manual on the Laws of War on Land*, as well as Henry Fawcett's *Manual of Political Economy* – which would help China adopt Western ways.[122]

Contesting "Autonomy"

Qing officials increasingly feared that Western states would act to confer the status of autonomy upon the various peoples that the Qing considered part of their *Badarangga Doro*.[123] Alongside Vietnam and Ryūkyū, the threat of a collapse of Qing influence also arose during the 1880s with respect to Joseon (aka Korea), Tibet, and Burma. In the case of Joseon, internal political conflicts and Japanese pressure had combined to create a state of turmoil, raising the prospect of another lost tributary. In the 1876 Treaty of Ganghwa, the Meiji Empire had applied pressure to open formalized diplomatic relations with Joseon, with the treaty's first article reading "As the Kingdom of Joseon is an independent (*jishu/zizhu* 自主) state it possesses equal rights/authority to those of Japan" (朝鮮國ハ自主ノ邦ニシテ日本國ト平等ノ權ヲ保有セ).[124] Over the coming years, the prospect of Joseon's rulers, either voluntarily or under Japanese duress, putting into effect this stipulation of the Treaty of Ganghwa and thus following a similar course to that of Vietnam vis-à-vis France, remained a major concern.

During this period, a young military officer named Yuan Shikai first rose to prominence, having been appointed to serve as the commissioner of trade at Seoul and then helping to put down the 1884 coup hostile to Qing influence, while coordinating military training and seeking to ensure the maintenance of traditional tributary ties. In repeated memorials over the course of the 1880s Yuan advised the court of the risks that Meiji-backed factions in Joseon would seek to turn its status of "independence" or "self-rule" into a reality.[125] Yuan would serve in Korea until 1894, being promoted by Li Hongzhang for his contributions to stabilizing the situation under something at least resembling the status quo, and preventing a repeat of Vietnam or Ryūkyū – while also avoiding open conflict with Japan.

Meanwhile, after a century of progressive annexations and conflicts with Burmese rulers, the British colonial administration unilaterally abolished Burma's monarchy in 1885.[126] In the face of unrest, the British sought to ensure a stable situation for their newest colonial possession, and handled this matter along with the questions of frontiers between British India and Tibet in the "Convention relative to Burmah and Thibet" of July 24, 1886.[127] This agreement stipulated China's acknowledgment that "in all matters whatsoever appertaining to the authority and rule which England is now exercising in Burmah, England shall be free to do whatever she deems fit and proper."[128] In return, Burma's new rulers would ensure that tribute missions to the Qing would continue to be sent.[129] Article 3, meanwhile, stipulated that the parties would subsequently sign a later agreement to demarcate territorial borders. Qing officials such as Zeng Jize protested this "usurpation of Burma's authority of self-rule" (*duo qi zizhuquan* 奪其自主權),[130] but, in the aftermath of the war with France, intervention was out of the question.

By the 1890s, Japan, too, would fully take up its role as a colonial power. It finally succeeded in prospectively ending consular jurisdiction in its territory via the 1894 Anglo-Japanese Treaty of Commerce and Navigation, prompting some international lawyers in the West to look back to the debates of the previous two decades. This renunciation of extraterritorial consular jurisdiction in Japan by European powers was disturbing to some respected scholars of international law influenced by Martens' worldview, as it was the "first occasion on which Oriental diplomacy has triumphed in its long war on the Consular jurisdiction," by means of which, "the position of all Europeans [had] been shaken."[131]

By the mid 1890s, many Western jurists were far less interested in the optimistic visions of East Asia's cooperative, mutually beneficial opening to trade and civilization that had earlier stimulated men like Burlingame or Field. More had come around to the view that "the true policy of Europeans in the East is one of solidarity."[132] Many in the 1890s, such as the German jurist Paul Heilborn, turned specifically to Lorimer's version of the levels of civilization to define duties owed to civilized peers (against whom interventions were presumptively unjustified); half-civilized states like China, Turkey, or Japan (against whom they might be justified based on context); and lastly "tribes" (*Stämmen*), against whom they were presumed justified.[133] This schema was increasingly standardized in legal texts during the 1880s–1890s, with China now firmly taking up a role as the "semicivilized" state par excellence.

Conclusion

The liberal and cosmopolitan ideals that featured in many international lawyers' discussions of China's opening during the 1860s were far less apparent over the subsequent decades, which coincided with a global depression and renewed colonial expansionism. As David Harvey has argued, "[h]eightened competition under conditions of crisis has coerced capitalists into paying much closer attention to relative locational advantages, precisely because diminishing spatial barriers give capitalists the power to exploit minute spatial differentiations to good effect."[134] The relative value of colonial outposts – whether in Korea, Vietnam, Taiwan, or elsewhere – increased for the foreign empires that were no longer as optimistic about the future of free trade, peace through law, and global commerce as they had been in more prosperous years.

Domestically in many Western countries, cheap Chinese labor came to be characterized as a scourge rather than an economic boon, leading to racist attacks by white workers against foreign competitors and racially restricted immigration policies across the English-speaking world. At the level of the international community, both Qing tensions with France and Japan in its coastal frontiers and with Russia over Central Asia incentivized assertions by the latter states to claim the greater rights of "civilized" vis-à-vis "half-civilized" powers. Japan's own escape from the latter status, which many Western jurists still attributed to it even as late as the very last years of the nineteenth century, would only be fully achieved after its military conquests of Qing territory. Meanwhile, discussions of non-Western states' status by jurists at the *Institut de Droit International* and in other such elite venues ultimately mirrored, and justified, the geopolitical power dynamics that increasingly put China in a position of formalized subordination to the Western family of nations.

Part II
Asserting Sovereignty, 1895–1921

4

The Public Law of Planet Earth

As the limited success of the Qing Dynasty's "self-strengthening" policies became apparent, reformist Qing officials like Xue Fucheng argued more vigorously for the importance of building up diplomatic expertise, establishing more legations abroad, making use of Western diplomatic and political forms, and pursuing policies closer to those of the Western great powers. As early as 1880, Xue had lamented that: "In our dealings with England and France they have always put aggressive militarism before diplomacy. We have been coerced as well as deceived, suffered great harm to our interests, and often been cast out from the public law of planet Earth [*wang wang you chu diqiu gongfa zhi wai zhe* 往往有出地球公法之外者]."[1] Major changes would be needed to escape this predicament. Xue had called for far-ranging modernization policies, as well as following up on the consolidation of Xinjiang and Taiwan as provinces by actively going abroad to set up colonies, perhaps in Southeast Asia, after the Western fashion.

Some other officials and intellectuals began to articulate similar views in the late 1880s and early 1890s, with a notably increased engagement with the concept of sovereignty. The reformist businessman/official Zheng Guanying, for example, wrote in opposition to China's sacrifice of economic policy autonomy in the treaty regimes and via the administrative role of the Maritime Customs Service (MCS).[2] Like Xue, as well as Sheng Xuanhuai, and others who saw *liquan* or economic authority as closely related to the polity's ontological security, Zheng argued for a more resolute and less accommodationist position vis-à-vis foreign capital and domination of China's trade.

Over the course of the 1880s and early 1890s, Xue's concern about ostracism became all the more apt. By 1887–1888, for example, Qing officials debated whether China should accede to the International Telegraph Convention of 1865, thus further embedding itself into the web of Western-centric global rules and governance. Ironically, while skeptics pointed to the novel language of "territorial autonomy"/sovereignty (*zizhu tudi zhi quan*) to justify *refusal* to join the convention, at least one proponent of the treaty invoked the more traditional relational value of *guoti* to argue in favor of China's adherence to global legal norms. *Guoti* could here be redefined to the fear of being treated by the West as a "pariah state" (*shuyuan zhi bang* 疏遠之邦), potentially subject to further military incursions.[3] Preserving stateliness, in some uses, by now included proactive engagement with international law, not just imposing limits on its application.

While China could potentially become more diplomatically excluded from the Western international community, it was without doubt ever more economically intertwined with it. Telegraphs, rail, and steam had by the turn of the 1890s made China far more permeable to foreign capital and personnel and cognizable as an object of both technical and legal regulation. By the early 1890s, Friedrich Engels was predicting that Western imperialists would inevitably push further into China as "[t]he last new market which could bring on a temporary revival of prosperity," radically disrupting traditional society and likely leading to a further "flooding of America, Asia and Europe by the hated Chinaman," blamed for unfair economic competition.[4]

A Shifting Status

The most significant geopolitical and ideological shock that altered both China's domestic intellectual climate and its position in global hierarchies was the disastrous Qing defeat in the First Sino-Japanese War of 1894–1895. It was with this victory that Meiji Japan finally obtained internationally recognized sovereignty over Taiwan, as well as its chance to assert membership in the highest rank of "civilization," that of expanding colonial empires, rather than the precarious middle zone. Amidst the ensuing international rush for new rights and concessions, the Qing state found itself consistently relegated to a third-party status in dealings that were carving out spheres of influence in its own territory.

The role of the First Sino-Japanese War in accelerating the reception of international law concepts was clearly demonstrated in official discourse at the highest levels. This process is strikingly embodied in one largely forgotten episode. In early 1895, Emperor Guangxu advised Li Hongzhang that "Taiwan could not be abandoned," and referred to a "petition written (or signed) in blood" (*xue shu* 血書) that had been submitted by Han Chinese gentry and commoners living on the island, asking imperial officials to defend it against foreign conquest. The content of the blood petition, meanwhile, invoked §286 of Bluntschli's *Das moderne Völkerrecht der civilisirten Staaten als Rechtsbuch dargestellt* (in its 1880 Chinese translation), which required annexation of one state's territory by another to have "recognition by the politically enfranchised population that dwell in the separated territory."[5] In Guangxu's message, there was almost certainly the very first instance of a sitting Chinese ruler directly invoking the text of a source of international law (in this case, Bluntschli's treatise) as a legitimate, noncoerced legal authority.

The Qing defeat of 1895, and specifically the Treaty of Shimonoseki that ended hostilities, was also the event that consolidated the term and concept *zhuquan*/“[territorial] sovereignty” into the Qing public law lexicon. Indeed, the Treaty of Shimonoseki was the very first international treaty or public law authority of any kind in which the Qing were forced to agree to a clause concerning *zhuquan* – albeit, even now, only in the Japanese version of the text. Just as had been the case in the dealings of the 1870s, it was again the expanding Meiji Empire that forced Qing interlocutors to directly confront the notion of “sovereignty” as a clear legal demarcation of exclusive (and alienable) dominion over territory.[6] Nonetheless, the Chinese version of Article 2 of the Treaty remained ambiguous: “China will perpetually hand over authority as to the following places . . . to Japan (中国将管理下开地方之权 . . . 永远让与日本).”[7] Meanwhile the Japanese text specified: “The Qing Empire will perpetually separate [from itself] and hand over to Japan . . . *shuken*/*zhuquan* over the below-listed territories (清國ハ左記ノ土地ノ主權 . . . ヲ永遠日本國ニ割與ス).”[8]

Those territories, the island of Formosa, the Pescadores island group, and the southern part of Manchuria known as Guandong/Kantō, were treated as alienable in a way incompatible with any claim to Qing influence. The more absolute Western notion of territorial sovereignty, reliant upon exclusionary state authority, was clearly conveyed in the Japanese invocation and description of *tochi no shuken* (literally, “sovereignty over territory” – a phrasing influenced by the German *Gebietshoheit*), but was still invisible in the Chinese version’s simplistic reference to a mere, vague “authority” (*quan* 權). In order to “avoid any future confusion,” meanwhile, the treaty also indicated that, while the Japanese and Chinese texts were both valid, so too was an English translated version that was drawn up at the same time, which would be treated as authoritative in case of any disputes over language. For the quoted part of Article 2 that differed so markedly in the Chinese and Japanese versions, the English version reads: “China cedes to Japan in perpetuity and full sovereignty the following territories,”[9] thus corresponding most directly to the Japanese version of the text with respect to the form of “authority” at stake.

As with the Ōkubo communiqué of 1874, the Treaty of Shimonoseki of 1895 sought to compel the Qing state to recognize sovereignty as the only meaningful legal status to describe territorial administration. In addition to Article 2 on sovereignty, Article 1 pledged China to “recognize . . . definitively the full and complete independence and autonomy of Korea,” and specified that this entailed that “payment of tribute and the performance of ceremonies and formalities by Korea to China, in derogation of such independence and autonomy, shall wholly cease for the future.”[10]

Another parallel with the Qing–Japan crisis of the 1870s was the role of the United States as mediator, in this case particularly via John Watson Foster, who had stepped down as US secretary of state in 1893 and had also recently participated in the landmark *Bering Sea* arbitration in Paris.[11] Foster neatly combined his far-ranging diplomatic and international law activities with a strong interest in global commerce – specifically, lobbying activities in

Washington on behalf of US firms looking to expand abroad.[12] Foster entered into the negotiations to end the Sino-Japanese War as a consultant for the Qing government, accompanying Li Hongzhang who led the Chinese side in the proceedings. Unlike Ulysses S. Grant in 1879, Foster was eager to take an active role in ending the dispute.[13]

There soon followed a hastened end to hostilities due to both a failed assassination attempt against Li by a Japanese extremist, and US efforts to maintain regional stability. Similar concerns would soon motivate the so-called Triple Intervention of Russia, Germany, and France to prevent Japanese control over Port Arthur (Dalian) in southern Manchuria.[14] During this period, the United States began to play a regular role as a kind of de facto "protector" of Chinese interests in the face of more aggressive moves by both European states and Japan as they looked to carve out their own spheres of interest in Qing territory.[15] In the mid 1890s, the Qing ambassador to the United States facing these issue was the trusted establishment official Yang Ru.[16]

During Yang's time in the United States, he represented China in the negotiation of the Gresham–Yang Treaty of 1894, in which the Qing recognized the post-1882 American restrictions on Chinese immigration but obtained exceptions for officials, teachers, students, and merchants, among others, to enter the United States.[17] This compromise position was endorsed by the Zongli Yamen, though ten years later when it came up for renewal it would prompt a major popular boycott movement in protest. The issue of discriminatory migration restrictions, in the eyes of both officials and the populace in general, implicated China's stateliness – but it soon appeared the public was much less willing to compromise over such issues than the court.[18]

Following his tenure in the United States, Yang was then dispatched to Russia to serve as the Qing representative in St. Petersburg. This coincided with a period of extreme pressure on China from multiple sides, as Russian plans to achieve a hegemonic position in Manchuria were accelerated with the coerced lease of the Liaodong Peninsula, the German occupation of the Jiaozhou Bay territory following yet another missionary case, and other such incidents. Though the lease of Liaodong to Russia was only for a term of twenty-five years, the Jiaozhou Bay agreement was for ninety-nine years, a figure soon to be demanded by and granted to Britain in Hong Kong's New Territories, as well as to France in Guangzhouwan.[19]

Already working in St. Petersburg when Yang arrived in 1896 was a twenty-five-year-old interpreter named Lu Zhengxiang, a French-language graduate of the *Tongwenguan*.[20] Born into a Protestant Christian family from Jiangsu, Lu first entered the service of Yang's predecessor in the post, Xu Jingcheng, in 1893.[21] Both Lu and Xu combined a self-denying ethos of diplomatic service to their state with similarly intense Christian religious sentiments. In a memoir written late in his life, Lu would recall how the Catholic Xu called on him to immerse himself in this "most ancient branch of Christianity," which was the real "strength of Europe," and to bring it into China.[22] Lu was also influenced in this regard by his Belgian wife, whom he married in February 1899. In May of that same year, he would join Yang Ru as the two became China's first ever delegates to a major international law conference, the First Hague Conference convened by invitation of Russian Czar Nicholas II.

A Consolidated "International Community"?

The nineteenth century had seen a general trend in international law toward ever-increasing use of the form of multilateral conferences to legislate new legal norms. Though consensual in principle, such events had since the 1815 Vienna Congress, which inaugurated the new order of the "public law of Europe" (*droit publique de l'Europe*), also served as meetings to establish compromises among leading states, based upon and in furtherance of notions of the balance of power and often deciding the fates of weaker neighbors.[23] Both India's fate and the history of Congress Poland as both a product and eventual victim of *Realpolitik* would, by the 1890s, serve as particularly potent symbols for some Chinese intellectuals of the lack of any true restraints of justice upon the principle of survival of the fittest in world affairs. Only more rapid and thorough modernization (despite different ideas as to just what that might entail) would prevent extinction.

As a young Xiong Xiling, a future premier of China, wrote in a memorial to the viceroy of Huguang in 1896: "If we [fail to develop local steamship trade] our fate will be like that of the blacks. Your Excellency is loyal to the state . . . you cannot hope for Hunan to become another India or Poland."[24] Such worries were par for the course among the reformers of the late 1890s. In their writings exhorting the adoption of Western scientific and commercial practices, and gradually extending into the arenas of law and politics, this new generation of reform advocates also generated interesting, and at times quite incisive, reflections on international law. For example, one of the coeditors of the reformer journal *Xiang Xue Bao* 湘学报, Yi Zongkui, suggested that China should send a memorandum to all of the Western states declaring its desire to be included in multilateral conferences, and should in the future rely explicitly upon international law whenever rejecting foreign demands or trying to advance China's positions.[25]

Others made related but distinct arguments, such as Xiong and Yi's firebrand collaborator Tang Caichang, who suggested that only by allying with and emulating Britain and Japan, despite their imperialist depredations, could China gradually be accepted as a geopolitical equal.[26] The notion of cooperation with and emulation of Japan was, in fact, typical of this milieu, a fact noted by W. A. P. Martin to his chagrin as he saw the West (and himself) being pedagogically displaced by a non-Christian power.[27]

Another new trend was the emergence of explicitly critical perspectives on international law and its function as part of the networks of Western power.

Another of the influential Hunan-based reformers, Pi Xirui, provided the incisive, darkly sardonic assessment that:

> Europeans stress international law, treating savage states unlike the civilized. To kill the former's people or take their land is not "inhumane." So when Westerners wipe out a state and take its territory, they first issue reports about how savage it is.[28]

For some influential reformist thinkers such as Kang Youwei, however, the new ideas about world order being imported from the West contained some genuinely admirable elements that could be merged with the essence of China's traditional thought.[29] International law and the Confucian ethics of benevolence, along with modern science and other forms of learning, were each complementary elements of a coming "Great Unity of the World" (*shijie datong* 世界大同), as presaged in the ancient *Book of Rites*.[30] In Kang's idiosyncratic ideas, there is perhaps for the first time a thorough religious/ethical valorization of international law from the perspective of Chinese philosophy, going beyond pragmatic accommodation. Some advocates of such views also still referred to Martin's arguments that modern Western international law echoed the interstate practices of ancient, preunification China.[31]

Hunan was an early center for the critique and reform discourse of the 1890s, but its clear national significance in the years after China's defeat in the First Sino-Japanese War led to a more general critical reflection on the limitations of the Late Qing self-strengthening policies. The ill-fated "Hundred Day's Reform" of the Guangxu emperor in mid 1898, in which he endorsed many aspects of the reformers' agendas, seemed to presage a Meiji-like shift for China. However, this movement was eventually suppressed by Cixi and the conservative faction at court, with Guangxu rendered effectively powerless, while many leading reformists were either imprisoned, executed, or went into exile. This failure would serve to swiftly catalyze more radical movements, shifting their aims from reform to outright revolution.[32]

Like the reformers, however, even the most powerful Qing officials were grappling with questions of China's proper approach to the Western system of international law. This is apparent, for example, in a major 1898 publication by the official to whom Xiong had addressed his memorial on steamships, Zhang Zhidong. In his 1898 imperially endorsed essay *Promotion of Learning*, Zhang included a brief discussion on "Refuting Disarmament" (*Fei Mibing* 非弭兵).[33] He pointed out that it would only be after China developed a modern military on par with those of the warring great powers that it could begin to speak of "disarming" on an equal basis with them. He noted that "some devoutly believe in international law [*duxin gongfa zhi shuo* 笃信公法之说] and claim it can be relied on, but this is foolish . . . law emerges from a balance of power, whence comes this law if states are not matched in strength?"[34]

Although he does not use the term *zhuquan* in this essay, Zhang's references to a "state authority" (*guoquan* 國權 or *guojia zhi quan* 國家之權)

whose practical contents depend on the balance of power very clearly point in this direction. Meanwhile, Zhang displays a striking *lack* of interest in comparing China's situation with that of other non-Western states or as part of a group of marginalized states. Such ideas of solidarity would begin taking further root over the next decade.[35] In any case, the idea that China should take the lead in implementing newfangled ideas of disarmament or pacifism – as was being advocated in some missionary publications of the late nineteenth century – was a nonstarter. As Zhang put it: "If we, who have so few arms to speak of, put on a big display of disarmament, won't we simply become a laughingstock?"[36] Nonetheless, when plans for the Hague Conference of 1899 were announced a few weeks after Zhang's essay was printed, there was no significant internal disagreement that China should accept the unprecedented invitation it received to participate.

Scholars today often remember the Hague Conferences as "an important inflection point in the evolution of expectations about participation and shared governance," which inaugurated newly universalist ideas and methods in the formation of international law.[37] The inclusion of states like China, Japan, and Persia did indeed broaden the scope of the conference form. On the other hand, the actual experience of non-Western states at these conferences, and especially their subsequent encounters with ongoing colonial pressures and incursions, suggest that expanded participation was ironically accompanied by an even more united front by the great powers of the West vis-à-vis intervention against those provisionally included in their new structures.

Geopolitically, alongside the appropriation of African territory, the ongoing contest among Western states, as well as Japan, for influence in East Asia was one of the factors going into the idea for a new conference to set global rules that limited intra-great power conflicts. Among the officials who participated in the initiative on the Russian side, Foreign Minister Muravyov had been the main architect of the aggressive policy of expansion into Manchuria. Fyodor Martens, of course, had been advocating Russia's right to occupy Chinese territory and that of other "noncivilized" states since the 1870s.[38] Meanwhile, Sergei Witte expressed the view around this time that all of North China would eventually be firmly ensconced in Russia's sphere of influence.[39] British leaders, including Prime Minister Lord Salisbury, at times expressed willingness to consider such arrangements as well – for example, a situation in which British control over the economically crucial Yangzi River Delta was exchanged for Russian dominance in North China down to the Yellow River.[40]

For China in 1899, the prospect of the Hague Conference was one of risk, as the development of new international doctrines posed both possible benefits – if they could really mitigate future aggressive incursions – as well as threats. This was reflected in the internal debates that the conference stimulated within the Zongli Yamen and in officials' interactions with the Qing Court. Since the start of the decade, missionary-run publications had introduced into Chinese journalism the ideas of the international pacifist movement and its Universal

Peace Congresses, adopting the traditional Chinese term *mibinghui* 弭兵會, or "disarmament conference." This originally referred to a diplomatic venture that occurred during the sixth-century rivalry between the Jin and Chu states, as recorded in the *Spring and Autumn Annals*, but many Qing intellectuals, and even officials, were willing to see the analogy with modern multilateral conferences as an appropriate one.[41] There were, of course, limits to such parallels, as had already been suggested in Zhang Zhidong's skeptical commentary of the previous year.[42]

Yang Ru suggested that entering the mainstream of international conferences could mean that "we will not be marginalized [any longer] . . . [t]his is truly a great turning point for [our] contemporary foreign relations."[43] He was chosen by the Zongli Yamen as the lead Qing delegate to the Hague Conference, along with Lu's former classmate at the *Tongwenguan* Hu Weide as second delegate, and Lu serving as interpreter. The Chinese delegation was the first to take up residence in the Scheveningen area, the raising of the Qing yellow silk dragon pennant at a hotel near the shore being one of the first visible signs that the event was soon to begin.[44]

If Qing officials hoped that the Hague meeting would help their state avoid marginalization, however, they were soon to be disappointed. Little if any attempt was made by the Western delegates to include China's representatives in substantive conversation, and there was also no one on the Chinese side with real expertise in international law. By contrast, Japan had dispatched as part of its delegation Professor Ariga Nagao, an internationally recognized legal scholar who had studied in Berlin.[45] Influential Western jurists present included T. M. C. Asser for the Netherlands, Martens for Russia, and James Brown Scott for the United States.[46]

In general, Western delegates were apt to contrast the "backward" Chinese – an impression only exacerbated by the country's geopolitical situation, and by the quashed reform efforts that had recently made headlines worldwide – with the "modernized," diplomatically active, and militarily ascendant Japanese. Qing diplomats had no discernible influence on the key outcomes of the conference – the formal adoption of new rules of land and maritime warfare and extension of those stemming from the 1864 Geneva Convention; the prohibition of exploding bullets, aerial bombardments, and poisonous gases as weapons of warfare; and, most ambitiously, the establishment of the Permanent Court of Arbitration (PCA), an official roster of arbitrators available to states to seek peaceful resolution of disputes (albeit on a purely voluntary basis – unlike the compulsory adjudication some advocates had hoped for).

On the level of personal interaction, meanwhile, Yang found the Hague a considerably less welcoming environment than Washington. In a recollection published two decades later, Austrian delegate and future minister-president Heinrich Lammasch critically recalls a mean-spirited joke among some Western Hague delegates that Yang had simply arranged for one of the translators next to him to pull his queue back and forth whenever he should shake his head "yes" or "no."[47] In a similar spirit was the American lawyer and Hague delegation secretary Frederick Holls' "humorous" account of Yang Ru saying at one point that the meetings were "too much talkee-talkee, too little do-ee do-ee."[48] This, of course, sounds just like the crude caricatures of Chinese-inflected English sometimes featured in American newspapers and fiction of the time.[49] Nonetheless, Holls' story about what he mockingly referred to as "Oriental philosophy" was widely circulated and dutifully recorded in the pacifist journalist William Stead's record of the conference, and even, quite remarkably, continues to be reprinted today verbatim and without any caveats in mainstream academic accounts in the West.[50]

It is, of course, possible that Yang might have said something to the effect that the meetings were all talk and no action, but that itself seems very unlikely. Yang and the Zongli Yamen were actually quite apprehensive, not optimistic, about the forms of "action" that might be taken by the assembled delegates. Unlike the delegations of the great powers, who were setting rules for the ongoing process of colonial appropriation of the non-Western world, China was in every sense on the defensive during the summer of 1899. Qing officials' eagerness to participate in international conferences was matched with a sense that such events could very easily contribute to joint action by Western states against the rest: Might the Hague end up as something like another Berlin West Africa Conference, this time with its target being China's vast and still-unexploited interior?

As Guo Songtao had noted a quarter of a century earlier, China was one of the few remaining areas still left for Western expansion, and any minor commercial or missionary incident might produce an opportunity for annexation of wide swathes of its territory. This had been amply displayed in events since 1894, in Qingdao, Weihaiwei, Guangzhouwan, and elsewhere. As remembered by Heinrich Lammasch, one joke at the Hague that actually was made *by*, rather than about, Yang Ru was that the delegates assembled should simply go ahead and determine a ratio for exactly what number of square miles of territory China should lose every time a European happened to die on its soil.[51] That dark witticism, though, did not find its way into any contemporary Western accounts of the event.

Inclusion and Subordination

At the meeting, aside from career diplomats, several delegations or their entourages included other notable figures such as the US naval captain and historian Alfred Thayer Mahan as well as members of the *Institut de Droit International* and others in the *avant-garde* of the international legal profession, legal academia or other areas of scholarship, and the pacifist movement. While at the Hague, Yang and the other Chinese delegates made the acquaintance of the influential peace activist Bertha von Suttner, who recorded with interest her interactions with the Chinese visitors. In her memoirs, von Suttner noted Yang's cordial communications, as well as a conversation with Lu Zhengxiang in which he stated that "precisely for us [Chinese], the achievement of the goals of the conference would be the most valuable . . . for we are those threatened the most by the European politics of force [*Gewaltpolitik*]."[52]

However, von Suttner evidently took the greatest interest in Yang's Manchu wife who had joined him at the conference, writing about her on several occasions as a kind of *objet d'art*: "a pretty young woman, but wholly of the type that one finds in Chinese porcelain" (elsewhere, she refers to her as "like a wooden doll").[53] Von Suttner also remarked on how the couple's young children would "no more grow up as true, unadulterated Chinese [for b]ehind their Wall lies from now on a piece of the World . . . One after another all of the Chinese walls will fall – and there are so many besides the ones in the Middle Kingdom itself. We already see them crumbling."[54] Such rhapsodizing indicates the way that, even for peace activists such as von Suttner and Stead, China's presence at the First Hague Conference was something to be noted in a symbolic register, rather than one of active participation or concrete contributions.[55]

Both of these pacifists praised China as an example of peaceful culture to contrast with the greed and aggression of modern empires – Stead, for example, lamented how Russia was aggressively pursuing self-interest in Manchuria and "inoculat[ing] the Yellow Race with the destructive virus of militarism," even as it pursued the cause of peace in name. Yet, in Stead's own comments on world affairs published in advance of the conference, his assessment of China's predicament vis-à-vis the West had led him to argue the acceptability of "a protectorate of China by any one European power, subject to three conditions – free trade, free religion, and no armaments." Those were, of course, more or less the same conditions that had been applied to the Belgian Congo in 1885, though Stead at least added the proviso that maintaining the status quo (which after all promoted all three of those universal goods) was a preferable policy.[56]

The fundamental logic of the international system that was reflected in and formalized via the First Hague Conference was still in many ways that of the post-1815 Concert of Europe, premised on ideas regarding the balance of power. The humanization of warfare that was embarked on at the Hague, reaffirming developments in codifying the law of war in which *Institut de Droit International* members and the International Committee of the Red Cross (ICRC) had played lead roles, addressed solely issues of *ius in bello* – law during wartime – rather than *ius ad bellum*, or law governing legitimate and illegitimate forms of conflict.[57] Any perceived violation of a duty, customary or treaty-based, could be treated by Western states as the basis for a "reprisal."

Qing officials were aware of such potential dangers. Following the conference, the agreements regarding creating a PCA, requiring the mediation or arbitration of interstate disputes, and creating new rules for the laws of war were debated by court officials. Yang suggested that, at least with regards to the PCA and the Red Cross Convention,[58] China should swiftly sign and ratify, given that: "This is the first time China has joined such a conference, if we do not sign and ratify, the foreigners will suspect that China wishes to remain an isolated region, and when there are future public conferences, they might not be willing to associate with us."[59] The fear of being a pariah, "cast out from the public law of planet Earth," remained a source of great concern.

Yet so too did the potential ramifications of adhesion to the new treaties. The First Hague Convention, creating the PCA, was a matter of particular debate. Officials of the Zongli Yamen expressed the (prophetic) concern that:

> Although the arbitration agreement is a means for reducing conflict and easing disputes when they arise, if all the foreign countries unite together, it is to be feared that when war approaches the situation will revert to one in which the strength of the two sides decides the matter.[60]

Indeed, they feared, China's very adherence to the PCA could itself result in further concessions being extracted if it was decided by Western powers that China had violated the provisions of the Hague Conventions, or their interpretation by arbitrators. To address such concerns, Yang emphasized in his submissions to the Zongli Yamen the voluntary nature of arbitration – mandatory arbitration having failed to be adopted during the conference.[61] Similarly, he presented the Red Cross Treaty of the original 1864 Geneva Convention as a great "benevolent act" (*shanju* 善举), adopting a term that was widely used in the Ming and Qing eras to refer to charitable actions taken either by private individuals and groups (such as merchant associations) or by state authorities.[62] Where Western lawyers and diplomats referred to the development of international humanitarian norms and institutions as cutting-edge instantiations of legal progress by a civilizational elite, Qing officials found them comprehensible within a traditional framework of imperially sanctioned philanthropic behavior – just as the Peace Conference itself had been (very roughly) assimilable to the Spring and Autumn Era notion of a *mibinghui*, and, decades earlier, favorable trade rules had been assimilable to the magnanimity of the Son of Heaven who maintained stateliness while giving up tariff revenues.[63]

On the other hand, some of the new rules of war that had been agreed in 1899 seemed to be a different matter. Yang Ru recommended against signing the new Hague treaty on land war, as "China's armed forces are still not fully versed in Western customs of warfare," which could give rise to accidental violations.[64] The new provisions added in 1899 included extensive regulations covering issues such as treatment of surrendered combatants, looting, bombardment of undefended towns and harbors, among others. Given the still-tenuous (and decentralized) character of China's military structure, it was likely a valid concern whether the central government was capable of ensuring compliance with these rules.

Yang also felt that the (third) convention extending the 1864 Geneva Conventions to naval warfare would be difficult to implement because China's various ports lacked Western medical personnel and equipment, as well as hospital ships, and other such accoutrements of humanitarian aid that would be required. As regards the new rules for land warfare, Yang's superiors agreed that "an incident at the borders" could easily arise that would possibly prompt foreign powers to accuse China of violating its new commitments, and thus provide grounds for exacting harsh forms of redress.[65] However, they felt that this was risk was not dispositive with respect to the convention extending the existing Geneva provisions to naval war, for:

> All around the globe people consider [the naval warfare provisions] as a *shanju* ... it is difficult to be a lone dissenter in this situation, and would be better to show charity to our fellow men and display a willingness to put our moral virtue into practice.[66]

As is evident, the traditional concept of *shanju* provided not just a category that facilitated discussion of the Red Cross and its functions, but also played a role in shaping the substance of official debate. This is on display in the contrast of views regarding the convention on naval warfare. While Yang pointed to the worry that this could be applied as a legalistic rule-set invoked to justify punishment of China by foreign powers, the Zongli Yamen officials instead redirected discussion of this convention back to the category of imperial charity compatible with Qing *guoti*. The example of Japan also played a role in deliberations regarding China's proper approach to such agreements, but less as an ethical model to be emulated than as a demonstration of survival strategies in a hostile world. In late 1899, Yang again opted for ancient analogies in conveying the importance and the nature of the new treaties to the Qing Court: "the situation of great powers around the globe today is just like the Spring and Autumn era."[67]

China's situation was, nonetheless, far different from Japan's. The latter was now a near-peer, partner, and competitor with the Western commercial empires. The Qing realm was, by contrast, above all a space in which those powers saw ongoing opportunities to expand. Chinese experience since 1894, especially, had given officials reason to fear that "while the European states all lying on the same continent may distrust one another, when it comes to their shared relations with the East it is to be feared that they will join together as one in scheming against us."[68] Who was not to say that the expansive new rules agreed upon at the Hague, including the provisions for arbitration of interstate disputes, might not simply "claim to promote peace and tranquility while in fact carrying out forcible restraint [of China]"? The question of actively participating in these new forms of international legal organization was one that "called for sagely wisdom and far-thinking."[69] However, China would be given very little time for such contemplation before its officials' fears were realized.

Joint Invasion and Occupation

Although the Qing signed the First and Third Hague Conventions of 1899 on December 27 of that year (while postponing approval of the extensive new rules of warfare introduced in the second convention),[70] they did not have a chance to ratify any of these agreements before the next major crisis, which would see many of the court's worst fears realized. The so-called Boxer Rebellion (in Chinese usually called the Yihetuan Movement), which was an armed insurrection that aimed to eliminate the Western presence in areas of north China that were subject to increasing foreign encroachments since the mid 1890s, erupted in late 1899. This uprising divided Qing officialdom, with some conservatives favoring endorsement of the rebels, while more moderate officials, including Yuan Shikai and Zhang Zhidong, aimed to contain the situation.[71]

The disastrous conflict of the following months entailed killings of some Westerners resident in the capital, an initial Qing attempt to suppress the Boxers followed by an official split over their cause, and then bloody intervention and reprisals by the foreign Eight Nation Alliance, which easily defeated the insurgents and then imposed harsh terms on China via the Boxer Protocol of September 7, 1901.[72] The conflict and its resolution were highly significant as international legal precedents. First, this "eight nation" intervention was the most internationalized use of force in modern history thus far. The extension of foreign economic interests into Chinese territory was by now so advanced that they required both joint policing and a kind of constitutionalized set of transnational guarantees to ensure their future security.

Second, the agreement ending the conflict was also highly innovative as a treaty text, introducing forms of normative obligation and enforcement with few precedents. Among other provisions, the Boxer Protocol imposed crippling financial indemnities on the state and also assigned their collection to the foreign-managed fiscal bureaucracy of the MCS;[73] China would be prohibited from importing arms and ammunition for at least two years;[74] the Legation Quarter in Beijing would "be considered as one specially reserved for [foreign states'] use and placed under their exclusive control, in which Chinese shall not have the right to reside"; the Qing would have to destroy the forts at Taku and any "which might impede free communication between Peking and the sea";[75] the Qing would have to allow foreign powers to militarily occupy strategic points (again, "in order to ensure free communication between Peking and the sea");[76] China would have to "prohibit forever, under the pain of death, membership in any anti-foreign society";[77] and the Zongli Yamen would be converted into a "Ministry of Foreign Affairs" (*Waiwubu* 外務部) that would rank above the other central government ministries that it had previously stood alongside.[78] Taken altogether, these protocol arrangements gave foreign powers collectively greater administrative control than some enjoyed even in explicit protectorates.

Also important was the innovation of largely unprecedented international prosecutions for "crimes against the laws of humanity" against mid-ranking officials accused of aiding the Boxer movement.[79] These investigations, prosecutions, and (capital) punishments were initiated before the signing of the protocol, beginning toward the end of 1900, and were coordinated by the multinational forces and the occupation government of Tianjin. The trials themselves, conducted at the city of Baoding, were *sui generis* proceedings held in closed sessions, and the trial body itself was at times referred to as an "international tribunal" and at other times as an "international commission of inquiry" (a form of legal procedure that had been given formal status at the Hague Conference), or other such terms. The impact of these prosecutions on the subsequent history of international criminal law was largely indirect, although they did indicate an important, transitional form of institutional "experimentation" in Chinese space by the international community so recently formally constituted at the Hague.

Third, the Boxer Intervention came to embody an important point of international law doctrine: the extent to which a justified international "intervention" could be undertaken against a state without turning into a condition of "war" with corresponding rights and duties between the belligerents. This is for example evident in the references to the Boxer conflict by Lassa Oppenheim in the first edition of his classic treatise on international law, where he uses the Boxer Intervention as a key example of legitimate armed reprisal, that is, "legalized self-help of . . . single States against one another," which could permit states whose interests were harmed due to wrongs committed by another state "through reprisals . . . [to] compel the delinquent State to comply with its international duties."[80]

As noted a few years before Oppenheim by the Berlin scholar of international and criminal law Franz von Liszt, this general notion of "peaceful means of self-help" (*friedlichen Mitteln der . . . Selbsthilfe*) could extend even as far as "armed collective interventions" like that of 1900–1902.[81] The "occupation of the territory of the state violating the law [i.e. China]" by the Eight Nation Alliance was warranted as a form of "direct self-help," and did not have to give rise to a "state of war" in which the various recently codified humanitarian legal norms would notionally apply.[82] Instead, "the measure of the permitted hostilities is in such a case only determined through the principles of Christianity and humaneness, not through international law."[83] Despite the fact that the hostilities had involved tens of thousands of deaths, and the occupation of vast swathes of its territory, they were considered by leading jurists as falling outside of legal restraint – except those self-imposed by the victors. Neither the occupying powers nor most international lawyers considered the massive intervention as a "war" in a legal sense; and the William McKinley administration was especially adamant to avoid this label.

Of course, the events of 1899–1902 had also raised the general question as to whether China should even be considered a member of the international community in the first place. To that question even W. A. P. Martin, by now in official Qing service for nearly four decades, gave a largely negative response. He left China in 1900 after personally being involved in early clashes with Yihetuan supporters at the legation district in Beijing; upon arriving in New York with a rifle slung across his back, he told local porters he had used it for "tiger hunting." Capitalizing on his sensational recent experiences by quickly publishing another book, Martin drew on a now-prevalent trope for the title, *The Siege in Peking: China against the World*. In it, he lamented that the West had not, as he had suggested in the 1850s, supported the Taiping rebels and undertaken to split China up into a more manageable set of subunits.[84]

If this was the view of longtime foreign "friends," prominent jurists in Western capitals were all the more negative in their assessments of China's right to membership in the global community. As the leading German public law scholar Georg Jellinek wrote in October 1900:

> One will surely not hear protests by China against violations of international law . . . It has shown through its own actions the denial of Western international law, and it will not fall to it to invoke this international law . . . Violations of international law always presume a subject that feels the violation. The proposition 'no violation without a victim' also applies without exception to international transactions.[85]

Of course, for Jellinek, as for many other self-understood progressive or liberal public lawyers at the time, this lack of status in international law was something that could be overcome eventually, as Japan (uniquely) had now accomplished. Were China to make similarly profound transformations and reforms, "the time would come when China would be accepted into the community of international law [*in die Gemeinschaft des Völkerrechts wird aufgenommen werden*]." Like many jurists, Jellinek advised that the occupying powers, though under no strictly legal obligation to do so, should behave humanely to bring that far-off goal somewhat closer.[86]

Jellinek, Martens, Holls, and other progressive international lawyers made arguments for maintaining China's territorial integrity, but not for treating it, or its demands to overturn unequally imposed treaty conditions, as serious interlocutors in matters of international law. The logic of the protocol – defending and further elaborating a solidarity of the "joint interests" of Western states (plus Japan) in Chinese territory – was something to be endorsed. Indeed, it was these very joint interests themselves that argued against any formal splitting up of China into annexations or formal spheres of influence, for under such circumstances, "the [existing] commercial treaties may become valueless." Far better was to repeat the kind of joint consensus on "the settlement of the Eastern question at the Congress of Berlin" of 1878, where the Ottoman Empire had had its territorial rights and status decided by a joint consensus of Western powers. A "similar general international arrangement might secure the peaceful development of China in the basis of the 'open door' policy."[87]

One significant question that arose before the hostilities had terminated was whether the new international institutions developed in 1899 should have any bearing on the situation unfolding in China. During the occupying powers' negotiations over the postintervention treaty, the prospect was raised of turning over the specific question of the indemnity amounts to the newly established PCA. This suggestion was initially brought up by the Russian side, but was then embraced by the United States, and endorsed to the other eight occupying states by Secretary of State John Hay and President McKinley.[88] Some of those who had been at the Hague, including Frederick Holls, also highly approved.[89] In the end, skepticism from the other powers, Germany in particular, blocked what would otherwise have been the first-ever use of PCA jurisdiction.

Martens, too, emphasized the need for an internationalized approach to China in the wake of the Boxer Intervention, and specifically called for maintaining the country's territorial integrity.[90] He reminded Western lawyers that "no treaty is in being in virtue of which we could abolish the Chinese state and nation." Of course, Martens' own arguments on behalf of Russian occupation of Chinese territory and the imposition of consular jurisdiction in the 1870s and 1880s made his current position somewhat anomalous, a fact that he subtly acknowledged by pointing out that "Circumstances have changed a great deal since 1872." At the same time, Martens continued in his other writings to be dismissive of China as a "state that, by all of its traditions and its *raison d'être*, is the very incarnation of absolute immobility [as opposed to progress] in political matters."[91]

Aftermath

Already in the midst of the Boxer conflict, it was clear to moderate Qing officials both that the conservative policies had decisively failed and that incursions from the West would likely grow ever more extreme. Yang Ru commented on such matters in an open letter, translated into French, that he sent to Bertha von Suttner and her husband.[92] This letter was published in various European newspapers, and drew some attention as a "Chinese perspective" on the events unfolding. In it Yang recalls the noble intention of the previous year's Hague Conference and refers to his wide travels around the world – the United States, Peru and other states of South America, Austria-Hungary, Germany, England, Spain, France, Holland, Japan, and Russia – and how his study of admirable administrative institutions and technology in the West had also led him to notice a spirit of "incessant rivalry and . . . jealousy manifested among all nations."[93]

In terms of the West's relations with China, meanwhile, Yang's view was that the basic problem leading to crises like the current one was the premise that China could only be accepted as an equal if its people converted to Christianity. Western policies on such matters were as counterproductive as it would be "to seek to force the people of the various countries to embrace the Confucian doctrine."[94] Such gunboat proselytization had given rise to counterreactions and their disastrous consequences, and so Yang suggested that "commercial relations between China and the foreign powers may be developed to any desired extent; but as for the question of religion, it would be more prudent to allow each to respect his own as he understands it."[95]

Bertha von Suttner indicated sympathy with Yang's views,[96] yet she also believed that "[t]he Chinese conflict has forced the civilized powers to enter upon the path which the peace party [had earlier] suggested . . . namely, union, the foregoing of their rival interests . . . in the name of their common interest." Meanwhile, the "international force" formed "spontaneously" to defend these joint interests in 1900 was but a poor proxy for what should have been some form of international "constabulary."[97] Nor would any lessons about the dangers or excesses of intervention per se be internalized by international lawyers in the wake of the bloody occupation of northern China. To the contrary, it would be widely cited by leading publicists as a precedent for just how far the right to intervene and occupy a foreign state could go without giving rise to obligations to declare a legal war (or accord the target corresponding rights).[98]

Meanwhile, in St. Petersburg, Lu Zhengxiang was deeply troubled by the events unfolding in China, not only the disastrous invasion of the country and the imposition of the harsh protocol – which he would describe in his memoirs as "one of the most cruel, unjust, and myopic acts in the diplomatic history of the world"[99] – but also by the policies of the Qing Court. Early on during the crisis, several critics of the conservatives' approach, including Lu's diplomatic and spiritual mentor, Xu Jingcheng, had been chosen as scapegoats for its escalation and executed.[100] Using the same epithets to characterize his country's ruling authorities as he had the foreign invaders, Lu asked himself "what is the point of serving rulers so unjust, blind, and self-interested?"[101] The general difficulty of representing China abroad during the ensuing period is described by Lu in terms redolent of self-denial and asceticism:

> [I learned that I should] not attach myself to the declining regime, neither to follow it, nor to condemn it, but instead limit myself to doing my duty and, in observing the most distinguished officials of the European countries, to create my own program of life and of action. To this end, [I would have to] learn to be silent, whatever might be the humiliations and the snubs that were inevitably inflicted on me by, on the one side, the Chinese dignitaries who despised all those who did not flatter them and, on the other, the European officials and society that called the whole Chinese state a "sick man" and regarded every Chinese as a devalued being.[102]

Largely due to American influence between 1899 and 1902, the European powers and Japan were deterred from demanding outright territorial concessions. The notion of an "open door" for multinational trade in China, which had been raised by US Secretary of State John Hay in September 1899, was now adopted as a general rule of organization for Qing territory.[103] The problem of how to administer the vast political and economic space of China was, now as always, a matter of great interest for political elites and intellectuals in the West. As the Boxer crisis was unfolding, the American naval historian Mahan, who had crossed paths with Yang and Lu at the Hague, published a book on *The Problem of Asia*, remarking upon how "[e]very step forward in the march that has opened China to trade has been gained by pressure; the most important have been the result of actual war." Amidst the current crisis, it was necessary to "prevent . . . preponderant control [of China] by any one external state" as well as "insist . . . upon the open door," both in terms of commercial activity and religious/cultural influence – with instilling Christianity a vital aim.[104]

Mahan also warned that, despite China's current weakness, it could one day expand across the Pacific and challenge American interests, including the territories newly acquired following the Spanish-American War. It was thus "difficult to contemplate with equanimity such a vast mass as the four hundred millions [sic.] of China concentrated [in the future] into one effective political organization, equipped with modern appliances, and cooped within a territory already narrow for it," unless it were "civilized" by the proper influences. Reflecting a frequent topic of discussion among those interested in further international efforts to develop China, Mahan suggested that "the outer world of maritime states can most readily and beneficially act upon China" in the Yangzi River and its vast delta region – while making full use of "sea power in the military sense . . . to maintain their position and rights in the trade of China."[105]

In line with such discussions, American positions emphasizing territorial integrity and the "open door" remained distinct from those of the other powers that had been part of the intervention, which rather more blatantly sought to maximize their influence and authority over various slices of China. Russia in particular initiated with renewed vigor its push for a formalized hegemony over Manchuria. Much of the subsequent pressure over the negotiation of intensified Russian demands fell on Yang Ru, who resumed his position as Chinese envoy to St. Petersburg after the Hague Conference. Bitterly divisive negotiations between the Russian foreign minister Vladimir Lamsdorff and Yang were conducted to determine the terms for a "reestablishment of the authority of the Chinese government in that region."[106]

The Qing records of this talk portray the intensity of coercion that the Russian side brought to bear in seeking explicit recognition of its dominance over Manchuria. The negotiations over the course of 1901 to early 1902 were so intense that, according to Lu Zhengxiang, the stress resulted in Yang's health deteriorating. This was followed by incidents of outdoor collapse that could have been either due to a stroke or (as reported by a few newspapers) possibly a physical altercation outside of Count Lamsdorff's offices with the latter's aides after an especially testy exchange. As the bedridden Yang's health deteriorated despite expert medical attention, Lu and Hu Weide continued negotiations with Russia, leading to the 1902 Convention; Yang passed away soon after, cementing his status as an early martyr for Chinese *zhuquan*.[107]

Conclusion

The Boxer intervention and Protocol were, in their way, as major steps in the "progress of international organization" as the 1899 Hague Conventions, and many at the time certainly saw them that way. But the former, unlike the latter, are now almost wholly absent from the professional memory of international law. In reality, from the Qing perspective, it was always apparent that increased international organization in the form of multilateral, legislated international norms, like those being pioneered at the Hague, could also imply collective forms of punishment and discipline for weak states. The Qing reticence over signing or ratifying new agreements was reflective of precisely these concerns, even if the specific rules being adopted appeared as "acts of charity" or *shanju*.

Moreover, the personal experience of China's delegates Yang Ru and Lu Zhengxiang, in which they were effectively excluded from taking any meaningful part in the proceedings and even turned into objects of ridicule by some other delegates, underscored this dynamic of subordination and lack of agency in diplomatic settings. The increasingly illusory character of China's state authority in the eyes of foreign great powers was then put on full display in the Boxer Protocol, where, to a greater degree than ever before, powers of *dominium*, including control over tariffs and public finance in general, were "internationalized" in foreign-dominated structures. The hundreds of millions of dollars worth of new public debt being accrued by the Qing state over the course of the interventions of the 1890s and, especially, after the imposition of the Boxer Protocol, were for the most part serviced by the ever-more important MCS.

Meanwhile, the concept and term *zhuquan*, which as we have seen was not emphasized in elite Qing discourse until repeated introductions from Meiji sources, now came fully into prominence. The erstwhile nineteenth-century focus on "stateliness" now rang very hollow in contrast with the Meiji achievement of recapturing domestic authority and a status of (near) parity with the West. Japan's *shuken* had been won, primarily, through its entry into the leading ranks of a violent and exclusionary family of nations, and this model increasingly preoccupied China's intelligentsia.

5

The Problem of Equality

In the words of one Chinese reform activist commenting on the "Boxer" crisis of 1899–1901, the failure of China's Manchu rulers to properly manage relations with the Western great powers had led to the disaster of "an occupied capital, people dead, soldiers slaughtered, land expropriated, payment demanded, and the state almost non-existent." Some Chinese domestic reformers after the crisis blamed Qing leaders for allowing China to be classed as an "enemy of all the world's states," thus giving pretexts for both intervention as well as the radical administrative and financial obligations imposed in the 1901 Protocol.[1]

From 1902, even within Qing officialdom, there was at last general agreement both as to the need for a program of domestic reforms and that skillful, permanent representation abroad was equally necessary. It was with these aims in mind that Qing officials had begun to dispatch high-performing students overseas to engage in the study of constitutional and international law in leading jurisdictions such as the Britain, Germany, France, the United States, and Japan in order to contribute to China's legal development.[2] Domestic education would also be restructured to promote the understanding of Western law, including international law. Diplomats, for the first time, started to engage closely with the subject, seeking inclusion in conferences. Meanwhile, with this post-Boxer aim to learn about international legal order, the idea of framing a "Chinese perspective" on international law also began to draw focused attention. The Second Hague Conference of 1907, where the Qing would for the first time send a delegation conversant with Western law,[3] sat at the nexus of these efforts.

New Students and New Teachers

The intervention of 1900 had seemed to many jurists and pacifists in the West as the first great "police" action of a more legally regulated world community.[4] The lessons for the Manchu Court and its subjects, however, were quite different. It was only in 1904 that the Qing authorities ratified the Hague Conventions on the use of force and dispute settlement that they had signed after the conference of 1899.[5] At the same time, and especially following the imposed Protocol of 1901, staying fully insulated from such developments no longer seemed a feasible goal.

Domestically, the 1898 reformers' agenda of Meiji-style constitutional monarchy, and the importation of related public law ideas, now rapidly gathered pace. The same was true for international law study – by the next decade, nearly the entire former lexicon of international law in Chinese, initially coined primarily via Martin's Tongwenguan translations, had been replaced with terms drawn directly from Meiji receptions of Western thought.[6] The profound albeit belated shift in ideas of public law was also embodied, *inter alia*, in the end of the millennia-old imperial examination system in 1904, which signaled a turn toward higher education that was focused on "modern" Western/Japanese practices, including basics of diplomacy and international law.

Even in the final imperial examinations themselves, meanwhile, this intellectual turn is already apparent. So too is the patently critical sensibility that young Qing scholars brought to the subject. International law – then still most often translated using the traditional term *gongfa* 公法 – was a frequently mentioned topic in essays by the last students ever to take China traditional Confucian exams. In their comments can be detected a sharp, critical gaze: "In the nineteenth century, there was no *gongfa*, only power," writes one, citing the examples of India, Egypt, and Turkey. "There is no *gongfa* for weak states," writes another. "*Gongfa* does not exist among unequal states [*bu pingdeng zhi guo wu gongfa* 不平等之國無公法]," writes a third. Rather, he continues, "international law is used by the Great Powers to obtain their interests from those outside [the community], and the [latter] weak states cannot call on international law to oppose this because they have already lost their interests to those inside of [the] international law [community] [*yi shi liyi yu gongfa zhi zhong* 已失利益於公法之中]."[7] Not only for radical revolutionaries, but even for the Qing state's own most promising young institutional insiders, the first years of the twentieth century had instilled a stark realization that China risked being cast out of the society of states by those "within *gongfa*": the Great Powers.

Some of the most promising students now began to engage in legal studies abroad, including several who would go on to influence both the international legal system itself and on China's role within it. One of those, who would eventually become China's first international judge and one of its most important twentieth-century jurists, was a brilliant student from Hong Kong who came from a line of Cantonese Lutheran pastors. That student happened to be the grandson of Wang Yuanchen (still alive at this time), who almost six decades earlier had been among the first and most devoted of Karl Gützlaff's converts. Wang Chonghui, born in Hong Kong in 1881, became the valedictorian of the first graduating class at the recently established National Beiyang University in Tianjin in 1900, just as the city faced foreign occupation. He is considered the first student ever awarded a Western-style university diploma from a Chinese university.[8]

After graduating, Wang then went to Japan to study law in 1901, where he also became involved in the revolutionary activities of overseas Chinese students. This stint in Japan was followed by studies for a Doctor of Civil Law degree at Yale between 1904 and 1905. Two years later, Wang produced the first full translation into English of the German Civil Code, at 600 plus pages; it remained the standard reference for the code in English for decades.[9] Continuing his legal studies in Britain, Germany, and France, Wang also found time to coauthor writings with Sun Yat-sen, becoming a cofounder of his Tongmenghui organization.[10] Wang would go on to become one of the key figures in China's republican/nationalist movement, as well as one of the very few leaders well-regarded across bitter factional lines and seen as having undisputed personal integrity. One of the more widely spread anecdotes about his early years seems to reflect the devout upbringing that seems to have informed his personality: When a Japanese maidservant at the inn where the twenty–three or twenty–four-year-old Wang was staying propositioned him – showing up in his bedroom one evening in a state of undress – his reaction was to run out to the hallway shouting for help from his student delegation head. Those who worked closely with Wang would also later recall a diligent work ethic and a lack of interest in material wealth.[11]

A very different but equally important figure (and, as it would turn out, the man who would be the last international judge appointed by the Republic of China) was the dapper and urbane Wellington Koo (aka Gu Weijun). Koo was born in Shanghai in 1888 and during the Boxer crisis was just beginning his studies at the Anglican-run Saint John's University, which he concluded in 1904. He then successfully applied (with Boxer indemnity funding) to Columbia University, where he would finish his undergraduate degree in three years with excellent grades, serve as editor-in-chief of the *Columbia Spectator*, become a debate-team star, serve on the student board, and pen letters to the *New York Times* and other publications about matters such as, in one case, unfair police profiling of Chinese in the United States. Over the next years, Koo would go on to pursue a PhD in international law from Columbia University under the prominent international lawyer John Bassett Moore, resulting in a 1912 thesis on consular jurisdiction and *The Status of Aliens in China*.[12]

Another student who would go on to become one of China's important international jurists was Zhou Wei, who in 1900 was living with his mother in Jiangxi following the death of his father, an instructor at a government academy. Zhou dedicated himself to the study of foreign languages that he began during the time of the Boxer Intervention and, after achieving top academic marks, was recommended by provincial authorities for further state-sponsored study at the reconstituted foreign affairs ministry's School of Translation (i.e., the *Tongwenguan*, reestablished in 1903 as the *Yixueguan*).

Soon after, he was dispatched to France, where he studied both law and civil engineering at the University of Paris and at Lille.[13] Zhou would soon become one of the first Chinese jurists to make a prominent impact on the field in the West.

Also studying abroad during the post-Boxer years was Zhou Gengsheng (no relation), a talented Hunanese student who left for Tokyo's Waseda University in 1905. Like many overseas Chinese students in Japan, Zhou became involved in the revolutionary movement. Though he took a more roundabout route to his eventual doctoral studies in international law (which he would begin at the University of Paris only after the collapse of China's first post-Qing national unity government in 1913), Zhou Gengsheng later came to be seen as one of the main founders of the international law discipline in China, especially in the People's Republic of China. From the very beginning of his legal studies and commentary, he also worked, like Wang and Koo, among others, to promote recognition of China as an equal of the Great Powers.

Similar concerns motivated the studies of China's earliest law PhD students at the University of Berlin, Ma Derun and Zhou Zechun, who would receive their doctorates in 1907 and 1910, respectively. Both focused their doctoral work on questions related to China's status vis-à-vis the "community" of Western international law. Ma's thesis dealt with "The Entry of the Chinese Empire into the League of International Law" [*Der Eintritt des chinesischen Reiches in den volkerrechtlichen Verband*], while Zhou's was on the recent Qing reforms to "Constitution, Administration, and Judicial Interpretation," with reference to corresponding European approaches.[14] These and other early doctoral students in public law abroad were notable for taking part in the dissemination of Western legal thought – Ma and Zhou, for example, created a short-lived but influential publication that included translations of Rousseau, Bluntschli, and other such sources – and for impacting discussions of China abroad.[15] By July 1907, when Ma graduated with his dissertation, a major Berlin newspaper carried a front-page summary of his arguments that "an unbiased evaluation of the essence of international law would make one realize that China has already recognized its main legal principles, and that China's entry into the international law league of the West has already been accomplished."[16]

Ma's doctoral project was intended to show that China was a part of an *Interessengemeinschaft*, or "community of interests" with Western states, and thus should be treated as an equal subject of international law. Zhou made similar arguments in his own work, and introduced such notions to Chinese readers.[17] This language of *Interessengemeinschaft* was particularly drawn from the work of one of Ma's and Zhou's teachers in Berlin, Franz von Liszt, who was the author of one of the most prominent international law textbooks of the period. In the editions of this work since 1888, Liszt had continued to refer to China, alongside Siam and the Ottoman Empire, as "half-civilized" polities, not fully part of the family of nations.[18]

New "Protectors"

The aspiration for equal agency in the Eurocentric "family of nations" was, in the post Boxer Protocol years, increasingly associated with the term *zhuquan*, now associated with its Bluntschian and Meiji-derived implications of full territorial control, aka *Gebietshoheit*. Dealings with Britain over Tibet between 1904 and 1906 especially helped to underscore for Qing officials the need to preserve the status of *zhuquan*,[19] and a similarly powerful message was sent by ongoing Russian–Japanese conflicts over Manchuria. Russia had sought to impose a formal hegemony over the zone in the wake of the Boxer conflict, and now a rising Japan sought the same. The Russo-Japanese War of 1904–1905, with its clear victory for Japan, radically changed the regional balance of power, with legal repercussions.

However, this success could not fully override Japan's stated commitments to the multilateral principles of the open door policy of the United States, announced by President McKinley's secretary of state John Hay in 1898: guaranteeing China's "territorial integrity" along with equal commercial opportunity for all foreign states. At the same time, Japanese officials saw major US figures, even President Roosevelt himself, as potentially supporting a kind of Asian Monroe Doctrine.[20] With the latter's interpretation of the original doctrine as conferring an "international police power" to sanction any "[c]hronic wrongdoing, or … impotence which results in a general loosening of the ties of civilized society" among states in the Western Hemisphere,[21] any similar application to East Asia had clear implications for interventions in China. Other great powers had, indeed, already adopted similar approaches in advance of the collective Boxer Intervention. The Anglo-German Yangtze Agreement of 1900, for example, had been key to ensuring cooperation in the joint occupation of China during the suppression of the Boxer movement. Like a Monroe-style arrangement, it had purported to preserve China's territorial integrity, but only on the basis of a framework of rules, and grounds for intervention, conferring agency on the "protecting" powers. While China was the third-party *object* of that agreement, it was not admitted to it as a contracting partner nor able to exert influence as an interlocutor during its negotiation process.

Chinese leaders as prominent as Empress Dowager Cixi herself had praised the United States, in the person of Roosevelt's just-assassinated predecessor, as "profoundly just and faithful in diplomatic relations, helping to preserve us during [the Boxer] crisis."[22] However, that sense of reliance was increasingly in question. When John Hay issued Roosevelt's call in 1904 to convene another Hague Conference (delayed due to the Russo-Japanese War), the plan was met with wariness from numerous quarters, some Qing officials included. An attaché in Berlin, for example, reported to the court the "subtle views" of German Chancellor von Bülow, who praised the initiative while regretting that "in this world of fierce competition" little progress toward pacifism could be expected.[23] The Qing diplomat also noted that the United States' own recent behavior in the Spanish–American War belied its claims to abhor imperialism.

Despite some trepidation over international law innovations emerging from the Anglo-American world, the Qing Court encouraged participation in the Second Hague Conference, where, for the first time, it deployed a delegation including several officials with legal training and/or previous experience at international conferences. Attended by forty-four states compared with the first conference's twenty-six, and now encompassing most of Latin America along with the independent states of the Middle East and East Asia, the 1907 Second Hague Conference clearly heralded "a new era in international relations."[24] It was apparent that, as the German jurist Carl Schmitt would much later phrase it, "the atmosphere and ambience" of the Second Conference was no longer as "purely European" as the first: "those who ought to have been carried out the door now already stood before it."[25] At the Hague, Qing delegates would play a significant role in confronting Eurocentrism, but also faced new prospects of formalized global hierarchy.

The leading Chinese delegate, Lu Zhengxiang, was the most important individual in the formulation of Qing positions at the Hague as well as, later, in framing the resulting reflections on and initiatives regarding China's role in global legal order. Shortly before being elevated into this position, however, Lu had evidently lost all faith in the Qing regime. As of 1906, he had recently experienced the dismissive attitudes he faced as a subordinate attendee at the First Hague Conference in 1899, the execution of his former diplomatic mentor Xu Jingcheng as a scapegoat for pro-Boxer officials in 1900, the Western occupation and the Boxer Protocol, and a variety of state and personal crises surrounding the Russo-Japanese conflicts fought in and over Chinese territory by two foreign great powers, with China a mere spectator. It was at this point that he, like other reformists and revolutionaries of "Young China," symbolically cut off the queue imposed on all Han Chinese by the Manchus. In a sign of the times, his fellow Han diplomats abroad quietly tolerated this rebellious gesture.[26]

Ironically, Lu was just then appointed as the Qing special envoy to the Netherlands and to the planned Second Hague Conference, thus being instantly elevated several grades in rank. He was recognized for his able performance in diplomatic settings, not least as to facility with the French and Russian languages, for which he had been praised by foreign officials.[27] However, he did not have a background in international law, except for limited exposure during his studies at Martin's academy for translators (Martin himself was at this point no longer in official service, having returned to missionary work after alienating the Qing government with his post-Boxer condemnations). Soon after gaining a role within the Qing foreign policy elite, Lu began to advocate for fostering a cadre of international law specialists able to engage with the West at the highest levels of legal discourse. As he suggested in a cable of December 22, 1906, it was imperative both to cultivate advanced students and to translate more works: "Given the present circumstances of our country, even if we master the study of international law, we may still be unable to make full use of it – let alone if we fail to master it."[28]

Lu also made specific suggestions as to the kinds of works that should be translated. As he informed his superiors at the Office of Foreign Affairs, "there are two great schools of thought on international law, one of which is represented by England and which places sea power over that of the land, the other of which is represented by Russia, Germany, and France, which emphasizes the land over the sea."[29] In Lu's view, China as a great continental power with limited maritime activity was "aligned with the latter school."[30] While this was hardly a fully formed intervention on the issue of framing a "Chinese" (or "Asian") position on international law, it did reflect a nascent opinion as to the need for progress toward formulating such a position – and the experiences of the conference would do much to reaffirm Lu in this conviction.

China as a "Third-Class" State?

The Qing delegation to the Second Hague Conference comprised Lu Zhengxiang, along with Qian Xun, the military delegate Colonel Ding Shiyuan, and a team of others including, far in the background, the recent Yale graduate Wang Chonghui.[31] Coequal with Lu and at times acting as China's main representative was American diplomat and former secretary of state John Watson Foster, who had previously engaged in several other international dealings in the service of the Qing government.[32] Also quietly in attendance was Foster's nineteen-year-old grandson John Foster Dulles,[33] then a student at Princeton, who many years later would follow in his grandfather's footsteps as US secretary of state, in his case during the high Cold War years of 1953–1959.

For China, the climax of the Second Hague Conference was what became infamous as the "third-class state" incident of 1907, which, while generally forgotten in the Global North, was also a major episode in international legal history for a number of other then-marginalized states, including in particular those of Latin America.[34] This imbroglio involved plans for the creation of a truly permanent international court, to supplement or replace the limited and voluntary arbitral jurisdiction of the 1899 Permanent Court of Arbitration (PCA). Though F. F. Martens himself raised this general suggestion in the early days of the conference, it was not until August 1 that two separate plans, one American and one Russian, were formally shared with the various delegations.[35] As a court of general jurisdiction over international disputes with a standing judiciary (unlike the PCA with its requirement of case-by-case consent and appointment of arbitrators by both parties) the "Court of Arbitral Justice," as it was eventually dubbed, would have been a major step in the legalization of international relations. It also gave rise to heated contestation over the court's powers and how exactly its "global judiciary" would be constituted.

At the First Subcommission meeting of August 1, the American plan was announced by Joseph Choate and explained in detail by James Brown Scott, who suggested that the new court should have full jurisdiction over disputes referred to it by common agreement, for example, in multilateral treaties as well as on a voluntary basis. As to its judiciary, Scott declared his view that while all nations had an equal interest in justice, there was nonetheless "a great difference between nations considered from the standpoint of *material* interests"[36] (emphasis added), and that the latter would be the only proper basis for deciding the composition of the court. Population, alongside other factors, could be used as a proxy for each state's relevant "material interests." Scott quoted Supreme Court Justice John Marshall for the statement that "[n]o principle of general law is more universally acknowledged than the perfect equality of nations," but argued that a court consisting of forty-six judges, one from each state at the Hague, would be "unwieldy."[37]

At the same meeting, Martens provided perhaps the most stirring defense of the idea of a permanent international court – as he said, during the age of the Crusades, there had been the cry "To Jerusalem! God wills it!", but since 1899 this had been replaced by the updated version: "To The Hague!"[38] However, his proposal was somewhat less ambitious than that of the United States, building instead upon the existing PCA roster, which he argued should meet regularly to elect among themselves a standing tribunal to hear cases. Despite skepticism from many quarters over what Scott vaguely referred to as the "actual and natural principle" of population as the planned main factor for assigning judicial posts in the new tribunal, the full proposal that the United States unveiled on August 17, with the backing of Britain and Germany, did generally follow that approach – with the crucial caveat that the proper mode of calculation was "the population with the colonies," ensuring the highest status for the great powers in the planned judicial panel of sixteen or seventeen members, of whom eight (those of the great powers) would sit permanently. The rest would rotate in terms of ten, four, or two years, or, for the lowest-ranked group, a single year. China, despite being generally considered to have the largest population of any state in the world, found itself in the third class: able to appoint judges only for four years out of each twelve-year rotation.[39]

In his Hague news diary, the peace activist and journalist William T. Stead, who less than a decade earlier had argued that China should be made a protectorate of a Western power or be managed by them jointly, now noted critically that "China, which had belonged to the major powers, [was now] relegated to the third tier."[40] At the August 17 meeting, even before the plan was formally announced, Lu Zhengxiang was the first delegate to speak, pointing out that the "principle of population" had clearly not been followed with respect to China.[41] Lu tactfully praised the "real forward step in the way of progress" that the push for a permanent court represented, connecting it to

China's own "pacific spirit," but argued that the distribution of judges was patently unfair. Instead, he suggested taking the existing dues paid to the PCA's International Bureau – a population-based measure by which the eight great powers would retain their position, while China would stand alongside them as an equal, and other low-ranked states would not – as the proper way to assign the maximum judicial terms.[42] This would, he said, "remov[e] all inequality in the distribution of the judges."[43]

In messages to the Qing Court, Lu expressed his view that what was at stake was not so much the judicial tribunal itself, but rather "all kinds of further potential losses in coming years" that could follow on from this new "plunge" in China's status.[44] He continued to oppose the judicial-ranking proposal, though the most prominent opposition came from Latin American states. The Venezuelan delegates referred to the ranking scheme as "in evident contradiction with the principle of equal representation of states," the Mexican delegation protested against it as "contrary to the equality of nations," and Brazil's Ruy Barbosa referred to full equality as the "primordial condition for peace among nations."[45] It was Barbosa that most consistently, vociferously, and publicly opposed the ranking scheme, issuing repeated calls in strong language seeking, for example, to "reestablish equilibrium of justice between the weak and the strong."[46]

On August 20, Barbosa supplemented his critiques with an alternative Brazilian plan for the proposed court, which would allow all states to appoint a judge and have the panel hearing each particular matter be determined based on case-by-case selection.[47] While this proposal did not win support, an increasing number of states did continue to join in expressing their rejection of the "inequality" built into the US–British–German proposal.[48] China maintained its opposition while Barbosa repeatedly invoked equality and the delegates of Persia, Mexico, and Romania, amongst others, gradually expressed similar views. By September 18, the court plan for a rotating judiciary was abandoned, not without acrimonious scenes between Barbosa and the US delegates.[49] "Joseph Choate, of U.S., Beaten at Hague by Brazil Delegate in Hot Word Duel," newspapers reported shortly afterwards.[50] Not deterred by criticism from some of the great power delegates, including Choate's statement that "he bores me so," Barbosa delivered an address on October 9 on "The Equality of Sovereign States," reinforcing his firm position.[51]

Meanwhile, before and alongside the contentious plans for the Court of Arbitral Justice, another new judicial institution was also being planned. The latter was far more specific in its aims than the arbitration court, but just as (or, in a certain sense, even more) ambitious, and raised some of the same issues. It would act as a compulsory court of final jurisdiction over *all* matters connected with the law of maritime "prizes," or capture of ships and property during naval warfare. This court plan, too, divided member states up into categories, in this case, based on the size of their merchant fleets and (especially) naval forces, and again put China in a "third-class" position.[52] There could hardly be a more literal illustration of the idea that "sea power" (as 1899 Hague delegate Alfred Thayer Mahan had phrased it),[53] or the lack of it, decided a state's relative status in the increasingly Anglo-American–dominated international order.

Two plans for a permanent International Prize Court had initially been deposited by Germany and Britain, respectively, at the meeting of the conference's First Commission on June 22. These two proposals differed especially in respect of the adjudicatory mechanism. Where the German plan would provide for each party to a naval prize dispute to select arbitrators after the fashion of the PCA,[54] it was the British version that called for creation of a permanent judicial body – one that if created would be the first-ever "international court" (few expected the more grandly conceived and contentious general jurisdiction court plan to precede the prize-specific court).[55] The eighty-year-old British lead delegate Edward Fry, who was a highly respected former judge and had served alongside F. F. Martens on the panel of the very first PCA arbitration in 1902,[56] explained the ambitious new plan and its ramifications:

> In the present state of things, each nation proclaims for itself what it believes to be international law. The courts of each country thus feel bound by their national system of jurisprudence in regard to prizes. In order that an International Court may apply the veritable international law [sic], its members must be free from all prejudices and from all partiality.[57]

The question as to what exactly constituted the "veritable international law" would seem to be obviously a matter admitting differences of opinion. For Fry and the other British delegates, however, it was an operating assumption that there was some universally correct standard for adjudicating naval prize disputes. The problem at hand was just ensuring that this standard could be elaborated and applied. Against early objections of the French delegate Louis Renault that "you could have no court until you had a code of law to administer,"[58] Fry insisted that, after the fashion of the common law, the court itself would make any legal norms that it might find lacking. Like many diplomats and international law scholars before his time and after, Fry was "struck by the greatness of the idea of really constituting a court above all national courts, thus making a great stride forward in the conquest of law over force."[59]

Conveniently, this noble internationalist idea would also work out to serve Great Britain's parochial national interests. Creating a new body to handle naval prize disputes was "a most important matter to England, seeing how ill our ships had fared in the courts of Russia and Japan."[60] Fry's fellow Hague delegate Ernest Satow – who had been consul general of the British occupying force at Tianjin during the Boxer Intervention and until the previous year had represented Britain in attempts to force Qing acceptance of mere "suzerain" status over Tibet[61] – wrote that on the prize court and related issues, "Edward Fry took a leading part, as became the First Plenipotentiary of a Great Power, and as befitted his eminence as an authority on law."[62]

As to the protests of Brazil and other states over the inequality of judicial terms in the ranking plan, Fry wrote dismissively that some of them "were more anxious to put their existence and their greatness in evidence before the world than influenced by any motives of wide philanthropy . . . To meet in the eyes of the world on equal terms with the greatest nations of the earth flattered their self-esteem."[63] That the people of these states might have sought existential security by influencing the international legal rules that bound them (and that had made them subject to such severe sanctions as China experienced in 1900–1901, or as Venezuela had narrowly avoided in 1903) does not seem to have crossed the mind of the Quaker veteran diplomat. Meanwhile, there were also limits to the solidarity among the marginalized states themselves: Just as Lu Zhengxiang had advanced a proposal for judicial spots on the Court of Arbitral Justice that would rank China among the great powers but not grant the same promotion to any other states, Barbosa on August 22 submitted his own suggestion that Brazil's large merchant fleet should entitle it to a first- rank position, and specifically pointed out that Brazil should outrank China, as well as other states lacking large merchant marines.[64]

Nonetheless, there was cooperation among the various marginalized states when it came to voting – with the low-ranked powers issuing reservations over the prize court's crucial article on judicial staffing – and some degree of ideological solidarity also developed over the course of the events. In his own telegrams home to the Brazilian government, Barbosa notes, for example, on August 7 that some of his country's "friends," including China, had passed on word about the judicial-ranking scheme in advance of its public release; later, on August 24, he mentions a conversation with the Chinese "ambassador" (presumably Lu) in which the latter supported his stance on sovereign equality.[65] In Lu's own later comments to the Qing Court, he mentioned Barbosa as an inspiration and also tied the latter's example to China's urgent need to reform its domestic law and politics and improve its standing in the world:

> The Brazilian delegate to the meeting said at one point: "Now I realize that there is no just principle under Heaven. After this meeting ends, I can only return home and implore my countrymen to commit themselves to the pursuit of military power. Please wait until the Third Hague Conference, gentlemen, and see whether Brazil is a strong country or a weak one, a large country or a small one." As I listened to [Barbosa's] remarks, I privately felt a sense of grand resolve . . . By the time of the Third Hague Conference, there will most likely be a great number of newly rising states . . . China too has already had the Empress's Decree to prepare for enacting a constitution, to be promulgated at a set date and gradually implemented. In matters of state interest, after all, one cannot rush too quickly and achieve success. It is only that your clumsy servant estimates that the Third Hague Conference will be held very soon, yet we can still implement our new constitution before then, and, in particular, use this to shut the mouths of the various countries and overcome their wicked designs.[66]

Encountering the Limits of International Law Reform

The judicial ranking schemes raised at the Second Hague Conference both failed, though in the case of the naval prize court this was only due to a reservation by the offended states that could, perhaps, be circumvented by the great powers should they choose to do so. Indeed, that was precisely the course of action that the powerful states embarked on soon afterward. In the follow-up conference held at London in 1908–1909, which revived the prize court project, most of the lesser powers, including China, were simply not invited in the first place and thus could offer no resistance.[67]

Both Anglo-American and some Continental jurists remained highly enthused about the naval prize court project. The pacifist international law scholar Hans Wehberg, for example, would later say that the prize court was "much nearer to the ideal of an international judicial court" than the plans for the Court of Arbitral Justice, both because of its compulsory character and because it had been intended not only to settle disputes but also "develop international law by its judicial decisions," and lead to "the organization of an international judiciary."[68] Articulating the more conservative view then more prevalent on the Continent, Berlin law professor Franz von Liszt, however, felt that "the establishment of a permanent court of justice having jurisdiction independently of the consent of the parties involves an encroachment upon the sovereignty of states, and consequently an alteration of the foundations of international law."[69]

The leading advocates of the scheme, of course, sought precisely such an alteration. Even after the opposition from various quarters, Fry had still declared at the close of the conference that "of all the projects we have adopted, the most remarkable in my opinion is that of the Prize Court, for it is the first time in the history of the world that one organizes a truly international Court."[70] This would, he predicted, make a "system of truly international laws" out of the present mere "chaos of opinions" that constituted the field.[71]

For court advocates, the resistance of dissenters could be portrayed as mere crude nationalism, or in any case as backward defenses of "chaos" over "progress." Despite occasional favorable commentary on Barbosa's eloquent appeals, public opinion in the West was not often on the side of the weaker powers. *The Times of London*, for example, published on September 14 a critical account of the prize court resistance that openly rejected the principles of equal representation and consensus: "By a diplomatic fiction, China, Persia, and Turkey are supposed to stand upon the same plane of cultivation as the nations of the West."[72]

Marginalized and especially non-Western states, it was clear, could in the eyes of most Western commentators act as either obedient cooperators or as agents of "chaos." The idea that they could *originate* international law proposals was hardly envisioned. Nor were such attempts seriously engaged with when they were initiated. Chinese delegates experienced their marginalized status at the Hague in this regard as well. One incident that takes on stark resonance in light of (much) later developments in international law was Western delegations' rejection of a suggestion by the Qing military delegate Ding Shiyuan to draft a legal definition of "war." Ding, one of the first Qing officials with legal training from the British Inns of Court, raised this issue on July 12 in response to a French proposal on rules for the formal declarations of war, arguing:

> [I]t would [also] be very important to settle the point as to whether a declaration of war can be considered by the State toward which it is directed as a unilateral act and whether the latter can regard it as [legally] null and void. It might be well, moreover . . . to define what is meant by the term 'war,' for it has often been made under the name of an *expedition* as may be learned from numerous instances that can be found in the history of my own country [emphasis added].[73]

The official records of the conference proceedings give no indication as to how Ding's intervention was received, skipping over the response by other delegates. However, the memoirs of John Watson Foster provide additional detail. He notes that "[t]he military delegate of China established a great reputation as a wit, notwithstanding he was one of the most serious-minded of the members and never consciously attempted a joke."[74] The way that Ding achieved this "reputation as a wit," Foster writes, was simply by making his suggestion that war should be defined, on July 12 as well as on another occasion during the conference. As Foster recalls:

> While the subject of the formal proclamation of war was under consideration, he asked the Commission what should be done when one nation declared war against another if the latter did not wish to fight. At another session, when the same subject was under discussion, he stated that he regarded it as important that the Conference should define accurately what constituted a state of war, for, said he, "my country has had its navy destroyed, its ports bombarded, and its capital occupied by foreign troops, when the aggressing nations declared that their acts were not war, but only expeditions," referring to the French hostilities of 1885 and the allied occupation of Peking in 1900. The only answer he received to his inquiries from the Commission was a hearty laugh from the delegates, who regarded them as sallies of wit or sarcasm on the part of the Oriental member.[75]

Thus, while Ding had obviously intended a very serious intervention regarding the legal definition of "war" – bringing the point up on two separate occasions during the discussions – this attempt was literally laughed out of the proceedings by the assembled Western delegates. Ding was, however, ahead of his time. The idea of delegitimizing uses of force constituting unilateral aggression would be taken up after World War I, continued through the Kellogg–Briand Pact and, decades later, incorporated into the United

Nations Charter as a core provision. Meanwhile, the project of providing an exact legal definition of aggression would finally be taken up at the United Nations General Assembly via Resolution 3314, adopted on December 14, 1974.[76] Though Ding's brief intervention certainly involved no such detailed proposals, he clearly suggested the need to both define and limit states' recourse to uses of force, and to legislate global *ius ad bellum* norms. His remarks were also closely related to the views being advanced by some Latin American delegates, including Argentine foreign affairs minister Luis María Drago, who had since 1902 advanced the "Drago Doctrine" that military force could not be used to collect state debts. A weakened version of this rule was adopted by a number of states in 1907, albeit with ambiguity as to its scope.[77]

Closer to the vein of Ding's comments, though, was the intervention of Santiago Perez Triana, appearing for both Colombia and El Salvador, who had with the other Colombian delegates floated a proposal earlier in July for an agreement stipulating that:

> The signatory powers declare that if states involved in disputes have recourse to hostilities without having allowed a period of thirty days to pass since their rupture [of relations], or without having made use of (Art. 2) Good Offices, (Art. 8) Special Mediation, (Art 9) Commissions of Inquiry) or (Art. 16) Arbitration in order to reach a peaceful solution to their dispute, such states will be declared guilty of a violation of international law, and will be treated as internationally outlawed enemies of the human race [*comme des proscrits internationaux ennemis de la race humaine*]; and that during the full duration of the hostilities following the violation of this convention, the signatory states will by all means in their power prevent their subjects from lending money to these delinquent outlaw states.[78]

This strong condemnation of all wars undertaken without good faith efforts at peaceful dispute resolution, and attempt to impose real financial sanctions on those waging such wars, never saw the light of day in the formal conference proceedings, undoubtedly because of a lack of potential support. Indeed, even among Latin American delegates, there were sharp divisions over matters regarding the use of force, with Barbosa, for example, rejecting the Drago Doctrine as in reality permitting an "abuse of sovereignty" in the form of bad faith contracting, and, in his reports home, criticizing the "ridiculous panegyric" of Perez Triana in Stead's news journal.[79] It is curious, nonetheless, that the strikingly worded, legally sophisticated, and innovative Colombian proposal was not even mentioned in James Brown Scott's or other leading memoirs of the event. Ding's subsequent, less fully developed comments about providing "war" with a clear legal definition undoubtedly would have gone similarly unmentioned afterward – had they not been recorded as "humorous" incidents.

For their parts, both Foster and cott, who also recorded the great power delegates' laughter at Ding's serious suggestion, seemed to feel the exchange reflected poorly on the West.[80] At a different session around the same time, however, Foster took it upon himself to issue on China's behalf "a remarkable appeal in favor of the neutrality of the high sea,"[81] including the claim (after minimal consultation with the other delegates) that China's "government would rejoice from any proposition that could give more freedom to free trade."[82] As had often been the case since the 1860s, acceptance of China as an equal member of the international community was premised upon issuing, in its name and even as a form of outright ventriloquism, an endorsement of unrestricted commerce heavily weighted toward Western interests. By late summer, Foster had been compelled to leave before the conclusion of the conference, though seemingly still on amicable terms.

Questions of equal status for marginalized peoples and nations also figured in another mid July incident that, though occurring on the sidelines, was perhaps the most dramatic event of the conference. This was the attempt of an unofficial delegation from Korea – then being treated as a Japanese "protectorate" – to attend on an equal basis with the other invited states. Japan had used the unofficial norm of "blackballing" unwanted weak states (which Italy had previously used with regards to the Vatican in 1899) in order to ensure no independent voice for the Koreans. When a small group of delegates arrived and sought out meetings with those present, they garnered no official acceptance but did create something of a media stir, especially when one member, Yi Jun, died at the Hague in what was taken for an act of protest by suicide. Stead's *Courrier* and other more mainstream publications all reported with sympathy for the Koreans' plight.[83]

The Qing delegates, too, paid careful attention to the situation of Korea and made lengthy reports on the subject to the court.[84] The radical loss of autonomy on display was another sign of what could happen to states that failed to achieve parity with the great powers. As Lu Zhengxiang reported back to the court in cynical terms, the gradually progressing annexation of Korea by the Japanese Empire, like the recent British conquest of South Africa, and the *de facto* recognition of these steps by the other great powers was a sign that "there are no public principles in the world, only power" [*Tianxia shi zhi you qiang quan, ben wu gongli* 天下事只有強權, 本無公理]. Korea, after all, was hardly like the Congo region, which had had "no ruler" before Belgium was entrusted with temporary authority over it (sic), yet it had now met the same fate with the approval of the West's leading public lawyers.[85]

Yet another issue implicating questions of equality in international legal order was that of extraterritorial consular jurisdiction. This topic was actually not raised by any of the countries that were still subject to this institution (or by Japan, which had only recently overcome it), but rather by Britain, which sought to include an article, 16 *l*, that would exempt consular jurisdictional matters from a proposed agreement on obligatory arbitration.[86] In some of the final meetings of the conference, the inclusion of this article was bitterly opposed by the delegates of states that had been forced to provide extraterritorial jurisdiction to Western powers.

When the vote on Article 16 *l* came up on October 7, the Persian delegate Samad Khan Momtaz os-Saltaneh protested this move to compromise the convention by denying equal justice to all parties.[87] Following this, the international lawyer Corragioni d'Orelli, who had been appointed to represent Siam, stated agreement on the latter's behalf. Lu Zhengxiang then spoke, in his most elevated rhetoric at either Hague Conference, calling for the elimination of Article 16 *l* and "ask[ing] of the Commission to perform before this altar of the God of Right and of Justice . . . an act of international equity and justice, by eliminating this article which, according to our point of view, contains a striking inequality."[88] When it came to a vote, the article retained support from Britain and France, but was opposed by thirty-six states, including all in attendance except for Greece, Portugal, Sweden, Switzerland, and Japan (which had abolished foreign consular jurisdiction in its own territory but now had such arrangements in place for its own citizens in China).

Two Ideas of Equality in International Law

All of these vivid lessons in power politics and hierarchy at the Hague prompted powerful protests to the Qing Court from officials decrying the slow pace of constitutional reforms. On September 22, 1907, all of China's leading diplomats in Europe issued a joint memorial to the Qing Court, seizing upon the "third-class state" incident to call for "enlightened law reform in order to preserve sovereignty."[89] As Lu simultaneously argued in his own personal reports to the throne, the diplomatic corps now jointly emphasized that it was "necessary to immediately implement major legal reforms, or else we do not know what sort of treatment we will be accorded at the Third Hague Conference."[90]

Similar views were reflected in another joint memorial that December, this time by the domestic legal reform ministers, that suggested to the Foreign Affairs Office (and thus, indirectly, to the court) the need to further combine Chinese diplomatic efforts with the project of dynastic reconstruction. Thus, they noted, "although laws are a matter of internal policy, in reality they are bound up intimately with international relations."[91] This international dimension was "all the more significant for the current legal revisions, which have as their great purpose the recovery of domestic legal jurisdiction and police powers from the Westerners."[92] It had already been argued by reformists that domestic law was tied to China's status in world affairs, but the Second Hague Conference had shown such status could directly depend upon foreign views of China's legal system: "The various countries pay close attention as to whether or not the steps we take conform to the public principles of the world [世界公理]."[93]

Although, as Lu had earlier lamented, the "public principles" of international law might often just be a cover for *Realpolitik*, diplomats thus still saw as potentially significant foreign perceptions of a state as conforming to or violating such principles. The steps advocated by the Qing diplomatic corps, along with revision of the laws themselves, included sending more students abroad to learn public law, building relations with other "small states" like those of Latin America, and also inviting more foreign scholars to help plan China's future reforms. With the Qing Court's approval of these moves, the project of constitutional monarchical reform was subsequently rapidly accelerated.

While it is certainly the case that the most significant impact on Chinese law from the Second Hague Conference was acceleration of domestic constitutional reform, another element involved exploring the sort of aims that, viewed today retrospectively, could be characterized as "Third World" organization. Lu Zhengxiang actually emphasized this aspect in his early 1908 memorial to Emperor Guangxu. After referring again to domestic constitutional matters, Lu returned to the topic of extraterritorial jurisdiction, and the common front that had been developed among Asian attendees at the conference (besides Japan). This led him to point out how:

> [T]here was an invisible atmosphere among the delegations [consisting in that]: while there has been an "American faction" [mei wei yi pai 美為一派] and a "European faction" [ou wei yi pai 歐為一派] there was originally no "Asian faction"; however when the topic of extraterritorial consular jurisdiction emerged, the Persian and Siamese delegates came to be closely aligned with us, and so an "Asian faction" [yazhou zhi pai 亞洲之派] was formed during these meetings.[94]

One of the key lessons Lu derived from his experiences at the Hague was that it would be necessary to take action toward further developing this sort of "Asian faction" (a term also translatable as "Asian school") in international law settings. However, there would be little concrete progress in this effort before the fall of the Qing Dynasty four years later. In the ensuing "warlord" era, meanwhile, ideas of pan-Asian solidarity would most often become associated with imperial Japanese messaging in favor of Monroe-ist protectorates over China and the region.

By contrast, the aim of claiming an equal voice and position in international law on the basis of national sovereignty remained consistent in official Chinese positions across various regimes after 1908. This idea also continued to become ever more significant in nascent approaches to international law elsewhere across what would later be called the Third World.[95] Based on a close reading of the events of 1907, it appears a shared aim among marginalized states of "decolonizing" international law could have taken hold much earlier than is usually assumed to be the case. That such an aim failed until much later to turn into a concrete form of multilateral organization in Asia, as it was beginning to in the Americas, may be more due to factors of *contingency* – not least the cancellation of the Third Hague Conference due to the outbreak of world war and the turn toward formal international organization with the League of Nations system – than to any inherent structural logic in the progress of international legal history.[96]

At the time, meanwhile, the Latin-Asian resistance on the basis of equal sovereignty had very different impacts in the West. Public and juristic opinion was as noted by no means generally on the side of China or other marginalized "weak" states in their demands for juridical equality, whether in terms of the court plans or extraterritorial jurisdiction. However, the "problem of equality" did become a topic of discussion for some leading jurists in the immediate wake of the conference.[97] There was no immediate consensus, though, as to whether the marginalized states had been right to insist upon equality as the "primordial condition" for peace and law in international relations. Did state sovereignty, *per se*, imply the right to equal agency in legislating new global norms?

A particularly strong advocate in favor of this view that now emerged was the Swiss jurist and diplomat Max Huber, who had been Switzerland's delegate to the 1907 Conference. In his 1909 essay on "The Equality of States" (*Die Gleichheit der Staaten*), Huber turned to the example of the world court debacle at the 1907 Second Hague Conference to make a broader conceptual point.[98] He opposed views like those of the *Institut de Droit International* member Thomas Joseph Lawrence, who considered the weaker states' positions in 1907 as symptoms of a "fetish of absolute equality."[99] Rather, Huber thought it only natural that weaker states had resisted any attempt by the great powers to formalize their status, and regrettable that should mean a rejection of progressive international law development in general. Far better would be to field proposals acceptable to both great and small states, for no advancement could come from "attempts to set up norms and to introduce institutions that are unacceptable … [either due to] restriction of the large states by the majority of the small states or the subordination of the latter to the great powers."[100]

This view might mean a more modest role for international law than that envisioned in terms of new global courts and other such institutions. But the move to such institutionalization itself could also easily resurrect the "hegemonic" character and ideas of the nineteenth-century Pentarchy. The "non-great powers," China included, "could not be reproached for basing their perspective on the [notion of] equality underlying the community principle, which is the palladium of their independence." Moreover, international law could "still develop a great deal on the basis of mere community and equality," provided that there was a situation of mutual trust.[101]

Huber did not in this essay explicitly call for China to be considered part of the civilized family of nations. However, he did so the following year in another essay, where he also explicitly tied this status to the issue of consular jurisdiction. Following Japan's entry into the community of international law (*Völkerrechstgemeinschaft*), Huber argued, the "old concept of *pays hors Chrétienté*" had become "meaningless." China, Siam, and many Muslim states were now also in such close contact with the rest of the world that they should be counted as true members of the global legal community. Only for "a few states such as Abyssinia, Morocco, Liberia and Afghanistan," Huber thought, could membership in the *Völkerrechtsgemeinschaft* still be unclear. For the other non-Western states still currently subjected to consular jurisdiction, such hierarchical regimes had to be regarded as clashing with their just claims to equal status.[102]

Despite his continued use of the "community of international law" and civilizational/ethical heuristic, then, Huber sought to increase its inclusivity to encompass more than just the sole exception of Japan. In his correspondence with Swiss officials over diplomatic questions, as well, Huber referred to both the "principle" and the "problem of equality" (*Gleichheitsprinzip*; *Gleichheitsproblem*) as being critical if future international law conferences were to achieve any better outcomes than had the Second Hague Conference.[103] Nor was Huber entirely alone in taking up this point of view. At the annual Lake Mohonk Conference on International Arbitration, for example, advocates of pacifism and international law not infrequently called for more inclusive approaches to China, and criticized excessive interventionism. At times, this even extended to recognizing China's and other weak states' rights to more equal representation in newly envisioned institutions like the planned world court.[104] But, as had been the case in earlier decades, speakers in these very same pacifist venues could also just as easily refer to acts such as the post-Boxer Intervention and occupation as an example of the kinds of "international action[s] which must grow as intercourse increases."[105]

Despite Huber's emerging notions about the *Gleichheitsproblem*, few others in the global international law profession or diplomatic communities were then advocating such strong views. Indeed, even China's own diplomats abroad were not yet consistent vocal defenders of this principle. When the Qing envoy to the United States Wu Tingfang appeared at the 1909 Mohonk Conference, for instance, he issued a strong appeal for compulsory arbitration in advance of an eventual "international court of justice," but said not a word (at least, in his published remarks) about the issue of equal status in judicial appointments.[106] As China's sole PCA arbitrator, his words on the subject might have carried particular weight; it is likely, though, that he sought to avoid controversy that might arise from directly contradicting the official positions of the United States.

Nor did the US government under either Roosevelt or his successor Howard Taft make China's "equality" as a matter of international legal status a priority in the same way it emphasized China's *de jure* territorial integrity as well as the commercial "equality" of foreign states and merchants in that protected space. At a public event commemorating Ulysses S. Grant in May 1910, for example,

Taft noted that the United States welcomed the "friendly reliance" of China and looked forward to fostering the investment of American capital, including via railway loans, but that it would in turn require China to engage in currency reforms and to abolish the internal *likin* taxes that "weigh … against our trade."[107] Noting that America's foreign trade in general now surpassed US$ 2 billion annually, Taft said that the "State Department could not … justify a [ny] policy which would in any way withhold a fostering, protecting, and stimulating hand in the development and extension of that trade."[108]

Taft concluded his remarks on US foreign policy with an endorsement of both the prize court and Court of Arbitral Justice plans that the United States had put forward at the Hague, and specifically for eventually "evolving" a version of the latter out of the former. The embrace of the envisioned great power court did not, however, deter Taft from also endorsing unilateral sanctions and interventions against Latin American states with "tyrannical and unprincipled" leaders, such as Nicaragua and Venezuela.[109] In a similar vein was an address to the American Society of International Law (ASIL) in 1910, in which Elihu Root reaffirmed that with respect to "governments whose control is inadequate for the preservation of order," it was now an "international custom for the countries having the power to intervene directly for the protection of their own citizens, as in the case of the Boxer Rebellion in China."[110] This "custom" applicable to both China and Latin America was to be considered valid, even though, admittedly, as an "impeachment of the effective sovereignty" of the targeted state, intervention "leads to many abuses."[111] As to extraterritorial consular jurisdiction, too, affected states "must be content to stand in an intermediate position between those incapable of maintaining order, and those which conform fully to the international standard."[112]

With these various hierarchical and asymmetrical elements very much included, the American principle of the open door continued to play a dominant role in both the geopolitical and international juristic imagination regarding China and its territory in the years after the Second Hague Conference. In one significant example, International Law Association member, Oxford academic, and Liberal politician Sir Thomas Barclay, for example, included in his expansive 1907 treatise *Problems of International Practice and Diplomacy* a "Draft Convention for Establishing a League for the Preservation of the *Status Quo* and the 'open door.'"[113] Barclay's proposal would have meant almost the opposite of Lu and his fellow officials' aspirations for the forthcoming Third Hague Conference; rather than conferring greater sovereign agency on China, this draft convention would have meant an entrenched and formalized globalization of the law and political economy framework established via the Boxer Intervention and Protocol.

Barclay sought to have great powers mutually guarantee in *all* of their colonies, protectorates, and even mere "spheres of influence" the same rules of "equal" commercial access and basic maintaining of the territorial status quo as had been explicitly applied to China through the development of the open door policy since 1898. In his draft convention, Barclay thus included the provisions that:

> whereas in China, Central Africa, and Morocco, the principles of equality of treatment, without distinction of nationality, has been permanently adopted as a fundamental condition in connection with economic expansion in these regions, and whereas most of the powers have already expressed their attachment to this principle of equality . . .
>
> In case any [state party] shall acquire dominion or any dominant influence over territory outside Europe, by way of annexation, protectorate, lease, sphere of influence, or otherwise, such acquisition shall be subject to the condition that absolute equality of treatment, whether by way of import or export duties, concessions, privileges, and in economic matters of all kinds, shall be granted, maintained, or recognised, as the case may be, in regard to the subjects and citizens of all States without distinction.[114]

Meanwhile, not only were disputes between parties to this draft convention to be subjected to compulsory arbitration, but "all matters relating to [it]" were to be "centralised at the offices of the Permanent Administrative Council of the Hague Court."[115] Though never realized, Barclay's 1907 proposal reflects the great significance that many international jurists attached to the open door system and the "principles of equality" it was based on (so different from and perhaps incompatible with Barbosa's "primordial condition" or Huber's *Gleichheitsprinzip*). For Barclay and other prominent commentators on international law, the "community of interests" that was the rational basis for states' mutual legal obligations was still best expressed by the shared interest of Westerners in expanding their trade and civilization into non-Western spaces. This was neither the first nor the last time that an ambitious scheme of "global cooperation" was drawn up against the ostensibly blank canvas of China's internationally regulated territory without any local involvement. After 1907, however, such plans would confront local projects that also made use of the conceptual toolkit of international law, aimed at preserving sovereignty for successive Chinese regimes over the full extent of Qing territory, and linking that "sovereignty" to agency within global norms and institutions.

When the Permanent Court of International Justice (PCIJ) was established in 1922, with the 1907 Hague attendee Wang Chonghui appointed as a deputy judge, he took his seat alongside more than half a dozen other representatives of "minor" (European or Latin American) states, who actually outnumbered the appointees of the great powers.[116] On the other hand, this more equal arrangement hardly turned the PCIJ into a vehicle for the radical adjustment of existing legal arrangements (including those of the 1901 Boxer Protocol) that many in China, including Wang himself, still viewed as deeply unjust.[117] Those more radical changes would later come via war and revolution, not conferences.

Conclusion

The Second Hague Conference of 1907 remains today mostly an afterthought in the international law profession's historical memory. When it is discussed, it is still most often in connection with the "failure to reach agreement on all too many vital issues" that heralded a period of resumed *Realpolitik* and then global warfare.[118] At the time, as well, it was widely considered, from the point of view of the great powers, as a "fiasco."[119] Nonetheless, some internationalist jurists, such as Germany's Walther Schücking, saw the event as an important incremental step toward "the organization of the world" and even a "World Confederation [*Weltstaatenbund*]."[120] As we have seen, China's own lead delegate, Lu Zhengxiang, went so far as to hope that the event would mark the founding of an "Asian school" (or "faction") of international law alongside Persia, Siam, and eventually perhaps even Japan.

When accounts of the Second Hague Conference to date have sought to go beyond great power–centric notions of it as a "stepping stone" toward later organizational forms, they have not unjustly emphasized "the much-celebrated story of Ruy Barbosa."[121] However, alongside Barbosa's star turn, many other factors and actors influenced the contestations of the idea of equality during and around the time of the conference. Gerry Simpson has noted that 1907 was also a turning point at which one form of inequality, that of "antipluralism" or exclusion, was temporarily replaced by another: "inequalities of status," based on the great powers' aim to set up "formal legalized hegemony."[122] This was indeed a novelty – for weak states, a novel threat – that was experienced as quite radical at the time and which prompted important reflections.

Conversely, as China's role at the conference suggests, this was also a moment that brought different ideas of "equality" into conflict. In the quasiinternationalized Qing space, foreign powers' moves to formalize norms of "equal commercial access" and legalized dispute resolution suggested intensified hierarchical subordination. Against this background, the Qing encounter with hegemonic legal initiatives at the Hague spurred a new emphasis upon making use of Western public law concepts, in both domestic constitutional and international legal contexts, to assert genuine agency. Domestic public law efforts, however, greatly overshadowed diplomatic initiatives, and Lu's early ideas of (what would later be called) Third World solidarity were not substantially pursued for many more years.

These encounters also stimulated more immanent critique in China of the ways that "pervasive and structural economic inequalities [persisted] in a system that claimed to provide formal political equality."[123] The later rise of socialist internationalism, pan-Asianism, and even fascist-adjacent political movements in China all involved condemnations of a world order denying the state equal status, and often shared an emphasis on asserting national sovereignty despite otherwise clashing ideas. In the years after 1907, discourses of *commercial equality* among the foreign powers active in China had to confront emphatic ideas of *equality of agency* among states, which made China's burdened sovereignty seem ever more anomalous, contingent, and subject to change. At the time of the Second Hague Conference, the students who had gone abroad to study international law after the Boxer Intervention were still too young to play key roles. In the ensuing years, however, they would very quickly take center stage.

6

Reconstituted Hierarchies

The sudden fall of the Qing Dynasty in 1912 following the Xinhai Revolution – most immediately spurred by a divisive plan to grant foreign investors control over China's railway system, but building on years of revolutionary activism – did not mean a radical break with its existing foreign policy. Rather, the core of the diplomatic community, now centered on Lu Zhengxiang,[1] maintained a high degree of continuity with the Qing's last years. This began a long-lasting pattern whereby the elite nucleus of diplomats (and international lawyers) served various successive regimes, forming one of China's "strong institutions in [a] weak polit[y]."[2]

The ideas and aspirations of this community would define China's changing role in international law as it entered a new era both in terms of the domestic public law of the state – now "Asia's first republic"[3] – and the international legal order to be remade in the wake of World War I. The notion of territorial *zhuquan* had by this point seeped into public discourse and, increasingly, also appeared in official diplomatic contexts. But it was only in the period between 1912 and 1921 that it would take up its role as the dominant paradigm for public discourse of China's international legal status and its rights as a legal subject.

Transforming the Polity and Consolidating Territory

In the post-Boxer period of uncertainty preceding the dynasty's fall, maintaining the (formal) territorial integrity of the Qing polity had already become a dominating concern for officials and intellectuals. Already in 1904–1906, the Qing had engaged in high-stakes diplomacy with Britain over Tibet's international legal status. In those negotiations, the British side, under the veteran diplomat and Japanologist Ernest Satow (who had previously clashed with Chinese officials as consul general at Tianjin during the Boxer occupation and would soon do so again at the Second Hague Conference) had repeatedly pushed for an attribution of China's status in Tibet as that of "suzerain" – while Qing officials (after some internal discussion over these confusing Western terms) tried to insist on describing their position as "sovereignty" – *zhuquan*.[4]

At the urging of the diplomat Tang Shaoyi, a fluent English-speaker who had pointed out to the court that there was a vital, if subtle difference between "suzerainty" and "sovereignty," the Qing side in 1906 had settled on excluding both terms from the agreement.[5] Structuring that dispute had been the fact that the concepts of "suzerainty" and of "near-sovereign" status in international law itself were both being innovated precisely as the Qing were forced to grapple with them: They did not in fact constitute a coherent body of existing doctrine.[6] As Lassa Oppenheim's influential international law treatise of 1905 noted: "the relation between the suzerain and the vassal always depends upon the special case, exclud[ing] the possibility of laying down a general rule as regards the position of vassal States with the Family of Nations."[7]

In the last year of the Qing's existence, the British jurist John Macdonell made a similar point in a general entry on the topic in the *Encyclopaedia Britannica*, stating that "in modern times the term [suzerainty] has come to be used as descriptive of relations, ill-defined and vague, which exist between powerful and dependent states; its very indefiniteness being its recommendation."[8] While it was certainly clear to anyone with knowledge of recent history or current affairs that suzerainty implied a lesser form of authority than sovereignty, there was no clearly understood doctrine regarding the relationship between the two concepts: "All definitions of suzerainty are of little use. Each instrument in which the word is used must be studied in order to ascertain its significance."[9]

The understanding of *zhuquan*, meanwhile, was also undergoing major changes. In its sense as the "highest authority over the state," it was incorporated into Article 2 of the Provisional Constitution of the Republic of China of 1912: "The sovereignty of the Republic of China belongs to the people."[10] However, the nature of that sovereignty's legal significance and reflection in the state's public law architecture – or its relationship with the notion of "sovereignty" as applied in diplomatic contexts – was quite ambiguous. For Sun Yat-sen's movement, popular sovereignty meant some form of democratic oversight of government; for Yuan Shikai, who emerged as president from the political dealings that established the new republic and quickly displaced his allies of convenience, there was no such implication.

Tang Shaoyi was appointed as the new regime's first premier but resigned in June 1912 amidst the political turmoil between Yuan and the Guomindang; meanwhile, Wang Chonghui, as a close ally of Sun Yat-sen, followed the same course with brief stints as minister of foreign affairs and then minister of justice, before stepping down to work as an academic at Fudan University. He was replaced as minister of foreign affairs by Lu Zhengxiang, who also took over as premier for three months between June and September 1912, until a suitable replacement was found. Lu then returned to focusing on foreign affairs, and also sought to officially promote the study of international law.

In the fall of 1912, Lu organized the Society for International Law (*Guojifa Hui* 國際法會), China's first organization, state or civil, devoted specifically to the field.[11] Writing in the *American Journal of International Law*, James Brown Scott saw Lu's initiative as a promising sign that China's leaders recognized that "the principles of international law must be studied and mastered by leaders of thought, and ... appropriate organs should be created for their study and dissemination."[12] The organization also spanned political fault lines. Despite the fact that Tang Shaoyi and Wang Chonghui had quit Yuan's government, they joined Lu's new association. So too did a twenty-five-year-old from a Shanghai-adjacent district of Jiangsu Province who had recently studied at Japan's Waseda University, Zhang Junmai. Zhang would soon again leave China to study in Germany and, later, become one of China's leading public law scholars.

These young scholars were at the cutting edge of imported "modern" political and legal thought. International law in general, though, was less pressing than immediate questions of consolidating China's territorial status. A crisis over such issues arose soon after the revolution with the declaration of an independent state in Mongolia by local officials and soldiers, with Russian support. On November 3, a treaty was signed between Mongolia and Russia that began with a Mongol declaration of independence "to maintain the national and historic constitution of their country," and stating that the "old relations between Mongolia and China ... came to an end," while also obliging Chinese troops to evacuate the new state.[13] Article 3 of the agreement, meanwhile, required "the consent of the Imperial Russian Government" for the conduct of future treaties, including those with China.[14] It seemed a likely Vietnam redux.

After Tang's departure, he was succeeded as premier by Lu Zhengxiang, who was already serving as the new regime's minister of foreign affairs (now referred to in the Japanese style as the *Waijiaobu* 外交部). Lu left the office of premier as soon as was feasible, returning to his diplomatic position, just as the Mongolia situation was reaching the crisis point, with military clashes ongoing and the threat of a more widespread war being unleashed. From the end of 1912 through the first half of 1913, Lu and his diplomats engaged in intensive discussions with Russian representatives over the terms of a new agreement regarding Mongolia's status.

Initially, the official Chinese position was that the most that could be promised was that "the old Qing system" of indirect management would be maintained, rather than transformed under the new political order. The question as to whether China should accept any explicit role for Mongolian self-rule – or representation in the diplomatic process – was a highly contentious one. In the eyes of some nationalists, any agreement that did not assert China's sovereign authority without qualifiers would cause an "invisible separation" between China and Mongolia.[15] Such views were also articulated by politicians, as in the case of a letter from the Yunnan provincial assembly chairman Li Zhengfen to the Ministry of Foreign Affairs on January 7, 1913. Li advocated that a "passive" (i.e., peaceful and diplomatic) approach could be taken with Russia, while an "active" approach should be taken with the Mongols:

> This Mongolian matter is different from the India [i.e., Britain]–Tibet Treaty. Then, the Tibetans were not scheming for independence and so gradually the situation could be recovered. If the Mongols are really able to achieve and maintain independence it will be a truly serious matter . . . our country believes that peace is most precious. However, we cannot make peace just for its own sake. For "[territorial] sovereignty" [*zhuquan* 主權] means the ability to repel encroachments, and "imperium" [*tongzhiquan* 統治權] means the ability to compel enforcement of orders. Why shouldn't today's problems be solved by employing both "Hague" and "Blood and Iron" [*Haiya yu Tiexue* 海牙與鐵血]?[16]

The solution for Li was to accelerate the process by which Mongolia was "turned into a province," like Xinjiang had been in 1885. The new regime's approach should be to actively incorporate the frontiers and their peoples into a modern, territorially homogenous nation-state. Specific norms regarding diplomatic and commercial rights for foreign powers could then be negotiated on the basis of this assertion of uninhibited territorial dominion, in the sense of exclusive ownership, and administrative imperium, in the sense of actual administrative control.[17] *Eisen und Blut* – the catchphrase of nationalist state-building *Realpolitik* and assertive foreign policy associated with former German chancellor Otto von Bismarck – had since the 1890s become a popular trope in Chinese nationalist discourse.[18] "Hague," meanwhile, appears here as a metonym for international law as such.

Just a few days after this memorial, the frontier situation took another turn as a treaty of friendship was signed in Ulaanbaatar between representatives of the new Mongolian regime and Tibetans claiming to represent their own independent state.[19] At the same time, the internal discussions of the Ministry of Foreign Affairs reinforced the need to insist on full territorial control. Its negotiators made notes such as that "[*zhuquan* is] also translated as *tongzhiquan* 統治權: the foreign term is *souveraineté*."[20] The Russian side, however, was insistent on prohibiting any use of that term, leading the Chinese negotiators to turn to the vague *zhuguo* 主國 – "ruling state" – which lacked any foreign equivalent or indeed clear meaning in Chinese.

The deadlock continued through the summer of 1913. By June, Lu Zhengxiang had left the post of minister of foreign affairs and the country in general was in crisis over the deepening conflict between Yuan and the Guomindang. The National Assembly's vote to reject the first agreed-upon draft agreement with Russia led to the latter coming back to negotiations with a more recalcitrant attitude and new demands. Russian threats to deal exclusively with Mongolia on a bilateral basis if China did not accede to the basic framework of Russian demands proved successful. In the end, the Chinese side agreed to sign a declaration in which the official text included both a reference to Outer Mongolia's "autonomy" and to China's "suzerainty" (the former rendered in Chinese as *zizhiquan* 自治權 and the latter as *zongzhuquan* 宗主權).[21]

This was the first time that "suzerainty" appeared in the text of a legal instrument signed by, not just about, China. Clarifying provisions for just what this ambiguous term might denote were included in a subsequent exchange of notes. The new foreign affairs minister Sun Baoqi successfully insisted on the provision that "Russia recognizes that Outer Mongolia is part of the territory of China."[22] With the aim of reasserting Beijing's position, some officials advised the use of "persuasion and enticement" rather than force,[23] however, the prevailing policy favored the rapid military suppression of separatists. At the same, there also appeared a new interest in using diplomatic and legal means to settle such interstate disputes in a way sure to be regarded as legitimate by the global community. Possible arbitration with Russia via the Permanent Court of Arbitration was raised, on multiple occasions, by Yuan Shikai himself.[24] Between mutually recognizing states, there could be "Hague" – international law and diplomacy – while for contested frontier spaces, there was "blood and iron." This was not far from the mainstream practice of the great Western empires.

Internationalism in the Service of National Destiny

While the protracted negotiations with Russia over Outer Mongolia were being conducted, other initiatives in international law were being undertaken by the new regime. These included, notably, the preparations for the Third Hague Conference – the topic that had so occupied China's diplomats after the "ranking" incident of 1907 and spurred their protests to the Qing Court. Under the auspices of Lu Zhengxiang's Ministry of Foreign Affairs but officially as an "Organ Appointed by the Special Authority of the President," the "Preparation Committee for the Third Hague Conference" held dozens of meetings between November 1912 and October 1914.[25]

Among those involved were Berlin law PhD-holder Ma Derun, the high-level military leader Xu Shuzheng, Chen Lu, a diplomat who had studied law in Paris and accompanied Lu Zhengxiang to the Hague in 1907, and, in one of his first major roles, a twenty-five-year-old Wellington Koo, fresh from receiving his PhD under John Bassett Moore at Columbia (and having married the prominent statesman Tang Shaoyi's daughter earlier the same year). These young officials debated the positions that China should take on the likely subject matter of the planned conference – and whether it should come forward with its own initiatives for legal reform. This was China's first-ever organized body of trained international lawyers. They had diverse academic backgrounds and also made use of resources, such as recent Japanese international law texts, recommended by officials abroad.[26] The group was endowed with significant authority; for example, in its early meetings, it sent to Yuan effective recommendations to ratify several Hague Conventions on humanitarian law that China had not yet adopted.[27] Another of the committee's contributions was to standardize international law terminology, often drawing on the by now already widely used Japanese lexicon.[28]

The issue of extraterritorial consular jurisdiction, of course, was a matter of special concern. Might the Third Conference build on the initial Asian-state cooperation on this issue of 1907 by securing a partial or full recovery of the surrendered jurisdiction? In one of the group's final meetings, Koo argued that Chinese delegates should either seek to have extraterritorial jurisdiction fully revoked or propose doctrines to gradually limit its scope.[29] In the thesis with which Koo had just earned his PhD at Columbia, he had argued that the West should give up "the folly . . . of entwining international politics with international commerce,"[30] implying a Chinese-initiated embrace of free trade to entice Western states to relinquish their treaty powers. Another delegate cited Belgian international lawyer Ernest Nys to argue that "ultimate sovereignty over leased zones remained with China," suggesting China could possibly simply take back this *zhuquan* under the right circumstances; a position that Koo endorsed in principle. Ma Derun argued instead that "sovereignty over leased territories was jointly shared" by both China and the lessee states,[31] and it would thus be seen as a breach to make unilateral changes. In the end, though, this meeting concluded with consensus on Koo's second suggestion, of proactively but gradually limiting extraterritorial jurisdiction.[32]

The beginning of war in Europe, of course, affected the tenor of the planning meetings. At the same time, Japanese prime minister Ōkuma Shigenobu and his cabinet initiated a more active project of hegemony in northeast China, in particular via the so-called Twenty-One Demands, which took the form of an ultimatum to Yuan requiring that Japan obtain a de facto sphere of influence over the administration and economy of Manchuria and Shandong, as well as recognition of Japan's obtaining of Germany's concession of Jiazhou Bay. Yuan's government, "incapable of meeting [Japan] in a military contest," increasingly reliant upon it financially, still locked in struggle with the Guomindang, and concerned with its tenuous grip on Tibet and Mongolia, acceded to several of the key demands.[33] Returning to the post of minister of foreign affairs, Lu Zhengxiang signed a set of agreements on May 25, 1915 that would confer to Japan most of its primary objectives.

Yuan's sense of the precariousness of his position both domestically and internationally also helped to prompt his decision, at the end of 1915, to launch a transition back to an imperial system with himself as the new emperor.[34] To defend his aspirations, Yuan borrowed recent Japanese imperial constitutional theory that took the traditional Chinese concept of *guoti* (*Kokutai* [Jp.]) and infused it with new sensibilities in part derived from German public law notions of "*Staatsform*" – that is, a robust notion of regime type. *Guoti*, with its new Meiji connotations of an inherent constitutional structure (the unassailable position of the monarchy), soon became Yuan's watchword. However, his imperial restoration seemed to many intellectuals and politicians quixotic and regressive. Over the next year, his short-lived Empire of China was rent apart by a broad coalition forming a "constitutional protection movement," and he died in June 1916 having expressed to the Chinese people profound contrition for his "lack of virtue."[35]

Even amidst Yuan's imperial venture, the Chinese study and practice of international law had been progressing. By 1915, Lu Zhengxiang's Society for International Law had fallen into desuetude given escalating factional strife in the Beiyang government, but he now replaced it with the Chinese Social and Political Science Association. Wellington Koo, recently appointed Yuan's minister to the United States at the age of only twenty-sseven, also played a role in the new group.[36] As president of the new association, Lu actively sought to further study Western public law ideas, including those of international law. Meanwhile, more radical ideas of internationalism were also beginning to be imported into China. Publications such as *Xin Qingnian*, founded in 1915 by the radical anti-Yuan intellectual Chen Duxiu, became transmission sites for new ideas of socialism and world revolution, which Chen continued to explore after being appointed as a professor at Peking University in January 1917. This institution had partly grown out of the Tongwenguan that W. A. P. Martin had helped to found, but was wholly transformed by the time he passed away in Beijing, in December 1916.

Just as new internationalist discourses were beginning to permeate the Chinese intelligentsia, Western jurists were finally beginning to revise their ideas about denying China recognition as a full member of the "family of nations." In the 1915 edition of Franz von Liszt's influential textbook *Das Völkerrecht Systematisch Dargestellt*, he notably modified his previous classification of China as a "half-civilized" land, adding a mitigating footnote citing to Ma Derun's Berlin PhD dissertation for the counterargument that China had indeed entered international legal community's *Interessengemeinschaft*.[37] In the same note, however, Liszt also adds somewhat apologetically that leaders of the field such as Lassa Oppenheim and Ernest Nys remained "firmly against" recognizing China.[38] Despite this conservative conclusion, Liszt's reference to his erstwhile student's argument is a clear example of how international law doctrine could be affected by personal encounters, and how the first generation of Chinese international lawyers were starting to shape views of their homeland.

The year 1915 also marked the first significant publications of a figure later considered the "dean of Chinese international law scholars," Zhou Gengsheng. Though he had returned to China from his studies in Japan by the first year of the republic, he left again in 1913 as Yuan's struggle with the Guomindang was intensifying, going on to doctoral study in law first at Edinburgh and then the University of Paris.[39] Zhou's 1915 writings touched on important national issues including neutrality in wartime, republican government, and the definition of "suzerainty."[40] This last topic continued to occupy him over the coming years, resulting in a major 1918 piece on the subject.[41] Zhou put China's experience in the context of a long-term phenomenon whereby suzerainty, originally an obsolete concept from medieval European feudalism, was suddenly "rediscovered" in the mid nineteenth century and applied to "the new context of international law, [in order] to characterize foreign states and their territories." In employing the label of suzerainty, Western states had been able to relativize the authority of the Ottoman Empire over its constituent peoples, while purporting to treat it as an equal power. It had more recently been turned upon China, as seen in Tibet and Mongolia. Zhou drily stated that he "could not but be awed by the subtle shrewdness of diplomats in making use of this discarded item for new purposes."[42]

While Zhou Gengsheng was beginning to articulate this incisive critique of recent developments in international legal order, another emerging Chinese scholar of international law came up with a proposal to revolutionize it in its entirety. Giving up his erstwhile dream of pioneering an aviation industry for China, Zhou Wei had moved during the war from Paris to the University of Fribourg, in Switzerland, for doctoral studies in law under the prominent jurist and politician Émile Bise.[43] After some minor writings on consular jurisdiction and commercial law issues, in 1917 he published an influential book titled *Essay on the Juridical Organization of International Society* (*Essai sur l'organisation juridique de la Société international*), which attracted considerable attention.[44]

Zhou Wei's *Essai*, published at a climactic point in the war, appeared at just the right time to capture the imagination of Western international lawyers.[45] As Émile Bise wrote in his preface to the book, its subject was one "upon which contemporary developments have conferred an exceptional relevance."[46] Of course, the basic idea of a structured global federation was already not new when Kant articulated it in 1795. More recently, the German jurist Walther Schücking had emphatically explored the "organization of the world" in various writings, including suggestions for pan-European and eventual "World Confederation."[47] In the United States, Theodore Roosevelt and his political allies had been volubly advocating an organized "league" of great powers since 1914.[48] Yet, as of 1917, very few if any jurists had gone as far as the lawyer-engineer Zhou in imagining a detailed architecture for such an organization.

Zhou articulated a Montesquieu-esque "three powers" schema for the constitution of an international organization. In this plan, three "organs" would be responsible for the application of international law: The "international parliament," "international tribunals," and an "international administration." The first of these would elaborate the international laws and codes applicable to all "states, nations, and individuals," the second would provide decisions in cases of disputes and assign penalties for violations, and the third would "execute, *manu militari*, all international legal decisions and judgements."[49] Each of these organs was dealt with in detail in its own section, with reference to relevant legal norms currently in effect, the historical development of those norms, and desirable modifications that could now be pursued.

Zhou's *Essai* was carefully triangulated between the Anglo-American and Continental jurisprudential traditions, helping it to attain broad appeal; in addition, he even introduced at various points commentary making (sometimes strained) analogies between the new structures he called for and ancient Chinese thought or institutions.[50] Overall, Zhou's contribution marked a striking new development in Chinese intellectuals' engagement with international law. Unlike previous work by others in the first generation of Chinese scholars trained in Western law, Zhou's monograph was not intended either to merely display mastery of Western legal norms or to "defend" China's interests in its terms. Even "sovereignty" received little mention in the book. Rather, it constituted a major intervention seeking to reform existing international law itself by proposing new cosmopolitan norms. The book also closed with a set of concrete proposals intended for the (now indefinitely postponed) Third Hague Conference.

These proposals included, most notably, efforts at handling the difficult problem of enforcement of international law against noncompliant states. What level of intervention should be appropriate for any newly created "international administration" or executive authority? One of the main suggestions that Zhou's *Essai* introduces is a centrally coordinated "general judicial boycott" against norm-violators that would "close off [to the offending state] the financial markets of the world"; "annul all loans already contracted with foreign creditors"; and "cease all commerce ..." with the offender.[51] Zhou's vision of such an "outcasting"-based enforcement regime for international law was both original and prescient.[52] Overall, Zhou's *Essai* seems to have been more widely read in the West than any other original work by a Chinese author on a legal topic up to that point – or for many years thereafter. The book would be in large part responsible for Zhou's inclusion in China's delegation to Versailles in 1919 as well as his induction, in 1921, as the first Chinese *associé* of the *Institut de Droit International*.[53]

The Legal Organization of the World

At the war's end, two separate Chinese delegations arrived at Versailles. One was the group sent by the internationally recognized, post-Yuan Beijing government, headed by Lu Zhengxiang in his final major diplomatic mission, and the other was the delegation of the Guomindang government based in Guangdong, headed by Wang Zhengting, who had studied international law at Yale and was a dedicated Guomindang member. The delegation from Beijing featured, in addition to Lu, Wellington Koo, China's minister to Britain Shi Zhaoji, minister to Belgium Wei Chenzu, and over two dozen lesser-ranked delegates, secretaries, and technical experts. Among the latter group was Zhou Wei, as a secretary for international legal issues.[54]

Although the joint Chinese group would end up having a significant impact on the results of the Peace Conference, this was hardly easy to foresee in advance. Indeed, it was notable that, Zhou's *Essai* notwithstanding, most of the extant proposals for a new international organization before the meeting at Versailles had involved plans that "would create an artificial body of eight Great Powers – the old six European Great Powers, with the United States and Japan added, but China excluded."[55] The old logic of "civilization," consolidated in the international law texts of the 1880s and afterward, was still very much in effect for many jurists and politicians in the West. Many saw it as entirely consistent to create a new architecture of legal "progress" that would also "eliminate from the League . . . what they call backward or half-civilized States."[56]

China's young Western-educated international jurists would help to change these still-widespread notions. Despite their different rankings within the diplomatic hierarchy of the delegation, Koo and Zhou would both serve as China's representatives on the important League of Nations Commission of the Peace Conference, during which plans for the organization were concretized.[57] They would confer in this capacity with Woodrow Wilson, Jan Smuts, Léon Bourgeois, and other architects of the League. A widely circulated photo of the commission includes both members of China's new generation of lawyer/diplomats; the well-connected diplomatic wunderkind and Ivy League debate champion Koo stands near the center, while the lower-ranked and more retiring Zhou peeks out from the left-hand corner.

Indeed, Zhou did not play a major direct role in the proceedings of the conference. Koo, however, was an active participant on a number of issues. This was no easy feat given that China's representation on the commission in the first place had only achieved after a vote in which it (and a few other "weak" states) managed to edge ahead of Romania, Portugal, Poland, and Czechoslovakia.[58] Lu Zhengxiang had also invoked "the principle of equality of sovereign states" to demand Chinese representation on the commission and other decision-making organs.[59] The hierarchical dynamics of 1907 were very much still in place, but little concrete progress had been made in solidarity or organization among the weak.

Koo was remembered by the American delegate David Hunter Miller as having "made a distinct impression by his ability," and as making "one of the best speeches of the commission" on the issue of small powers' representation.[60] This speech, at the second meeting of the commission on February 4, entailed a number of arguments as to why more states than just the planned five permanent members (Great Britain, France, the United States, Italy, and Japan) should be allowed representation on the League Council.[61] Such representation would prevent "secondary powers [being made] to feel that they were outsiders"; avoid incentivizing the provocation of disputes as the only to have their cases brought before the council; facilitate settling disputes among the five powers; and also would be essential for the League's ability to serve all of its members' interests: for "no one great power had interests greater than the aggregate interests of all the so-called secondary powers."[62]

Koo's address was the last before Léon Bourgeois signaled France's agreement to the need for some representation of groups outside the great powers on the council, effectively deciding the matter. Another issue on which Koo represented China's interests was the proposed Article 21 of the League Covenant, which established a recognition of "regional understandings" like the US Monroe Doctrine, declaring them compatible with the League framework.[63] Koo sought to include revisions that would lessen the risk of this provision providing a legal basis for Japanese claims to any analogous "Monroe Doctrine for Asia," that would justify interventions into Chinese affairs.[64] Although he managed to achieve some textual changes to help allay these concerns, here Koo ran into a third rail of American politics – it was widely known that any perceived threat to the Monroe Doctrine would immediately be seized upon by Republican opponents to justify resistance to Wilson's foreign policy initiatives. Moreover, the president himself evidently felt strongly about the doctrine: It is recorded that his lips "quivered" with indignation while listening to it be denounced by the French representative. The Article was retained in the final draft.[65]

The Japanese proposal for a provision explicitly recognizing the doctrine of racial equality (understood by those present to be most directly relevant to discriminatory immigration quotas) was supported by the Chinese delegation, but eventually defeated due to, in particular, Australian opposition.[66] This was despite the concession made by the Japanese delegates in changing their proposal from one of "racial equality" (*zhongzu pingdeng* 種族平等) to one instead focusing on "national equality" (*bangguo pingdeng* 邦國平等) – seemingly limiting its application to the realm of interstate responsibility for equal treatment of foreign nationals.[67]

Outside of the commission, the rest of the Peace Conference also turned on issues that were also closely related to national rank and power. Unlike Japan or the other leading allied states, China's delegates were for the most part invited only to meetings directly related to their own state's interests.[68] Above all, the "Shandong Question" was the central problem facing the two Chinese delegations, each of which faced pressure to pursue the reclamation of China's sovereignty over the Jiaozhou Bay concession that Japan had seized from Germany early in the war. As in the commission, it was Koo's "impressive" speeches on this topic that made the biggest impression on foreign delegates, as well as in domestic media.[69] However, the policy of absolute insistence on China's sovereignty over Shandong was ultimately formed organically, with large contributions by communities of overseas Chinese and study-abroad students that publicly protested over the issue. In Paris, Zhou Gengsheng joined students and workers to literally surround China's delegates and demand that they refuse to sign any agreement that failed to return the territory to Chinese control.[70]

Neither Wilson nor the other great powers were willing to apply pressure on Japan toward this end, however. In response, the two Chinese sides presented a united front, even issuing joint declarations and explanatory materials on China's position – namely, that the German concession rights had been terminated with China's declaration of war on the side of the allies, and could not be passed onto any other power. Ultimately, both Lu Zhengxiang and his counterpart in the Guomindang delegation, Wang Zhengting, jointly refused to sign the resulting treaty – the only major delegation to do so.[71] Lu had qualms about this extreme step – he lamented in a letter to his wife that "months of hope and labor have been reduced to a sublime absence of China from the concert of civilized nations."[72] Yet he found the decision vindicated after the other delegates then returned to a China erupting with the popular demonstrations of the May Fourth Movement, mostly stimulated by general anger over the Beiyang government's failure to regain sovereignty over Shandong. This entailed more a general climate of political ferment and cultural reassessment than a unified movement advocating a unitary agenda.

Some elite observers in China were also highly skeptical of the League organization. Zhang Junmai, who had been a member of Lu's international law association, was by now an influential political theorist based at Peking University. Arguing that "China was sacrificed [by Wilson] for the birth of the League of Nations," Zhang criticized the terms of Versailles but gave a more restrained (if by equal measures cynical and prescient) analysis of the League itself:

> We can think of only one way to save China, that is, to make China united and strong[,] and the League of Nations can do nothing good for us, although it can do no harm. Anyhow, it is not strong enough to prevent the aggressive ambition of our neighbor, Japan. Believe me.[73]

Over the coming months, Zhang continued to criticize the League's "unjust" transfer of Germany's Shandong possessions to Japan, however, he also saw in it, or an organization like it, elements of "an international legal and ethical order that would protect the weak ... from the powerful" that China's own emerging nationalist movement would need to engage.[74] Sharper condemnations of the League were being articulated by the new generation of political activists and organizers who emerged during the May Fourth Movement and its aftermath. A twenty-one-year-old student at Nankai University in Tianijn named Zhou Enlai, for example, led campaigns to boycott Japanese goods and demand Beijing stand firm on Shandong. A twenty-five-year-old Mao Zedong, newly returned to Hunan from a period working at the Peking University library, was also harshly critical of recent events. In his first widely circulated writings, Mao combined nationalist critiques over the Shandong issue with a heavier focus on global issues, seeing the entire proceedings at

Versailles as a cover for a new phase of imperialist expansionism. It was striking, he thought, that Germany was being asked to disarm but there was as yet no corresponding plan for disarmament by the allied powers.[75] The allies' treatment of the defeated Germany, he thought, was hardly different than Napoleon's after his victories.[76]

Mao also pointed out the hypocrisy of claims regarding the norm of "national self-determination." Poland might be able to restore its statehood, and Arabs to gain some political independence, because this fit the allied powers' interests vis-à-vis weakening Germany and Turkey. But why for example should the League ignore Koreans or Central Asians, "so many of whom have died, and whose lands are in chaos"? This was "some national self-determination!"[77]

China's new class of international lawyers, of course, were among those most involved in assessing the League and its merits. Zhou Gengsheng, for example, gave a speech to the Paris Chinese Students Association, in which he lauded the League idea. Zhou emphasized to his fellow scholars that the Chinese people should distinguish between the self-interested acts of the Allies and those aspects of the postwar settlement that were genuinely in the best interests of humanity. Understanding the Great War meant looking back to a recent international history in which most of the human race had been "the objects of international relations [while] Europeans were the subject of international relations." The imperialist competition between European states had eventually fostered instability in Europe and the rise of sentiments of "blind nationalism" that had proven their destructive character in the recent conflicts. Bitter experience had now demonstrated that there was a need for a radical change in the organization of global politics. However, the success of the new efforts would depend on a shift of mental paradigms:

> If there is no transformation in the psychology of average citizens towards the outside world the League of Nations will have no great effect. But if there is such a psychological transformation without having a League of Nations organization in existence, then there will still be no effective realization of any cooperative world order ... Even though there are many unjust elements of the peace treaties, this plan for the League of Nations embodies an achievement of pacifism. We have great hopes for it.[78]

In his writings, Zhou Gengsheng argued in favor of the League as a matter of principle, suggesting that sovereignty and international legal organization should be seen as mutually consistent.[79] Indeed, more international organization was necessary to combat the aggressive forms of imperialism to which China had long been subjected.[80] Reiterating a point that Chinese reformers had begun to favor in the 1890s, he too connected international law and organization with the ancient ideal of "Great Unity," or *datong* 大同.[81] Meanwhile, he continued to leaven his positive appraisals of the League with critiques and suggestions for improvement. The worst feature of the covenant, he thought, was its lack of clear and compulsory rules regarding the adjudication of international disputes.[82] This was a criticism that Zhou Gengsheng would continue to articulate over the remainder of the League era, even as he was also helping to pioneer the Guomindang's policies of "revolutionary diplomacy" (*geming waijiao* 革命外交).[83]

A similarly mixture of internationalist sentiments were expressed by some high-level Guomindang party figures, including Wang Jingwei, a leading figure on the intellectual "left" of the Guomindang, who published a book on *China and the World after the European Peace Conference* that included positions drawing on those already expressed by Zhou Gengsheng.[84] Indeed, the latter made reference to Wang's book in his own subsequent comments to Chinese students in Paris, recommending that they consult it as part of their efforts to understand and spread "the ideology of international cooperation."

Zhou Wei was also a firmly committed advocate of the new plan that so resembled, in spirit if not in all particulars, his widely noted book of 1917. On January 12, 1919 he had presented his views on the plans for a League to a gathering of overseas Chinese students in Shanghai. There, he argued that China, having the world's largest population, oldest civilization, and its own traditions of peace and cosmopolitanism in Confucian thought, had a "duty" to aid in preserving world peace. In his view the "civilized and tolerant attitude of the Chinese race, and its peaceful and just methods, could be broadcast to the world" by means of China's participation in the new organization.[85]

China's membership in the international community as a notional equal (at least in a technical juridical sense) was indeed now closer to a matter of general consensus. Yet hierarchies persisted. In the 1920–1921 edition of his *International Law*, for example, Lassa Oppenheim situates himself between those who describe international law as applying to all humanity, on the one hand, and those who still limited its reach to Christian states, on the other. He thus includes a table of the world's states, which describes Asia as comprising:

Great power	Japan
Smaller states	Afghanistan
	China
	Hedjaz
	Persia
	Siam
Half-sovereign states	Mongolia
	Thibet[86]

Unlike the jurists of 1907, Oppenheim in 1920 considered it misguided to assert any legal permanence to such hierarchies. As Japan had shown, a state could rise to become a great power; the examples of Germany or Russia showed how the status could be (temporarily) lost as well. The attribution of "sovereignty" was not to be seen as insulating a state from geopolitical pressure and intervention, or ensuring full territorial jurisdiction (*dominium*) or personal supremacy (*imperium*) of the state over its own citizens.[87] For "there is not, and never was, unanimity regarding this conception [of "sovereignty] ... there can be no doubt about the fact that there are semi-independent States in existence, [and so] it may well be maintained that sovereignty is divisible."[88] Peoples that failed to attain "full sovereignty" would, Oppenheim mused, "be more or less overshadowed by other States" within the Family of Nations.

At the end of the 1910s, following World War I and the treaties that brought it to a close, the *Gleichheitsprinzip* in Huber's sense had made only marginal advances. One form of "equality," though, did receive redoubled emphasis in diplomatic contexts: equal commercial access to underdeveloped markets. In response to proposals that had been floated for a joint American–Japanese loan to China, a group of the leading US banks submitted to US secretary of state Robert Lansing, John Watson Foster's son-in-law, a proposal for an international banking consortium that would internationalize Chinese finances as never before. "Through cooperation of England, France, Japan and the United States," the bankers wrote, "much can be accomplished for the maintenance of Chinese sovereignty and the preservation of the 'open door'; and, furthermore, such cooperation might greatly facilitate the full development of the large revenue sources from only a very few of which China at present realizes a satisfactory income."[89] Great power officials expressed enthusiasm for the idea of "throw[ing] open the whole of China without reserve to the combined activities of an International Consortium."[90]

Throughout the early 1920s, Wellington Koo would continue to serve as China's leading representative in League affairs. Wang Chonghui, as well, was highly active in the early meetings of the League, specifically with respect to the consideration of possible amendments to its covenant. He continued pursuing the initiative to limit the role of "regional understandings" that had been introduced via Article 21. Like Koo at the commission sessions, however, he found limited success in this effort – various other states, especially Japan and the United States itself but also some in Continental Europe, saw in the idea of "regional understandings" a vehicle to advance their own interests. Chinese anxieties over the Japanese project of a "Monroe Doctrine for Asia," were left unheeded, even as the latter grew more explicit.[91] Such ideas, and Article 21 itself, would indeed play a major role in eventual Axis efforts to overturn the League system.[92]

At the League Assembly meetings of 1921 considering the issue, Wang Chonghui sought in vain to raise the objection that "there might be regional understandings which were contrary to the letter and spirit of the covenant," and so there should at least be added a limitation along the lines of "provided such engagements or understandings do not prejudice the rights or interests of the Members of the League not parties to them."[93] However, even this calculated invocation of the *pacta tertiis* principle of legal interpretation was unpalatable to the great powers, and was not included. The assembly eventually reaffirmed the existing language, albeit paired with a resolution nodding to China's proposal by means of a milquetoast assertion that the League should promote only those understandings "tending to the maintenance of peace."[94]

Amidst these setbacks, however, China's diplomats were more successful in proposing another norm, regarding a "continentalist" (*fenzhouzhuyi* 分洲主义) representative system in allocating nonpermanent seats in the League of Nations Council to ensure equal representation of world regions. [95] Though this arrangement, too, failed to achieve formal adoption by the assembly, it would be continuously advocated by China during the League years, and became an unofficial norm of council elections (helping to ensure China's own ongoing membership). This "Continentalist" rule also significantly aided in efforts to counter Japanese claims to formal regional hegemony. The potential meaning of Article 21, meanwhile, remained an open question. So too was the fate of Shandong, as well as any plans for disarmament aside from the unilateral obligations placed upon Germany.[96] These unresolved issues vital to the League's future would all be addressed outside its ambit, at the Washington Naval Conference of 1921–1922.

A "Magna Carta for China"?

Among the initial outcomes of Versailles was the rise to national and global prominence of Wellington Koo. In 1921, the first year of China's participation in the League, he succeeded in obtaining its election as one of the nonpermanent members of its council. Subsequently, at the Fourteenth Council Session, held August 30–September 3, Koo himself was elected to the rotating position of council president.[97] This was, of course, an unprecedented conferral of global prominence to a Chinese statesman, and reflected Koo's networking skills as well as his palatability to the United States (which many European diplomats still hoped would eventually find its way into the League). It would have seemed fantastic only a few years before.

At the time that Koo first represented China on the council, and during his own presidency of it from the end of August, the council was dealing with some of its major early disputes over the disposition of Imperial German territory after the war. Most pressing were the issues of the status of the Saar Basin, contested between France and Germany for decades, and of Upper Silesia, to which a revived Poland now laid claim. Koo played a significant role in the Upper Silesia matter, although the council's special deliberations on the issue were presided over by his predecessor as president, the Japanese League delegate Viscount Ishii.[98] The key hearings were, in fact, assigned by the larger council to a smaller group of four including Koo himself and the representatives of Belgium, Spain, and Brazil, as "minor" powers who would have fewer interests in German territorial questions.[99] The four diplomats conducted investigations involving the extensive review of evidence, testimony, and the reports of on-site experts. The ultimate decision, to partition the region into German and Polish zones, was, of course, still largely based on the positions of the great powers. Nonetheless some German nationalists bitterly resented "a Chinese" deciding on the partition of *Reich* territory.[100]

Despite its firmer basis to claim the status of an active participant in the international legal order, China after 1919 remained a weak state heavily reliant upon great power support. This was fully on display in the eventual resolution of the Shandong issue via the 1921–1922 Washington Naval Conference. Wilson's failure to get the Republican-majority Senate to ratify the League Covenant and his party's subsequent loss of the White House in the 1920 election had set the stage for another major shift in US foreign policy. The Harding administration, as represented by Secretary of State Charles Evans Hughes working alongside Senator William Borah and Elihu Root, organized the conference as a kind of alternative to the League under US Republican auspices. Not coincidentally, it also marked a return to a more explicit, Vienna-style great power club to handle several crucial issues – including Shandong but also disarmament and the naval balance of power – that had proved "unsolvable" at Versailles.

At Washington, China's large delegation included Wang Zhengting, Wellington Koo, Wang Chonghui, and a number of other Chinese recent graduates in international law from Western institutions; the future international judges Zheng Tianxi and Xu Mo, in particular, now made their first major impacts in the field. Zheng, whose family came from Guangdong and who had spent his youth in Hong Kong, studied law at University College London between 1907 and 1915. He had then graduated with honors and was called to the English Bar, as well as joining the Grotius Society, and in 1920, the group that had been founded by David Dudley Field in 1873, now called the International Law Association. His private law-focused thesis on *Rules of Private International Law Determining Capacity to Contract* was published soon after his graduation.[101] The younger Xu Mo, meanwhile, had recently graduated from the National Peiyang University in Tianjin when he was dispatched to Washington to serve as a diplomatic aide while continuing his studies. He would receive his Master's degree in international law from George Washington University in 1922. Under the coordination of the joint delegation head Wang Zhengting, both helped to develop arguments for the return of Shandong, along with tariff autonomy and the end of extraterritorial jurisdiction.

In the event, however, only the first of these objectives was achieved, with vague promises from the United States and other Western powers to eventually address the latter two. Ultimately, important agreements on naval arms reduction were reached among Britain, France, Japan, Italy, and the United States in a "Five Power Treaty"; a "Four Power Treaty" of these states minus Italy entailed recognition of the territorial status quo in Asia; a "Nine Power Treaty," which also included Belgium, the Netherlands, Portugal, and China, reiterated that status quo with additional obligations; and, finally, a separate "Shandong Treaty" between Japan and China transferred that territory along with Chinese pledges to recognize certain Japanese economic and security interests.[102] Geopolitics and law intertwined throughout these stacked agreements. Root, in particular, played an active role in seeking to ensure the inclusion of provisions favorable to Japan, hoping to reconcile Chinese aims with the need for Japanese acceptance.[103]

While the open door policy of combining preservation of China's territorial integrity with open access to its markets was reaffirmed, the arrangements of the conference also formalized its hierarchically subordinated relationship vis-à-vis the great powers, especially Japan and the United States. This was especially brought to the fore over the question of extraterritorial jurisdiction, which Wang criticized on November 25 as a "derogation of sovereignty," as being perceived by the general public as a humiliation, as giving rise to legal uncertainty, and as based on a state of affairs – foreign views regarding the legal system of eighty years previous – long since superseded by the facts. It would be inexpedient, he said "for China to open her entire territory to foreign trade and commerce" until the system was abolished. In response, Hughes pointed to the treaty texts of the post-Boxer period that premised abolition of extraterritorial jurisdiction on Western "satisfaction" at Chinese progress in judicial administration. The only outcome acceptable to the United States or other great powers at this stage was appointing a commission of inquiry, thus postponing any changes, perhaps indefinitely.[104]

China would thus not be accorded full *imperium* over its own territory at this United States-led meeting.[105] However, it was supposedly to be placed on the trajectory of development toward that goal. Charles Evans Hughes announced that the conference was intended to serve as a "Magna Charta for China" which would open a "new era of good feeling in the Far East."[106] On the one hand, the conference would serve as a legal framework to ensure the political independence and territorial and administrative integrity of China while imposing upon it obligations to ensure the interests of the great powers and their citizens. It would also, however, help China to progress toward modernity. Hughes lamented that, as one "one of the tragedies of human evolution," "the fine civilization which had developed in China and which had spread to other lands of eastern Asia was of necessity withered by contact with our more material western system of living," causing China to require international guidance in order to develop in step with the rest of the world.[107]

Another aspect of China's treatment over the previous decades that the delegation hoped to overturn was the foreign assertion of (formal or informal) spheres of interest in Chinese territory. Wang argued that this was a violation of Chinese sovereignty, but the great powers were more concerned with the threat to open door principles of equal commercial access. The International Banking Consortium was invoked repeatedly during the Washington

Conference as a panacea to competition over spheres of influence (inasmuch as it would internationalize project financing and investment), though the British and Japanese agreement on excluding Manchuria and Mongolia from the consortium arrangement cast some doubt on these two state's full commitment to the stated goal "to abolish spheres of interest and throw open the whole of China to the activities of an international financial combination."[108] Modifications to reflect Japanese "special economic and military interests" were ultimately accepted.[109]

Writing decades later, the American international lawyer Charles G. Fenwick described the Nine Power Treaty of 1922 as an effort to make "effective the principle of the 'open door' in China," and as following in the spirit of Wilson's Fourteen Points – not, however, with reference to the principle of self-determination, but rather that of the "removal, as far as possible, of all economic barriers and the establishment of an equality of trade conditions."[110] Reflecting a pattern that was as old as the first treaties between China and the West, Fenwick saw (and applauded) in this an application to China of the same economic principles being applied to the colonial world; specifically, the "equal opportunity for trade and commerce" in certain territories placed under the League Mandate system.[111] If only the "economic disarmament" that the great powers undertook at Washington regarding Chinese space had been applied to the entire globe, Fenwick implies, interwar rivalries might never have erupted again into world war.[112] The idea of China as an "empty" field for cooperative institution-building by the West was again in play.

Critics of the new order for China, too, saw it as a watershed in the appropriation of international law forms for projects of political economy. Thus, for example, the Austrian-born Marxist economist Rudolf Hilferding, who would become Weimar Germany's minister of finance in 1923, wrote during the conference:

> The content of the treaty is collective capitalist expansion, and its object is China. Competitive struggle will be switched off, and the Powers will mutually guarantee their acquired rights in the Far East. They will pledge to handle all differences via collective conferences and will assist each other in event of a threat [to their shared interests]. As to China itself, the details are still being worked out, but it is clear that the giant empire will be made available, by mutual accommodation, for the unified capitalism of the great powers.[113]

Hilferding pointed to an essential contradiction in the new multilateral initiative to "settle" questions of regional order in East Asia. As had always been the case, China with its vast population and market potential was the focal point. Yet the new path in 1921, like those of the past, turned ultimately upon foreign agreements *about* China. There had now been enough elevation of its status to at least give it a seat at the table. But Chinese diplomats could still only seek change to the authority structures of inherited treaties if they had American backing and overall acceptability to the great powers. To obtain a measure of security for its status as a territorially sovereign state like those of the West – or to even begin conversations about the repeal of extraterritorial rights and concessions – China had first to confirm unequivocally its availability as a permanently open market, the lights kept always on for Western merchants and lenders. In this sense, the status quo in 1921 was not so distant from that of 1860.

Views along these lines were widely shared in the socialist press of Europe. The French Communist Party daily *L'Humanité*, for instance, referred continuously to the Washington Conference as making China "the prey of all imperialisms," subject to a "general pillaging."[114] And, gradually, this way of looking at things was also finding its way into China itself. At the time of the Qing Dynasty's fall a decade earlier, there had still usually been only the most general of senses that the course of China's recent history was not an idiosyncratic set of disasters, but rather one iteration of a global phenomenon of expansion by Western imperial powers and their interests. Since the beginning of the war, though, more detailed critiques had been imported into China for several years in publications such as Chen Duxiu's *Xin Qingnian*, and Marxist writings from Japan were also being translated in growing quantities, while Comintern personnel in China made sporadic efforts to spread ideas of world revolution.

By the summer of 1921, after the experience of great power politics at Versailles but before its sublation into the new stacked arrangements at Washington, a small coterie of intellectuals held a formal national congress of the Chinese Communist Party in Shanghai.[115] Among the earliest publications of the new party would be a pamphlet translating critiques against the Washington Conference by the Japanese Marxists Yamakawa Hitoshi and Sakai Toshihiko.[116] A few years later in Paris, a young Zhou Enlai would write: "The United States at the Washington Conference ended the decades-old pattern of foreign states' carving out spheres of influence in China, forging a new path of collective invasion and profit-sharing."[117] Zhou and a number of other radical students destined to become major Party leaders, including Deng Xiaoping, had arrived as students in France in the wake of Versailles. In their protests and publications, they began to argue for a full embrace of Soviet-style proletarian internationalism in rejection of what they saw as a corrupt, bourgeois imperialist world order undergoing mostly cosmetic changes in the new treaty regimes.

The mainstream of young intellectuals at the time, though, were less radical. As recalled by Jiang Tingfu, later a highly influential historian and diplomat who would serve as the Republic of China's long-running ambassador to the United Nations during the early Cold War, although Chinese students congregating in Washington at the time of the conference loudly protested and chanted slogans to demand China's full equality, many of them were overall happy with the "progress … in recovering sovereignty" achieved by multilateral recognition of China's formal title to Shandong – despite the lack of any real change to tariff and extraterritoriality rules. In general, more students abroad now also began to incorporate international law into their studies, the importance of the field being clearer than ever. For example, many Chinese students at Columbia, where Jiang had started his PhD in history in 1919, now flocked to take John Bassett Moore's course on international law, and hear Moore's praise of former star pupil Wellington Koo. The general atmosphere of fervent but ideologically undirected nationalism among his fellow students, however, Jiang found to be at times misguided. He wrote that he "could never share my compatriots hatred for imperialism," for "I felt that if China was only willing, it also had the ability to achieve organization, politics, and economical progress like that of Europe . . . at the very least, [it] could replace unilateral control by others with equal and mutually-beneficial relations."[118] Achieving "stability" and order at all costs would naturally lead to prosperity and power, improving China's status – or so thought a more vocal right wing.

Conclusion

The dramatic reorganization of global geopolitics and international legal order after the end of World War I had profound implications for China's role within the latter. Meanwhile, the emergence of a Chinese international law collegium, heavily represented in its fledging diplomatic corps, also began to lead to regular expressions of (limited) external agency. Among this first generation of international lawyers trained in the West, Wang Chonghui, Wellington Koo, Zhou Wei, and Zhou Gengsheng made especially key contributions not only to the articulation of their own country's national interests, but also to the field's doctrines and ideas globally. While Zhou Wei's *Essai* was a notable (and now unaccountably forgotten) intellectual intervention that exerted influence at a moment of profound transformation, others of these figures' contributions were made primarily in face-to-face diplomatic contexts.

Between the conferences at Versailles and Washington, Chinese delegates struggled to reach a modus vivendi preserving the now-republic's *zhuquan* over its full territorial domain and reclaiming some aspects of administrative authority, such as court jurisdiction. However, there was only so far such efforts could go under the semiprotective umbrella of the United States' open door policy. The ultimate resolution achieved at the Washington Naval Conference tended to still further accentuate the distinction between sovereignty as *imperium* over subjects combined with territorial integrity, while alienating *dominium* more than ever with the "removal, as far as possible, of all economic barriers."

Like the seminal moments of transformation of 1860 and 1901, the 1919–1922 treaties reorganized China's public law framework both at home and internationally, and did so on a multilateral basis that was explicitly in the interests of the great powers and global capital. Dissatisfaction with Western aspirations for a "Magna Carta for China" along these lines, and China's continued vulnerability to traditional imperialist aggression were by now becoming clearly articulated positions for intellectuals on the left, influenced by socialist thought and, especially, by the new example of the Soviet Union. With the final collapse of both the Qing Dynasty and successive imperial restoration attempts, China's political and legal future now seemed like a blank page to many radical intellectuals, with those on the right exploring postimperial strongman politics and those on the left associating their country's pursuit of "equal" sovereignty with new intellectual currents of antiimperialism, or even world revolution.

Part III
Internationalisms, 1922–2001

7

Changing Circumstances

The international institutions created in the wake of Versailles often straddled the line between law and geopolitics. The Permanent Court of International Justice (PCIJ) was certainly no exception. Nonetheless, with its founding in 1922, there was now created, for the first time, a true "international court" with general jurisdiction over members' disputes. Unlike the previous efforts by the great powers in 1907 that had encountered the joint opposition of Asian and Latin American states, there was now a more equal plan of judicial appointments by open election of "independent judges . . . regardless of their nationality."[1] Of course, its eleven full and four deputy judges still had to be recommended by the states parties to the Court. Meanwhile, there was a general admonition that "the whole body also should represent the main forms of civilization and the principal legal systems of the world."[2]

During the meetings of the Advisory Committee of Jurists deciding on the new Court's structure, the experience of 1907, and the various schemes mooted since by international lawyers, were discussed in detail.[3] Several of the participants on the committee had intended to incorporate a formal hierarchy in its design like that of the earlier proposals – in the words of Japanese representative Adachi Mineichirō and the British delegate Lord Phillimore during the session of June 19, 1920, this would simply be giving consideration to "actual facts."[4] However, the decision to appoint judges regardless of nationality was taken following careful arguments on this point by Rafael Altamira of Spain and Albert de Geouffre de La Pradelle, the latter having pointed out that "[t]he great Powers had no need to claim representation on the Court. They would obtain it automatically. Would it not be better therefore for them to obtain those mandates spontaneously?"[5] Elihu Root's agreement with this version of the "principle of equality" on behalf of the United States then played a decisive role in settling the question.[6]

The approach of election "regardless of nationality" that was adopted could then, as Gerry Simpson has pointed out, "be claimed as a victory for a softened form of sovereign equality while lurking in the background was the de facto veto power of the Great Power-dominated Council," thus "melding . . . soft legalism with a basically hierarchical structure."[7] The different points of view articulated during the meetings of the committee, in particular, the exchange of June 19 between *Institut de Droit International associés* Adachi and Phillimore and *membre* La Pradelle,[8] showed the process by which this "softened" version of hierarchy was articulated and encoded into the Court. The panel that was ultimately chosen was indeed unprecedented not only in the nature of its institutional stature and jurisdictional authority but also in its diversity. Its initial composition was as follows:

Judges: Rafael Altamira (Spain); Dionisio Anzilotti (Italy); Ruy Barbosa (Brazil); Robert Bannatyne Finlay (United Kingdom); Max Huber (Switzerland); Bernard Loder (Netherlands); John Bassett Moore (United States); D. G. Nyholm (Denmark); Oda Yorozu 織田萬 (Japan); Antonio Sanchez de Bustamante (Cuba); André Weiss (France)

Deputy Judges: F. V. N. Beichmann (Norway); Demètre Negulesco; (Romania); Wang Chonghui (China); Michailo Yovanovitch (Yugoslavia)[9]

Thus, on February 15, 1922, two Asian judges and two Latin Americans were among those scheduled to take up their seats on the new World Court, at the Great Hall of Justice in the Peace Palace at the Hague. However, Wang Chonghui was unable to attend its opening ceremony as he was still in the United States for the Washington Naval Conference. Among the line-up were some judges who had made favorable connections with Chinese diplomats and jurists, including Max Huber, who had been an early advocate of China's formal entry into the international legal community; John Bassett Moore, who had been Wellington Koo's PhD adviser at Columbia; and also Ruy Barbosa, who had collaborated with Lu Zhengxiang and other non-Western states at the Hague in 1907, although he died before taking up the position.[10] Judge Nyholm of Denmark, on the other hand, had recently published a monograph – while serving as vice-president of the Mixed Tribunal at Cairo exercising extraterritorial jurisdiction – that suggested a world court with a ranking scheme, like those of 1907, put China in the "third class."[11]

The notion of accepting China as a juridical equal was, thus, hardly a self-evident proposition for international jurists, even as of 1922. However, in Wang, China now had a jurist exercising a theoretically equal role with the judicial representatives of the great powers. In his involvements with legal questions via the PCIJ, multilateral conferences, and at the proceedings of the League, Wang would be in a position to take up an active role in the articulation of new international norms. Arguably, he had already done so in the years prior to his PCIJ appointment, with his advocacy for the Chinese proposals on "continentalism" for nonpermanent council seats. Though this norm was never formally adopted by the League, it was followed informally with enough consistency that the precedent would eventually turn into an explicit rule in the United Nations (UN) Security Council (and other UN organs).[12] It was Wang who, as a member of the League's Advisory Committee of Jurists and its commission for covenant revision, led the effort to revise covenant Article 4 to reflect the "continentalist" principle. Similarly, his attempts to ensure that

Article 21 could not be invoked by Japan to justify projects of hegemony in Asia had failed – he was unable to get the great powers to endorse application of the *pacta tertiis* principle to "regional understandings" like the Monroe Doctrine – but would later be vindicated in the (eventual) multilateral rejection of Japan's interventionism in China throughout the 1930s.[13]

At the beginning of the 1920s, though, the record did not seem to bode well for international acceptance of China's normative goals. In April 1922, Wang wrote to the Ministry of Foreign Affairs that, during the attempts at covenant revision, "the great powers unified their interests and cooperated in opposing us. The weaker countries considered these affairs as irrelevant to them, and didn't dare to defy the powers. Thus . . . the resolution [on Article 21] passed without our addendum."[14] Earlier, he had written in a more emotional register, expressing to Beijing his "profound guilt and regret" at the failure to revise the League Covenant.[15]

In light of these concerns, the Court, and the newly continuous task of codifying international law in which it and the League's Advisory Committee of Jurists found themselves de facto engaged, offered another possible path toward existential security for the Chinese state. The close connection between the international legal system and China's domestic political ontology was frequently on display. Wellington Koo had embodied these concerns in his remarks on December 13, 1920, during the twenty-first plenary meeting of the League Assembly Committee drafting the statute of the PCIJ. Koo lauded the Court as "a pillar of support in the great edifice of universal peace which we all want to see built up and forever maintained," but added that he and China's other delegates were fully in favor of compulsory jurisdiction for the Court, as embodied in the so-called Optional Clause by which some states had accepted jurisdiction over all disputes of a legal nature having to do with (1) interpretation of treaties; (2) questions of international law; (3) existence of any fact that, if established, would constitute breach of international obligations; and (4) the nature and extent of reparations to be made for the breach of an international obligation.[16] To have all such matters go before the Court would have obvious benefits for China, given its history of having territorial authority stripped away unilaterally by foreign states on the pretext of such disputes.

Koo expressed his hope that "all the Members of the League, and other States as well, may see their way, when signing or ratifying the protocol . . . to declare their acceptance of compulsory jurisdiction," and further elaborated that:

> My hope is all the more earnest, because China's faith in the ultimate supremacy of reason as contrasted with force is unbounded. Moreover, the compulsory jurisdiction referred to in Article 36 . . . is not of an all-embracing nature, but, on the contrary, is expressly limited to certain classes of questions, which are all of a justiciable character. I believed, therefore, that concerted recognition of compulsory jurisdiction in these questions would constitute a modest but very

desirable beginning in our common effort to discourage the use of force in international dealings, and to extend the reign of law everywhere in the family of nations.[17]

This "effort to discourage the use of force in international dealings" that Koo referred to in December 1920 was more than mere rhetoric. Rather, it was a consistent aim pursued by Chinese representatives in various international forums – and a rational prerogative for a weak state threatened by both internal conflicts and foreign encroachments. As a judge of the PCIJ and active participant in the juristic affairs of the League, Wang Chonghui became a central figure for Chinese efforts in this direction.

His real judicial work began in 1923, when he was involved in deciding a number of important matters before the PCIJ, including the *S.S. Wimbledon* case – which produced the Court's first actual judgment – and the important advisory opinion request as to the Finland–Soviet *Eastern Carelia* dispute. As part of the majority in both cases, Wang endorsed the principle articulated in *Wimbledon* of the capacity for international treaties to override preexisting contradictory rights and obligations (i.e., Germany's rights and obligations as a "neutral" state in the Polish–Soviet War). He also supported, in *Eastern Carelia*, both the important premise that the Court should be able to decide on its own jurisdiction in terms of advisory opinions, and that it would not be appropriate to issue such an opinion presently vis-à-vis a non-League-member state (the Soviet Union) that had not consented to that jurisdiction.[18]

In his memoirs, Max Huber recalled how he, Wang, Moore, Anzilotti, and Finlay had committed to this view before the deliberations started, and even planned a joint dissent should they be in the minority.[19] In another advisory opinion of the same year, the geopolitically important *German Settlers in Poland* matter, the Court found that German minority residents in Poland were entitled to the protection of "civil rights," including rights of property, and that there "must be equality in fact as well as ostensible legal equality in the sense of the absence of discrimination in the words of the law," with regards to policies protecting such rights.[20] That judgment "was drafted by Moore, Wang, and myself," Max Huber later wrote in his memoirs.[21]

In general, Wang's involvement in the Court tended toward promoting its institutional autonomy and powers of judicial review, independent from mandates by the council. In a brief article of 1926, he elaborated on his views regarding the Court's function in international society, expressing, like Koo six years earlier, his regret that "none of the great powers has as yet admitted the compulsory jurisdiction of the Court," but that, nonetheless, "the Court … has become an indispensable international institution" with its six decisions and twelve advisory opinions to date, and prospect for much more such work. He also expressed the need to promote "moral disarmament" – in his definition, "to be free from prejudice, to have good-will for all, and to believe that war is detrimental both to the victor and to the vanquished."[22]

As a member of the League's newly created Committee for the Progressive Codification of International Law, Wang was also personally involved in the codification effort that had been approved by the League Assembly in 1924. At its first session in Geneva, April 1–8, 1925, Wang emphatically called for adopting a "broader sense" of codification, which should also involve "proposals for the alteration of existing rules, either by modifications or additions."[23] At this first session, Wang was also appointed to two of the eleven subcommittees studying specific issues. These were the eighth subcommittee, which contemplated an international convention on piracy, and, more importantly, the sixth subcommittee, which would examine:

(1) Whether, and in what cases, a state may be liable for injury caused on its territory to the person or property of foreigners; and
(2) Whether, and, if so, in what terms it would be possible to contemplate the conclusion of an international convention providing for the ascertainment of the facts that may involve liability on the part of a state, and forbidding in such cases recourse to measures of coercion before the means of pacific settlement have been exhausted.[24]

The aim of "forbidding ... recourse to measures of coercion before the means of pacific settlement have been exhausted" was a highly ambitious inclusion. Here, if anywhere, was an example of Wang's "codification in a broader sense." His fellow subcommittee member, El Salvadoran lawyer and politician José Gustavo Guerrero, later to be the first president of the PCIJ's successor court, the International Court of Justice (ICJ), had very similar aims.[25] Ultimately the full committee somewhat reluctantly agreed to include the query in the parameters of the contemplated codification conference, and at its second session in early 1926 adopted for reference purposes the resulting "Guerrero–Wang Report" that presented the two authors' strong position in favor of limiting state responsibility and restricting practices of military coercion.[26] For the sixth subcommittee, this was quite a notable success, especially given that of the eleven issues opened up for the initial study, state responsibility was one of only three to progress to final consideration at the Hague Codification Conference in 1930. The others were nationality and the territorial sea.

Recapturing Autonomy

Wang's participation in efforts at codifying international law came at the same time that he was heavily involved in efforts to dramatically reform China's own domestic legal system. This task was, of course, also directly connected with China's international position, given that the Washington Naval Conference had endorsed a commission to "study" possible abolition of extraterritorial rights and concessions. Indeed, a few months after the first meeting of the committee, Wang was called back to China by the Beiyang government to oversee contentious multilateral negotiations for judicial treaty revision and tariff autonomy.[27] It was at this point that the Beiyang government also finally began to take seriously the push for intensified domestic legal reform, including the formulation of a Chinese Civil Code, and Wang was also appointed to lead these domestic legal codification efforts, among many other duties.

These overlapping efforts came at a time when China's overall political situation was in turmoil. The recent Second Zhili–Fengtian War, between two rival political factions in the north, had culminated in the ascendance of Manchurian warlord Zhang Zuolin's Fengtian clique, the defeat of the Zhili faction that had favored closer relations with the West, and, importantly, a decline in northern strength in general vis-à-vis the Guomindang government in the south. However, the Guomindang was also in a state of profound uncertainty following the sudden severe illness of Sun Yat-sen in late 1924 and his subsequent death on March 12, 1925. When Sun passed away, he left behind a Guomindang organization that was more cohesive and disciplined than any political grouping in the north, but that was also nonetheless split between its own rival factions with different political networks and highly distinct ideological emphases. The United Front policy of cooperation between the Guomindang and the Communist Party was a deeply divisive issue, with Wang Jingwei and the Guomindang's left seeking to maintain the alliance, while Chiang Kai-shek and the Guomindang's right-wing favored a decisive break, some degree of revival of China's Confucian traditions, and the courting of Western powers.

Sun himself had by this point cast serious doubt on the possibility for help from the West. In his last major speech, delivered in Kobe, Japan in November 1924, he endorsed ideas of Pan-Asianism as well as cooperation with the Soviet Union. Criticizing the way that "the Westerners . . . only consider their own civilization logical and humanitarian," he told his audience in Japan that "other [non-Western] peoples with any culture or independent ideas are considered as Barbarians in revolt against Civilization." It would be natural, then, for China and Japan to work together to define their own relations on a basis of equality and "the way of kingship" (*wangdao* 王道), based on shared moral principles rather than *Realpolitik*.[28] At the same time, Sun had also argued that the Soviet Union was "a new country in Europe which has been looked down upon and expelled from the Family of Nations by the White races." Linking communist ideology with the era's racialized geopolitics, Sun characterized Russia as "join[ing] with the Orient and separat[ing] from the West," which had made Europeans "afraid that [Soviet] principles, when put into effect, would overthrow their rule of Might. Therefore they do not accept the Russian way . . . but denounce it as contrary to world principles."[29]

The increasingly widely shared position that only a radical change to global order could restore agency to China and other non-Western states, and the increasing conviction that the great powers had no intention of giving up their "rights" in China, sparked a sharp rise in radical activism among both the nationalist and communist movements. This included protests, strikes, and clashes like the May 30 Incident, in which British police fired on demonstrators in Shanghai's International Settlement, killing several. With tensions rising between the south and foreign powers, particularly Britain, the Canton government soon after initiated a general strike and boycott against British goods that "caused very grave injury to the colony of Hong Kong and British trade in general."[30]

The south's confrontational posture incensed the British Foreign Office and troubled officials in Washington, but the north too was growing newly assertive. The Zhang Zuolin–dominated government hoped to bolster its own legitimacy by finally delivering on the promises of treaty revision and the attainment of tariff autonomy, and in furtherance of these aims, Wang Chonghui was appointed the lead figure in the late 1925 negotiations for a Special Tariff Conference as well as on matters of extraterritorial jurisdiction.[31] When the Special Tariff Conference opened in Beijing on October 26, 1925, Wang and other Beiyang representatives took a strident line on the principle of "tariff autonomy" (*guanshui zizhu quan* 關稅自主權).[32] After tariffs, Wang hoped, there might finally be a basis for the potential revision of extraterritoriality treaties that had been promised at Washington three and a half years earlier.[33]

Western governments were generally in agreement about the need to hand ultimate control over tariffs back to China, with January 1, 1929 envisioned as a completion date.[34] However, two related issues prevented a more substantive set of agreements – first, the question of whether and how China would be obligated to abolish the *likin* taxes on internal trade, and second, just how high its new "autonomous" tariff rates should be permitted to go.[35] Divisions among Western states persisted, with the United States taking firm positions on these issues.[36] Leaving the tariff commission to focus on extraterritoriality negotiations, Wang Chonghui in November 1925 remarked publicly that China was "no longer willing to be led by the hand" and was "no longer interested in treaty technicalities" – a significant statement from a PCIJ judge and a bold new tone for the many foreign statesmen that knew him primarily as "China's foremost jurist."[37]

Despite early promise, the practical success of the tariff negotiations was limited. About a year after the general agreement, a British diplomat in China, Victor Wellesley, lamented that "the powers were [still] determined to extend foreign control over the whole of China's customs revenues,"[38] and hoped to convince Foreign Secretary Austen Chamberlain and Prime Minister Stanley Baldwin that, in line with the positions being advanced by the Beiyang side: "We should no longer insist on the strict letter of treaties which are admittedly out of date," but rather that "[e]ach case of invasion of the privileged position hitherto held by the foreigner in China should be considered on its merits."[39] Such flexibility, if really adopted, would be a significant shift.

Meanwhile, however, Wellesley was also involved in the ongoing use of Britain's overwhelmingly superior naval power to intervene regarding its "rights" in other matters. Piracy issues in Hong Kong, for example, had prompted calls from the governor and naval officials to launch raids into Chinese territory involving "destruction of villages" that were believed to harbor pirates. Some moderate diplomats argued this would spur criticisms of British aggression or "barbarous treatment of innocent villagers" – particularly as it was hard to guarantee that all or any targets would really be pirates – but the use of force as such was still viewed as basically discretionary.[40]

More sensational was the "Wanhsien Incident" of August 1926, stemming from an apparent attempt by a Guomindang official to commandeer British ships moored in Chongqing. The ensuing clash between British vessels and Nationalist forces had resulted in, by British estimates, "less than 100 civilians killed, 140 injured and 20 houses destroyed," while per Chinese statements "more than 100 police ... were killed, nearly 1,000 civilians killed and wounded, and over 1,000 houses and building destroyed by gunfire." On the British side, there had been three officers and four seamen killed.[41] Despite the extremely uneven casualty figures, there were calls among British officials for further reprisals such as a "blockade of Szechuan."[42] A string of such incendiary incidents accompanied the progress of the Guomindang's "Northern Expedition" to reunify China, launched in June 1926.

Foreign powers were faced with the disturbing prospect of a revolutionary party with ties to the Soviet Union managing to unite China and, very likely, unilaterally abolish foreign treaty rights and privileges. The risks to existing foreign property rights, contracts, and debt held in China, along with the prospects for future market expansion, were palpable. So too was the rapid delegitimization of the Beiyang government in the face of Nationalist success. Even the apparently significant preliminary agreements reached at the Special Tariff Conference went unimplemented, as the government that had contracted them on the Chinese side fell apart. Nonetheless, the proceedings, and the attention that they generated in national media, had contributed to making "tariff autonomy" or "tariff sovereignty" a household word across China.[43]

The planned conference on extraterritoriality, meanwhile, had finally been convened in January 1926, but to little effect. Preparations had been undertaken since shortly after the Washington Conference – Wang's future successor at the PCIJ Zheng Tianxi, for example, had published a collection of Supreme Court decisions intended to show Western observers the maturity of China's judiciary and its determination to enforce valid foreign treaty rights even after the termination of extraterritorial jurisdiction. Indeed, the Beiyang government's Supreme Court had even explicitly asserted the principle that "the validity of an international agreement is superior to municipal law," as well as direct applicability of treaty law in domestic courts.[44]

At the conference, Wang Chonghui was elected as honorary president of the commission and presented a questionnaire to the representatives of the other signatories of the Washington Naval Treaty. Wang's four questions asked the commission to assess the current state of Chinese legal system and functioning of the judiciary, then to provide recommendations for the proper timeline to end extraterritoriality.[45] Following its initial meeting, the commission met in full on another twenty occasions, the last of which was on September 16. In the end, the commissioners of the powers were unwilling to sign onto anything more than a general set of recommendations regarding judicial independence, legislation, and prison reforms, and a vague promise that "the powers concerned ... might consider the abolition of extraterritoriality according to [a] progressive scheme" once such the "principal items" of such reforms had been completed.[46] The evident prerequisite for finding that China's state was "mature" enough to provide security for foreign rights, Carl Schmitt would later suggest, was nothing less than the "full Europeanization" of its legal system.[47] With few better options, Wang signed the document, but added a reservation that his signature should not be taken as endorsing all of its findings.

Wang's efforts in 1925–1926 to restore China's jurisdictional autonomy by multilateral agreement thus proved largely in vain. Wellington Koo, meanwhile, came into the service of the Beiyang government in 1926 and by October had been chosen by Zhang Zuolin to fill the office of foreign minister as well as acting premier. Despite the extreme precarity of both the regime he represented and his own position within it, Koo spent his time as titular head of government with a great deal of energy. As acting premier, Koo sought to convince the great powers to reopen tariff negotiations, employing hardball tactics such as allowing local governors to unilaterally seize "surtaxes" equivalent to those that would have been granted under the stalled 1925 plan. When challenged on this point by US diplomats, Koo shocked them by saying "the Foreign Office could not expect to turn the provincial leaders away from so obviously a just action."[48]

At the same time, Koo sought to finally bring the Maritime Customs Service (MCS) under Chinese control. The old "synarchic" institution was, by this point, the indisputable foundation of Chinese public finance generally and the collection of customs revenues in particular.[49] It was also essentially the only bureaucracy to function on a national level across all jurisdictions – collecting duties, managing debt payments, and administrating state infrastructure. Above all, it functioned as a kind of domestic interface and enforcer for China's international debts.

While the Guomindang was pursuing an even more assertive policy than Koo with respect to claiming "surtaxes" on foreign imports, its approach to the MCS was actually considerably less confrontational. Minister of Finance T. V. Soong (Song Ziwen) and other officials hoped eventually to bring the service – "the backbone of China's credit" – under national control, but not before reuniting China under a centralized regime. Moving too hastily might risk serious economic consequences.[50] This position was also likely calculated in order to avoid incentivizing the foreign powers to accede to Koo's demands for new tariff negotiations, which would damage Guomindang legitimacy and thus "convert the Chinese Maritime Customs from a politico-fiscal organ into an engine of war-finance and foreign intervention."[51] At the same time, the Guomindang cooperated with the MCS to collect "inland tax" (*neidishui*), and even ended the Canton–Hong Kong strike/boycott as part of an understanding worked out mainly with the British Foreign Office.[52]

Koo, meanwhile, used his time in office to transform the MCS. He pursued a policy of treating the service in fact as what it purported to be in name, that is, an organ of the central government in Beijing subservient to national policymakers. Koo clashed repeatedly with the MCS inspector general, Francis Aglen, over the promulgation of new policies including, above all, the imposition of the surtax and its free use as a revenue source by the Beiyang government. Aglen resisted these moves, to the extent of engaging in close personal negotiations with the Guomindang. In the end, he was forced out of office by a decision of the Beiyang cabinet and his ultimate successor, Frederick Maze, would for the first time initiate a policy of placing genuine policy control over MCS activities in the hands of China's political rulers.[53]

Such moves came as unwelcome surprises to foreign diplomats, who at times portrayed this newest iteration of the Beiyang regime as an even greater threat than the Guomindang – though the Soviet influence upon the latter, and the idea of a spread of "Bolshevism" in China, remained the most potent fear for both business and political leaders in many capitals.[54] Another aspect of Beiyang policy under Koo that presented a fundamental challenge to the geopolitical status quo touched more directly upon international law doctrine. This was the bilateral dispute that arose in relation to the Sino-Belgian Treaty of 1865, which had extended to Belgium the extraterritorial jurisdiction rights and favorable tariff rates that were accorded to other leading commercial powers following the Arrow War. The treaty had provisions for renewal every ten years but only accorded the Belgian side the right to initiate revisions. In April 1926, the Chinese side declared its intention to revise the treaty on equal terms. In the face of Belgian insistence upon the letter of the agreement, Koo declared the intent to unilaterally abrogate it unless a new *modus vivendi* could be reached in advance of a revised agreement.

In connection with the Belgian dispute, Koo's government drew on the expertise of international jurists that he and Wang had already formed connections with during their diplomatic activities in the West. Among those consulted to help frame the Beiyang government position and its potential arguments before the PCIJ were Walther Schücking, Giuseppe Motta, Nicolas Politis, and Robert Lansing. Schücking and Politis, in particular, advocated variations of the view that China could embrace the principle *rebus sic stantibus*, or changed circumstances, though it should be careful to portray this move "as a last resort" based on Belgian refusal to negotiate a new treaty.[55] The Belgian side itself, Schücking suggested, must have noticed its vulnerability to the application of this doctrine.[56] However, even if international jurists were optimistic about China's chances, these dealings too aroused Western "doubt of [Beijing's] sense of responsibility in regard to foreign obligations," as the American envoy to China complained.[57]

Many doubted that Beijing would truly take the unprecedented step of unilaterally abolishing treaty rights, even against a minor power. In the face of Belgium's insistence upon its treaty rights, however, Koo issued (as acting premier) an order to himself (as foreign minister) that declared the treaty to be ineffective. The Belgian side then took the matter to the PCIJ. Although the Beijing government did not acknowledge the PCIJ proceedings, Court President Max Huber did issue preliminary orders for the "protection" of Belgian interests in China in advance of the matter's resolution, including the need for judicial procedural rights consistent with the treaties and also that "property and shipping [must be] protect[ed] against any sequestration or seizure not in accordance with the generally accepted principles of international law."[58]

Although the Belgians hoped for support from the great powers in presenting a united front against Chinese treaty revision, this was not forthcoming. Other, more dramatic concerns occupied the leading states with interests in China, as when Nationalist forces allowed locals to storm the British concession at Hankow (today part of Wuhan) in January 1927, provoking the British Foreign Secretary to condemn this "unjustifiable attack on the long-established rights of the British commercial community," and his government's subsequent decision to dispatch considerable forces to China and to ensure that the events "shall not be repeated at Shanghai." The success of Chiang's Northern Expedition and his suppression of his erstwhile communist allies in mid 1927 led to a new situation. China proper was now, for the first time since the Qing era, nominally united. Although it was under a revolutionary and ostensibly left-wing regime, the West could, perhaps, now incentivize a rightward turn and the protection of foreign capital, not to mention continued payments on a public debt that had by then ballooned to an estimated US$2.5 billion, of which about three-quarters was foreign-owned and mostly secured by the MCS, salt taxes, and railway revenues. Meanwhile, Chiang's regime found it entirely in their interests to pursue this rapprochement that might ensure foreign recognition, along with more lending.[59]

Many of China's leading diplomats and its first generation of international lawyers joined the new Guomindang-led government after 1927, especially those like Wang Chonghui who had long-standing connections with the party but also many, such as Koo, Zhou Wei, Zheng Tianxi, and Xu Mo, who had not been part of Sun's movement. However, the Chinese international law field's spiritual forerunner Lu Zhengxiang, who was at this point still representing China at the League of Nations in Geneva and who at fifty-six years old might have served for several more years, did not follow suit. With the death of his Belgian wife and the change of government, Lu decided to retire from public life, becoming a Catholic lay friar at a Benedictine monastery in Bruges.

At around the same time, a thirteen-year-old in Fujian began to develop a deep interest in international law. Wang Tieya, later one of China's most influential jurists, would recall his interest in the subject first being stimulated by animated discussions over the PCIJ Belgian treaty case between his father, a diplomatic official who had studied law in France in the Qing era, and a cousin newly returned from serving as a diplomat in Belgium. From that point forward, he decided, he would pursue a career in this exciting field.[60] In Jiangsu, meanwhile, a fifteen-year-old named Han Depei, who had been raised by an elderly grandfather he called "Daddy Whiskers" that had served in his youth as a soldier for the Taiping rebels, borrowed money from his uncle, a Buddhist monk, to study at a prestigious local middle school. There, he would first encounter the progressive writings of May Fourth Movement intellectuals and begin an academic career that would also bring him to the forefront of a future generation of international lawyers.[61]

China, State Responsibility, and the Use of Force

While both of China's dueling governments pursued newly bold policies in asserting sovereignty during 1925–1927, some of China's other internationally active jurists were also proposing reforms to international legal order in the pursuit of autonomy and security. At the 1926 annual meeting of the *Institut de Droit International*, Zhou Wei echoed Wang and Koo's efforts in proposals to his fellow members of the leading body of international lawyers. Particularly notable was his call for an official *voeu* to condemn the use of military force as a means of reprisal for international wrongful acts.[62]

Such a rule could be seen as a natural evolution of the Calvo and Drago Doctrines, which had earlier sought to restrict applications of unilateral military sanctions to collect state debts.[63] However, Zhou sought a considerably stronger formulation, that "measures of coercion or reprisal, that is a provocation that could give rise to an international war, should be excluded forever from modern international law."[64] Military reprisal as such would thus be prohibited – and, should the institute produce such a suggestion, this would very likely help to shape the international law codification efforts ongoing under League auspices. In the end, however, the institute adopted a far weaker position, "tending to exclude as much as possible [use of] war and diplomatic measures," as sanctions before domestic remedies for injured aliens had been exhausted and/or agreement was reached between the aggrieved and offending states.[65]

During this same session in 1926, Zhou also sought to include in the institute's draft proposals a clause "excluding responsibility of states in which a revolution has suddenly erupted or a civil war has persisted for some time,"[66] but this too was watered down considerably to the position that state responsibility might be "limited based on the circumstances," where there are "areas infested with brigandage," sudden outbreaks of violence out of state control, or prolonged conditions providing prior warning of local dangers.[67] Another important suggestion, that "the state is not responsible if the acts of its officials [giving rise to harm to foreigners] were aimed at safeguarding national security or the sovereign rights of the state," received the endorsement of the Italian institute member Scipione Gemma, but was rejected by the other members.

Though Zhou's specific suggestions were diluted into more anodyne forms, his critique of armed reprisals did seem directly responsible for the institute's agreement to engage upon a further study of "coercive measures," which it defined as "diverse measures of retorsion and reprisals (boycott, embargo, angary, pacific blockade, etc . . .)." This category of international uses of force "short of war" – which had been so central to China's experiences of coercion by foreign powers – had by this point only just started to be given a clearer legal definition, beginning with the League Council's handling of the *Corfu* incident of 1923.[68] That matter had resulted in an opinion from the League's Commission of Jurists to the effect that

> Coercive measures which are not intended to constitute acts of war, may or may not be consistent with the provisions of Articles 12 to 15 of the Covenant, and it is for the Council, when the dispute has been submitted to it, to decide immediately, having due regard to all the circumstances of the case and to the nature of the measures adopted, whether it should recommend the maintenance or the withdrawal of such measures.[69]

Notably, at the time that the League had the *Corfu* matter under consideration, the threat or use of armed interventions and "reprisals" was very much still in vogue among the great powers. Most obviously, France and Belgium were at the time engaged in an ongoing occupation of Germany's Ruhr Valley over the issue of unpaid war reparations.[70] Meanwhile, the United States was involved in a long-term occupation of Nicaragua and other regional interventions under the Monroe Doctrine. The United Kingdom had always considered armed reprisals as a vital part of its toolkit in expanding and protecting its global influence and interests. Japan had carefully emulated these approaches to the use of force in its own policy of expansion.[71] Very soon after the *Institut de Droit International*'s 1926 meeting, however, the issue of prohibiting or restricting armed reprisals became a common theme for lecturers at the Hague Academy of International Law.[72]

The issue of state responsibility, including the related topic of appropriate measures that could be taken by states against others "violating" their (or their private citizens') rights, was under consideration by various groups contemplating responses to the questions raised by the codification committee, most notably the team working on the so-called Harvard Research in International Law.[73] This group's branch considering questions of state responsibility included the traditionalist Yale international law professor Edwin Borchard (who served as reporter), recent US secretary of state and soon to be chief justice of the Supreme Court, Charles Evans Hughes, PCIJ judge Manley Hudson, and Quincy Wright of the University of Chicago, among others.[74] Most were also members of the American Society of International Law (ASIL) and, specifically, its Standing Committee on the Codification of International Law.[75]

Like the *Institut de Droit International*, the team working on the Harvard Research was not prepared to formulate a clear denunciation of coercion and reprisal. They did, however, include an addendum to a proposed article regarding compulsory PCIJ jurisdiction over disputes lamenting that "claiming states [using reprisals] are not bound to resort to the judicial process and have on occasion constituted themselves plaintiff, judge, and sheriff in their own causes. This is one of the principal and justifiable grievances of certain states."[76] In the context of the Guerrero–Wang Report, it is clear that the "certain states" whose grievances are alluded to would include, in particular, the states of the report's two authors. The overall thrust of the Harvard Research approach, of course, did not tend to substantively address such concerns, however, it did explicitly critique how reprisals for alleged violations of foreigners' rights led to cases in which force was used by (and against) "a whole people on behalf of a single citizen or corporation – a primitive form of collective action which survives in practically no other branch of public law."[77]

As we have seen, by the mid 1920s, both the Beijing and Guangzhou regimes were largely unanimous in asserting the territorial integrity of the Chinese state, its autonomy with regards to fiscal and judicial policy, and its rejection of the legitimacy of unilateral uses of force. The notion that China's international status was indeed anomalous, and thus in need of "correction" to match with its titular sovereignty, was by the end of 1920s also becoming more common among international lawyers and diplomats. At the same time, however, the notion of a "united front" of the West (and sometimes Japan) against China still had major adherents. Both views were put into open contention during an important discussion at the 1928 Berlin meeting of the Interparliamentary Union (IPU), as it debated resolutions regarding the issues of state responsibility, the adjudication of disputes, and the new efforts of legal codification.[78]

Its longtime secretary general Christian Lous Lange, a Norwegian internationalist, connected these topics while specifically invoking China at multiple points in his remarks. As he noted, "[i]t is above all in China that the question of the rights of the foreign powers vis-a-vis national authorities creates dangerous situations and brings up difficult problems."[79] With its, increasingly anomalous, capitulations still in place, China was the chief example of how "[s]ome states, considered in law as independent and sovereign states, are in fact submitted to a regime of tutelage that is at times quite broad, and may be exercised either by a single state or by a limited number of powers."[80] For Lange, this was not a state of affairs deserving condemnation or radical reform. Rather, this was an example of the sort of "tutelage" (*tutelle*) that could be applied to "members of the [international] community that are not yet capable of managing their own affairs." Like pacifists around the time of the first Hague Conference, the influential pacifist Lange thirty years later could still see in China an object for what he called "an organization of international tutelage," now to be developed on the basis of the League Mandate system.[81]

Later in the same report, this leading internationalist jurist again invoked China as a sort of test case for another creative initiative in global governance. This arose in connection with the provisions of the League Covenant prohibiting military aggression among members, and committing them to collective defensive action in such situations. After referring to skeptical "adversaries" of the League who had long considered its centralization of military force as impractical, Lange commented that:

> It is above all with regards to events in China that one hears lately these voices of adversaries, and it is difficult not to admit that they are to a great degree well-founded ... One can ask, in any case, if it would not be possible for *multiple* members of the League to cooperate to invoke Article 11 in common before situations as grave as that which has developed in the Far East.[82]

The idea of Boxer Intervention–style Western "solidarity" trumping Chinese agency was thus still alive and well. At these same Berlin meetings, however, other delegates presented very different views. The Swedish socialist politician and judicial magistrate Carl Lindhagen raised the prospect that the general language regarding threats to peace under Articles 10 and 11 could lead to unjust outcomes, such as, for example, if China were to demand the return of a piece of territory under European control. Should the European power holding that territory refuse to turn it over, "[s]hould all other European powers [then] rush over in order to suppress a just claim for freedom, and to uphold an unjust occupation?"[83] The Indian-British MP and Communist Party member Shapurji Saklatvala listed China alongside India, Egypt, Nicaragua, and Iraq as regions regularly subjected to interventions by Western imperialists.[84] Meanwhile, another representative to the IPU meeting from the colonial periphery, the Egyptian political leader Wissa Wassef-Bey, spoke in similar terms about British abuses of the "right of intervention" in his country. Taking issue with Lange's neutral descriptions of capitulation rights, Wassef-Bey portrayed them as aspects of a general system of domination that imperial powers like Britain had deployed in calculated fashion to ensure political and fiscal control over subject peoples the world over.[85]

Walther Schücking, acting as president of the session by virtue of its German setting, also challenged Lange's defense of Western intervention in China. After recalling how he had provided his report to the Chinese government in 1927 regarding its right to invoke *rebus sic stantibus*, Schücking noted "with great pleasure" that foreign states were increasingly ready to negotiate with China. The issue to which Schücking raised this example was Article 4 of the IPU's draft declaration with respect to the rights and duties of states. Specifically, the question at issue, which was debated vigorously during the meeting, was whether or not the draft clause "Treaties establish law among states" should modify the word "treaties" with the limiting phrase "freely consented to."[86] This clause was ultimately voted down, though another related addition was made – that treaties could be derogated not only by agreement of the parties involved, but also in ways "otherwise conforming with international law." This, in context, would have had to be taken as referring to invocations of *rebus sic stantibus*.

On the topic of uses of force, meanwhile, the Berlin IPU session over which Schücking presided produced a draft article (Article 6) that went far beyond the Kellogg–Briand Pact "renouncing war as an instrument of national policy" that was then being signed in Paris. The IPU draft article read: "States do not have the right to do justice by themselves. All armed aggression constitutes a crime. Guilty (*coupables*) *individuals will be prosecuted* in conformity with international law."[87] Had this norm been adopted instead of the relatively weak (and reservation-ridden Kellogg–Briand Pact), it would have anticipated by two decades the clear prohibitions on all unilateral uses of force contained in the UN Charter.[88] China's history of interventions by the Western powers, and the ongoing efforts of its regimes and popular movements to change the international legal status quo, seemingly played a major role in establishing the discursive context for these bold new visions for the outlawry of aggression (even when passed off as reprisal) that would eventually come to fruition within the UN system.

Indeed, the following year, Schücking again returned to the topic of the renunciation of the Belgian treaty in an article where he framed it in light of China's struggle for recognition as a "full member" of the international legal community.[89] Among other sources, he cited the diplomat Zhou Zechun's 1910 Berlin PhD thesis, and the sympathetic views of some Continental jurists, such as Karl Strupp, for the argument that China's "full membership" should now, at long last, be recognized along with the corresponding autonomy its people demanded.

New Discourses of International Order

Despite the rapidly shifting views of some leading reformers of international law, as of the late 1920s, the premise that China was a coequal sovereign state deserving of full autonomy was not universally shared in the West even among internationalists. Along with Lange, other prominent jurists also saw China mainly as a field for the innovation of new projects of global governance. The influential Columbia University historian and Carnegie Foundation officer James Shotwell, for example, came up with his own set of quixotic suggestions about a structure by which the United States and other treaty powers could agree to hand over consular jurisdiction.

Shotwell's plan was presented as a study for a session of the Institute of Pacific Relations held at Kyoto, Japan, in late 1929. It would entail a five to ten year period during which "a limited number of special courts [would be established] in a half-dozen places where foreign business is most largely carried on or where foreigners are most largely congregated." These "special courts," including a separate court of appeal, would be staffed by a unique group of what Shotwell called "judges or jurisconsults," to be selected by a panel of experts nominated either by the PCIJ or the Permanent Court of Arbitration (PCA), and which would originate with "lists prepared by the law associations of the countries concerned in some agreed proportion."[90]

Shotwell was of the view that such a system would allow a transition away from extraterritorial jurisdiction while assuaging foreign powers' concerns about the quality of administration of justice. He suggested that in terms of the eventually resulting judicial appointments, "Chinese jurists would have an equal chance with foreigners," but also that "only those jurists be appointed who would have personal and direct familiarity with the law and practice of the Western nations."[91] Obviously, most of the judicial appointments resulting from such a system would be of foreigners, and, in Shotwell's view, the PCIJ should be given the power not only to make such nominations but also to determine the appointees' salaries and working conditions. After all: "The World Court, representing nothing political, but solely the juristic life of the civilized world, could not come under suspicion of political aims."[92]

Nor should the innovative system subjecting China to an unprecedented globalized judiciary be seen as a "derogation of Chinese sovereignty," but rather as the modern incarnation of the ancient Roman *ius gentium*, by which notionally "universal" legal rules were formulated within Roman law and over time contributed to the development of Rome's civil law corpus. Of course, Rome had never had a body of foreign judges deciding cases and developing jurisprudence outside the administrative authority of its own rulers. Nonetheless, Shotwell rather grandiosely suggested that "[t]he opportunity has now come to China to do the same thing for the modern world which Rome did for the jurisprudence of Europe."[93] His earlier use of the curiously antiquated word "jurisconsults" to describe his envisioned group of centrally administrated transnational legal technocrats was thus clearly quite considered. For Shotwell, China was a zone in which new legal norms could be developed alongside the growth of globalized trade. The cause of internationalism and the growth of foreign commerce in what remained a vast and only partially unexploited market would proceed hand in hand.

There was never a chance that the Nationalist regime would accept such an arrangement, so closely resembling in spirit the League's Mandate system for "uncivilized" territories. Somewhat remarkably, nevertheless, in January 1930, the Hoover administration actually did propose to the Nationalist government's minister to the United States, Wu Chaoshu, a system bearing close similarities to Shotwell's project. This draft agreement called for a body of "legal counselors or jurisconsults," nominated by the PCA and receiving from it their salaries and conditions of payment, acting primarily not act as judges, but monitors over cases involving foreign nationals. A special Court of Appeal would also be established. If cases involving foreign interests were seen as inadequately handled, there could even be "evocation" (transfer) of the matter to a foreign tribunal.[94]

In response, Wu, speaking quite definitively for the Nationalist government, politely shut down these suggestions. He reserved his most strident objection to the principle of evocation, which was likely "to die of desuetude even in Siam where it originated."[95] Meanwhile, in response to the US suggestion that there should now be held the long-delayed multilateral conference to consider the revision of extraterritorial jurisdiction, Wu replied laconically that "China's experience with conferences had been unfortunate."[96] Multilateral legislative settings, he implied, had tended to privilege the united interests of the great powers, while China's recent advances had been mostly due to unilateral initiatives.

At around the same time, matters of international organization were discussed in Zhou Wei's next major publication on international law topics, 1930's *The New International Law*.[97] This book focused on the role of the League and the PCIJ as agents of gradual transformation of the international legal order. Though occasionally noting where the League had fallen short of earlier visions of international organization (such as his own 1917 *Essai*), Zhou was, characteristically, still quite positive about the role of international law in promoting China's security, and its consistency with ancient Chinese thought.[98] Zhou's book also included a preface by Wang Chonghui, who called it an excellent compass for the study of international law. He agreed with Zhou's reiterated claims that in the spring and autumn period there had been some notions that approached those of modern international law, but also pointed out drily that China since the Han era had "despised distant peoples as *manyi*," leaving it completely unprepared when modern Western forces finally invaded.[99] Another preface was by the sitting minister of foreign affairs, Wang Zhengting, who also affirmed Zhou's expertise in modern international law doctrine as well as his clear explication of its importance. However, like Wang Chonghui, he cast doubt on the old trope Zhou carried over from Martin and Late Qing thinkers that linked international law and ancient Chinese practices. Ancient Chinese, Wang wrote, "did not even want to use law for domestic affairs, let alone apply it to the international level."

Both in his public writings and in reports to the Guomindang government, Zhou Wei noted a set of achievements that he and other Chinese delegates had accomplished in the course of their League activities. In particular, he thought, the "consistent and ever more firm" promotion of "Continentalism" via the League Council rotation system had helped to ensure that China would not be relegated to second-tier status. Also important was maintaining China's support from other "weak" states, such as those of Latin America. Carefully citing Sun Yat-sen for the benefit of his new Guomindang superiors, Zhou closed a 1930 memorandum on League affairs with the quote "as the former Premier said, we should unite with and strive alongside all the peoples of the world who treat us as equals . . . and only thus can we demonstrate the culture and capability of the Chinese nation."[100]

Zhou Gengsheng, meanwhile, continued to adopt an approach that focused upon the popular sentiments and collective rights of the Chinese people. In 1929, he had been appointed as the chairman of the departments of Political Science and Law at the newly renamed and restructured National Wuhan University, which he would over the course of decades shape into, eventually, China's leading center of international law scholarship. While an academic and administrator in one of the core educational institutions of the new Guomindang government, Zhou was also emerging as the leading public representative of a nationalist perspective on matters such as treaty revision and tariff autonomy, and his name was tied closely to the legal critique of "unequal treaties" as inherently invalid.[101]

As for the League, Zhou Gengsheng doubted its use as a forum for the restoration of China's foreign relations to conditions of full equality. Foreign diplomats had merely been "placating" China when saying that matters of treaty revision could be referred to the League, and, moreover, due to the League's waning influence, it was doubtful that it would really change matters on the ground even if it were to decide in China's favor.[102] Given the League's inability to override the self-interest of powerful states, and recent proof of the futility of multilateral negotiations with the West, Zhou advised that unilateral action and bilateral negotiations "based on the unique circumstances of relations with each counterpart state" would be the best path forward for restoring China's equality.[103] Like Wu Chaoshu in his dealings with US diplomats, Zhou Gengsheng portrayed Western plans as reiterating patterns of foreign regulation of China, not according it true autonomy and a sovereign status coequal with Western states themselves.

Emerging Chinese jurists of younger generations were similarly committed to the idea that the international system had to change in fundamental ways. For example, Li Shengwu, a Shandong-born Master's student in international law under J. L. Brierly at Oxford University who had previously studied in Tokyo, wrote around this time that "[a]nyone passing through London can feel how . . . this little island is the headquarters of the British empire, central office of the world's colonies, appraisal department of global industry, and slaughterhouse of backward peoples."[104] Though he did not advance to complete a doctorate under Brierly,[105] upon his return to China, Li taught at Fudan University and took on stints as an official in the Ministry of Foreign Affairs and as chief editor of the influential *Eastern Miscellany* magazine, promoting a strongly pan-Asianist tone in the publication. Similar sentiments had recently been expressed at the 1927 International Congress against Colonial Oppression and Imperialism held in Brussels, where Jawaharlal Nehru represented the Indian National Congress to begin pursuing cooperation with the Guomindang, though such prospects would be sharply limited by the latter's turn to Western rapprochement.[106]

Conclusion

The interwar period saw radical transformations in China's society, intellectual life, and geopolitical environment. The League of Nations provided, for the first time, a formalized international legal status for China within the contours of an organized international society, as opposed to the ad hoc, idiosyncratic multilateral frameworks applied ever since 1860. Yet the Washington Naval Conference and its resulting Nine Power Treaty of 1922, which dealt with the most important questions of Chinese sovereignty and territorial integrity, had instead been precisely a continuation of the earlier trend. From the recovery of Shandong to the stymied attempts to end extraterritorial jurisdiction, to the later invasions by Japan and ultimate participation in plans for another postwar order, China's transformations would still be handled in (unequal) "dialogue" with great powers, above all the United States.

At a time when China itself was in a state of ideological ferment, with nationalist, Marxist, liberal, neotraditionalist, fascist, and other perspectives entering the public sphere, scholars of international law exhibited some corresponding diversity of views. Effectively all of them were united, however, by the claim that China had been both unduly subordinated and existentially threatened by the Eurocentric international law order of the past several decades, and that it needed to insist further upon equal status in the international community. The consistency of that position was testimony to a firmly entrenched shared belief that the extant world order was denying China essential dimension of its sovereignty. For the first time, moreover, Chinese jurists now had the opportunity to assert the principle of the coequal sovereignty of weak states as contributors to a more general nascent global shift away from nineteenth-century doctrines of cosmopolitan *dominium* rights and corresponding powers of intervention.

8

New Orders

On September 17, 1930, three new full judges were admitted as members of the Permanent Court of International Justice (PCIJ). These were Wang Chonghui, Walther Schücking, and Frank Kellogg[1] – each of whom had, in recent years, been highly visible as an "activist" in projects for the reform of international law. In the five years to come, Wang would take part in a number of important cases,[2] and contribute to PCIJ deliberations, but would later return to a China undergoing full-scale invasion by Japan and in which questions of world order, and China's role within it, were being hotly debated.

Earlier, Wang had been appointed as minister of justice – a strong vote of confidence from Chiang Kai-shek, then consolidating his rule as the dominant figure in the Guomindang and in the country – but he asked to turn down the position in order to make his return to the Court. This also marked a reassertion of China's presence in international legal affairs after three years in which revolution had raised major anxieties abroad. Rapprochement between the Guomindang and the West, especially the United States, had however been made much easier by suppression of the party's left wing and Chiang's new efforts to exterminate the Communist Party.[3] That rapprochement paid various geopolitical and financial dividends, but did not lead to agreement on projects of international law reform. This was made clear at the Hague Codification Conference of 1930, though the dynamics of such meetings would change radically as the world careened back toward total war and the general reimagining of the global legal order.

Codification, Equality, and Security

When delegates met at the Hague, they had before them suggestions regarding the issues of nationality, the territorial sea, and state responsibility. They also had the initial reports on these subjects produced by the respective subcommittees. But in the case of state responsibility, the main responses provided were very much in the opposite spirit to that of the Guerrero–Wang Report, which had sought to sharply limit states' liabilities to foreign citizens and companies. The choice between these two approaches – reinforcing the legal umbrella protecting capitalist globalization, or curbing it in the interest of state sovereignty – was not resolved in 1930.[4]

In the end, no agreement was reached even in principle by the delegates discussing the state responsibility or maritime law. However, China's lead delegate, Wu Chaoshu, brought his country's experiences since the 1830s to the fore in defending the principle of state sovereignty. As he argued, standards for the treatment of foreign nationals had long been so vague as to allow application of "two standards: one a higher one, one a lower one . . . depending unfortunately in some cases on the relative strength, prestige and influence of the disputing nations."[5] Wu startled his Western interlocutors at the Hague by continuously insisting on amendments that returned to the principles of the Guerrero–Wang Report. As he argued in terms clearly drawn from Chinese experience, no nation "legally and morally invites foreigners to come to its soil; [rather] foreigners go there of their own accord. Why, therefore, should the Government of that country be saddled with a heavier responsibility than that which it has towards its own nationals?"[6]

Assuming that foreigners would be given all of the rights of legal recourse that are available to nationals, Wu continued, the only disparity that could possibly justify a higher standard of responsibility toward aliens would be that they lacked the ultimate "right of redress" possessed by locals – engaging in revolution against an unjust regime. However, foreigners had an even "better right of redress than that of revolution . . . the right of absence."[7] Those aware of unstable conditions in a country, or who found its standard practices for policy implementation or the administration of justice unpalatable, could stay away just as easily as those who were troubled by its weather and climate conditions. These arguments, as Wu must have expected, did not convince his Western interlocutors – many now believed that globalized commerce now made interpenetration of state liabilities an irreversible aspect of the international community.

Reflecting on the conference subsequently, the Yale international lawyer Edwin Borchard, who had coordinated the Harvard Research draft on state responsibility, reproached Wu and his supporters for their proposal of a "categorical rule" of equality with nationals as the maximum for states' required treatment of aliens.[8] He noted, however, that both the Hague draft and the International Conference on the Treatment of Foreigners, held in Paris late the previous year, had "broke[n] down on the issue of equality."[9] Borchard portrayed Chinese anxieties concerning the potential use of international law obligations as pretexts for foreign aggression (something the country had experienced on various occasions) as exaggerated. Yet, while he suggested such views were held only by China and a "minority" of states in attendance, the actual numbers on the vote – 17 to 23 – showed that many did agree with Wu's concerns.[10] Notably, all of the Latin American states at the conference voted in favor of the "equality" draft but one, Cuba, which abstained.[11]

The "South" position formulated in the Guerrero–Wang Report, then espoused by Wu and other delegates from "peripheral" states, served to limit international obligations in principle and thus asserted state sovereignty. At the same time, it did not do so on the basis of an opposition between sovereignty and international law as such. This point is demonstrated in the comments Wu had made at the second meeting of the Committee on Nationality, for which he acted as vice-chairman. There, he took note of the clause included in the Basis of Discussion that "nationality laws are within the sovereignty of each State." While that might be true, he added, "[a]t the same time, . . . this sovereignty is not unlimited [and] each State must nevertheless take account of certain principles generally recognized." On the specific issue of nationality, he remarked on behalf of the Chinese delegation that:

> [W]e believe it is extremely desirable that, in those cases where the nationality legislation of the different countries still embodies provisions which are discriminatory as regards certain nationalities, races or religions, those provisions should be removed as soon as possible. They have, in the past been fruitful causes of conflict between races and nations, and for the future peace and comity of nations, it is very desirable that they should be suppressed.[12]

Eleven years earlier, the Chinese and Japanese delegations had exhibited rare unity at Versailles over Japan's racial equality proposal, even as they contested bitterly over Shandong. Now, Wu pressed the same issue (with its implicit condemnation of America's Chinese Exclusion, the "White Australia" policy, and similar immigration regimes), and linked it with extraterritoriality on Chinese soil. Due to Western opposition, however, racial equality (or gender equality, which went unmentioned) was not addressed in the final agreement.[13] During the proceedings of the Committee on Nationality, Wu Chaoshu seems to have played the role of a consummate diplomat, as opposed to the more assertive position he had carved out on state responsibility. Indeed, Chinese–US cooperation, in particular, seems to have helped the Committee on Nationality to achieve its final consensus. At the closing session, the chairman, Nicolas Politis, praised Wu for his "high idealism combined with practical insight."[14]

Upon his return to China, Wu went back to work in tandem with the left wing of the Guomindang associated with Wang Jingwei, Sun Fo, and others. The increasing marginalization of and pressure from Chiang against this side of the party, however, led him to retire from public life. Also playing a role was his disillusionment with the Western (chiefly US) decision to sponsor Chiang's Nanjing government, and supply it with arms, in order to promote the political unification of China on terms friendly to Western capital. During the early 1930s, the domestic political scene in China was preoccupied with this internal dissent among the Guomindang factions, and the dramatic escalation of Japanese intervention that was embodied in the move, in 1931, to establish a puppet state in Manchuria. Coming about as the result of a venture by Japan's aggressive "army faction," the occupation of Manchuria and later "recognition" of the new state of Manchukuo (*Manshūkoku*) were defended by Japanese diplomats post hoc as necessary uses of force to protect Japanese citizens and "legitimate interests" from local threats – just the sort of unilateral intervention Chinese diplomats had actively sought to limit in their contributions to international law debates throughout the 1920s.

Despite Japanese appeals to traditional justifications for uses of force, and continued lip service to US open door principles, the international stand-off over the de facto annexation of Manchuria would gradually mark a paradigm shift in legal doctrine surrounding the use of force. That shift, though, was not immediate. The response from the League Council on December 10, 1931 was the appointment of a commission of inquiry headed by Lord Victor Bulwer-Lytton, a former governor of Bengal and viceroy of India. The Lytton Commission would travel to Manchuria and investigate the recent conflict, the nature of the newly established regime, and proper responses, if any, by League members. A key concern for Lytton and many members of the commission was whether Japan's actions in the matter had violated the Nine Power Treaty of 1922 with its promises of "territorial integrity" and rejection of spheres of influence.

Though the commission criticized Japanese forces' actions and the "non-spontaneous" character of the new regime's establishment, they did not go as far as to label the incident an act of aggression or call for sanctions. For many in China, the League failure over Manchuria led to increased skepticism of the Western great powers and their supposed humanitarian turn since 1919. Remaining pro-Soviet figures in the Guomindang found some of their arguments bolstered. The Berlin-educated warlord scion, jurist, and diplomat Xu Daolin, for example, though anti-Soviet in his own sympathies and having recently befriended the radical conservative German legal theorist Carl Schmitt, pessimistically warned German readers that the question now facing China was no less than "*Genf oder Moskau*?"[15] Japan's exit from the League in the face of criticism over its actions did little to assuage such concerns, given acceptance of the status quo by the great powers. Nonetheless, from 1931 on, practices permitted for centuries in international law under the veneer of "protection of nationals" or defense of legitimate state interests, and so on, would come to be considered as presumptively illegitimate – and the prototypical case that set this shift in motion was that of Japan in Manchuria.[16]

Wu's main deputy and alternate at the Hague Codification Conference had been the twenty-seven-year-old junior diplomat and former judge of the Provisional Court in Shanghai's International Settlement, Liang Yunli. Liang, born in 1903 into a family of Qing literati in Zhejiang, had mastered English and French before studying law at Nanyang University in Shanghai and then at Soochow University, taking classes day and night to hasten his progress. It was a testament to the advancement of legal education in elite eastern Yangtze Delta institutions by the mid 1920s that this background, along with his subsequent judicial work between 1926 and 1929, prepared him adequately to begin engaging with some of the West's leading jurists. Liang's contacts in diplomacy and international law over the coming decades would generally remember him as talented and learned, though the British historian-diplomat Charles Kingsley Webster, who would encounter Liang during the planning conferences of the United Nations (UN), saw him as "tiresomely clever." The focus of Liang's later career was the codification of international law, in which he would play a major role for decades after World War II.[17]

At the time of the 1930 Hague Codification Conference, however, Liang felt that the event's failure had called into question the entire "future of such a method [of codification via periodic conferences]." The conference had successfully shown that existing rules were in many cases outdated, but had been unable to generate "consensus on new rules."[18] Following the conference, Liang spent several years in the United States completing advanced studies at George Washington University and Harvard Law School, where he worked closely with several jurists who had been involved in the Harvard Research project. His continued study of codification and state responsibility, combined with events unfolding in Manchuria, led Liang to focus his attention on the legal status of uses of force in the wake of the Kellogg–Briand Pact.

International Law in Exceptional Times

Liang Yunli's research on the Kellogg–Briand Pact and its legal implications dovetailed with his ongoing diplomatic duties, which entailed serving as a lead delegate for the special League sessions having to do with the Manchuria conflict. He was also prominently cited in the press regarding the latter.[19] In public writings and statements in the United States and in China, Liang vocally endorsed US secretary of state Henry L. Stimson's rejection of Japanese military intervention in China, and sought to explain its legal significance in detail.[20] For Liang:

> The meaning of the word "war" in the Second Hague Conference in 1907, for example, was necessarily different from what it is now. At that time, war was considered as a permissible means of redressing international wrongs. Now it is an illegal thing, as Mr. Stimson calls it. Whatever runs counter to the settlement of disputes by pacific means is war, and as such must be considered as in violation of the Kellogg pact.[21]

These and other positions articulated by Liang in the early 1930s were entirely in keeping with the general view among Chinese political and intellectual figures that Japan's moves were illegitimate. But Liang went further than most in seeking to define the exact nature of their illegality – indeed, with his claim that the Kellogg–Briand Pact prohibited *all* non-Pacific settlement of disputes, he also went beyond Stimson's rather vague positions about force as such (the United States was, notably, still involved in unilateral interventions in Central America at the time). He also excoriated the League, which had not only failed to protect China from invasion but, to the contrary, generated "hypnotic melodies" that had lulled it into a false sense of security. At the same time, while the League was undoubtedly "an imperialist camp," it was also the only then-available forum for China to pursue its aims of transforming international order.[22]

Upon returning to China in 1933, Liang remained highly involved in diplomacy for Chiang's government and also engaged in promoting international law research and study. His unique approach was reflected in his 1934 review of the book *Public International Law Theory* by Li Shengwu, who was by now an official at the Ministry of Foreign Affairs. While praising Li's book as "detailed, logical, and better than most international law textbooks," he added:

> [I]n the next volume, I hope that the author can speak less about the so-called "law of war" and more about the development of the anti-war conception, legal restraints on war, the dividing line between war and legitimate self-defense, the definition of aggression, the theory and practice of the League Covenant and to write more about enforcing sanctions against war based on the Kellogg–Briand Pact, and other such issues.[23]

In his lectures and writings of the 1930s, Liang continue to advocate providing all unilateral uses of force with clear definitions and legal consequences.[24] He also criticized the majority of writers on international law in China who relied on restating existing doctrine, without recognizing that "some classic theories of international law have already been eroded by time and will be overturned." The "painful history of the last 60 years," he said, was in large part because "Chinese have either looked at treaties as scraps of paper or as magical instruments."[25] The best approach, Liang thought, would be for China to seize on the most progressive elements in international law at a global level, and add its own weight to further such existing trends.[26]

One example was Soviet foreign commissar Maxim Litvinov's recent comments at the Geneva Disarmament Conference of 1932–1934, where he had pushed for both more radical disarmament and more specific legal restrictions on warfare.[27] Liang argued that China should be at the forefront of pushing for such progressive transformations of international law, rather than relying primarily on shifting geopolitical alliances and interests for its security. A growing number of other jurists followed suit with similar arguments.[28] The notion of framing a "new international law" became a new watchword among China's young community of international lawyers. Already in 1930, Zhou Wei had anticipated this trend with a book that had that precise phrase as its title.[29] By just a few years later, though, others were going much farther in arguing that there had to be not just evolution, but wholesale replacement of existing doctrine. As it was phrased by a young Wang Tieya, one of Zhou Gengsheng's students of international law at Beijing: "[Lassa] Oppenheim has an extremely consummate theoretical system. It can only be overturned from the foundations, rather than just amended and revised."[30]

Some of the major influences on this new generation of international law scholars were works such as Politis' *Nouvelles Tendances du Droit International*[31] and, especially, the so-called Austrian school of "legal monism" associated with Hans Kelsen. In Kelsen's highly influential thought as developed since 1920, domestic and international law had to be regarded as part of a single, unified structure of authority resting atop a *Grundnorm*, or fundamental legal rule. Wherever generally valid norms conflicted in this unified system, Kelsen gave priority to international law. He thus chose for his *Grundnorm* the traditional legal principle *pacta sunt servanda*: Agreements should be complied with by the parties bound to them.[32] Future generations of legal scholars have been mixed in their appraisals of Kelsen's thought and his *Grundnorm*, and indeed in his own late work he revised its content to be that "states should behave as they have customarily behaved." While both the first and second versions of the *Grundnorm* were dismissed by some other theorists as little more than "tautologies," the first *Grundnorm* and the monist idea of law it supported remains influential to this day among international law practitioners and scholars.

Zhou Gengsheng was particularly acclaimed for embodying a theoretical turn in his 1934 book *New Developments in International Law*, which a fellow jurist would soon after describe as "the first thorough representation in Chinese intellectual circles of the theories of Kelsen, Liszt, Oppenheim, Strupp, Triepel and Verdross."[33] In reality, though, the turn to theory in general, and to notions of monism and limited sovereignty in particular, was a more general intellectual trend among Chinese scholars of law and politics. This might seem puzzling – after all, since the time of the Boxer occupation Chinese diplomats and lawyers had been ever more vocal in calling for protection of China's *zhuquan*. This term had also attained a near apotheosis in the popular reaction to the Treaty of Versailles.

By the early 1930s, however, international lawyers and other scholars were frequently critical of what they viewed as muddled and confused usage of the term. The London-based diplomat Qiu Zuming, for example, had complained in a 1928 essay about widespread imprecise usage of the term *zhuquan* in China. Many, he lamented, used the term to refer simply to "ownership," even that of individuals over personal property and chattels. In reality, he had argued, sovereignty had three genuine components: (1) independence; (2) *dominium*, that is, territorial sovereignty; and (3) *imperium*, that is, political sovereignty or administrative authority over persons.[34] Chinese citizens had to be clear that *zhuquan*'s meaning depended upon context, as well as which of these three aspects were being emphasized.[35]

In his 1934 book, Li Shengwu had articulated a similar complaint, noting that "[i]n conversation, we might sometimes say that a certain item belongs to me by stating that 'I have *zhuquan* over it.'"[36] This led to unrealistic notions of absolute ownership (i.e., private law *dominium*) when translated to international law. Instead, he argued, the real problem was that:

> The sovereignty of the great powers is overextended, and that of the weak states is overly diminished. This is what gives rise to conflict. What public international law needs is for the sovereignty of all states to be protected on an equal basis, and at the same time for sovereignty itself to gradually give way to international law.[37]

Outside of the international law arena, as well, many scholars in other areas of law and political theory were influenced by recent Western trends of deconstructing sovereignty. Critics of the concept such as Harold Laski and Léon Duguit were by now widely influential. As one scholar of politics summarized the emerging *sensus communis* among liberal and socialist intellectuals: "This 'sovereignty' thing is really an abstract term; it's hard to describe the naked truth of it. The only way that we can know it is via the reflection of all the state's various activities into our brains. That's how we experience that there is such a thing as 'sovereignty.'"[38]

The critical analysis of the notion of sovereignty was also promoted by developments such as the ruling of the PCA in the Nanjing government's dispute with the Radio Corporation of America (RCA) over concession rights based on a 1928 agreement. In this historically significant arbitration that marked the extension of PCA jurisdiction to a case involving non-state parties, the PCA ruled that China was indeed bound by its agreement with RCA, and that the latter imposed "obligations . . . upon the Chinese Government of efficient cooperation with the RCA in maintaining [its] privileged position" as a service provider as specified in the agreement. Meanwhile, RCA's claim as to the exclusive nature of the agreement was rejected, as the PCA would not presume a state to limit its inherent sovereign rights without clear textual evidence. That allowance for sovereignty, of course, was less significant than the principle of enforcing a private company's claims against a state that the other parts of the decision entailed. The *RCA* v. *Republic of China* arbitration thus presaged a later age of investor–state dispute settlement arbitrations that, many have argued, limit the autonomy of newly decolonized states.[39]

An increasingly critical perspective on the coherence of absolutist doctrines of state sovereignty made sense for jurists in a state whose territory was as of the early 1930s still subject to foreign military incursions based on vague international law doctrines and whose policy autonomy was still sharply limited by agreements with Western states (and, now, corporations). The notion of *coequal* sovereignty within the framework of international legal relations and institutions such as the League was far more relevant than a notional unrestricted autarky. The ultimately successful invocation of *rebus sic stantibus* in the Belgian dispute, and the mixed outcome in the RCA matter, like the fate of Manchuria in the League debates, underscored for jurists that it was through reforms to international law doctrine and practice, not the setting up of a simplistic sovereignty/international law distinction, that China's autonomy might be secured.

Nonetheless, the same jurists espousing such views continued to insist that China's coequal status in international law and in particular its *territorial* sovereignty, that is, its *dominium eminens*, had indeed been regularly violated by foreign states and most recently by Japan in Manchuria. Zhou Gengsheng maintained his status as the most energetic exponent of China's "revolutionary diplomacy" on the basis of popular sovereignty by calling for boycotts of Japanese goods, international economic sanctions, and/or nonrecognition of Japan's claims by foreign states as legitimate forms of reprisal for its violations of the legal prohibition on unilateral aggression.[40] Although such views became ever more prevalent among jurists and the general intelligentsia, they coexisted with other tendencies that lay in radically different directions. If Zhou and others on the Guomindang "left" and liberal flanks still placed their emphasis on the people as *pouvoir constituant*, and constructed their legal arguments on this basis, the ascendant Guomindang right wing surrounding Chiang Kai-shek sought to invoke state sovereignty as a basis for personalistic rule and dictatorial authority – almost as Yuan had done in the 1910s.

Several jurists found themselves pressured to support these efforts, sometimes being dragooned into turning their studies into sources of legitimation for Chiang's rule. This was particularly common for those whose studies had been conducted under the auspices of Guomindang funding. At Nanjing's National University of Governance in 1933, a student from a poor background named Zhou Ziya became one of the institution's first graduates in its new foreign relations and diplomacy program, which included the study of international law. He and three others soon after accompanied the Guomindang's ambassador to Nazi Germany, where Zhou studied international law at the University of Berlin from 1936 to 1938, and found himself upon returning to China compelled to write alongside his scholarly work encomiums to justify Chiang's political dominance in National Socialist–style terms of "One Ideology, One Government, One Leader."[41] Other jurists and diplomats in wartime Chongqing had to balance similar demands of showing political fealty with use of their academic expertise.[42]

Another young international lawyer who completed advanced study in Berlin, Jiang Haichao, also demonstrated the unique position of his profession at this time. While in Germany from 1929, Jiang had studied in Frankfurt under Karl Strupp, who was a leading theorist and historian of international law with a sociologically informed approach.[43] Though Strupp was dismissed in 1933 for his Jewish ancestry, Jiang continued his studies and graduated with a PhD in 1936, then went on to conduct research at the prestigious Institut für Völkerrecht und ausländisches öffentliches Recht at the University of Berlin. In internal Guomindang personnel files, Jiang capitalized on connections with prestigious 1930s German legal figures like Walter Simons, Heinrich Triepel, and Carl Schmitt via his research at the institute. Such elite foreign connections and public law expertise were praised by his Guomindang superiors, and they approved of his study of "Theories of Authoritarian Politics" – "authoritarian" being used here in a highly positive sense.[44] After the breakout of all-out invasion by Japan in 1937, Jiang and other jurists in wartime Chongqing simultaneously wrote in (often perfunctory) support of Chiang's dictatorship and called for increased steps toward internationalism, such as founding an Association for International Law and International Relations Research to focus on the "new international law" that China should proactively help to shape in the coming postwar era.[45]

If many international lawyers under the Guomindang negotiated these political pressures, others reacted made more radical decisions. Zhou Wei went to work for the Wang Jingwei collaborationist regime after the bloody occupation of Nanjing,[46] perhaps viewing Japan as the lesser of two evils in a coming East–West confrontation. He had recently argued that equal to Japan's incursions was how "[Western] foreign naval vessels can sail into the Yangtze, all the way to Sichuan."[47] Li Shengwu, too, who had been regarded as one of China's most promising new scholars of international law, also went to work for Wang and would eventually rise to the position of foreign minister.[48] On trial after the war, he would claim, implausibly, that he had in fact sought to undermine the puppet regime all along. Ding Shiyuan, by now a general and elder statesman, decided to go into service for the Manchukuo regime. All three found themselves swept up into Japanese projects of regional hegemony in Asia that were justified in terms of a "great space" order along the lines of the US Monroe Doctrine, or by invoking the Weberian trope of a "community of fate" (*unmei kyōdōtai*) among Asian peoples – under Japan's "leadership."

That path was, of course, rejected by most rising young international lawyers, even if they shared a distaste for the Chiang regime and its ongoing efforts toward dictatorial rule. Among those who would later exert great influence were Li Haopei, Wang Tieya, and Han Depei, who all went to elite Western institutions to study international law. Li and Wang arrived at the London School of Economics in 1936 and 1937, respectively. When, upon arrival, Wang met the prominent international lawyer Hersch Lauterpacht, he was asked by the latter "Why do so many of you Chinese students want to study the law of treaties?" Wang replied to the effect that "China has been oppressed by unequal treaties for many years, and the joint aspiration of the whole people is to overcome these treaties; accomplishing that historical mission is the reason for us to study this subject." He would later recount that Lauterpacht had found this a convincing response.[49] Han, meanwhile, began his studies at the University of Toronto in 1939 and then from 1942 continued his research as a fellow at Harvard Law School, where he studied and wrote on former dean Roscoe Pound's sociological jurisprudence and Hans Kelsen's pure theory of law. At the same time, he and other Chinese students read publications such as Mao Zedong's "On New Democracy" and debated the best path forward for China's political future.[50]

From the Atlantic Charter to the Pacific

Somewhat removed from the changing discourses of international law during the 1930s was Wang Chonghui. At the end of his PCIJ term in 1935, Wang was replaced on the body by Zheng Tianxi, the fellow Hong Konger with whom he had collaborated at the Washington Conference and in the subsequent, ultimately stymied attempts to overturn extraterritoriality. Wang then served again as minister of foreign affairs and then, from 1938, as secretary-general of the Supreme Council of National Defense.[51] His return to domestic politics at the highest level was a delicate proposition, given infighting within the Guomindang and his own tenuous relations with Chiang. Nonetheless, while based in Chongqing, he continued working actively to promote internationalist ideas about which Chiang himself was ambivalent but that were shared by other scholars and diplomats, many of them remnants of the Guomindang left.

In 1942, Wang responded to the new developments in international law heralded by Franklin Roosevelt and Winston Churchill's signing of the Atlantic Charter the previous year – with its renunciation of "territorial changes that do not accord with the freely expressed wishes of the peoples concerned" – by again publicly advocating the need for a clear definition of war and firm legal restrictions of aggression.[52] As the war came to a close, these and other aims important to Chinese internationalists would translate into initiatives to influence postwar order.

In a speech at the Yale University Dining Hall in New Haven, Connecticut on June 9, 1942, recently appointed Chinese foreign minister T. V. Soong informed students and alumni that "China, with all other liberty-loving nations, will gladly cede such of its sovereign powers as may be required" to create "an effective world instrument to dispense and enforce justice." The content of that justice, though, he proceeded to define differently from the mainstream of Anglo-American discourse. Though never contradicting the policies articulated in Roosevelt and Churchill's recently signed Atlantic Charter, his remarks, delivered upon receiving an honorary law degree, focused on rereading the charter's text to support "political freedom and economic justice for Asia." Rather than Asia continuing to serve for the West as a realm "of concessions [or as] a source of raw materials," he advocated "the freedom of all Asiatic nations." Soong drew on language such as that of Article 3, which asserted "the right of all peoples to choose the form of government under which they will live" and the "wish to see sovereign rights and self-government restored to those who have been forcibly deprived of them."[53]

Since the charter's signing, however, its applicability to non-European questions was being called into question. In parliament on September 9, 1941, Churchill had even assured MPs that the charter "does not qualify in any way the various statements of [existing] policy ... about the development of constitutional government in India, Burma or other parts of the British Empire."[54] Rather, it had been aimed at "the restoration of the sovereignty, self-government and national life of the States and nations of Europe now under the Nazi yoke."[55] Even the premise that the charter was meant to apply globally, which Roosevelt had certainly intended, was now being called into question by the British side.

By this point, the charter had, however, already sparked various "creative" readings and appropriations, like Soong's, by representatives of marginalized states and peoples around the world. Nelson Mandela, for example, was also invoking the charter in the name of his African National Congress Party's efforts to achieve self-determination for non-whites in South Africa.[56] Mohandas Gandhi, too, sent a letter to Roosevelt in July 1942 in which he noted that Western slogans about freedom and democracy "sound[ed] hollow, so long as India, and for that matter, Africa are exploited by Great Britain, and America has the Negro problem in her own home."[57] Earlier that year, Chiang had made a trip to India in which he met with Gandhi and Nehru, and sought to build on the latter's enthusiasm for an "eastern federation," previously expressed during a visit to Chongqing in 1939. Given China's reliance on Western support to win the war, however, the prospects for any radical anticolonial solidarity were limited.[58]

Nonetheless, internal planning at high levels of the Guomindang in 1942 explored the possibility of taking concrete steps in this direction. In July, Wang Chonghui reported to Chiang on the need to supplement the Atlantic Charter with a "Pacific Charter" that would address the concerns of China and states in its region. Taking note of Churchill's attempts to limit the Atlantic Charter's scope and preserve Britain's colonial empire, Wang described the Roosevelt–Churchill document's explicit content as entailing no more than a "passive self-determination." By contrast, China's interests and values would require developing a principle of "positive self-determination," for: "There are a vast number of colonies in the Pacific region. We deeply hope that after the war this situation can be adjusted on the basis of the principle of the self-determination of peoples."[59] Wang's July 7 draft of a "Pacific Charter" included three articles:

(1) The principles of the Atlantic Charter, particularly relating to the disarmament of aggressor states and national self-determination, among others, are applicable at the global level.
(2) Japan's territory is to be restored to its state in 1894, before the initiation of its policies of conquest.
(3) All peoples and all races are equal. All are key elements of world peace and progress.[60]

Policies of decolonization, which had received only indirect and contestable endorsement in the Atlantic Charter, were here made concrete. Clearly, the text focuses primarily on Japan's expansionist aggression, including the specific proviso of territorial adjustment back to the country's 1894 borders. Yet, especially articulated at a time when it was Japan that occupied the vast majority of Asian territory, the juxtaposition of territorial sovereignty with principles of self-determination, and of racial equality, also set forth a challenge to the general prewar status quo. A handover of colonies back to their European masters would not meet the region's aspirations. In a more detailed proposal for postwar organization that Wang outlined in an address to the Chinese Political Science Association in Chongqing, he laid out the positions that:

> a "United States of Nations" should be organized with the objectives of: (1) peaceful settlement of all international disputes; (2) strict prohibition of the use of force between nations; (3) a clear-cut definition of aggression; (4) establishment of a permanent machinery for the implementation of sanctions, whether diplomatic, economic, or military; and (5) reconsideration of treaties which became inapplicable and consideration of international conditions whose continuance might endanger peace.[61]

There were few illusions among China's foreign policy and international law community about the scope of the charter as formulated, but there was some hope that it could be built upon. Zhou Gengsheng also became a staunch advocate of the idea that China should seek both to promote full Japanese demilitarization and take the lead in establishing a regional association – perhaps even a "United Nations of the Pacific" (*Taipingyang Lianheguo*) – that could both promote stability and security and also, in the long-term, help to spur decolonization.[62]

As part of Wang's mid 1942 plan, he also called for an "international police organization" that could enforce sanctions against norm violators. This perceived need for a strong international executive authority was by then a consistent theme for China's diplomats. T. V. Soong, too, advocated the need for an "Executive Council" for the new organization.[63] In a speech at Wellesley College, the alma mater of the Soong sisters, Hu Shih noted that "any attempt to set up a jural order of the nations without some overwhelming force to back its own law and judgment will inevitably be scrapped in face of determined armed aggression."[64] It was only in July of the following year that the idea of an "Executive Committee" for the UN would clearly appear in the Draft Constitution of International Organization produced by the US State Department's Special Subcommittee on International Organization.[65]

The emphasis on a global executive authority was vividly on display at the Cairo Conference of November 22–26, 1943, where Chiang met Roosevelt and Churchill to discuss wartime and postwar plans. Earlier that year, the State Department's chief of the Division of Far Eastern Affairs Maxwell Hamilton had emphasized the importance of keeping China in the war. To do so, he raised a stark hypothetical: "China's continuance as an active belligerent on the side of the United Nations is the best insurance that the present war not become a race war."[66] These concerns over race were, he thought "extremely important not only for the present but for the long future as well."[67] Anticolonial struggles now burgeoning in the region had showed that any stable postwar order would need a non-Western power as one of its linchpins.

At Cairo, Roosevelt affirmed China's status as one of the "Big Four" of the projected postwar order. The notions of decolonization and racial equality that Wang had included in his Pacific Charter draft were not endorsed at Cairo. Indeed, Chiang's delegation itself seems to have diluted its demands in this regard, as the official memorandum of the Chinese government handed by Wang to US diplomats on November 24 did not press these issues. Instead, it only alluded to decolonization by recommending that "[f]or the settlement of questions relating to territories in the Pacific, China, Great Britain, and the United States should agree upon certain basic principles and also establish a Committee of Experts to make recommendations for the settlement of these questions."[68] Perhaps, under the auspices of such a committee, the principle of self-determination could be further concretized. However, in the event, even this softened plan could not win the assent of the United States and Great Britain. The final communiqué instead simply indicated that:

> Japan shall be stripped of all the islands in the Pacific which she has seized or occupied since the beginning of the first World War in 1914, and that all the territories Japan has stolen from the Chinese, such as Manchuria, Formosa, and The Pescadores, shall be restored to the Republic of China. Japan will also be expelled from all other territories which she has taken by violence and greed.[69]

The fate of former colonies once Japan was "expelled" was not spelled out. Moreover, rather than 1894, the communiqué only asserted that Japan's territorial gains since 1931 would be reversed (although Formosa's handover seemed to constitute a de facto adoption of the former date). On one point, though, Chinese suggestions clearly influenced the outcome of the communiqué. Rather than make any reference to "trusteeship" over Korea, its text explicitly declared that "[t]he aforesaid three great powers, mindful of the enslavement of the people of Korea, are determined that in due course Korea shall become free and independent."[70] If, however, Wang's draft had stood for a general principle of self-determination that would apply to colonial possessions, such as, for example, Hong Kong, Vietnam, or Indonesia as much as to Korea, such possibilities were now basically invisible in the final text. Indeed, as late as 1945, Winston Churchill would reject US suggestions regarding the handover of Hong Kong to China, going so far as to declare that "Hongkong will be eliminated from the British Empire only over my dead body." When challenged on the basis of Atlantic Charter language on self-determination, he would reply that "Britain is not bound by the principles of the Atlantic Charter at all."[71]

Diverging Visions

Back in China, the domestic political order was undergoing shifts alongside those now unfolding in the global war situation. In March 1943, Chiang (likely via a team of ghostwriters) had produced a long tract entitled *China's Destiny and Chinese Economic Theory* (*Zhongguo zhi Mingyun* 中國之命運), which laid out an official account of Chinese history, the "national shame" (*Guochi* 國恥) and crisis endured since the Opium War, and Chiang's vision for restoration.[72] The potent variant of nationalism that informed the work included various critiques of the effects of Communist activities in the country, which Chiang blamed for economic collapse through disruption of existing economic structures in rural areas (i.e., land redistribution), among various other ills – although the war had by then forced him into renewed Nationalist–Communist cooperation. Chiang countered leftist economics with a vision of national planning that directly drew on the conservative-protectionist thought of Friedrich List and Othmar Spann, and praised the latter's corporatist philosophy as more suited to China's traditions than liberalism or communism.[73]

Overall, the vision of *China's Destiny* suggested a strong executive leading a polity that was disciplined into obedience along vaguely Confucian lines, while pursuing rapid economic development and modernization (implicitly under the direction of those closest to the regime). The Chinese Communist Party, and its sympathizers abroad such as the American communist journalist Phillip Jaffe, frequently described this Guomindang-rightist vision as "feudal-fascist."[74] In one of many acts of compelled subservience to Chiang, Wang Chonghui was obliged to attach his name to the book's official English translation,[75] though there is little indication that he approved of its ideas about China's future course.

Ideological views and geopolitical preferences were, however, still diverse at the very pinnacle of the regime, indeed even within the Chiang/Soong extended family. Despite his longtime status as China's leading banker, T. V. Soong, in his public comments, often advocated Soviet-style economic planning and even spoke of a "present world trend . . . away from capitalism and toward general social and economic justice in which the common man would have greater rights and greater powers."[76] As with decolonization, his views on economic matters (and corresponding openness to improved Sino-Soviet relations) were more radical than those that Chiang was willing to publicly endorse.

On a number of issues, Soong found himself excluded from policymaking, often replaced by his brother-in-law, vice premier and minister of finance H. H. Kung (Kong Xiangxi), who since 1933 had also been Soong's successor as governor of the Central Bank of China. As husband of the eldest Soong sister, Soong Ai-ling, Kung had been part of the Guomindang's "ruling family" since 1914, and came from a line of Shanxi bankers that claimed Confucius as a direct ancestor – by the 1930s, he was widely known as both a seventy-fifth-generation descendant of the Sage and as China's richest man, with views on Confucian morality and staunch anticommunism befitting both personas.[77] At the first annual ceremony to worship Confucius on the Sage's birthday that the Chiang regime instated in the summer of 1941, Kung referred to Roosevelt and Churchill's recent Atlantic Charter as simply reiterating what Confucius "had already seen 2,400 years ago" in his advocacy of *datong*.[78] Neither cooperation with the Soviet Union nor the promotion of decolonization was a feature of Kung's vision of China's global role.

During the war years, Kung worked as one of Chiang's most trusted representatives, and was also responsible for significant efforts in foreign policy. His successful negotiation in 1942 of a US$500 million interest-free loan from the United States under the lend-lease program, including US$220 million in gold bullion, was often regarded as "saving" the wartime economy and would go on to form the basis for the Republic of China's postwar finances.[79] T. V. Soong, however, suggested somewhat darkly in public comments soon after that what China faced was "a bigger job than even $500,000,000 or a billion dollars can do"; unless China could receive US$5–10 billion–worth of credit, it would be unable to complete meaningful reconstruction.[80]

Kung does not ever seem to have adopted such a confrontational tone. Overall, he displayed an ingratiating approach when he led China's delegation at the UN Monetary and Financial Conference held at Bretton Woods, New Hampshire on July 1–22, 1944. There, Kung closely collaborated with American treasury secretary Henry Morgenthau, Jr., serving as chairman of the Committee on Rules and Regulations while his fellow Chinese delegate, Jiang Tingfu, chaired the important Committee on Purposes, Policies, and Quotas. Overall, the Chinese side played an important supporting role, endorsing US objectives both rhetorically and during most votes. The official conference materials even listed Kung's status as a "75th generation descendant of Confucius," and he hosted a number of events intended to foster *esprit de corps* among attendees. In remarks on July 7, 1944, he noted that while China faced massive postwar challenges, he would "take this opportunity to assure you that China will offer her foreign friends opportunity for investment and provide protection for such investment."[81]

At the conference, Kung's only major divergences with Anglo-American views came over two issues. One was the size of China's allocated quota, which represented both voting power and borrowing rights from the International Monetary Fund that was to be established. On July 15, Kung issued a reservation over China's "insufficient" quota, though he dropped it five days later, after lobbying from the United States and Great Britain, saying that "[w]e made the reservation because we are facing real difficulties but … China is ready to make further sacrifices and to cooperate with the friendly nations 100 percent in order to make this Conference a complete success."[82]

Though Kung and other conservative elements in the Guomindang were still strong in mid 1944, they were forced to collaborate with left-leaning and liberal figures, and minority parties, who had their own visions of both the future domestic and international order. Among the efforts from these circles was, in mid 1944, the birth of a new dedicated association for the study and advancement of international law. The China Society of International Law (*Zhongguo Guoji Fa Xuehui* 中國國際法學會) was founded on May 12 in Chongqing, with Sun Yat-sen's son, the sitting president of the Legislative Yuan, Sun Fo, serving as the group's chairman.[83] Its Executive Committee included Wang Shijie, Guo Taiqi, Hsieh Guansheng, and Wang Chonghui, who was also head of its Research Division. Members had to have studied international law for at least ten years, and to have produced well-regarded publications on the subject. These strict requirements, but above all the leadership by Sun and other high-level political figures, gave the new society a prestige that could conceivably come to approach that of the American Society of International Law (ASIL) in the United States (upon which it was modeled). Indeed, at about the same time, Wang Chonghui was also made an honorary ASIL member, the first Chinese person to receive this distinction.[84]

Overall, the organization's stated goals included focusing on promoting consistency between domestic and international law, sponsoring research and study, including via library constructions and scholarships for students in the field, and also holding public-oriented informative lectures and events involving foreign diplomats and scholars.[85] At its inaugural meeting of about forty members, however, Wang articulated a more ambitious vision, including the hopes that:

> International law would undergo a fundamental transformation; that after the war it would be possible to compile a Code of International Law (*yi bu guoji fadian* 一部國際法典); that international morality and custom could be turned into enacted norms of international law.[86]

At the same inaugural event, Guo Taiqi, who would later be appointed as China's first permanent representative to the UN, issued another call for genuine sanctions to enforce international law, such that it could have real compelling force between states. These and the other aims of the society's members would very soon have new forums for their expression, albeit not infrequently being frustrated by geopolitics.

From Dumbarton Oaks to San Francisco

During the Bretton Woods meetings, preparations for the Dumbarton Oaks conversations to determine the shape of the planned postwar organization for international peace and security were already well underway. Chinese officials tried to ensure meaningful representation at this important forum, but faced the problem of continued Soviet neutrality vis-à-vis Japan – the same pretext that had left them excluded from the Tehran and Yalta conferences, at the latter of which Chinese claims to Outer Mongolia had been rejected and Russian naval use of Dalian (Port Arthur) promised to Stalin. Though coming before the latter developments, anxiety over the possible repercussions of an all-Western parlay at Dumbarton Oaks is patent in Chiang Kai-shek's June 2 note to Roosevelt, in which he stated that "If there is no representative from the Orient, then this meeting will lose [all] significance for half of the human race."[87]

Nonetheless, the Chinese side had little choice but to accept the plan of a two-phase conference, the first involving the United States, Great Britain, and the Soviet Union from August 21 to September 28, and the second involving China, the United States, and Great Britain from September 29 to October 7.[88] It did not escape the notice of Chinese participants, meanwhile, that this arrangement tended to heavily favor the United States and Great Britain over the Chinese side (and to a lesser degree the Soviets) as far as attaining consensus upon their respective objectives. Indeed, the key structural aspects of the UN, such as the basic designs of the Security Council and General Assembly, were already decided by the start of the sessions that included China. Nonetheless, there was hope that China's delegation, led by Wellington Koo, would be able to influence key features of the new organization.

In advance of the meetings, officials on the Chinese side conferred over the positions that China should adopt. T. V. Soong noted that it was likely the Security Council would be expanded beyond just the Big Four allied powers, and suggested that China might support Canada, Brazil, the Philippines, and/or liberated France as members.[89] The first two, in particular, had long had relatively favorable relations with China – much more so than Australia with its "White Australia" policies, for instance. However, a key question was the status of regional organizations, which Latin American states had sought to ensure would retain a substantial degree of autonomy. For Soong, based on recent trends, it now seemed very unfavorable for China that a regional organization be established in the Asia-Pacific region. Rather than only reaching agreements with the United States, Great Britain, and the Soviets, China would then find itself negotiating with "Australia, New Zealand, France, Holland, and India" on regional matters.[90]

A formal regional framework, Soong now thought, would in the end actually dilute China's role and status. It would be better to "pursue other approaches to try and attain hegemony/leadership authority in the Far East (*yuandong lingdaoquan* 遠東領導權)," such as creating a regional consultative mechanism based in Chongqing.[91] There was some tension between these ambitions for Chinese "leadership" and the more egalitarian version of decolonization that Soong articulated in his public statements, though given China's experiences with the various colonial dominions on its doorstep, it made some sense that he might be concerned that a regional institution would allow it to be outvoted by unfriendly interests. Half a year later, Soong would summarize China's "three [main] proposals" at Dumbarton that had been accepted by the other parties:

> 1) that international disputes should be settled on the basis of justice and public international law; 2) that the codification of international law should be pursued; 3) that there should be educational and cultural cooperation and exchange.[92]

These and other points were brought up by Wellington Koo at the October 3 plenary session of the conference, in the Chinese delegation's most comprehensive set of proposals. They focused overwhelmingly on international law and, in particular, on restricting the use of force. As a vastly weaker state compared with the United States or Soviet Union, or even the beleaguered but still potent British Empire, China could not count upon its own wealth and power to ensure territorial integrity or autonomy. The replacement of the League with a new organization seemed to China's delegates like a chance to build in true legal safeguards against aggression by strong states against their weaker peers.[93]

Most dramatically, China's delegates reiterated the proposal for an "international air force" that could centralize legitimate uses of force under the direction of the UN, rather than leaving deployments of force up to the discretion of individual states. Unlike some other iterations of such a plan, the Chinese version of 1944 also involved abolishing national air forces. This would, of course, have been the most radical measure of multilateral disarmament in world history, before or since.[94] This proposal, which had had some support from the Soviet side (though they had had internal reservations), was effectively vetoed by the two Atlantic powers.[95]

Another proposal, for including in the UN Charter a commitment to the compulsory adjudication of international disputes via the new International Court of Justice (ICJ), was also rejected by the United States and Great Britain. In their view, the natural result of such a clause would be that the Security Council would in some instances become a mere enforcement arm of the Court, making the judicial body into the most powerful institution in the international system. Such important *Realpolitik* features of the new arrangement as the Security Council veto would then be relativized or nullified. This was far too much "rule of law" to handle.[96]

Similar themes related to the restriction of aggression characterized another proposal. This was to include an explicit commitment in the UN Charter to member states' "political independence and territorial integrity." Such language had previously been found in League Covenant Article 10, which included a positive commitment by members "to respect and preserve as against external aggression the territorial integrity and existing political independence of all Members of the League." This Article had been at the center of several of the intra-League disputes that ultimately prompted its dissolution. Against such a background, Koo's "Article X phraseology" seemed to the Western delegates like a repeat of one of the covenant's mistakes: Too much legalization of the existing status quo, too little room left for "peaceful change" by adroit diplomatic consensus.[97] They also argued that political independence and territorial integrity were already implicitly protected in Article 2's prohibition on aggression.[98]

This, however, was the whole point of the Chinese side's position: Article 10 of the covenant had indeed prohibited "external aggression" as early as 1919. Yet this had not saved China from subsequent uses of force by great powers – especially Japan, but also, if on vastly smaller scales, various incidents or threats involving each of its current postwar allies. Moreover, in its experience of international law ever since the 1830s, China had been subjected to interventions and occupations that invariably were given justifications as something other than war per se: usually "reprisal" or defense of nationals. As of 1945, there was still no satisfying response to the point Ding Shiyuan had first raised at the Hague in 1907 to a chorus of laughter from the Western delegates, and that had since occupied many Chinese diplomats and lawyers: Could uses of force, as such, be multilaterally defined and limited in such a way as to prevent aggressors from portraying their own acts as justified?

The last of China's proposals rejected by the United States and Great Britain was directly related to this issue. This was, simply, to provide a clear definition of "aggression" in the UN Charter.[99] The Soviet Union had previously made such a proposal, only to face Anglo-American stonewalling. The same fate befell the Chinese attempt, including Koo's proposal that specific examples of aggression could be explicitly agreed upon in order to facilitate identification of future cases. The United States and Great Britain objected to the constraints this would place upon the Security Council, which should instead determine such matters on a "case-by-case basis."[100] The political institution of the Security Council would be entrusted to handle such matters, not lawyers or judges.

There was, however, one more opportunity to make a last-ditch effort at establishing a true binding effect for international law, especially in relation to interstate disputes. This comprised the meetings of the Committee of Jurists that met from April 9 to April 20, 1945 to finalize a draft statute of the new ICJ, which would then be presented for a vote at San Francisco. During these discussions, Wang Chonghui represented China (based on T. V. Soong's nomination),[101] and he became one of the most vocal advocates for a stronger Court. Indeed, he boldly tried to reintroduce into the ICJ statute the same norm the United States and Great Britain had already rejected at Dumbarton Oaks: compulsory adjudication of disputes, "chang[ing] from an optional to a non-optional basis."[102]

The key proceedings at which the noncompulsory nature of ICJ jurisdiction was decided were on April 12 and 13. At the sixth meeting of the committee, Article 36 of the statute, on jurisdiction, came up for a discussion that began with an American draft providing for optional jurisdiction similar to that under the PCIJ. Wang argued that due to changing public opinion, the vast majority of states having already adopted the optional clause, and support from legal groups such as the American and Canadian bar associations, the time had come for truly compulsory jurisdiction. He was supported by the representatives of Brazil, Turkey, Ethiopia, and various Latin American states, among others, but encountered joint US, Soviet, and British opposition.[103]

Indeed, the Soviet representative was one of the first to reject Wang's position, because "the majority of authorities on international law were always inclined in favor of a voluntary and not compulsory jurisdiction," and, moreover, "he could also [just as easily] cite reverse views of American lawyers on this matter" to those that Wang had mentioned.[104] It is deeply ironic that not only were the Soviet Union and United States standing together in April 1945 to deflect Third World states' demands for compulsory Court jurisdiction – the Soviet side even pointed to the prevailing views within the elite of America's bourgeois legal profession in order to do so.

In supporting Wang's position, the Mexican delegate Roberto Cordova argued that "[t]he discussion at San Francisco would be political. Here we should not hesitate to draft that kind of document which seems best from a juridical point of view."[105] The Ethiopian representative Ambaye Woldemariam also made the point that "no substantial changes have as yet been made in the Statute [from that of the PCIJ], and ... it would be a disappointment to humanity if the Statute were to go without the improvement ... [thus] we must be a little braver."[106] Lopez-Herrarte of Guatemala supported the measure saying that he "agreed with the representative of China that the world was ready for changes in the direction of achieving real justice."[107]

Following a lack of resolution of the question that afternoon, it was picked up again the following morning. However, a dramatic event cast something of a pall over the ensuing discussion: President Roosevelt had died the previous afternoon. Opening the April 13 meeting with commemorative remarks, the US delegate Green H. Hackworth awkwardly but emphatically tied this news to the ongoing dispute over compulsory jurisdiction:

> I am glad we did not vote last evening and I trust that we shall not now vote on this particular issue ... I should very much dislike to see us at this particular time take sides on this issue ... I should not like to see this group so sharply divided ... After all, what we are trying to do is to frame a plan for a court which all of the United Nations will be able to accept. None of us would wish that our work should have the result of making it impossible for any state represented here to join in supporting the International Court.[108]

Far better, Hackworth thought, would be for the jurists to adopt the advice that had been given by Elihu Root to American delegates to the Second Hague Conference: "In the discussions upon every question, it is important to remember that the object of the conference is agreement and not compulsion."[109] Next to speak was Wang Chonghui, as representative of those advocating compulsory jurisdiction. He tactfully but firmly refuted Hackworth's strained invocation of the American diplomatic policy of 1907 to embody the will of the international community in 1945: "We could not pay a higher tribute to this great man [Roosevelt]," Wang said, "than by doing our best to contribute toward the realization of his cherished ideal of an international organization for peace and security based on justice and sovereign equality of all peace-loving nations."[110]

However, it was clear that the matter was at an impasse. A number of delegates who had initially expressed support for the compulsory jurisdiction idea subsequently declared that they would stay neutral on the matter given the US–Soviet opposition and the uncertain atmosphere after the president's death. An unusual compromise approach was reached whereby a special subcommittee would be created to draft a potential alternative version of Article 36, which would be presented to the San Francisco Conference alongside the American version. That subcommittee was created the same afternoon, with Wang Chonghui and the delegates of Brazil, Mexico, Cuba, and Venezuela as members. Wang was elected as chairman, and the final proposed language of the draft article was nearly identical with what he had earlier suggested.[111]

The "alternative" article that followed was, of course, regarded as merely symbolic by the delegates that had not supported it. Another proposal that Wang made on the same day, though, was more successful. At the April 13 session, he suggested that the General Assembly (in addition to the Security Council) should be given the explicit right to independently request advisory opinions from the Court, thus continuing the League precedent. As to this, perhaps mindful of the need to manage the anger of Third World delegates whose jurisdictional ambitions had just been overridden by the great powers, Hackworth said he had "no objections ... [and] no strong conviction."[112] There followed a vote of 27 in favor and none opposed.

For neither of Wang's proposals was he able to count on any aid from his fellow former PCIJ judge Manley Hudson of the United States, who had joined the Court in the term after Wang's 1935 departure. Though Hudson did not take the floor to oppose Wang's proposal for compulsory jurisdiction, he was specifically asked by fellow delegates to share his views – and in response simply stated that he had no opinion.[113] Given the lenient voting threshold for amendments, support for his bench colleague from Hudson might well have secured compulsory jurisdiction a place in the draft – though it would have still faced difficulty at San Francisco.

On the eve of the San Francisco Conference, Secretary of State Stettinius made the following summary of the "proposals put forward by the Chinese Government" that the other three leading Allied powers had accepted for inclusion in the UN Charter:

(1) The charter should provide specifically that adjustment or settlement of international disputes should be achieved with due regard for principles of justice and international law.
(2) The Assembly should be responsible for initiating studies and making recommendations with respect to the development and revision of the rules and principles of international law.
(3) The Economic and Social Council should specifically provide for the promotion of education and other forms of cultural cooperation.[114]

While these three principles were indeed incorporated into the charter, with regards to the issue of compulsory jurisdiction, politics won the day just as Cordova had predicted. The subcommittee's draft article was not adopted. However, the final version of the statute did include Wang's suggested right of the General Assembly to request advisory opinions. In the time since, this has become an important means for the development of international law on issues not yet litigated before the Court – one whose full impact may have yet to be felt.[115]

Conclusion

Throughout the interwar period, Chinese diplomat/jurists' attempts to increase China's agency and consolidate its status independent of management by foreign powers (usually) coincided with an aim to increase international law's role in world affairs and further its development in general. The career of Wang Chonghui, particularly from his roles at Versailles and Washington through his appointment as China's first international judge and then his important contributions at the ICJ planning conference, was emblematic of this synergy. So too, though, were the international law writings and advocacy of those who followed very different political paths and who embraced different visions of possible future regional and world orders. Perhaps the most important global trend, and one in which a number of Chinese jurists played an outspoken role, was that of shifting the scales of discourse on issues of state sovereignty.

The consistent antiinterventionist Chinese position took on a greater conceptual significance with the development of ever more clear and technical positions on international law, peaceful dispute settlement, and the use of force: the absolute prohibition on wars of aggression; the need to clearly *define* aggression; the creation of an international air force to centralize global policy decisions on the use of military force; and, in general, the promotion of international law (and ICJ jurisdiction) as core features of the new UN framework. In the Chinese context, these aims were perceived as consistent with the by-now fully entrenched aim of protecting *zhuquan* – indeed, they helped to endow the latter with its concrete meaning.

At the same time, there were still diverging ways of approaching this concept. Freedom from external military intervention and the formalization of global decision-making according to legally defined norms, processes, and structures could indeed add real substance to the often empty assurances of Chinese *imperium* and territorial integrity that were *de rigueur* since 1901. Though something of the balance between *imperium* and *dominium* had been shifted in China's own domestic context by the time it finally emerged as one of (and much the weakest of) the Big Four Allied powers, there remained very little independent agency available to Chinese actors in the global economic sphere. The coming renewed civil war between the Communist Party and the Guomindang would see the contest of different forms of internationalism, ideas of sovereignty, and property relations.

9

Perpetual Peace

When the United Nations (UN) Charter was adopted on June 26, 1945, China's delegates were given the honor of being the first to sign, as their country had been at war longer than the other powers.[1] The signers were, in order: Wellington Koo; Wang Chonghui; Wei Daoming, the sitting Chinese ambassador to the United States; Wu Yifang, a prominent politician and president of Ginling Women's College; Li Huang, a leader of the Guomindang-aligned China Youth Party; Zhang Junmai; Dong Biwu, a moderate intellectual member of the Communist Party Central Committee, later to serve atop the People's Republic of China's (PRC's) Supreme People's Court and as a titular head of state; and Hu Lin, the editor of the left-leaning but technically unaffiliated *Da Gong Bao* newspaper. The third-party delegates found themselves situated uncomfortably between the Guomindang and the Communist Party in a tense postwar climate. Taken as a whole, China's young but increasingly vocal community of international lawyers found themselves in much the same situation.

The Monist Moment

The inclusion at San Francisco of representatives from Chiang's Communist rivals as well as the leading third parties was the result of both internal and external pressure, partially intensified by Chiang's (and Kung's) recent scandals, as well as the sense among some in the US State Department that the Communists might be induced to favor autonomy from the Soviet Union and limit their immediate aims for vying for power within a coalition government. The Communist representative Dong Biwu, who had studied law in Japan, frequently sought to reinforce hopes for a long-term united front. He spoke in particular of "coordinat[ing] my efforts [at San Francisco] with those of Mr. Li Huang and Mr. Carson Chang [Zhang Junmai]" of the third-party Democratic League, with the aim that "through our united efforts a democratic China can be realized. Otherwise there will be no permanent peace [or] freedom for the people of China or for the people of [the] world."[2]

Between August 1945 and April 1946, the Communist Party and Guomindang were engaged in negotiations aimed at determining the possibility and terms of a unity government. In the "double-tenth agreement" of October 1945, both sides agreed to recognition of each other's legal status and committed to pursuing constitutional governance. The next phase of negotiations came with the convening of the Political Consultative Conference (PCC), involving both parties and also, in key roles, members of third parties and other prominent individuals. Meeting in Chongqing between January 15 and February 1, 1946, the PCC produced a so-called Joint Program for Political Administration that reiterated in greater detail the shared commitment to constitutional government, democratization on a multiparty basis, and a range of other, more specific provisions on matters ranging from military issues to postwar economic policies.[3]

Among the new commitments was a set of jointly endorsed diplomatic principles, the first of which was "Adhering to the Atlantic Charter, the Cairo Declaration, the Four-State Moscow Declaration, and the UN Charter, and actively participating in the United Nations Organization, in order to preserve and secure world peace."[4] The UN, and its charter, took on major domestic significance. Notably, it was the Communist Party delegation, headed by Zhou Enlai and by Dong Biwu, that formally submitted these clauses for inclusion on January 17, 1946.[5] Two days earlier, the inclusion of the references to international agreements had been officially proposed by Dong on behalf of the Communist side.[6] His fellow Communist Party delegate, the philosopher Zhang Shenfu, also made similar proposals regarding "participation in the international peace organization" during the January 15 session, as did the China Youth Party cofounder Chang Naide.[7] While (liberal) Guomindang-aligned figures had led China's participation at Dumbarton Oaks and San Francisco, the Communist side and the minor parties were now the ones pushing to translate UN membership into domestic public law obligations. These were paired with a number of other fundamental policies that could be used as a foundation for cooperation across the various parties' vast ideological gulfs.[8]

From the end of January through April, the various basic policies agreed to by the PCC were then incorporated into a draft constitution. The Berlin-trained legal scholar/political theorist Zhang Junmai played an especially important role in guiding this drafting process both due to his acknowledged academic expertise and, in particular, his unique political profile at the head of the independent Democratic Socialist Party. Zhang's politics emphasizing both civil and political rights and socialist economic policies, combined with his record of criticism against both the Communists and Guomindang (which had led to harassment and imprisonment by the latter in the interwar years), now (briefly) made him a sort of ideal totem of compromise.[9]

The draft constitution produced by April, and agreed to in principle by all parties, was both qualitatively and quantitatively different from previous Chinese constitutional documents. It was considerably longer and more detailed than previous draft constitutions, and it also emphasized principles of the separation of powers, judicial independence, and individual rights protections more than its main predecessors.[10] Moreover, despite the great influence of the US constitution (which was also exerted in postwar constitutions drawn up elsewhere), the draft also contained significant elements drawn from other sources, such as the Weimar constitution that had impressed Zhang during his studies in Germany, as well as France's new 1946 constitution. Accordingly, the 1946 constitutional draft also included "the right of existence [and] the right to work," alongside civil and political rights, and also a commitment to "equitable distribution of land ownership and control of capital in order to obtain a well-balanced development of public economy and private livelihood,"[11] commitments to providing work opportunities and welfare benefits, and other such provisions meant to reflect progressive socialist ideals.[12]

The section of the draft constitution containing these commitments was itself something of an innovation. This was Chapter 13 of the constitution, "Fundamental National Policies" (*jiben guoce* 基本國策). Though brief, it contained mostly the same set of highly important commitments that had been agreed upon in principle during the PCC negotiations. In addition to the provisions on the National Economy and Social Security, there were articles covering National Defense, Education, Border Regions, and Diplomacy. In each of these areas, a set of basic commitments was articulated that comprised the shared policy agenda of China's various rival parties, at greater or lesser degrees of specificity. As to diplomacy, the new "fundamental national policy" clearly drew upon the principles of the PCC's Joint Program:

> Art. 141. The foreign policy of the Republic of China shall, in a spirit of independence and initiative and on the basis of the principles of equality and reciprocity, cultivate good neighborliness with other nations and respect treaties and the United Nations Charter in order to protect the rights and interests of overseas Chinese nationals, promote international co-operation, advance international justice, and ensure world peace.[13]

Some commentators on the draft constitution, particularly those with ties to the Guomindang's right wing, criticized the "fundamental national policies" as an aberration departing from usual constitutional practices. These critics asked how occasionally very general commitments (such as the use of the military solely for "safeguarding national security and preservation of world peace") could have any real determinate content. At times, however, they also criticized the implied constraints upon the national government's ability to freely determine policies. The inclusion of the clause on "respecting/adhering to . . . the United Nations Charter" was condemned by some as inappropriate for a domestic legal text.[14]

Many lawyers and diplomats, however, lauded the draft's embodiment of international law commitments. Zhou Gengsheng, who was himself a delegate to the Constitutional Assembly, argued that the "fundamental national policies" provision on foreign policy was likely to "draw the most attention" from observers abroad, and that it followed the "trend of modern constitutions," including the Weimar constitution, and then those of Austria, Republican Spain, and the new French Fourth Republic. While allowing that some in China were concerned over the possibility of an excessive self-limitation of sovereignty – "binding oneself up like a silkworm," per the standard expression – Zhou argued that, given how a Hobbesian "anarchy" among states had already caused China so much suffering, "peace must be organized."[15]

The joint delegates at San Francisco had embodied "the unified diplomatic position of the state," and now the constitutional clause on the charter would show that "the pursuit of perpetual peace in the world by means of an international organization can be considered a diplomatic policy that is the consensus of all citizens of the Republic of China."[16] Having himself played such a major role in denouncing the illegitimacy of *unequal* treaties, Zhou's words carried special weight when he told his readers that it was entirely appropriate for China to fully commit to viewing its *equal* treaties as binding in a manner equivalent to domestic public law. One of Zhou Gengsheng's academic hires at Wuhan University, the Harvard-trained legal scholar Han Depei, made similar arguments regarding the connection between the UN Charter and China's new constitution. He also invoked Hans Kelsen's monism to argue for this position.[17]

Some jurists, meanwhile, argued that the draft should go further. For example, Zhou Ziya sought to situate the new constitution against the backdrop of a transformed world order. As he had in other recent writings,[18] Zhou connected questions of international law's binding effect with the split between monism and dualism, with their respective "teachers": Kelsen and Verdross, on the one hand, and Triepel and Anzilotti, on the other. Explaining this divergence of views to his lay audience, Zhou argued that "the great trend in today's legal science is clearly . . . the blending of international and domestic law."[19] China now had the chance to become part of this global "trend" by ensuring that its new constitution explicitly embraced the monist view. Zhou thus recommended incorporating a clause modeled on Article 4 of the Weimar constitution, which read "[t]he generally accepted rules of international law are to be considered as binding integral parts of the law of the German Reich."[20] This more explicitly monist suggestion was, however, not adopted by the drafters.

Ultimately, increasing tensions between the Communist Party and Guomindang, worsened by distrust and military build-up in Manchuria, soon led to a collapse of the planned convention. Ultraconservatives in the Guomindang had greatly contributed to the breakdown in talks by taking a hardline stance on outstanding issues regarding party representation and regional autonomy during a party conference in March. By November, relations between the parties had worsened beyond repair and all-out conflict was again in full swing. It was only due to the need for third-party support, and in particular the lobbying and insistence of Zhang Junmai, that it was the early 1946 joint draft that went up for a vote at the year's end, instead of one more geared toward Guomindang dominance.[21] Despite the deteriorating situation, the constitution adopted by the Guomindang-dominated Assembly did include the provisions on "fundamental national policies." These features were little noticed, however, during a period of renewed and bitter civil war.

The New Era of Codification

The monist position that was suggested by the new constitution and explicitly endorsed by leading international lawyers in China was also embodied in the activities of the country's representatives within the new UN organization. As at Dumbarton Oaks and San Francisco, Chinese diplomats and international lawyers in the early years of the UN system were among the most vocal figures arguing for, and participating in, attempts to codify and better enforce international law. In these efforts, the former Shanghai International Settlement judge and by now well-known diplomat-jurist Liang Yunli was particularly active. Indeed, per his new role as director of the UN Secretariat Division of Development and Codification of International Law, he was the UN official most directly responsible for coordinating efforts in this arena.[22]

From the beginning of the division's work in early 1947 through to his retirement in 1964, Liang would be one of the driving forces behind international law codification. Liang's status as a leading voice in the movement for further codification of international law was further cemented with a 1948 course at the Hague Academy of International Law on "Le développement et la codification du droit international," which made him the first Chinese international lawyer ever to give one of these prestigious courses that helped to steer the intellectual direction of the field.

His most impactful efforts during this period, however, were certainly those connected with the establishment and operation of the International Law Commission (ILC).[23] Since its creation by the General Assembly, the ILC has been the most important expert body in the elaboration of international law norms, including both draft declarations or agreements on specialized topics (e.g., state responsibility), and research on general principles or features of international law. Liang, in his role as the UN Secretariat's point person on codification and progressive development, was a constant presence in ILC meetings and frequently intervened on both substantive and procedural questions. He also used public addresses and scholarly publications as venues in which to explain (or indirectly guide) the ILC's efforts, including many articles in the *American Journal of International Law*.[24]

Other Chinese jurists or diplomats were involved in similarly significant ventures. Perhaps most obvious to the layman was the new project of international criminal law, which immediately after its innovation at Nuremberg was applied to Japan at the Tokyo Tribunal of 1946, where Chiang's government fielded a team of elite jurists with largely American educations, including judge Mei Ru'ao, prosecutor Xiang Zhejun, and Ni Zhengyu as the head of their team of advisors.[25] The project of international criminal law was then largely abandoned by the Cold War superpowers for several decades, however. Nor did Chinese leaders or jurists place great emphasis upon the new, experimental field.

Meanwhile, the new idea for an "international health organization" that would become the World Health Organization was introduced via a joint declaration by the delegations of China and Brazil during the San Francisco Conference.[26] One of those involved with this effort was P. C. Chang (Zhang Pengchun), an educator, playwright, and diplomat who had most recently served as the Republic of China's (ROC's) ambassador to Chile from 1942 to 1945.[27] Soon after, Chang was also chosen to serve on the newly created UN Commission on Human Rights, where he made the contributions to international law for which he is today most well-known. At the first meeting of the commission in January 1947, Eleanor Roosevelt was chosen as the chair and Chang was elected as vice-chairman. He would go on to play a major role in the philosophical debates surrounding the proper content of the envisioned Universal Declaration of Human Rights (UDHR) and would also exert great influence during the drafting process.[28]

Overall, Chang was the commission's most consistent advocate for the idea that non-Western views should play a meaningful role in the UDHR. Though often comprising his introduction of Chinese values into otherwise Western-dominated debates, this idea also manifested at times in a more cosmopolitan mode. For example, Chang's arguments helped to shape Article 2 on the universal scope of the rights in the UDHR: "without distinction of any kind, such as race, colour, sex, language, religion, political or other opinion, national or social origin, property, birth or other status."[29] Other aspects of the UDHR that were particularly informed by Chang's views or interventions included Article 18 on the right to freedom of thought, conscience, and religion; Article 23, the right to work; Article 25, on the guarantee of a minimum standard of living for an individual and "his" (sic) family; Article 26 (2), on the right to education as comprising "full development of the human personality"; and Article 27, on the right to freely participate in the cultural life of the community. However, Chang failed in his attempt to include in Article 1 a reference to the Confucian *ur*-value of *Ren* 仁, translatable as intersubjective "benevolence,"[30] as well as in his proposals for human rights based on traditional Chinese institutions including the right to petition one's government and the right to employment in the civil service on the basis of impartial examination.[31]

Chang was also involved in the drafting of the Convention on the Prevention and Punishment of Genocide, as were several other Chinese diplomats. China's proposals with regards to the prohibition of genocide tended to emphasize broad definitions of the concept, as is evident in a Chinese draft version of Article 1 of the Genocide Convention submitted on April 16, 1948, which included not only "physical destruction of a human group," but "subjecting of a human group to conditions of life, or applying to it measures that were likely to result in . . . physical destruction"; "destruction of the institutions or of the culture of that group, or the suppression of its language"; and conspiracy or accessory liability to any of the above acts.[32]

China's delegates were, in fact, consistent defenders of the inclusion of "cultural genocide" in the definition of the concept, in the face of (eventually successful) opposition by those who sought to limit it to various forms of physical destruction.[33] A more idiosyncratic effort by the Chinese delegates was to include in the definition of genocide its potential commission by use of narcotics, as Japan had allegedly done by reviving the opium trade (and, implicitly, as Great Britain had done in the previous century). However, few other delegates were interested in picking up on this thread. As to "cultural genocide," China's delegates endorsed a specific set of concrete examples that would constitute this crime, including: "Prohibiting the use of the language and [/or] destroying systematically and by violence the libraries, museums, schools, historical monuments, places of worship or other cultural institutions and objects, of the group."[34]

As to "self-determination," however, Chinese delegates did not break with the general position advocated by the Western powers that embraced a highly limited version of this right. Under the general framework of the charter, there was no firm guarantee of independence as such for territories or peoples under foreign control. Even officially designated trust territories were to be given only "progressive development towards self-government or independence as may be appropriate to the particular circumstances of each territory."[35] Zones to be designated as trust territories were either former League mandates, areas occupied by the defeated Axis powers, or zones voluntarily given trust status by their sovereigns.[36] The various minority ethnic zones that Chinese representatives had sought to ensure sovereignty over since the Late Qing era thus faced no real prospects for recategorization in this schema.

Indeed, one of the Chiang government's few clear orders during the UDHR proceedings was to convey a lack of interethnic conflict in Xinjiang, and keep it out of the discussions.[37] Around the same time, meanwhile, Mao Zedong expressed the view that local unrest in Xinjiang and calls for independence were "triggered by the incorrect policy of [Chiang's] Chinese government, which does not want to take into account the national specifics of these nationalities, does not present rights of self-rule, [and] does not permit the development of the national culture."[38] In discussions with Soviet diplomats, and even with Stalin himself, Mao emphasized the need for a *modus vivendi* as to the status quo in Xinjiang – his abandonment of China's claim to Outer Mongolia, "respect[ing its people's] wish . . . to remain a sovereign state," was effectively presented as a quid pro quo for a Soviet withdrawal from Xinjiang and refraining from further support of local alternatives to Communist Party authority or Chinese *zhuquan*.[39]

A Profession in Transition

For the minority of once-prominent jurists and diplomats who had chosen to collaborate with Japan, the end of the war meant the end of any professional relevance. These figures now found themselves pariahs. Zhou Wei, for example, offered his services to the postwar authorities but was tried and eventually sentenced to fifteen years in prison for his wartime collaboration. While in jail in Suzhou awaiting trial, he attempted suicide, reportedly gutting himself in emulation of the Japanese samurai practice of *seppuku*.[40] Though failing in this attempt, he died of illness three years later, while detained in Nanjing. Thus ended the story of China's first member of the *Institut de Droit International* and its first author of an internationally influential text on general public international law topics.

Li Shengwu, too, had been found guilty of collaboration. Though sentenced to fifteen years imprisonment, Li was released early for medical reasons, and later moved to Hong Kong, where he became one of the first professors to teach international law for the newly established Chinese University of Hong Kong.[41] General Ding Shiyuan, who had first brought up the matter of defining aggression at the Hague in 1907, died of an illness in Manchukuo just before it was liberated in 1945, thus avoiding his own prosecution as a war criminal.[42] Along with some other scholars and diplomats who had perhaps seen in Japanese imperialism the chance to erect a new public law order based on "Asia for Asians," these figures were all but forgotten after the war.

Those who had been loyal to China during wartime and now celebrated the victory of the Allies, however, faced pressures of their own. Liberal or left-leaning intellectuals in general were targeted with renewed suspicion by Chiang's regime in the aftermath of the collapse of détente between the Communists and Guomindang by mid 1946. Along with the prospects for a unity government, there had also vanished any real hope for a monist legal order, or any meaningful constraint of Guomindang authority with reference to either alternative parties or shared policies. In a sharply critical essay published amidst this breakdown, Han Depei pointed out that the legal theories of ancient Chinese legalists such as Han Fei or National Socialist jurists such as Carl Schmitt might technically be *fazhi* 法治 ("rule of/by law"), but these were hardly the kinds of *fazhi* that China needed in order to become a progressive, democratic *Rechtsstaat*.[43]

Renewed civil war began in earnest in 1947, and very much overshadowed the official entry into effect of the constitution in December of that year. Soon after, the Guomindang-controlled National Assembly passed the highly Schmittian "Temporary Measures Effective during the Period of Communist Rebellion" of April 18, 1948, which suspended most of the democratic and separation-of-powers-related elements of the 1946 constitution, and would remain in effect until 1992.[44] Not only actual Communists, but also members of the third-party Democratic League were ordered to terminate their activities. Liberals and noncommunist socialists, including the various international lawyers who saw themselves in either of those camps, were under pressure.

Many of China's prominent international lawyers were torn between the sides of the renewed civil war. Zhou Gengsheng, had established a pragmatic cooperative relationship with Chiang, and the latter had reappointed him as president of the politically important Wuhan University in mid 1945. On several occasions thereafter, Chiang liaised with Zhou over the situation of "Communist rebellion" in the important city – that is, largely youth-driven protests.[45] During his tenure between 1945 and 1949 Zhou faced great difficulties appeasing Guomindang leaders while also confronting increasingly volatile local political sentiments, and was himself targeted at times by angry student protestors. Shortly after his 1947 meeting with Chiang, there occurred an incident that left a deep impression on the university community, when Guomindang security forces seeking Communist agents confronted an angry crowd of students and fired weapons, killing three bystanders. On June 22, Zhou presided over a memorial ceremony for the students who had been killed. Chiang sent a wreath and lamented "errors" by the local police.[46]

Although Zhou continued his public compliance with the Guomindang's policies until the Communist takeover of Wuhan in 1949, by his own account he grew increasingly disillusioned with Chiang's policies and increasingly sympathetic with the anti–civil war student movement.[47] The decision to stay behind in 1949 was one that he shared with a number of other prominent international law professionals (and legal and political academics in general), who often expressed similar motivations.[48] During the Civil War years of 1945–1949, the international legal profession based in China became a powerful source of critique of both the Chiang government and, especially, of the United States' relentless prosecution of early Cold War policies.

A number of figures who would later be instrumental in the "rebirth of international law" in the PRC after the Cultural Revolution made their decisions in favor of the Communist Party during this period of time. These included Zhou himself, Wang Tieya, Li Haopei, Han Depei, Zhou Ziya, Jiang Haichao, and also younger scholars such as Chen Tiqiang, who studied for a doctorate in international law under J. L. Brierly at Oxford between 1945 and 1948, and whose resulting dissertation on the law of state recognition, published in 1951, remains today one of the core modern works on that important topic.[49] Zhou Gengsheng continued to act as a guiding figure for general trends in this community, including his outspoken advocacy against Guomindang rightist attempts to revise the constitution toward a "presidential" system and in his criticisms of the "Sovietphobia" of some liberals who had compromised their beliefs in collaborating with Chiang's regime.[50]

Of course, most of China's leading intellectuals not affiliated with the Communist movement had been compelled to compromise their beliefs to some extent in collaborating with Chiang's regime, Zhou himself included. Now, though, there was a decisive intellectual turn against the Nanjing government that rapidly accelerated with its military missteps, continued inability to either stabilize the currency or procure new American loans, and a string of ill-timed scandals involving the American forces still present throughout the country. One such incident, a 1946 rape case involving American troops and a female student of Peking University, inflamed outraged press coverage nationwide and was remembered by Zhou Ziya as a pivotal moment in his turn against the Guomindang regime and its American backers. An essay he wrote at the time arguing for criminal jurisdiction over the foreign soldiers in Chinese courts, on the basis of China's sovereign rights, greatly raised his profile as a "patriotic" international lawyer.[51]

Many of these international lawyers also made more general critiques of American policy amidst the backdrop of the emerging Cold War. Wang Tieya, for example, wrote an essay on "Monroeism and Trumanism" in which he sought to demonstrate a direct link between the interventionist practices that the United States had developed in the Western Hemisphere on the basis of the Monroe Doctrine and its new claims to exert the same authority worldwide.[52] These criticisms of both "global Monroeism" and "Trumanism" were also on display in critical writings by a number of other jurists. Both Chen Tiqiang and Zhou Ziya, for example, also wrote about the legacy of the Monroe Doctrine and linked it with America's pursuit of global dominance.[53] Meanwhile, however, Chiang's government was relying on US backing to exert its own idea of a regional maritime sphere of power, issuing in December 1947 its "Eleven Dash Line" claim to much of the South China Sea, in which later claims by both Beijing and Taipei have their roots.

Many liberal intellectuals, international lawyers included, argued that there was a need for cooperation between the postwar superpowers. Speaking to students in Wuhan in 1948, Han Depei even called for China to act as a "matchmaker" for the United States and the Soviet Union, helping to restore the good relations that they had maintained in wartime.[54] It is this sort of middle path, focused on international institutions rather than a full tilt into either the American or Soviet geopolitical orbits, that seems to have been preferred by most international lawyers. Their theoretical interests continued to match this posture. In 1948, for example, Jiang Haichao envisioned a comprehensive remaking of world public law, including both the international legal system and domestic constitutions, with the aim to "instill monism" as a belief in all the world's peoples.[55] Introducing Kelsen's *General Theory of Law and State* to Chinese readers the same year, Han emphasized law's dual role as a system of interlinked norms in the world of "ought" and as a "coercive order" reliant on real sanctions to give it practical effect in the world of "is."[56]

Many of those involved in the field stayed behind in the Mainland after Chiang's forces fled to Taiwan, and the PRC was established on October 1, 1949. On the one hand, the new government was intended to begin with a clean slate; the provisional constitution adopted before the establishment of the PRC, the Common Program of the Chinese People's PCC, included as Article 55 the provision that "[t]he Central People's Government ... shall examine the treaties and agreements concluded between the Kuomintang and foreign governments, and shall recognize, abrogate, revise, or re-negotiate them according to their respective contents."[57]

On the other hand, jurists were, for a time, invited to contribute to the new diplomatic, administrative, and educational efforts being initiated in the early years of the new regime. Zhou Gengsheng, Wang Tieya, Han Depei, Li Haopei, Zhou Ziya, and Jiang Haichao, among others, would conduct teaching and research on international law topics in the early 1950s, advocating that the new Communist government in China, along with the Soviet Union, should uphold and build upon the "progressive" elements in existing international law. For both established figures like Zhou Gengsheng and newer members of the profession like Chen Tiqiang, the change of regime in 1949 seemed – at least at first – as though it would open up new opportunities to combine patriotism and progressive internationalism. When the Chinese People's Institute of Foreign Affairs was established in December 1949 as the new PRC's first major foreign affairs–related professional organization, its inaugural director was the political theorist Zhang Xiruo, whose first academic claim to fame had been for deconstructions of sovereignty in the 1920s.[58]

If many of China's leading international lawyers not directly affiliated with the Guomindang regime decided to stay behind in Mainland China after 1949, the jurists and diplomats at its highest levels generally made the opposite choice. Wang Chonghui turned from international law back to domestic public law as the president of the Judicial Yuan from 1948, helping maintain the ROC judiciary's autonomy to a significant degree, even amid the crisis of defeat and the regime's relocation to Taiwan, before passing away in 1958 at age the age of seventy-six.[59] Zheng Tianxi, who officially remained a judge of the PCIJ until the creation of its successor in 1945, stepped down to serve as the ROC ambassador to the United Kingdom between 1946 and 1950. At the end of Zheng's term, his son Bin Cheng (Zheng Bin) graduated from University College London with a doctorate in law – he would soon after become a leading advocate of the notion of "general principles" as a binding source of international law,[60] and later a highly influential founder of the newly emerging fields of air and space law.[61]

China's judicial position on the International Court of Justice (ICJ) went to Hsu Mo, who like Wang and Zheng combined high regard as a legal scholar and years of service as a high-level diplomat. Hsu also became, in 1948, China's second-ever *associé* of the *Institut de Droit International.* The third was Liang Yunli, in 1950, then in the midst of codification work at the UN

Secretariat, where he would remain until 1964. Wellington Koo served as ambassador to the United States until 1956, and would then take over Hsu's position at the ICJ with the latter's death that year, stepping down a decade later as the vice-president of the Court – while serving on it, he would in several rulings emphatically support the institution and new doctrines such as *jus cogens*, or a core of "compelling" legal norms that generates universal obligations for all states.[62]

Public Law in a Divided World

Cold War battle lines were now being drawn internationally and intensifying ideological conflicts within the state. According to Soviet records, Mao told Stalin in December 1949 that "the most important question at the present time is the question of establishing peace." He was of the view that "China needs a period of 3–5 years of peace, which would be used to bring the economy back to pre-war levels and to stabilize the country in general."[63] Soon after, however, the Korean conflict between the Northern and Southern regimes escalated into a bloody and costly three-year war. The Truman administration led efforts at the UN Security Council to classify the intra-Korean conflict as a threat to *international* peace and security sufficient to activate UN Charter Article 51, and thus permit an external intervention under UN auspices. With the Soviet Union boycotting the Security Council over the US-led refusal to switch recognition from Taipei to Beijing, Truman's plan for UN-based intervention went ahead.

After the ICJ's *Corfu Channel* case of 1947–1949 limiting the scope of "self-defense," the Korean War was the next great test of the UN Charter's hard-won new principles on the restriction of the use of force. Just how absolute was the prohibition on military intervention? Hans Kelsen, in an updated version of his major textbook on the UN, noted that:

> The formula used in the resolution of June 27 [on intervention in Korea] is justified only if the Security Council was of the opinion that the armed conflict in Korea at least before the Council recommended military intervention by Members of the United Nations was an international war between the Republic of Korea and another state.[64]

As an intervention into what was ultimately a civil war, "the action in Korea," Kelsen argued, was "inconsistent with the *old law* of the United Nations."[65] In a curiously realist coda, however, he then added that the intervention "perhaps, constitute[s] one of these cases of which we may say *ex injuria jus oritur* [law is born from violation]."[66] International lawyers in the Soviet Union and PRC were certainly willing to agree with the first part of Kelsen's assessment, if not the latter. Amidst the grueling Korean conflict, international lawyers in Mainland China now continued to refer to a point that had exercised their professional community for decades: the need for a definition of aggression. Surely, under the new UN system, it should at last be possible to clearly demonstrate who was an "aggressor" and who was not?

Unfortunately, as the ongoing conflict made clear, this was not the case – or, at least, norms regarding the use of force were still susceptible to highly contestable reinterpretations by major powers.[67] Very few in the Anglo-American international law world found fault with the Korean intervention; even Kelsen's protégé and fellow transplant to the United States, Josef L. Kunz, for example, argued that the Security Council could designate *any* situation as a "threat to international peace and security."[68] Defining the new zeitgeist, Myres McDougal argued at the Hague Academy of International Law that "any decision about the constitutionality of the Korean resolutions, whether for or against, must depend upon policy choices," rather than law.[69]

Chiang's government on Taiwan still held China's recognized UN seat and Security Council position, despite the United Kingdom's decision to recognize Beijing in January 1950. There were at this point two competing theories on state recognition, the so-called declaratory and constitutive approaches – the former considering state legal personality as purely fact-based, and the latter as originating in a decision to recognize taken by other states in the international community. Chen Tiqiang's monograph written under Brierly was to be an influential expression of the declaratory view that would clearly favor legal recognition of Beijing, though it did not appear in print until after the United Kingdom's switch of recognition. Hersch Lauterpacht was a recognized authority on the subject favoring the constitutive view; his advocacy of a "duty to recognize" despite the ultimately policy-based nature of the act helped to defend the United Kingdom's decision.[70] Yet neither argument would make much headway in the context of US international law discourse, where scholars and practitioners rarely questioned Washington's practice on matters of recognition of communist governments or its free-wheeling approach to deploying force to oppose them.

Its existence hanging by the thread of the US Security Council veto, Chiang's government certainly had no inclination to challenge the United States' flexible applications of legal doctrines such as the UN Charter rules on the use of force. However, some of its representatives in the organization continued to work for a more legalized approach, including on the problem of defining aggressive uses of force, which were foregrounded by the Korean conflict. Liang Yunli, by 1951 well-established as the UN Secretariat's point person for international law codification efforts, was heavily involved in the attempt of the ILC to compose a Draft Code of Offences against the Peace and Security of Mankind, among the commission's other projects, taking an active and engaged role.[71] At one early meeting, for example, Liang intervened into a discussion regarding whether the Draft Code's prohibitions should affect acts such as annexation of territory only to the extent that they were "inconsistent with the Purposes of the United Nations." Based on Liang's suggestion, it was decided instead to refer to the principles of the UN Charter; that is, the explicit prohibition of uses of force other than in self-defense. This was one of many occasions when Liang, in his capacity as secretary to the ILC, sought to keep its formulations in close consistency with the norms and language of the UN Charter.[72]

Liang's work at the UN Secretariat, participation in debates at the ILC and the *Institut de Droit International*, and voluminous writings in the *American Journal of International Law*, among other efforts, contributed greatly to the project of international legal codification in the 1950s and 1960s. Rarely if ever did his activities suggest any discernible preoccupation with narrowly defined interests of Chiang's embattled Nationalist regime. The same was not true, however, of the ROC representative on the ILC itself, former Guomindang delegate to the League Shuhsi Hsu (i.e., Xu Shuxi). At the sixty-first meeting held on July 5, 1950, Hsu called for "subversion" and "propaganda" aimed at the overthrow of a government to be included as crimes in the Draft Code.

As authority for this innovation, so suited to the Cold War zeitgeist, Hsu cited Truman's rationale for intervention against Communist "subversion" in Korea. When challenged that "propaganda" could just as easily go the other direction – the Pope, for example, having recently called on Catholic believers to resist communist regimes – Hsu responded with the simple declaration that "[i]f the Pope's propaganda was good, it was not subversive."[73] Though Hsu's proposal only made it into later iterations of the Draft Code in a diluted form (and was not later included in the Rome Statute), that this blatantly one-sided argument was not outright dismissed spoke volumes about how Cold War battle lines were impacting international legal discourse.

For the leaders of the newly founded PRC, meanwhile, the Korean conflict helped set the terms for "antiimperialist" struggles throughout the region, including the Indonesian Revolution of 1945–1949 and the struggle for independence in Vietnam. When the Party decided in 1950 to commit resources to support Vietnamese forces, Mao described the effort as a "glorious internationalist task."[74] In conversation with Ho Chi Minh, Liu Shaoqi acknowledged that Chinese support for the former might delay the PRC's recognition by the West, but that in any case recognition would be inevitable once China was strong.[75] After the Korean conflict concluded in the stalemate armistice of mid 1953, Beijing focused again on diplomacy and international law. The Soviet Union now initiated the idea of a five-power conference, among itself, the United States, United Kingdom, France, and the PRC, to settle the disputes roiling Asia. The PRC quickly signed on to this proposal, which would culminate in the Geneva Conference of 1954 where Zhou Enlai first engaged with these key Western powers.[76] Though failing to reach a mutual agreement on the end of the conflict in Vietnam, the Geneva meeting did arguably represent a PRC victory in its effort to prevent that conflict being "internationalized" (in particular, by a multilateral UN-based intervention) just as the one in Korea had been.[77]

Already in advance of the Geneva Conference, Zhou Enlai had articulated for the first time the "Five Principles of Peaceful Coexistence" during a meeting with Indian diplomats in December 1953. This reflected a significant effort to develop an alternative grammar of international legal rights and obligations that was centered on more absolute prohibitions on intervention or interference between states.[78] The limits of UN Charter Articles 2 and 51, asserting the illegality of aggression and the need for a "threat to international peace and security" as the only legitimate basis for military intervention, were on blatant display in both Korea and, increasingly, in Vietnam. Given its own security interests, Chiang's government on Taiwan was now supportive of Western interventions in the region; meanwhile, the PRC adopted its predecessor's erstwhile position of absolute prohibitions of military intervention.

The broader decolonization process offered an opportunity for China's new rulers to reframe international legal order around this central pillar of non-interference. In repeated efforts over 1954–1955, Zhou Enlai and Mao himself made efforts to join with regional neighbors – even some with staunchly anticommunist governments – to enshrine the nonintervention principles as the basis for regional cooperation going forward. To this end, Mao asked Indian prime minister Jawaharlal Nehru in October 1954: "What does Prime Minister Nehru think about convening a World Peace Congress in the near future? All the nations of the world may participate, and a sort of world treaty for non-aggression may be signed which may establish that no war should be fought [for] several decades."[79]

The Asian–African Conference convened at Bandung, Indonesia in 1955 reflected the background of such conversations among regional governments seeking to promote cooperation and self-determination.[80] At Bandung, which Nehru described as "an experiment in co-existence,"[81] Zhou Enlai took up an attitude clearly distinguishable from that of Soviet diplomats who tended to portray themselves as leaders in matters of both ideology and policy. Rather than putting forward a new general program, Zhou restricted his proposals to the Five Principles, which won the assent of the other delegates.[82] The African-American journalist Richard Wright commented that "[Zhou] did not say that he knew the way of eternal salvation . . . all he said was that he and his fellow Chinese were suffering, were backward, were afraid of war . . . No one could recall having heard a Russian Communist speak like that."[83]

Beijing's new role in helping to promote Third World legal organization helped to favorably shift views of Mao's government among some jurists who had originally been staunchly anticommunist. Li Shengwu, for example, who had vitriolically condemned the Communist Party while at Oxford and as a high-level collaborator with Japan, watched the events at Bandung from his exile in Hong Kong with enthusiasm. As his son would later recall:

> When he talked about the Bandung Conference, I saw for the first time the emotional side of a man obsessed by political ambition. He became so animated

> as he described Jawaharlal Nehru's speech that he had to be imagining himself in the audience . . . applauding the charismatic Indian prime minister's condemnation of colonialism.[84]

Of course, the Bandung program served a dual role in promoting the overthrow of Western colonialism and reinforcing the *imperium* of new sovereign states. Like the early PRC, many of the region's other states saw a tight connection between external security as guaranteed by well-protected sovereign borders, the consolidation of internal territorial control (including over internal minority groups), and state-led economic development. Indeed, the main initial impetus for Nehru and Zhou's platform of Five Principles had been reaching an understanding over Tibet's international status as part of PRC territory and the demarcation of the Indo-Chinese border. It was also in the same year as Bandung, 1955, that Xinjiang was officially incorporated into the PRC as an "autonomous region."

During these busy years of the early and mid 1950s, PRC jurists were involved domestically in establishing new associations and research initiatives in international law and diplomacy, publishing on topics such as the illegality of the use of force in the Suez Crisis, the law of the sea, and so on. As in the previous decade, such discussions overlapped with discourse regarding China's domestic constitution – now the Soviet-style constitution of 1954 that established a framework for a state government separate from, but still under de facto control by the Party. The jurists who had stayed behind after the defeat of the Guomindang participated in this process, with Zhou Gengsheng, for example, acting as one of the official consultants for the constitutional drafting process (though its tightly controlled, top-down procedure was criticized by some other international lawyers). At the time when Zhou subsequently joined the Communist Party in 1956, the prospects for the profession in the PRC still seemed positive. By the next year, however, many of its members had already been flagged as bourgeois rightist elements with insufficient loyalty to the orthodox Party line.[85]

Universalism and Ostracism

Despite the PRC's exclusion from most aspects of the still Western-dominated international legal order, the notion that some extant international norms (especially the prohibition on aggression) had a "progressive" character was never fully rejected. Indeed, following the promising Bandung moment, the middle of the decade saw the beginnings of a potential reconnection between the Mainland Chinese jurists and their counterparts abroad. One significant step in this direction was the August 26–September 2, 1956 meeting of the International Law Association (ILA) in Dubrovnik, then part of Yugoslavia. As the host state, Tito's government invited Soviet and Chinese lawyers to attend. For the first time since the PRC's founding, some of its jurists thus attended a meeting of international law specialists alongside delegates from the Western capitalist states. At the meeting, the issue of promoting "peaceful coexistence" was adopted as a topic for discussion and was included in the itinerary for the next meeting, to be held in New York two years later. David Dudley Field's organization, some eight decades after its founding, still seemed to display something of his own relative openness toward engaging with China on grounds of equality.[86] By the time of the ILA's 1958 meeting, however, Mao's Antirightist Campaign would be underway and Chen Tiqiang, who had attended at Dubrovnik, was one of its targets along with other leading international lawyers.

Even amidst these pressures, jurists continued to actively debate the question of a "socialist international law" and its continuity with the norms of the past. At a 1957 meeting of international lawyers in Shanghai, for example, the prevailing views held that some common rules among bourgeois and socialist international law systems had to be recognized, though their exact relationship and respective content was left open for further discussion.[87] Often, influential jurists harshly criticized Western international lawyers' recent moves in the direction of cosmopolitanism, while continuing to advocate the universality of at least some norms – a position that had, after all, received official Party endorsement via the principles of Bandung.

In a 1957 book review of the newest Hersch Lauterpacht–edited version of Oppenheim's *International Law*, for example, Zhou Ziya suggested that Chinese lawyers study the work closely in order to debunk Lauterpacht's arguments for "natural" legal principles that were, for Zhou, ultimately in the service of imperialism and Anglo-American "world hegemony."[88] Zhou Gengsheng articulated similar views at greater length in a 1963 pamphlet on the "modern trends" toward universal expansionism of Western international law norms and obligations; in his view, most such innovations that promoted "world law" were ways for bourgeois states to reassert forms of control that they had lost with the ongoing post-World War II wave of decolonizations.[89] At the same time, he and other leading jurists still called for the recognition of core norms of international law, such as the prohibition on aggression, equality of states, and mutual noninterference, that had genuine universal obligatory force. As Zhou Gengsheng suggested, citing the Soviet jurist Grigory Tunkin, "[to claim] it is impossible to have a general international law is actually an apologia for the 'position of strength' and the 'cold war.'"[90]

Among Western authorities, perhaps the most ambiguous position was held by Hans Kelsen. Though coming in for regular critique on the basis that his monist theory of law "was being used by American imperialism,"[91] his formalist emphasis on systematic rules remained clearly in conflict with the ad hoc "policy" view now gaining currency in the United States, or with the natural law tropes invoked by Lauterpacht.[92] During the early 1960s, Kelsen's views were even briefly cited twice in the *People's Daily*, regarding Hungary's right to reject UN observers as well as the PRC's right to China's UN seat.[93]

Soon after, however, several pieces by Party ideologists in the *People's Daily* attacked Western international legal thought at some length – and a special target was the "reactionary essence" of Kelsen's Pure Theory of Law. Kelsen's own writings criticizing state Marxism made him an easy target for such exposés.[94]

Meanwhile, in most mainstream early Cold War settings of Western international law and diplomacy, the PRC was still portrayed as an outlaw state, sometimes in grandiose terms. The influential economic and political theorist Wilhelm Röpke, for example, grouped the "Communist Pseudo-Islam" and National Socialism together as dangerous forms of messianic economic collectivism that had to be overcome in order to ensure that *dominium* – the global legal regime of private property ownership – would be insulated from states' political *imperium*. For Röpke, spreading such views from his professorial chair in Geneva, a 1954 course at the Hague Academy of International Law, and elsewhere, China's communist turn was the bursting of a "dyke" that had left global society in unprecedented peril. The Boxer Rebellion of 1899 he saw as a kind of antecedent to this modern threat to property, *dominium*, and civilization.[95]

Like many leading anticommunists, US secretary of state John Foster Dulles embodied similar views in his capacity as one of the key architects of US policy during the early Cold War. Perhaps more than any other official, Dulles worked to ensure that the United States would not give in to political reality by recognizing the PRC and allowing it entry into the UN. Indeed, in the face of British suggestions along these lines, Dulles even threatened to force the UN to move its headquarters off of US soil should Communist China enter the organization.[96] There was a need, he forcefully advised America's allies, for a "common approach by the Western World towards China."[97] Though threats to UN headquarters may have been bluster, the idea of "massive retaliation" against communist states themselves was not. Indeed, in 1958 Dulles signed on to Pentagon plans for potential nuclear strikes should Beijing advance against Taiwan, even merely by occupying coastal islands on the Mainland side of the Strait.[98] The "dyke-bursting" and domino theories ruled out any compromise with Beijing.

Meanwhile, the lack of a consensus on the PRC's international legal status was at times *the* central bone of contention obstructing many other forms of international legal cooperation at the global level. This was highly apparent when the first UN Conference on the Law of the Sea (UNCLOS) was held in Geneva in the spring of 1958, building directly on the codification work Liang Yunli had helped coordinate via the UN Secretariat and the ILC. At the opening of the very first plenary meeting on February 24, the Soviet jurist Tunkin protested the exclusion of the PRC and set off a lively debate on the topic, typical of diplomatic scenes during the period.[99]

Eastern Bloc countries noted that Beijing "controlled the territory of China and had been recognized by almost half of the countries represented at the

Conference," and, on a practical level, "the People's Republic of China, [as] a country with an immense sea-coast, could not possibly be excluded" from the proceedings if its resulting rules were to be seen as legitimate. India's delegate, the Nehru government's minister for law and justice Ashoke Kumar Sen, pithily assessed that "the absence of representatives of the Central Government of the People's Republic of China imparted an element of unreality to the Conference so far as the peoples of the Far East were concerned." If there was to be any prospect that "ideals of peaceful co-existence were to prevail," he continued, "the United Nations could not afford to exclude representatives of that government from its discussions."[100] The "unreality" would, however, last thirteen more years.

Throughout the PRC's long period of Washington-imposed ostracism from the UN system, both Chinese jurists and officials continued to argue for the state's right to membership the organization. As the Cold War progressed, though, Beijing was increasingly willing to emphasize views to the effect that, as an official statement put it in 1965, "[b]lind faith in the United Nations must . . . be liquidated . . . [It] is by no means sacred and inviolable . . . We can live on very well without it."[101] With the advent of Mao's Cultural Revolution in 1966, meanwhile, unprecedented restrictions were now placed on all dimensions of international law scholarship and practice, alongside all other "bourgeois" professions. Even activities such as Wang Tieya and Chen Tiqiang's translation of the eighth edition of Oppenheim's *International Law* could only be worked on in secret, published under pseudonyms, and made available only as "internal reference material" for Party cadres.[102] Ten years earlier, the Chinese People's Institute of Foreign Affairs had itself published an official translation of the seventh edition.

Similarly, Zhou Gengsheng's textbook *International Law* (*Guojifa* 國際法), which he had completed in 1964, also could not be published until after the Cultural Revolution.[103] However, Zhou, who passed away on April 20, 1971, missed seeing this publication as well as, if only just, the PRC's belated entry to the UN. At the time, the Nixon administration was in the middle of shifting the US approach to China, and secret talks between the two sides swiftly gathered pace. At a July 11 meeting in Beijing between Henry Kissinger and Zhou Enlai, the details for Nixon's seminal visit to China the following year were worked out. Among many issues associated with rapprochement and state recognition, the two sides focused on building mutual trust: something that, as Zhou Enlai remarked to his counterpart, was "very important in international relations."[104] In the end, it was Kissinger, not Kelsen, that provided an inroad to restoring Beijing's place in the late Cold War global system.

From Revolution to Globalization

The PRC's entry into the UN in October 1971 via General Assembly Resolution 2758 spurred the reemergence of China's international law profession, though it would be several more years before "bourgeois" professions like legal scholarship could be pursued in earnest. Nonetheless, China's diplomats and some high-level officials began to actively engage in international law settings soon after. The third UNCLOS could now, finally, operate in a far less "surreal" fashion than its predecessors due to the PRC's inclusion. At UNCLOS meetings between 1973 and 1982, and in other venues, Chinese delegates paired defenses of state sovereignty with "revolutionary" positions on the side of the Third World in general – for example, managing deep sea resources as the common heritage of mankind – that sometimes managed to overrule the former value.[105] On the other hand, Chinese delegates, including Wang Tieya at a 1979 meeting, also clearly expressed the position that consent from all parties would be required for any valid arbitration of territorial issues.[106]

Beijing's renewed legal Third World-ism also extended to rhetorically supporting emerging discourses regarding the need for a New International Economic Order and notions of a redistributive "right to development" for poor and formerly colonized states. However, already by the late 1970s, that rhetoric increasingly seemed out of pace with the actual changes on the ground in a post-Mao China newly reopening to Western international law, global capital, and the new ethos of "development." Immediately after UN membership, for example, the PRC had, despite the country's extreme poverty, engaged with the UN Development Program (UNDP) only as a donor state, rather than a recipient. By 1979, however, the country shifted its position to that of accepting much needed assistance. Among its important initial projects, the UNDP funded a six-week international study tour of six countries in the Asia Pacific region and Latin America focused on trade development and foreign investment, particularly Special Economic Zones, which was headed by Jiang Zemin, at the time the vice minister of the Administrative Commission for Foreign Investment.[107] Years later as state and Party leader, Jiang would claim that this mission had been key to "convinc[ing] other leaders . . . to change elements of . . . national policies in attracting foreigners and overseas Chinese to invest in such free trade zones and jumpstart the acceleration of foreign direct investment."[108]

In its other initiatives, the UNDP helped to formulate what have since become core features of Party policy with respect to the merging of GDP growth and various features of "sustainable development," such as environmental impact assessments and poverty alleviation. It also engaged closely with large-scale Chinese–foreign joint investment projects into natural resources in Xinjiang and other ethnic minority autonomous regions, as in the case of a projected natural gas pipeline to run from Xinjiang to Shanghai, for which the UNDP drew up plans showing that "relatively little had to be done to meet the expectations and demands of the poor local communities along the path of the pipeline."[109] Along with UNDP assistance, of course, the new international consensus on Beijing's legal status finally allowed it access to much-needed borrowing from the International Monetary Fund and the World Bank, beginning in 1980; its billions of US dollars worth of loans over the next decade would also greatly facilitate Deng's economic reform agenda.[110] Meanwhile, these organizations too served as conduits for the transmission of norms in the fields of law and political economy. The World Bank, in particular, organized major conferences connecting Chinese economists with leading foreign experts, some of whom vigorously sought to promote neoliberal agendas of "shock therapy" and rapid liberalization of market controls.[111]

With China's sovereignty seemingly secured by UN Security Council membership, a new period of identification between Chinese state interests and those of the still Western-centered "international community" had come about, which was reflected in Beijing's new tone on international law obligations, as well as in the rebirth of the profession. The founding of the Chinese Society of International Law (*Zhongguo Guojifa Xuehui* 中国国际法学会) in 1980 was led by jurists who had already been leaders in the field in the late 1940s and had decided to remain in the Mainland after 1949. By that point, these figures, including Wang Tieya, Li Haopei, Chen Tiqiang, Jiang Haichao, Han Depei, Zhou Ziya, Ni Zhengyu, and others, found themselves revered elders called on to help rebuild international law scholarship and practice. These scholars provided advice and expertise as Beijing began to actively engage with international treaty regimes, including (if at times warily) in the growing realm of international human rights law.[112]

Academic research and policy-focused work in international law now coincided more closely than ever before. Han Depei notably led the restoration of international law study at Wuhan University, where he founded the first Center for International Law at a PRC academic institution, and published important foundational works on newly important topics such as private international law and international environmental law.[113] Indeed, one of the main novel contributions of China's international law community during these years was spreading knowledge and skills regarding the rapidly evolving field of international economic law.

The new foreign capital coming into China had already started to produce some early investment disputes. One of the earliest such incidents involved a German–Japanese investment project involving up to US$2.5 billion worth of equipment and technology investments into four Chinese industrial centers (including the Karamay oil fields in the north of Xinjiang), which the PRC side sought to cancel in 1981. International lawyers Zhou Ziya, Han Depei, and Li Shuangyuan collaborated with the Ministry of Foreign Affairs to develop arguments in large part based on the 1980 UN Convention on Contracts for the International Sale of Goods, and successfully reduced the compensation claim to 11 percent, as opposed to the full contract value.[114]

All three jurists, along with Han and Li's colleague at Wuhan University, Yao Meizhen, would soon after be involved in a 1984 conference/workshop on international economic law at the Lushan mountain resort area in Jiangxi, which led to the founding of the Chinese Society of International Economic Law (CSIEL; Zhongguo Guoji Jingji Fa Xuehui 中国国际经济法学会). The CSIEL has ever since been heavily involved in the process of Chinese incorporation into global economic norms and institutions, in particular the World Trade Organization (WTO) system.[115] As Lushan workshop organizer Zhou Ziya, then affiliated with the Shanghai Academy of Social Sciences, had put it in a recent article where he yet again revisited Kelsen's monism, the development of legal norms to govern both the world's oceans and global trade had proved itself a "historical inevitability."[116] In line with this sentiment, Deng Xiaoping's China signed four bilateral investment treaties (BITs) in 1984, after have signed only one each (its first two) in the previous two years. Almost eighty more BITs would be signed by the time of Deng's death, thirteen years later; a pace that has largely continued.[117]

This new embrace of international economic law was matched with an effort to reach conciliatory formulae to resolve outstanding public law disputes and controversies, such as those surrounding the status of Taiwan and the return of Hong Kong to Chinese sovereignty. The negotiation of the Sino-British Joint Declaration in 1984 established the basis for the "one country, two systems" approach for Hong Kong that Beijing has also applied to Macau and (albeit unsuccessfully so far) to Taiwan. In such contexts, international lawyers balanced their arguments for engagement in global legal and economic institutions with statist defenses of China's territorial sovereignty; Han Depei, for example, refuted advocates of "self-determination" for Taiwan by noting a lack of norms in mainstream doctrine conferring effects to subnational independence referendums and, by contrast, the various treaties and other positive legal authorities that had already long-since identified Taiwan as part of China's territory.[118] At the same time, he energetically advocated active Chinese participation in a wide-range of new and emerging areas of international law, including maritime and international environmental law.

Another significant turning point in 1984 was China's return to the international judiciary. When elections for ICJ positions were held in 1984, the Beijing foreign policy establishment for the first time decided to advance a candidate: the respected and well-credentialed but always politically reliable Ni Zhengyu.[119] Earlier that year, the seventy–eight-year-old Ni had joined the Chinese Communist Party; a senior diplomatic official supported his application by saying that despite Ni's white hair, "his legs and torso were still healthy, and he could go out onto the battlefield."[120] Both his selection by the PRC Foreign Ministry and his ICJ election were secured without major opposition. Among the first cases he would participate in was the important *Nicaragua* v. *United States* matter involving the use of force. In his Separate Opinion on that matter, Ni sought to limit US invocations of multilateral treaty-based reservations to ICJ jurisdiction, as well as to restrict related appeals to UN Charter Article 51 collective self-defense as an exception to the rules against unilateral use of force contained in Article 2.[121]

Ni was the first Chinese international judge since Wellington Koo had retired as vice-president of the ICJ in 1967. On the eve of Ni taking up his seat at the ICJ, he visited Koo and the latter's family at their home in Manhattan, where they reminisced about the Beijing of decades past.[122] The friendly meeting served as something like a symbol of the ties between China's international lawyers, despite differences in ideology and allegiances. Or, as a 1988 textbook on international law would put it, "[t]he UN Charter was not something monopolized single-handedly by capitalist states, but rather was based on a universal demand by the peoples of all the world's countries. It was created by capitalist and socialist states together."[123] Commitment to the validity of existing positive international law within the UN system (if not an embrace of broad conceptions of dispute resolution or tribunal jurisdiction) was by the late 1980s an entrenched policy of the Party under Deng and his proxy reformer Zhao Ziyang.

The previous year, meanwhile, had seen the publication of another influential book, bearing the title *State Sovereignty* (*Guojia Zhuquan* 國家主權). Its author, a thirty–two-year-old professor of international politics at Shanghai's Fudan University named Wang Huning, was not a lawyer by training but had made an intensive study of modern international legal history, reflected in his first book and in a number of other writings on related subjects. Like Zhou Ziya and some other early advocates of international legal integration and globalization, Wang was in the late 1970s and early 1980s affiliated with the Shanghai Academy of Social Sciences. However, his approach to these topics was quite distinct from that of the internationalist jurists then in the process of enthusiastically rebuilding their profession – instead, Wang now called back, sometimes explicitly, to the critiques of "expansionist" Western international law thought that had been articulated by Chinese international lawyers in the 1950s–1960s. Taking aim at scholars such as Harold Laski, Hersch Lauterpacht, and many others who had sought to restrict sovereignty, Wang portrayed such discourse as a means of encoding the interests of Western monopoly capitalism at the expense of the Third World. The latter, he argued, had to find ways to defend their political, economic, and cultural sovereignty against new forms of imperialism.[124]

While endorsing the consensus view that sovereignty had to be limited with respect to legitimate aspects of international legal order, such as those in the UN Charter and the Bandung platform, Wang argued for greater caution toward Western initiatives in the areas of "human rights," culture, and economics, which could be used to build new power hierarchies at others' expense. His programmatic revalorization of sovereignty came at precisely the right time to impact mounting intra-Party debates over the proper scope of global integration and rapprochement, which in the late 1980s were reaching a major inflection point. Intra-Party tensions over increasing Western influences, and the extent to which China should adopt foreign models and prescriptions in both the economic and political spheres, would soon come to a head in factional strife exacerbated by mounting inflation and mass social unrest.[125] The ongoing transformation and future direction of China's economy was also the main preoccupation for leading voices in Wall Street and Washington, who were more concerned that China converge with Western intellectual property and other economic norms than with the ultimately stymied moves toward political liberalization during Zhao Ziyang's ill-fated administration.[126]

The essence of Wang's position, advocacy of a continued but more cautious, state-led economic globalization to promote development of the forces of production, combined with a firm defense of China's territorial, political, cultural, and (when necessary) economic *zhuquan*, was well-suited to the rapidly shifting ideological climate. Especially following the suppression of the Tiananmen protest movement in 1989 and the resumption of economic "reform" after Deng's famous Southern Tour in 1992, the general ethos of Jiang Zemin's post-1989 Party leadership merged a redoubled focus on economic development and liberalization with a newly emphatic assertion of China's sovereignty in civil-political and territorial matters, including in ethnic minority regions.[127] Wang was appointed in 1994 as the dean of Fudan University's law school, and then, soon after, began a decades-long career as a leading ideological authority in the Chinese Communist Party; He has since become a top leader at the national level.[128]

The freeze on domestic political reform after 1989 was paired with positions asserting state sovereignty in Hong Kong via the Basic Law drafting process that terminated in the final version's adoption by the National People's Congress in 1990, and with regards to Taiwan via the "1992 Consensus." When China ratified UNCLOS in 1996, it included statements of reservation regarding its territorial claims, adjustment of borders only via "consultations," and the right of coastal states to limit rights of passage for foreign warships.[129] On China's vast Western border, as well, the changes in Central Asia since the fall of the Soviet Union spurred newly insistent attempts to insulate Beijing's sovereignty from challenges by transnational networks – whether Islamist movements, Tibetan "separatists," or Western rights monitors.[130] One of many incidental symbols of the resumed emphasis on territory was the Lin Zexu Memorial Hall, complete with a statue of its namesake, erected at Ili in 1994.

The assertive position on *zhuquan* was also reflected in Beijing's approach to the newly resumed project of international criminal law. Two elder jurists, Li Haopei and Wang Tieya, took up judicial positions at the International Criminal Tribunal for the Former Yugoslavia (ICTY), where both promoted expansive conceptions of Tribunal jurisdiction and strict enforcement of norms against aggression, genocide, and crimes against humanity.[131] Soon after, when the Rome Conference to frame the prospective International

Criminal Court was to be convened in 1998, it followed a meeting in Beijing to which Wang Tieya had invited the ICTY president and other leading officials in an implicit effort to promote China joining the ICC.[132]

At that year's meeting in Rome, however, China's official delegate Liu Daqun opposed envisioned provisions for the new court's jurisdiction without Security Council action or the consent of a defendant's state. These features "violating the sovereignty of State parties" led to China's negative vote on the Rome Statute.[133] Though obviously rooted in an interpretation of the rights of sovereign states, these objections (like those articulated by Chinese delegates in many forums since the Second Hague Conference and the negotiations at Versailles) were based not on a simplistic opposition between sovereignty and international law but rather on a view emphasizing state agency and requiring active expressions of consent for norms' validity.[134] If translated into the register of general principles of law, that position overlaps with the traditional rule against states being bound by agreements to which they are not parties, *pacta tertiis*. Much the same basic position characterizes most of Beijing's objections to the use of multilateral frameworks to bypass the need for positive expressions of state consent to intrusive regulatory or dispute resolution processes in matters of jurisdiction, territory, and human rights.

This formalistic or positivist approach, centered on the UN Charter and giving free reign to the veto power held by China and other Permanent Five Security Council states, is the most salient feature of Beijing's pronouncements on major questions of international law interpretation. It is especially notable in official positions on matters regarding intervention in the name of ostensibly universal norms, for example, the United States' uses of force for "humanitarian intervention," but also the much softer "meddling" involved in the monitoring activities of global human rights bodies.[135] In the sphere of economic law and institutions, however, Beijing's embrace of multilateral norms and adjudication has been more radical and far-reaching. The "achievement" of WTO entry in 2001, especially, solidified the pursuit of economic globalization as a core element of Party policy. Yet, an initial swing in the direction of liberalization of domestic political/constitutional discourse was, as it had been in the late 1980s, relatively swiftly replaced by resurgent assertions of developmentalist authoritarianism and, most recently, an upsurge of interest in promoting a more Sinocentric regional economic and geopolitical order.[136]

Nonetheless, both before and after WTO entry, mainstream legal and political theory had firmly embraced in principle a multilaterally regulated world economy. As a graduate of the Central Party School put it in a successful 2000 PhD dissertation, citing Hans Kelsen for the point, economic law treaties should be considered as superior to ordinary legislation, and invalid only if they conflict with a state's domestic constitution. The WTO had thus provided China with "a basic frame for economic law."[137] Over the coming years, massive changes to legislation and policy in order to meet WTO requirements would see "[o]ver 2300 laws, regulations and departmental rules [being] drafted, revised and revoked at the central government level, and above 190,000 local regulations, rules and other policy measures [also being altered]."[138]

While experts in China and abroad have often differed in their assessments of China's "compliance" with WTO rules, it is a matter of general consensus that China has embraced the institution as the key forum for promoting its own preferred rule-sets for international economic governance, albeit one increasingly supplemented by its own multilateral initiatives.[139] As state media would declare two decades later:

> Economic globalization is an objective historical process driven jointly by the development of productive forces and changes to the relations of production; it is not determined by the will of man.[140]

The overriding concern for promoting GDP growth and global "stability" that undergirds such positions has, as noted, been paired with a stronger articulation of *zhuquan*, now encompassing both territorial control and selective autonomy from "excessive" foreign economic, cultural, and technological influences. Multilateral forums in which Beijing can play a coleadership role such as the Security Council, the WTO, and of course its own institutions often appear as the ideal places to balance these aims, allowing for what some observers have described as a turn to "institutional statecraft" at the global level.[141] Though the Communist Party remains committed in theory to an eventual Marxian future in which both class and national distinctions no longer divide up humanity, that future tends to be depicted as very far off indeed. It is one only to be reached via a long, historical process of state-led but market-driven "peaceful development" that may address capitalist excesses at the margins, for example, in line with the ideas of a "socialist market economy" and a recent turn to (nonredistributionist) aims of "common prosperity,"[142] but will not seek to radically disrupt the economic world system from which they emanate, or undermine its statist legal architecture. For, "as long as classes, nation-states, and private ownership of the means of production still exist, so too will sovereignty."[143]

Conclusion

From Object to Subject? China in a World of Institutions

Already by the sixteenth century, China had been in many ways embedded into the incipiently "global" economy by means of flows of silver, tea, silk, cotton, and other commodities. By the 1830s and 1840s, many of these flows had been transformed, with the British termination of the East India Company's monopoly, the rise of the opium trade, and comparative Western advantages of technology and maritime dominance setting the stage for new economic relations. International law, which had hardly featured into Sino-Western relations in previous centuries, now became the practical and ideological vehicle for reconstituting China's political economy. At first, this took the form of a *catena* of unequal bilateral treaties, agreed to on the Qing side by officials more concerned with "stateliness" than with legalistically construed state authority.

From the latter half of the 1850s, meanwhile, China was incorporated into Western international law not in the main as a mere partner to a set of *bilateral* agreements – however coercive or unequal – but rather as an object of *multilateral* regulation by a newly project-oriented, cooperatively expansionist, positivist-legislative community. The founding of the *Weltmarkt*, which Marx at this time identified as "the real task of bourgeois society," was coterminous with the creation of a *Weltrecht* that by 1860 encompassed the Qing *gurun*. With it soon came intensified local aspirations for "economic authority" as well as *zhuquan*, the "authority of rule" that would now come to be seen as an inherent attribute of the state.

Global law as a body of positive rules – as a vehicle for intentional "projects" of regulation – required as a necessary condition a set of *objects* for such norm-legislation.[1] The process by which China, along with other Asian states, was made into such an object was also that of recasting its state power as a restricted *imperium*, passive before the rising shoots of foreign *dominium* that used it as a support and scaffolding. This project, already at work in the 1830s "intellectual artillery" the missionary sinologist Karl Gützlaff brought to bear while promoting liberalism, Protestantism, the opium trade, and British power, was also the frame for William Martin as he arbitraged social capital between the nascent Western international law profession and Qing officialdom as a translator-pedagogue. Much the same project was also the primary motivation of the great imposed, multilateral, quasiconstitutional treaty regimes.

From the post-Convention of Beijing initiation of tariff-secured borrowing during Zuo Zongtang's suppression of rebellions in Qing Central Asia, this pattern was reiterated in the post-Boxer Protocol "open door" regime from 1901 and then in the consensus on China's territorial status secured in 1919–1922 between the conferences at Versailles and Washington. Genealogically related "consensus framings" for Chinese sovereignty and the rules of legal and market institutions that would shape its exercise were also put in place at the postwar planning meetings of the mid 1940s and even in many respects also after the People's Republic of China's (PRC's) "return" to the United Nations (UN) system in 1971, and to global markets from the end of that decade. Global institutions and capital flows have always framed modern China's *imperium*, and have in turn produced corresponding local aspirations to imbue *zhuquan* with a more robust sense of sovereign *autonomy*, but also of sovereign *equality*.

The Chinese international law profession, born in the post-Boxer years and coming of age in the ideological ferment between Versailles 1919 and Bandung 1955, reflected previously mentioned as well as various other intellectual influences. Judge Xue Hanqin, a successor to her countryman Wellington Koo as a former vice-president of the International Court of Justice (ICJ), has noted that:

> China [after 1949] was perceived as "an opponent, a challenger and a revolutionary" vis-à-vis the existing legal order. But it is important to understand that China did not opt to be an "outlaw." Although precluded from taking its seat, China expressly endorsed the purposes and principles of the UN Charter and principles of sovereign equality, peace and mutual respect. Its attitudes and practice towards international law manifest both realism and idealism.[2]

Indeed, as we have seen throughout, both interwar and postwar Chinese voices not only endorsed principles of "peace" and "sovereign equality," they were not infrequently among their most committed advocates and expositors in various important settings and interactions. During the period at which this book's account began, China was treated by encroaching Western commercial empires as a quintessential entity of the periphery, yet also, simultaneously, as a focal point for innovating new forms of global regulation. Meanwhile, by the end of this book's account, China had at last attained the status of a securely independent state in many ways central to world affairs and institutions. The paradox of today is that centrality, per se, does not imply unfettered agency. Nor has the radical challenge of Bandung been revived in an age when China's "rise" has been synonymous with its role as (again) the last frontier of global capitalism.

Worldmaking and Will

The Soviet legal scholar Evgeny Pashukanis and many of his later interpreters embraced a depiction of international law as a typical instantiation of "legal form": the assertion of apparently equal rights belied by underlying power disparities, directly reflecting the general form of relations of exchange in capitalism.[3] However, as B. S. Chimni and others have aptly criticized, "capitalism is a process of production, and exchange is merely part of that process."[4] A focus only on substantive inequality in bilateral relations (e.g., "unequal treaties" and their abolition) misses the distinctive dynamics typifying international law as a generator of world order. The form of law is, after all, linked not only to the alienation and exploitation of supposedly free labor but also the precedent "dispossession of the majority of people of the means of production."[5] In this light, the example of China in international legal order, or rather of the polity and economy of China and other states as *produced* by world-ordering legal regimes in various iterations since 1860, suggests the need to view international law as in a broader sense coterminous with the establishment of global capitalist relations of production, changes to those relations over time, and the moral superstructure of beliefs and values erected upon that basis.

When Georges Abi-Saab wrote in 1962 that "[t]he newly independent states are not the legislators of the world," he nonetheless noted an ongoing "transformation of very large parts of the globe, mostly in Africa and Asia, from objects to subjects of international law."[6] A very similar sentiment had been expressed decades earlier by Zhou Gengsheng, one of the founders of the international law profession in modern China, when he wrote in 1920 that China, along with most of humanity, had hitherto been "the objects of international relations [while] Europeans were the subject of international relations."[7] In between, Zhou Enlai and Jawaharlal Nehru's Five Principles of Peaceful Coexistence, and the form of cooperation by Third World states across ideological boundaries institutionalized at Bandung, sought to concretize this new subjecthood. Principles of territorial and popular sovereignty, and self-determination for majority nationalities in former colonial zones, were raised to the level of inviolable precepts in the context of Asian and African cooperation, in contrast to the hierarchically structured Cold War security blocs.

With China's reintegration from 1971, however, the notion of a radically different world system that had been intimated by the Bandung process was itself sublated. Rather than pursue a transformation of global order, China would rise, economically and geopolitically, to the apex of the existing order. Though it would maintain a rhetorical and at times even practical commitment to many elements of the Bandung agenda (not least the rejection of doctrines on the use of force that permit security alliances and humanitarian or preemptive interventions), the same could not be said for the subsequent notions of a New International Economic Order or a redistributionist "right to development," among others, that PRC diplomats still supported in the early years of the Deng era.[8] Indeed, even then, at the UN Commission on Human Rights, General Assembly, and other venues, PRC diplomats verbally supported such initiatives, but did not actively seek to supply their obviously missing component of real operable legal machinery.[9] As the Reform Era PRC subsequently embraced key aspects of the emerging neoliberal world economic system, radical change became ever less of a priority. By the time of China's World Trade Organization (WTO) membership in 2001, it was truly central to both global legal order and political economy – but not as a legislator.

Only in the last decade under Xi Jinping, as China cemented its status as the world's second largest economy (and largest by purchasing power parity metrics) and also began to articulate more activist visions for regional and global order, has this started to shift. However, despite the growing chorus of commentators who see in moves such as the vast Belt and Road Initiative (BRI) of development lending and investment, the founding of the Asian International Investment Bank, or the Regional Comprehensive Economic Partnership (the largest free trade agreement in history) intimations of a "Chinese new world order," the reality is rather less dramatic. Each of these new structures in significant part replicates, and sits atop of, a vast array of existing organs and agreements comprising what has been termed the "ordo-global" arrangement of economic globalization and global governance mediated by layers of "rules-based" – but decidedly undemocratic – institutions.[10] The BRI, for example, sits atop a large preexisting body of bilateral trade and investment treaties (145 as of 2021), which have at times embraced such neoliberal features as investor–state dispute settlement mechanisms.[11] After a long mid twentieth-century interregnum of failed alternatives, the encoding of *dominium* rights via transnational juridical authority has regained pace under Beijing's regional stewardship.

Similarly, China's growing influence within the UN system has relied almost entirely on the use of existing institutional forms of authority, from those of the Security Council to those of the Human Rights Council, and so on, and the promotion of initiatives aimed not at radical action but at defenses and entrenchments of the many aspects of the international status quo from which it has benefited in economic and security terms. Not revolution, but rather refinement and consolidation of existing orders, is the core message of the "human community of fate" (*renlei mingyun gontongti* 人類命運共同體) platform, first articulated by Hu Jintao in 2012 and then expounded to the world by Xi Jinping at a 2015 speech before the UN General Assembly. In this comprehensive international law/international relations platform, there is a reassertion of a strict interpretation of state sovereignty, both in respects to freedom from foreign military interventions and also criticism or sanctions on the basis of human rights, paired with a redoubled commitment to economic globalization and multilateral technocratic institutions.[12]

Notions of an international "rule of law" can be invoked for a vast number of different purposes. For example, Western states, led by the United States, have made it a regular practice to dispatch aircraft carriers in rejection of any possible Chinese claim to an exclusive maritime zone in the multilateral South China Sea dispute, while both Beijing and Taipei have agreed on the illegitimacy of the 2016 *Philippines* v. *China* tribunal, with its innovative "island versus rock" definition by a panel of arbitrators and decision to ignore reservations on sovereignty issues.[13] Meanwhile, the PRC's compliance with the nonsovereignty-implicating aspects of the ruling remain a topic of debate,[14] while its official nonrecognition of the tribunal and its outcome reiterates the behavior of other states in similar "security" contexts, notably those impinging on great powers' Monroe Doctrine-esque regional sphere of influence.[15] China and Russia have, indeed, recently begun to formally define an international law platform to reflect a shared focus on sovereignty,[16] which has also been encoded into the Shanghai Cooperation Organization and other Beijing-sponsored institutions. National *zhuquan*, regional security, one-party rule, and global capitalism remain locked in a sometimes tense, but often mutually reinforcing embrace.[17]

Meanwhile, no Chinese initiative to date has raised the same prospect that seemed briefly viable at Bandung – that of a world order wholly remaking its traditional focal points of power, wealth, and influence. Instead, whether in its role in the post-1945 architecture of global institutions or in creating new ones, Beijing's approach to global legal order has tended toward refining and entrenching extant structures of political economy and global governance. The sense of radical, world-remaking agency that animated decolonial struggles in the 1940s–1960s is not the dominant affect at the memorandum of understanding–signings and black-tie banquets of the BRI. Nor does it characterize the vast security state that is intertwined with them and that, as well, creates great structures of encumbering commitments and liabilities even as it facilitates new modes of statecraft.

What is clear, however, is that China has attained a position of centrality in global order in a way deeply reliant on a status quo of neoliberal globalization and relative stability. The process of "opening up" has meant wealth and power, but also new insecurities. To pair continued global integration with an ever-firmer articulation of the rules of "stately" deference on political and territorial matters that Beijing insists be observed by foreign states, corporations, and individuals may for many of today's officials and intellectuals seem the best of both worlds. For such a formalist legal order built atop an informal structure of "win–win cooperation" among developmentalist regimes, the central pillar of legal organization may be neither *pacta sunt servanda* nor absolutist ideas of sovereignty per se, but rather the principle *pacta tertiis*: That only formal consent can ground legal obligations, and that even "global" regimes cannot reach beyond such consent to bind third parties. Reviewing the long arc of international law encounters and aspirations since the 1840s, this rule may, perhaps, even seem to emerge as China's *Grundnorm*.

Rectifying Names in International Legal History

The premise that a state (or other group) can oppose certain aspects of a legal order, or find itself marginalized and even excluded from it, while still endorsing many of its fundamental norms or structures and thus being committed to a *version* of that order, is highly relevant today. The PRC is only one of many states that still occupies a position vis-à-vis international legal institutions that regards the latter as both existentially essential and at times inherently suspect, with their origins in large part contingent upon a history in which others – the great Western colonial empires – have played a dominant and often exploitative role. Lasting restrictions on the agency of the newly decolonized, experiences of attaining subjectivity only once the major decisions have already been made, trouble international law's legitimacy.

On the other hand, those empires did not play the only role. International law also changed and developed as it was being "introduced" to China, and this included varying degrees of influence by Chinese officials and jurists who sought agency within this imposed order. Their experiences raise important questions as to whether, and to what extent, the great legislative moments of international law, from the Hague Conferences to San Francisco, 1945 or the Rome Conference of 1998, offered only a "false contingency" – giving weak powers mere apparitions of agency or free will – as opposed to serving as fields for genuinely open-ended struggle.[18]

The meaning of the symbol "equality" in such contexts changed when non-Western actors became active participants in its invocation. The degree of agency available to Chinese engaged with questions of international law certainly transformed greatly from the time when a young Wang Chonghui sat in the audience at the Second Hague Conference as a recent Yale graduate, and (perhaps) heard his compatriot's proposal for a more specific definition of "war" being literally laughed out of the day's proceedings, to the time when, almost four decades later, he himself helped to lead advocacy for legal restrictions on the use of force and compulsory ICJ jurisdiction.

Of course, specific Chinese proposals on matters such as the international air force, compulsory jurisdiction of the ICJ, and indeed the more specific definition of aggression, were not successfully adopted in 1945. "Chinese monism" nonetheless played an important role in promoting the accelerated pursuit of endeavors such as the progressive codification of international law – as we have seen, references to international law were absent from the Dumbarton Oaks proceedings until Chinese insistence on their inclusion – but these efforts nonetheless faced sharp limitations arising from geopolitical realities. The same might be said for the initiatives undertaken in the postwar period by jurists on either side of the Taiwan Strait.

Nonetheless, these and other episodes of engagement in and contribution to the development of international legal order by Chinese actors deserve a larger space in the modern professional memory of international law. It is striking, for example, that as of the time of writing there is no reference to Liang Yunli on the website of the International Law Commission (ILC),[19] that Wellington Koo's Shanghainese given name is misspelled on the website of the ICJ, of which he was a former vice-president,[20] and that Holl's joke about Yang Ru calling the Hague Conference "too much talkee-talkee" still gets repeated in grave academic prose.[21] Wang Chonghui, China's Hong Kong–born first international judge, the leading advocate for compulsory ICJ jurisdiction during the planning meetings of 1945, and the person directly responsible for the General Assembly's ability to request advisory opinions, among other contributions, is now little known to international lawyers globally. Some of the figures discussed in this book, meanwhile, are all but forgotten not only in the West but also on either side (or in a few cases both sides) of the Taiwan Strait, for reasons having more to do with their political affiliations than their roles in the actual history of international law discourse.

International lawyers globally should engage with this history, as it is an important but often overlooked facet of the origins of our current legal, geopolitical, and economic architecture, and thus of a shared future whose contours are still unknown. It may well be that international law's expansive aims will be neither triumphant or defeated in the coming years, but rather that we will find ourselves in a world exhibiting a "multiplicity of universalisms."[22] More cosmopolitan forms of professional memory may thus be in order if international law's promissory notes of universal progress are to remain valid tender in a less Eurocentric world.

Glossary of Chinese and Japanese Names

Ariga Nagao	有賀長雄
Chang Naide	常乃悳
Chen Duxiu	陳獨秀
Chen Tiqiang	陳體強
Ci'an	慈安
Ci'xi	慈禧
Daoguang	道光
Deng Xiaoping	鄧小平
Ding Shiyuan	丁士源
Ding Weiliang (William Alexander Parsons Martin)	丁韙良
Dong Biwu	董必武
Gu Weijun (Wellington Koo)	顧維鈞
Guangxu	光緒
Guanzi	管子
Guiliang	桂良
Guo Songtao	郭嵩焘
Guo Taiqi	郭泰祺
Han Depei	韩德培
He Guiqing	何桂清
Hu Jintao	胡錦濤
Hu Lin	胡霖
Hu Shi (Hu Shih)	胡適
Hu Weide	胡惟德
Huashana	花沙納
Jiang Haichao	江海潮
Jiang Jieshi (Chiang Kai-shek)	蔣介石
Jiang Tingfu	蔣廷黻
Jiang Zemin	江澤民
Kang Youwei	康有為
Kong Xiangxi (H.H. Kung)	孔祥熙
Li Haopei	李浩培
Li Hongzhang	李鴻章
Li Huang	李璜

Li Shengwu	李聖五
Li Shuangyuan	李双元
Li Zhengfen	李正棻
Liang Yunli	梁鋆立
Liu Daqun	劉大群
Lin Zexu	林則徐
Lu Zhengxiang	陸徵祥
Muzhang'a (Mujangga)	穆彰阿
Ma Derun	馬德潤
Ma Jianzhong	馬建忠
Mao Zedong	毛澤東
Mei Ru'ao	梅汝璈
Ni Zhengyu	倪征燠
Nishi Amane	西 周
Ōkubo Toshimichi	大久保 利通
Ōkuma Shigenobu	大隈 重信
Pi Xirui	皮錫瑞
Prince Gong (I-hsin/Yixin)	恭親王
Qian Xun	钱恂
Qiu Zuming	邱祖铭
Qiying (Kiyeng)	耆英
Senggelinqin (Sengge Rinchen)	僧格林沁
Sheng Xuanhuai	盛宣懷
Soejima Taneomi	副島 種臣
Song Ziwen (T. V. Soong)	宋子文
Sun Ke (Sun Fo)	孫科
Sun Yat-sen	孫中山
Tongzhi	同治
Tang Caichang	唐才常
Tang Shaoyi	唐紹儀
Tsuda Mamichi	津田 真道
Tsutsumi Koshiji	堤殼士志
Ueno Kagenori	上野景範
Uryū Mitora	瓜生三寅
Wang Chonghui	王寵惠
Wang Huning	王滬寧
Wang Jingwei	汪精衛
Wang Shijie	王世杰
Wang Tieya	王鐵崖
Wang Yuanshen	王元深
Wang Zhengting	王正廷
Wei Daoming	魏道明
Wei Yuan	魏遠

Wu Chaoshu	伍朝樞
Wu Yifang	吳貽芳
Xi Jinping	習近平
Xianfeng	咸豐
Xiang Zhejun	向哲浚
Xiong Xiling	熊希齡
Xu Daolin (Hsü Dau-lin)	徐道鄰
Xu Jingcheng	許景澄
Xu Mo (Hsu Mo)	徐謨
Xu Shuxi (Shu-hsi Hsu)	徐淑熙
Xue Fucheng	薛福成
Xue Hanqin	薛捍勤
Xunzi	荀子
Yanagiwara Sakimitsu	柳原前光
Yang Ru	杨儒
Yao Meizhen	姚梅镇
Ye Mingchen	葉名琛
Yizhu (Iju/Xianfeng)	奕詝
Yuan Dehui	袁德輝
Yuan Shikai	袁世凱
Yi Jun (이준)	李儁
Yi Zongkui	易宗夔
Zeng Guofan	曾國藩
Zhang Junmai (Carsun Chang)	張君勱
Zhang Pengchun (P. C. Chang)	張彭春
Zhang Shenfu	张申府
Zhang Zhidong	張之洞
Zhao Ziyang	赵紫阳
Zheng Bin (Bin Cheng)	鄭斌
Zheng Tianxi	鄭天錫
Zhou Enlai	周恩來
Zhou Gengsheng	周鯁生
Zhou Wei	周緯
Zhou Zechun	周泽春
Zhou Ziya	周子亚
Zuo Zongtang	左宗棠

Notes

Introduction

1 For other challenges to one or more of these premises, see Otsuka Hirohiko, "Japan's Early Encounter with the Concept of the 'Law of Nations,'" *Japanese Annual of International Law* 13, no. 35 (1969): 35–65; Onuma Yasuaki, "When Was the Law of International Society Born?: An Inquiry of the History of International Law from an Intercivilizational Perspective," *Journal of the History of International Law* 2, no. 1 (2000): 1–66; Arnulf Becker Lorca, *Mestizo International Law* (Cambridge: Cambridge University Press, 2014).

2 Georges M. Abi-Saab, "The Newly Independent States and the Rules of International Law: An Outline," *Howard Law Journal* 8, no. 2 (1962): 97–121 (emphasis added).

3 See, e.g., Quentin Skinner, "Meaning and Understanding in the History of Ideas," *History and Theory* 8, no. 1 (1969): 3–53; Hayden White, "Foreword" in Reinhart Koselleck, *The Practice of Conceptual History: Timing History, Spacing Concepts* (Stanford, CA: Stanford University Press, 2002) (Todd Samuel Presner, trans.). Koselleck's approach "focuses on the invention and development of the fundamental concepts (*Begriffe*) underlying and informing a distinctively historical (*geschichtliche*) manner of being in the world" – in this case that of international law. Ibid.

4 Zhongguo Di Yi Lishi Dang'an Guan 中国第一历史档案馆 [First Historical Archives of China], "Qing Dai Zhong-Xi Maoyi Shang Qian An Dang'an 清代中西贸易商欠案档案" [Records Related to Debts in Qin Era Sino-Western Trade], *Lishi Dang'an* 4 (2020): 4.

5 Adam Smith, *An Inquiry into the Nature and Causes of the Wealth of Nations* (London: Printed for W. Strahan and T. Cadell in the Strand, 1776), vol. 1, 87.

6 Preamble, *Constitution of the People's Republic of China* (1982). Available at: www.npc.gov.cn/zgrdw/englishnpc/Constitution/node_2825.htm.

7 On center–periphery relationships within a hierarchically structured "world system" as emanating from unequal power dynamics in three distinct but linked dimensions of productivity, trade, and finance, see Immanuel Wallerstein, *The Modern World System II: Mercantilism and the Consolidation of the European World-Economy, 1600–1750* (New York: Academic Press, 1980).

8 See Ernst Bloch, "Nonsynchronism and the Obligation to Its Dialectics," *New German Critique* 11 (1977): 22–38 (Mark Ritter, trans.) (original publication

1935). Later interpreters have often applied this idea to, e.g., the persistence of feudal social forms even after widespread industrialization. See, e.g., Louis Althusser and Etienne Balibar, *Reading Capital* (New York: Verso, 1970) (Ben Brewster, trans.); Fredric Jameson, *Postmodernism, or, The Cultural Logic of Late Capitalism* (Durham, NC: Duke University Press, 1991), 307.

9 The "turn to history" in international law has been associated both with efforts to supplement professional/doctrinal memory with more accurate historical narratives and to account for ideological factors in the field's genealogy. See Martti Koskenniemi, *The Gentle Civilizer of Nations: The Rise and Fall of International Law 1870–1960* (Cambridge: Cambridge University Press, 2001); Martti Koskenniemi, "A History of International Law Histories" in Bardo Fassbender, Anne Peters, Simone Peter, and Daniel Högger (eds.), *The Oxford Handbook of the History of International Law* (Oxford: Oxford University Press, 2012); Thomas Skouteris, "Engaging History in International Law" in José María Beneyto and David Kennedy (eds.), *New Approaches to International Law* (The Hague: T. M. C. Asser Press, 2012), 99–121; Matthew Craven, "Theorizing the Turn to History in International Law" in Anne Orford and Florian Hoffmann (eds.), *The Oxford Handbook of the Theory of International Law* (Oxford: Oxford University Press, 2016); Ntina Tzouvala, *Capitalism as Civilisation: A History of International Law* (Cambridge: Cambridge University Press, 2020); Martti Koskenniemi, *To the Uttermost Parts of the Earth: Legal Imagination and International Power 1300–1870* (Cambridge: Cambridge University Press, 2021). Cf. Martin Clark, "Ambivalence, Anxieties/Adaptations, Advances: Conceptual History and International Law," *Leiden Journal of International Law* 31, no. 4 (2018): 747–771.

10 Some particularly useful recent studies of China's relation to key aspects of international order, international law, and Western public law concepts during the period under consideration include, *inter alia* James L. Hevia, *English Lessons: The Pedagogy of Imperialism in Nineteenth-Century China* (Durham, NC: Duke University Press, 2003); Pär Kristoffer Cassel, *Grounds of Judgment: Extraterritoriality and Imperial Power in Nineteenth-Century China and Japan* (Oxford: Oxford University Press, 2011); Stefan Kroll, *Normgenese durch Re-interpretation: China und das europäische Völkerrecht im 19. und 20. Jahrhundert* (Baden-Baden: Nomos, 2012); Gao Quanxi, Zhang Wei, and Tian Feilong, *Xiandai Zhongguo Zou Xiang Fazhi zhi Lu* 现代中国走向法治之路 (Beijing: Social Sciences Academic Press China, 2012); Peter Zarrow, *After Empire: The Conceptual Transformation of the Chinese State, 1885–1924* (Stanford, CA: Stanford University Press, 2012); Teemu Ruskola, *Legal Orientalism* (Cambridge, MA: Harvard University Press, 2013); Hans van de Ven, *Breaking with the Past: The Maritime Customs Service and the Global Origins of Modernity in China* (New York: Columbia University Press, 2014); Stephen R. Halsey, *Quest for Power: European Imperialism and the Making of Chinese Statecraft* (Cambridge, MA: Harvard University Press, 2015); Li Chen, *Chinese Law in Imperial Eyes: Sovereignty, Justice, and Transcultural Politics* (New York: Columbia University Press, 2015); Zhang Yongle, *Jiu Bang Xin Zao: 1911–1917* (旧邦新造 1911–1917) (Beijing: Peking University Press,

2016); Jenny Huangfu Day, *Qing Travelers to the Far West: Diplomacy and the Information Order in Late Imperial China* (Cambridge: Cambridge University Press, 2018).

11 Christopher Tomlins, "After Critical Legal History: Scope, Scale, Structure," *Annual Review of Law and Social Science* 8, no. 1 (2012): 31–68.

12 Matthew Craven, "Introduction: International Law and Its Histories" in Matthew Craven, Fitzmaurice Malgosia, and Maria Vogiatzi (eds.), *Time, History and International Law* (Leiden: Martinus Nijhoff Publishers, 2007), 1–26.

13 See, e.g., Ingo Venzke, "Introduction: Situating Contingency in the Path of International Law" in Ingo Venzke and Kevin Jon Heller (eds.), *Contingency in International Law: On the Possibility of Different Legal Histories* (Oxford: Oxford University Press, 2021).

14 Koskenniemi, *The Gentle Civilizer of Nations*, 5; Craven, "Theorizing the Turn to History in International Law," 3; Skouteris, "Engaging History in International Law," 103.

15 On this theme in relation to colonial expansion, see, e.g., Richard Tuck, *The Rights of War and Peace: Political Thought and the International Order from Grotius to Kant* (Oxford: Oxford University Press, 1999); Edward Keene, *Beyond the Anarchical Society: Grotius, Colonialism and Order in World Politics* (Cambridge: Cambridge University Press, 2002); Carl Schmitt, *The Nomos of the Earth in the International Law of the* Jus Publicum Europaeum (New York: Telos Press, 2003) (G. L. Ulmen, trans.).

16 See, e.g., Charles G. Fenwick and Westel W. Willoughby, *Types of Restricted Sovereignty and of Colonial Autonomy* (Washington, DC: Government Printing Office, 1919), 99–112.

17 For some useful recent studies, see Ma Ziyi, "Cong 'Tianxia' Dao 'Zhuquan': Cong Tiaoyue, Chuanjiao Kan Qingmo Shehui Guannian de Bianhua 從「天下」到「主權」——從條約、傳教看清末社會觀念的變化" [From "Tianxia" to "Zhuquan": Evaluating the Transformation of Concepts in Late Qing Society through Treaties and Missionary Activity], *Shilin* 6 (2004): 15–22; Zhang Yongxin, "Wanqing Zhongguoren de Zhuquan Guannian: Guojifa Shijiao 晚清中国人的主权观念－国际法视角" [Perspectives on Sovereignty of Late Qing Era China: An International Law Perspective], *Beijing Shixue* 10 (2004): 102–134; Maria Adele Carrai, *Sovereignty in China: A Genealogy of a Concept since 1840* (Cambridge: Cambridge University Press, 2019); Jin Guantao, Liu Qingfeng, and Qiu Weiyun, "Zhongguo Xiandai Zhuquan Guannian Xingcheng de Shuwei Renwen Yanjiu 中國現代主權觀念形成的數位人文研究" [A Digital Humanities Approach to Studying the Formation of the Modern Concept of Sovereignty in China], *Ershiyi Shiji Shuangyuekan* 172 (2019): 49–67.

18 Onuma Yasuaki, *A Transcivilizational Perspective on International Law: Questioning Prevalent Cognitive Frameworks in the Emerging Multi-polar and Multi-civilizational World of the Twenty-First Century* (Leiden: Martinus Nijhoff Publishers, 2010), 306.

19 Wang Tieya, "International Law in China: Historical and Contemporary Perspectives," *Recueil de Cours de L'Académie de Droit International* 221 (1990): 213–214.

20 Onuma, *A Transcivilizational Perspective on International Law*, 285.

21 See Ryan Martínez Mitchell, "International Law as Project or System?," *Georgetown Journal of International Law* 51, no. 3 (2019): 623–689. The system/project distinction in legal imagination, referring to the possible *a priori* interpretation of legal rules as either "natural" by-products of social organization or intention-bearing artifacts of human will, is drawn from Paul W. Kahn, *The Origins of Order: Project and System in the American Legal Imagination* (New Haven, CT: Yale University Press, 2019).

22 Qing Dynasty Imperial Examinations Collection (via Shu Tong Wen Guji Shujuku).

23 Ibid.

24 In addition to the recent works mentioned, see also classic studies including Hosea Ballou Morse, *The International Relations of the Chinese Empire* (London: Longmans, Green, and Company, 1918), vols. 1–3; Immanuel C. Y. Hsü, *The Ili Crisis: A Study of Sino-Russian Diplomacy 1871–1881* (Oxford: Clarendon Press, 1965); John K. Fairbank, ed., *The Chinese World Order: Traditional China's Foreign Relations* (Cambridge, MA: Harvard University Press, 1968); James Louis Hevia, *Cherishing Men from Afar: Qing Guest Ritual and the Macartney Embassy of 1793* (Durham, NC: Duke University Press, 1995); Lydia He Liu, *The Clash of Empires* (Cambridge, MA: Harvard University Press, 2004); Wang Hui, *Zhongguo Xiandai Sixiang de Xingqi* 中國現代思想的興起 [*The Rise of Modern Chinese Thought*], 4 vols. (Beijing: Sanlian Shudian, 2004); Immanuel C. Y. Hsü, *China's Entrance into the Family of Nations: The Diplomatic Phase, 1858–1880* (Cambridge, MA: Harvard University Press, 2013) (original publication 1960).

25 Cf. Quentin Skinner, "Meaning and Understanding in the History of Ideas," in James Tully (ed.), *Meaning and Context: Quentin Skinner and His Critics* (Princeton, NJ: Princeton University Press, 1988), 67 ("such histories [are] indispensably 'relevant', not because crude 'lessons' can be picked out of them, but because the history itself provides a lesson in self-knowledge. To demand from the history of thought a solution to our own immediate problems is thus to commit not merely a methodological fallacy, but something like a moral error. But to learn from the past – and we cannot otherwise learn at all – the distinction between what is necessary and what is the product merely of our own contingent arrangements, is to learn the key to self-awareness itself").

Chapter 1

1 Zuo Zongtang, "Preface" in *Lin Wen Zhong Gong Zheng Shu* 林文中公政書 [*Policy Writings of Lin Zexu*] (Shanghai: Shangwu Yinshuguan, 1935); cf. Peter B. Lavelle, *The Profits of Nature: Colonial Development and the Quest for Resources in Nineteenth-Century China* (New York: Columbia University Press, 2020).

2 Lin Zexu, *Lin Zexu Quanji: Riji Juan* 林则徐全集: 日记卷 [Complete Works of Lin Zexu: Memoirs] (Fuzhou: Haixia Wenyi Chubanshe, 2002), 537.

3 QSL, Xianfeng Shilu, Daoguang 30, Juan 20 (偽言熒惑。使朕不知外事).

4 FO 17/170.

5 See, e.g., FO 17/160; Thomas Francis Wade, *Note upon the Condition and Government of the Chinese Empire in 1849* (Hong Kong: China Mail Office, 1850), 1.

6 See, e.g., FO 17/172, 430–432 (letter to Lord Palmerston from the Chamber of Commerce and Manufacturers of Manchester advocating a permanent "British Mission at Pekin").

7 Long Xiaofei, "Qiying Waijiao Lilun Chu Tan," *Shoudu Bowuguan Congkan* 0 (1995): 30–36.

8 Li Guanghe, "Yapian Zhanzheng Qianhou Qiying Dui Wai Jiaoshe Lunshu 鴉片戰爭前後耆英對外交涉論述" [Kiyeng's Commentary on Foreign Relations before and after the Opium War], *Huaibei Meishiyuan Xuebao (Zhexue Shehui Kexue Ban)* 2 (1999): 3–5; CBYWSM, Daoguang Year 20, Juan 16 ("硃批以現在情形而論所辦尚是總要上不傷國體下不開邊釁").

9 See Li Yumin, "Wanqing Shiqi Guoti Guan de Bianhua Shitan 晚清时期国体观的变化试探" [Analyzing the Transformation of Perspectives on *Guoti* during the Late Qing Period], *Renwen Zazhi* 6 (2013): 71–90; Fan Xianzheng, "'Guoti' yu 'Zhengti' Zai Jindai Zhongguo de Yanbian yu Fenhua '国体' 与 '政体' 在近代中国的演变与分化" [The Development and Separation of "Guoti" and "Zhengti" in Modern China], *Xueshu Yanjiu* 3 (2014): 40–45.

10 See Luo Zhufeng, *Hanyu Dacidian* 汉语大辞典 (Shanghai: Shanghai Cishu, 1990).

11 Ibid. ("国之全体").

12 Ibid. A closely related set of implications would soon develop around the so-called *ti/yong* (i.e., essence/function) division that was applied to Western science beginning in the late nineteenth century, with the implication that *zhong "xue wei ti, xi xue wei yong* 中學為體，西學為用" [Chinese learning [remains] the essence while Western learning provides us with useful techniques]. Zhang Zhidong, *Quan Xue Pian* 勸學篇 [*Promotion of Learning*] (Changsha: Liang Hu Shu Yuan, 1898). Separately, by the early twentieth century, the term *guoti* would gain a new set of associations derived from its Japanese equivalent *kokutai* 国体 – the latter itself having been imbued with notions of a polity's fundamental structure derived from the German public law concept *Staatsform*. Today, *guoti* is in fact most often used in this sense, describing the most fundamental aspects of the state's constitutional order. Cf. Lin Laifan, "Guoti Gainianshi: Kuaguo Yizhi yu Yanbian 国体概念史: 跨国移植与演变" [The History of State Form as a Concept: Transnational Transplants and Evolution], *Zhongguo Shehui Kexue* 3 (2013): 65–84; Yu Zhong, "Suowei Guoti: Xianfa Shike yu Liang Qichao de Gonghe Zaizao Shike 所谓国体: 宪法时刻与梁启超的共和再造时刻" [The So-called *Guoti*: Constitutional Moments and Liang Qichao's Moment of Reforming the Republic], *Faxuejia* 4 (2015): 158–175.

13 See, e.g., QSL, Qianlong Shilu, Juan 139 for the term's use in a corruption-related context.

14 Clifford Geertz, *Negara: The Theatre-State in Nineteenth-Century Bali* (Princeton, NJ: Princeton University Press, 1980), 121.

15 Martin Loughlin, *Foundations of Modern Public Law* (Oxford: Oxford University Press, 2010), 187 (emphasis added).

16 See Peter C. Perdue, *China Marches West: The Qing Conquest of Central Eurasia* (Cambridge, MA: Harvard University Press, 2009), 433–436, 500–501 ("[T]he practical world of politics … is more evident in the non-Chinese texts").

17 In another of Qianlong's frequent invocations of the concept, he commented in 1788 upon the volatile relations with the Gurkha kingdom on Tibet's borders: "compare this with [the situation in] Annan, which has surrendered and offered tribute: that serves better to esteem *guoti* and display martial might." QSL, Qianlong Shilu, Juan 1411.

18 On *gurun i doro*, see Perdue, *China Marches West*, 111, 123; Nicola di Cosmo, "Nurhaci's Gambit: Sovereignty as Concept and Praxis in the Rise of the Manchus" in Zvi Ben-Dor Benite, Stefanos Geroulanos, and Nicole Jerr (eds.), *The Scaffolding of Sovereignty: Global and Aesthetic Perspectives on the History of a Concept* (New York: Columbia University Press, 2017), 102–123.

19 *Jimi* 羈縻 (bridling and reining) was a traditional term used to refer to successive Chinese dynasties' policies of pursuing pragmatic relations with particularly troublesome foreign peoples not easily susceptible to "moral transformation." See, e.g., Peng Jianying, "Zhongguo Chuantong Jimi Zhengce Lüelun 中国传统羁縻政策略论" [Overview of Traditional Chinese *Jimi* Policies], *Xibei Daxue Xuebao: Zhexue Shehui Kexue Ban* 34, no. 1 (2004): 104–108.

20 See, e.g., "Zhong-Mei Fu Meng Lu: 'Da Huangdi' yu 'Hao Pengyou,'" *Peng Pai*, July 11, 2018. Available at: www.thepaper.cn/newsDetail_forward_2254376.

21 As well, the official Qing practice of referring to China as *Dulimbai Gurun* – the Central State, i.e., *Zhongguo* 中國 – arguably combined the Sinocentric worldview with a more pluralistic political reality.

22 In the entire official *Veritable Records of the Ming Dynasty*, for example, the only imperial orders or court memorials that mention *liang guo* 兩國 (two states) do so in reference to two *other* states, besides China itself, which as a notionally universal polity, is not discussed in this manner.

23 For the Latin version, see Joseph Sebes, *The Jesuits and the Sino-Russian Treaty of Nerchinsk (1689): The Diary of Thomas Pereira, S. J.* (Rome: Institutum Historicum, 1962), 157; for the Russian, see Mikhail M. Speranskii, *Polnoe Sobranie: Zakonov Rossiiskoi Imperii s 1649 Goda, Vol. 3, 1689–1699* (St. Petersburg: Tipografiya Ego Imperatorskogo Velichestva Kantselyarii, 1830), 31–32; a transcription of the Manchu version is available in Walter Fuches, "Der Russisch–Chinesische Vertrag Von Nertschinsk Vom Jahre 1689: Eine Textkrische Betrachtung," *Monumenta Serica* 4, no. 2 (1940): 546–593.

24 The Manchu version of Daoguang/Kiyeng's message to President Tyler referred to the Treaty of Wangxia in specifically legal terms perhaps best translated as "the new imperial law" (Ma. *iqe kooli*), while the Chinese version's *tiaokuan* 條款 could refer to either agreements or domestically-promulgated codes and statutes.

25 On Lin's translation, see Rune Svarverud, *International Law as a World Order in Late Imperial China: Translation, Reception and Discourse; 1847–1911*

(Leiden: Brill, 2007). Jesuit scholars in the Ming era had previously translated at least excerpts from other texts on the law of nations, though apparently with very little impact.

26 Lin's interactions with the British side regarding obligations to punish sailors accused of crimes in Kowloon, for example, seemed to draw on some Vattelian premises.

27 Emer de Vattel, *The Law of Nations* (London: S. Sweet and A. Maxwell, 1834) (Joseph Chitty, trans.), 171–172; book 2, §100.

28 Ibid.

29 Cf. Reinhart Koselleck, "Staat und Souveränität" in Otto Brunner, Werner Conze, and Reinhart Koselleck (eds.), *Geschichtliche Grundbegriffe: Historisches Lexicon zur Politisch-Sozialen Sprache in Deutschland* (Stuttgart: Klett-Cotta, 1972–1990), vol. 6, 120.

30 Vattel, *The Law of Nations*, 171–172, book 2, §100.

31 Wei Yuan, *Wei Yuan Quanji* 魏源全集 (Changsha: Yuelu Shushe, 2004), vol. 7, 1981.

32 Vattel, *The Law of Nations*, §90.

33 Ibid., 131, §292.

34 Daniel Lee, "Sources of Sovereignty: Roman Imperium and Dominium in Civilian Theories of Sovereignty," *Politica Antica* 2, no. 1 (2012): 79–80.

35 Philippe-Antoine Merlin, *Répertoire universel et raisonné de jurisprudence* (Paris: Garnery, 1827–1828), vol. 17 ("Nul ne peut être contraint de céder sa propriété, si ce nest pour cause d'utilité publique, et moyennant une juste et préalable indemnité ... Au citoyen appartient la propriété, et au souverain l'empire ... Telle est la maxime de tout les pays et de tout les tems [sic] ... L'empire, qui est le partage du souverain, ne renferme aucune idée du domaine proprement dit.").

36 Vattel, *The Law of Nations*, 89, 111–112; §182, §244–245; cf. Henry Wheaton, *Elements of International Law*, 6th ed. (William Beach Lawrence, ed.) (Boston: Little, Brown, & Co., 1855), 366–367.

37 Koskenniemi, *To the Uttermost Parts of the Earth*, 151.

38 HC Deb April 8, 1840 vol. 53 cc. 749–837.

39 Jennifer Pitts, *Boundaries of the International: Law and Empire* (Cambridge, MA: Harvard University Press, 2018), 134–135.

40 Ibid.

41 Cf. Chun Yu, "Wei Yuan, Lin Zexu yu 'Haiguo Tuzhi' 魏源, 林则徐与 '海国图志'" [Wei Yuan, Lin Zexu, and *Haiguo Tuzhi*], *Wenshi Zazhi* 4 (2006): 26–30.

42 See Jessie Gregory Lutz, *Opening China: Karl F. A. Gützlaff and Sino-Western Relations, 1827–1852* (Cambridge: Wm. B. Eerdmans Publishing, 2008).

43 See Stephen R. Platt, *Imperial Twilight: The Opium War and the End of China's Last Golden Age* (New York: Alfred A. Knopf, 2018).

44 Ai Han Zhe [Karl Gützlaff], *Dong Xi Yang Kao Mei Yue Tong Ji Zhuan*东西洋考每月统记传 [*East and West Monthly Journal*] (Guangzhou: 1833–1838).

45 Gützlaff had distributed writings on political as well as religious topics from the very beginning of his missionary activities in China, and in a voyage to Tianjin in 1831 he had already distributed a "general account of the English nation that was eagerly received by all classes." It is likely that parts of the political lexicon

developed in his later writings, perhaps including "the principle of self-rule," were already developed in these earlier works.

46 Cf. S. Wells Williams, "Christian Missions among the Chinese" in *The Middle Kingdom*, vol. 2 (Leiden: Global Oriental: 2007), 275.

47 "On the one hand, Gützlaff saw himself as the insignificant tool of God, but on the other hand, he aspired to convert, not merely China, but all of East Asia in his own lifetime." Lutz, *Opening China*, 30.

48 Karl Friedrich August Gützlaff, *China Opened* (Cambridge: Cambridge University Press, 2015), 235

49 Wang Yuanshen, *Sheng Dao Dong Lai Kao* 聖道東來考 [*Treatise on the Arrival of the Holy Way in the East*] (Hong Kong, self-published, 1899).

50 See Ralph Covell, *W. A. P. Martin: Pioneer of Progress in China* (Washington, DC: Christian University Press, 1978); Anonymous, "The Life and Work of the Late Dr. W. A. P. Martin," *The Chinese Recorder* 48, no. 2 (1917): 116–123 (suggesting that Martin eventually objected to his own family's reliance on "slave labor").

51 William Alexander Parsons Martin, *A Cycle of Cathay: Or, China, South and North, with Personal Reminiscences* (New York: Fleming H. Revell, 1896), 19.

52 Ibid., 18.

53 Ibid., 21.

54 Lai Xinxia, *Lin Zexu Nianpu Chang Pian* 林则徐年谱长编 [*Chronicle of the Life of Lin Zexu*], vol. 1 (Shanghai: Shanghai Jiatong Daxue Chubanshe, 2011), 13.

55 Gregory Afinogenov, *Spies and Scholars: Chinese Secrets and Imperial Russia's Quest for World Power* (Cambridge, MA: Belknap Press, 2020), 243–255.

56 QSL, Xianfeng Shilu, Juan 23, Daoguang 30 (1850).

57 QSL, Xianfeng Shilu, Juan 40, Xianfeng 1 (1851).

58 QSL, Xianfeng Shilu, Juan 44, Xianfeng 1 (1851).

59 See, e.g., Pitts, *Boundaries of the International*, 144–146.

60 Afinogenov, *Spies and Scholars*, 248–252.

61 van de Ven, *Breaking with the Past.*

62 Cf. Mitchell, "International Law as Project or System?," 623.

63 Cf. History of the Chinese Maritime Customs Project, University of Bristol. Available at: www.chinafamilies.net/records/chinese-maritime-customs-service/about-the-project/.

64 See, e.g., Felix Boecking, "Tariffs, Powers, Nationalism, and Modernity: Fiscal Policy in Guomindang-Controlled China, 1927–1945" (PhD dissertation, Cambridge University, 2008).

65 On the circumstances surrounding the run-up to the Arrow War or so-called Second Opium War, see Morse, *The International Relations of the Chinese Empire*, vol. 1; John Yue-wo Wong, *Deadly Dreams: Opium and the Arrow War (1856–1860) in China* (Cambridge: Cambridge University Press, 2002); Hevia, *English Lessons*, 31–48.

66 Travers Twiss, *Two Introductory Lectures on the Science of International Law* (London: Longman, 1856), 42.

67 Wheaton, *Elements of International Law*, clxxxiii.

68 See, e.g., Johann Caspar Bluntschli, *Das moderne Völkerrecht der civilisirten Staten: als Rechtsbuch dargestellt*, 2nd ed. (Nördlingen: C. H. Beck, 1878), 62–63.

69 Heinhard Steiger, "Völkerrecht" in Brunner, Conze, and Koselleck (eds.), *Geschichtliche Grundbegriffe*, vol. 7, 123–124.

70 Robert Case Mowat, "'From Liberalism to Imperialism: The Case of Egypt 1875–1887," *The Historical Journal* 16, no. 1 (1973): 109–124; Peter J. Cain, "Character and Imperialism: The British Financial Administration of Egypt, 1878–1914," *Journal of Imperial and Commonwealth History* 34, no. 2 (2006): 177–200; Umut Özsu, "The Ottoman Empire, the Origins of Extraterritoriality, and International Legal Theory," in Anne Orford and Florian Hoffman (eds.), *The Oxford Handbook of the Theory of International Law* (Oxford: Oxford University Press, 2016), 129.

71 Cf. Mitchell, "International Law as Project or System?," 657–658, 666–668.

72 See Karl Strupp, *Ausgewählte diplomatische Aktenstücke zur orientalischen Frage* (Gotha: Friedrich Andreas Perthes, 1916), 86 ("Vertrag zwischen Österreich, Frankreich und Großbritannien, betr. Die Integrität Türkei, vom 15. April 1856").

73 Pramod Nayar, ed., *The Trial of Bahadur Shah Zafar* (Hyderabad: Orient Longman, 2007).

74 W. A. P. Martin, "The Recognition of the Nanking Government: Advocated in Two Letters to the Hon. Caleb Cushing," *The North-China Herald* (Shanghai), June 20, 1857, 186.

75 Ibid.

76 Ibid.

77 Ibid. (italics removed).

78 WJDA: 01-02-003-02-039 ("命桂良等逆夷所請於國體無傷者可從權辦理").

79 See description in Morse, *The International Relations of the Chinese Empire*, vol. 1, 518–523.

80 CBYWSM, Xianfeng Era, Juan 27. Shu Tong Wen Gu Ji Shu Ju Ku.

81 But for the different situation and interests of the Russian side, see Mark Bassin, *Imperial Visions: Nationalist Imagination and Geographical Expansion in the Russian Far East, 1840–1865* (Cambridge: Cambridge University Press, 1999).

82 WJDA: 01-02-003-02-039.

83 Chen Kaike, "Qiying Yu Di Er Ci Yapian Zhanzheng Zhong De Zhong E Jiaoshe 耆英与第二次鸦片战争中的中俄交涉" [Kiyeng and Sino-Russian Relations during the Second Opium War], *Jindaishi Yanjiu* 4 (2009): 60–76.

84 Cf. Liu, *The Clash of Empires*, 33–38, 61–66, 42–45, 98.

85 "Treaty of Tientsin" [Tianjin] (1858) in *Treaties, Conventions, etc., between China and Foreign States,* vol. 1 (Shanghai: The Statistical Department of the Inspector General of Customs, 1917).

86 "Treaty of Tientsin" [Tianjin] (Russia) in *Treaties, Conventions, etc., between China and Foreign States,* vol. 1 (Shanghai: The Statistical Department of the Inspector General of Customs, 1917), 97; CBYWSM, Xianfeng Era, Juan 33.

87 "Treaty of Tientsin" [Tianjin] (Great Britain) in *Treaties, Conventions, etc., between China and Foreign States*, vol. 1 (Shanghai: The Statistical Department of the Inspector General of Customs, 1917), 405.

88 Ibid.

89 Ibid., Article 3. On MFN clauses and their ambiguities, see Pär Kristoffer Cassel, *Grounds of Judgment: Extraterritoriality and Imperial Power in Nineteenth-Century China and Japan* (Oxford: Oxford University Press, 2011), 51–52.

90 WJDA: 01-02-003-03-060 (June 23, 1858).

91 Covell, *W. A. P. Martin*, 89.

92 See Morse, *The International Relations of the Chinese Empire*, vol. 1, 520–529; Covell, *W. A. P. Martin*, 83–89.

93 Covell, *W. A. P. Martin*, 89. This phrase is used by Martin specifically to describe the progress of Western penetration into China, but he separately characterized events in other non-Western realms in highly similar terms.

94 "Marx an Engels, 8. Oktober 1858," in Karl Marx and Friedrich H. G. Engels, *Karl Marx Friedrich Engels Gesamtausgabe* (MEGA), Part 3, *Briefwechsel*, Januar 1858 bis August 1859 (Berlin: Akademie Verlag, 2003), vol. 9, 123.

95 See Morse, *The International Relations of the Chinese Empire*, vol. 1, 532–534; Xing Zhiyu, "Cong 'Shuize Tanpan' Kan He Guiqing yu Zhongyang Zhengce de Boyi 从'税则谈判'看何桂清与中央政策的博弈" [Analyzing the Policy Struggle between He Guiqing and Central Authorities in Connection with the 'Tariff Conference'], *Xue Lilun* 7 (2019): 135–138.

96 QSL, Xianfeng Era, Juan 29 (advising Guiliang and Huashana: "wait patiently for the internally-determined approach"); see also Hsü, *China's Entrance into the Family of Nations*, 71–73; Li, "Yapian Zhanzheng Qianhou Qiying Dui Wai Jiaoshe Lunshu," 74–75.

97 Unfortunately, the edict containing the original text of the internally determined approach has been lost.

98 WJDA: 01-02-005-01-086.

99 QSL, Xianfeng Era, Juan 30; CBYWSM, Xianfeng Era Juan 3, 1130–1131.

100 Ibid. The term *liquan* had been used since ancient times, but dealings with the West since the First Opium War had by now endowed it with a very new set of associations relating to the permanent loss of autonomy on matters of economic policy.

101 WJDA: 01-02-005-01-107; WJDA: 01-02-006-02-005. Cf. Li, "Yapian Zhanzheng Qianhou Qiying Dui Wai Jiaoshe Lunshu," 73–74.

102 WJDA: 01-02-005-03-037 (October 21, 1858).

103 WJDA: 01-01-013-04-044 (October 21, 1858).

104 See van de Ven, *Breaking with the Past*, 36–39.

105 QSL, Xianfeng Era, Juan 30.

106 Ibid. (*Bu du wu yan dui Zhen, heyi dui Tianxia* 不獨無顏對朕，何以對天下?).

107 Liu Gengsheng, "Yixin yu Zongli Yamen de Jianli Shuping 奕䜣与总理衙门的建立述评" [Account of Yixin and the Establishment of the Zongli Yamen], *Lishi Dangan* 3 (1990): 93–98.

108 FO 17/331, 377.

109 FO 17/331, 376.

110 FO 17/331, 375.

111 FO 17/331, 307.

112 Liu Yi, "Lun Zongli Yamen de Jianli Ji Qi Lishi Diwei 论总理衙门的建立及其历史地位" [On the Establishment and Historical Role of the Zongli Yamen], *Suzhou Daxue Xuebao* 3 (1991): 116–120.
113 Ibid.
114 Ibid. ("疑臣等專辦通商，不與理事").
115 See, e.g., Hsü, *China's Entrance to the Family of Nations*, 126–128.
116 Wang Ruicheng, "The 'Outward Flow of Power' and the Evolution of the Late Qing Power Structure, 1855–1875," *Modern Chinese History Studies* 2 (2012): 28–46.
117 Koselleck, "Staat und Souveränität," 120.
118 See Dennis O. Flynn and Arturo Giráldez, "Cycles of Silver: Global Economic Unity through the Mid-Eighteenth Century," *Journal of World History* 13, no. 2 (2002): 391–427; Dennis O. Flynn and Arturo and Giráldez, *China and the Birth of Globalization in the 16th Century* (Farnham: Ashgate Variorum, 2010); Andrew B. Liu, *Tea War: A History of Capitalism in China and India* (New Haven, CT: Yale University Press, 2020).
119 See, e.g., Platt, *Imperial Twilight*, 12, 172, 245–257, 263, 268, 273.
120 See Twiss, *Two Introductory Lectures on the Science of International Law*, 42; Wheaton, *Elements of International Law*, clxxxiii; Johann Caspar Bluntschli, *Das moderne Völkerrecht der civilisirten Staten: als Rechtsbuch dargestellt*, 1st ed. (Nördlingen: C. H. Beck, 1872), 19; cf. Steiger, "Völkerrecht," 123–124.
121 See, e.g., Karl Haushofer, "Gesamtasiatische Fragen" in Karl Strupp (ed.), *Wörterbuch des Völkerrechts und der Diplomatie* (Berlin: Walter de Gruyter, 1924), vol. 1, 390–394; cf. Wilhelm Grewe, *The Epochs of International Law* (Berlin: Walter de Gruyter, 2000), 478.
122 See Charles Henry Alexandrowicz, "Some Problems in the History of the Law of Nations in Asia" [1963] in David Armitage and Jennifer Pitts (eds.), *The Law of Nations in Global History* (Oxford: Oxford University Press, 2017), 80 ("the elimination of the natural law principles of universality of the family of nations and of declaratory recognition and their replacement by a European Club of States endowed with power of constitutive recognition of non-members of the club outside Europe, provided a new legal pressure mechanism in the hands of the great powers").
123 Miloš Vec, "Sources in the 19th Century European Tradition: The Myth of Positivism," *European Journal of International Law* 16 (2005): 539–559.
124 Schmitt, *The Nomos of the Earth*, 197–199.
125 Karl Marx, *Grundrisse: Foundations of the Critique of Political Economy* (New York: Penguin Books in association with the New Left Review, 1973), 408.

Chapter 2

1 He Qinhua, "'Wanguo Gongfa' yu Qingmo Guojifa' 万国公法' 与清末国际法" [Wanguo Gongfa and Late Qing International Law], *Faxue Yanjiu* 23, no. 5 (2001): 137–148.
2 FRUS 1863, vol. II, 204.
3 See Zhang, "Wanqing Zhongguoren de Zhuquan Guannian," 108–112; Jin, Liu, and Qiu, "Zhongguo Xiandai Zhuquan Guannian Xingcheng de Shuwei Renwen Yanjiu."

4 See, e.g., Zhang Tingyu, et al., Ming Shi 明史 (via Shu Tong Wen Guji Shujku), Juan 188 ("自古奸臣欲擅主權必先蠱其心志" [since ancient times, when ministers seek to usurp *zhuquan*, they have always first sought to poison the [ruler's] will and aspiration]).

5 See Jin, Liu, and Qiu, "Zhongguo Xiandai Zhuquan Guannian Xingcheng de Shuwei Renwen Yanjiu."

6 John King Fairbank, "Synarchy under the Treaties," in John King Fairbank (ed.), *Chinese Thought and Institutions* (Chicago: University of Chicago Press, 1957), 204–234.

7 Cf. Jerry Norman, *A Comprehensive Manchu–English Dictionary* (Leiden: Brill, 2020); Hu Zengyi, *Xin Man-Han Cidian* 新满汉大词典, 2nd ed. (Shanghai: Shangwu Yinshuguan, 2020). The Chinese version was almost certainly also influenced by the phrase *wei shan bu tong, tong gui yu zhi* 为善不同, 同归于治, from the ancient *Book of Documents*, which signifies "Though the forms of worthy conduct may differ, all similarly leads to order."

8 Halsey, *Quest for Power*, 5–7.

9 CBYWSM, Tongzhi Era, Juan 16.

10 CBYWSM, Tongzhi Era, Juan 41.

11 Van de Ven, *Breaking with the Past*, 68.

12 Ibid.

13 Ibid.

14 William N. Goetzmann, Andrey D. Ukhov, and Ning Zhu. "China and the World Financial Markets 1870–1939: Modern Lessons from Historical Globalization," *Economic History Review* 60, no. 2 (2007): 302.

15 Cf. Ibid.

16 Lydia He Liu, "Legislating the Universal: The Circulation of International Law in the Nineteenth Century," in Lydia He Liu (ed.), *Tokens of Exchange: The Problem of Translation in Global Circulations* (Durham, NC: Duke University Press, 2000).

17 Svarverud, *International Law as World Order in Late Imperial China*, 107.

18 Halsey insightfully observes that interpretations of "sovereignty" in China "remained fluid prior to 1900," and suggests that the notion was more often "interpreted . . . as a form of absolute control over territory, people, or wealth rather than the final or ultimate authority of the state." Halsey, *Quest for Power*, 6–7. However, his description of the Qing approach to the concept as particularly oriented toward "zero-sum competition" or "absolute" control may understate the degree to which it has often been invoked in the West as well to justify such competition, along with its fluidity and contextually driven meanings regardless of setting. Cf. Koselleck, "Staat und Souveränität," 61–64, 83–88.

19 Wheaton, *Elements of International Law*, 45.

20 Ibid., 27.

21 Ibid., 27–28.

22 Henry Wheaton, *Wanguo Gongfa* (Beijing: Tongwenguan, 1864) (W. A. P. Martin, trans.), 12. In the original, "Prussia" is (more accurately in this context) rendered as "Germany."

23 Ibid., 51–54.

24 Ibid., 21–22.
25 See, e.g., QSL, Qianlong Shilu, Juan 103 (若屡化而不从。则国体所在。亦不可存姑息之心以酿祸也).
26 Wheaton, *Wanguo Gongfa*, 21–22.
27 Wheaton, *Elements of International Law*, 41.
28 Wheaton, *Wanguo Gongfa*, 17 (emphasis added).
29 Wheaton, *Elements of International Law*, 342–343.
30 Wheaton, *Wanguo Gongfa*, 91.
31 Wheaton, *Elements of International Law*, 217.
32 Ibid.
33 Ibid.
34 Wheaton, *Wanguo Gongfa*, 72.
35 CBYWSM, Tongzhi Era, Juan 23.
36 CBYWSM, Tongzhi Era, Juan 26, 155 ("在中國洋面扣船卽屬輕視中國").
37 Ibid.,146.
38 See *Treaties, Conventions, etc., between China and Foreign States*, 118–127.
39 Cf. Wang Yuanchong, "Defining Chosŏn: Qing China's Depiction of Chosŏn's Status, 1862–76," in *Remaking the Chinese Empire: Manchu-Korean Relations, 1616–1911* (Ithaca, NY: Cornell University Press, 2018), 121–143.
40 CBYWSM, Tongzhi Era, Juan 26, 167.
41 Li Yumin, "Wanqing Shiqi Guoti Guan de Bianhua Shitan 晚清时期国体观的变化试探" [Analyzing the Transformation of Perspectives on *Guoti* during the Late Qing Period], *Renwen Zazhi* 6 (2013): 71–90.
42 Ibid.
43 Wang Ding'an, *Xiang Jun Ji* 湘軍記 (Shanghai: Jiangnan Shuju, 1889), vol. 1.
44 *Qingdai Wai Zhai Shi Ziliao*: 1853–1911 *Shang* 清代外债史资料 1853–1911 上 [Historical Materials on Qing Era Foreign Debt] (Beijing: Zhonghua Renmin Gongheguo Caizheng Bu: 1988), 37–52.
45 CBYWSM, Tongzhi Era, Juan 54, 139–140.
46 Ibid.
47 Ibid., 84.
48 *Banquet to His Excellency Anson Burlingame and His Associates of the Chinese Embassy by the Citizens of New York, on Tuesday, June 23, 1868* (New York: Sun Book and Job Printing House, 1868), 6.
49 Ibid.
50 Ibid., 17.
51 Ibid., 12.
52 Ibid.
53 Ibid.
54 See, e.g., W. Travis Hanes and Frank Sanello, *The Opium Wars: The Addiction of One Empire and the Corruption of Another* (Naperville, IL: Sourcebooks Inc., 2002), 193–200.
55 *Banquet to His Excellency Anson Burlingame*, 17.
56 Ibid.
57 Ibid.
58 Ibid., 35–36.

59 Mathias Reimann, "The Historical School against Codification: Savigny, Carter, and the Defeat of the New York Civil Code," *The American Journal of Comparative Law* 37, no. 1 (1989): 95–119.

60 The International Law Association, *Reports of the First Conference Held at Brussels, 1873, and of the Second Conference Held at Geneva, 1874* (London: West, Newman & Co., 1903), 1–8.

61 American Free-Trade League, *Some Account of the American Free-Trade League and of Its Purposes* (New York: American Free-Trade League, 1869), back cover.

62 *Banquet to His Excellency Anson Burlingame*, 36.

63 Ibid., 37.

64 Ibid.

65 Hayden White, *Metahistory: The Historical Imagination in Nineteenth-Century Europe* (Baltimore: Johns Hopkins University Press, 2014), 8–9.

66 *Banquet to His Excellency Anson Burlingame*, 36.

67 "Additional Articles to the Treaty between the United States of America and the Ta-Tsing [Great Qing] Empire of the 18th June 1858" in *Treaties, Conventions, etc., between China and Foreign States*, vol. 1, 729–735.

68 Ibid., Articles 3–7.

69 Ibid. The term *yiti* is used in the brief treaty nine times and appears in five of its eight articles.

70 Ibid., Article 1.

71 Ibid.

72 *Some Account of the American Free-Trade League and of Its Purposes*, 5.

73 *Banquet to His Excellency Anson Burlingame*, 36.

74 Gerritt W. Gong, *The Standard of "Civilization" in International Society* (New York: Oxford University Press, 1984), 31–35.

75 Koskenniemi, *The Gentle Civilizer of Nations*, 101–105.

76 Tzouvala, *Capitalism as Civilisation*, 66–73.

77 See, e.g., Koskenniemi, *The Gentle Civilizer of Nations*, 42–47.

78 Ibid.

79 Ibid. On Romantic narrative in general, see White, *Metahistory*, 7–9 for his definition of the "Romance" emplotment of historical narratives that rely upon a figure of identification for the reader who "transcends" forces of opposition. The juristic "conscience" overcoming the barbarism internal to Western society, and then that of the rest of humanity, is certainly a narrative that can be examined through the lens of this emplotment.

80 Johann Caspar Bluntschli, *Allgemeine Staatslehre* (Stuttgart: G. Cotta, 1886) (original publication 1875), 88–89; cf. Johann Caspar Bluntschli, "Arische Völker und arische Rechte" in *Gesammelte kleine Schriften* (Nördlingern: C. H. Beck, 1879), vol. 1, 63, 89. For a major influence on Bluntschli's and other racial schemas of the period, see Arthur Gobineau, *Essai sur l'"inégalité des races humaines* (Paris: Didot Frères, 1853).

81 Ibid., 88.

82 Ibid., 89.

83 Johann Caspar Bluntschli, *Alt-asiatische Gottes- und Weltideen in ihren Wirkungen auf das Gemeinleben der Menschen* (Nördlingen: C. H. Beck, 1866), 160–161.

84 Francis Lieber, *Fragments of Political Science on Nationalism and Internationalism* (New York: Charles Scribner & Co., 1868), 22–23.
85 Ibid.
86 Francis Lieber, *Notes on Fallacies Peculiar to American Protectionists, or Chiefly Resorted to in America* (New York: American Free-Trade League, 1869), 6.
87 Gustave Rolin-Jaequemyns, "*Notes on Fallacies Peculiar to American Protectionists, or Chiefly Resorted to in America*, by Francis Lieber," *Revue de Droit International et de Léglisation Comparée* 2 (1870): 354–356.
88 Ibid.
89 See, e.g., Mitchell, "International Law as Project or System?"; Matthew Craven, "Between Law and History: The Berlin Conference of 1884–1885 and the Logic of Free Trade," *London Review of International Law* 3, no. 1 (2015): 31–59.
90 See, e.g., Umut Özsu, "Ottoman Empire" in Fassbender, Peters, Peter, and Högger (eds.), *The Oxford Handbook of the History of International Law*, 429–446.
91 Ibid.
92 The full list of cofounders of the institute was: Gustave Moynier, Gustave Rolin-Jaequemyns, Pasquale Stanislao Mancini, Emile de Laveleye, Tobias Michael Carel Asser, James Lorimer, Wladimir Besobrassof, Johann Caspar Bluntschli, Augusto Pierantoni, Carlos Calvo, and David Dudley Field.
93 Koskenniemi, *To the Uttermost Parts of the Earth*, 966.
94 CBYWSM, Juan 53, Tongzhi Year Six (1867).
95 Yu-qin Li, "Analysis of the Establishment and Operation of Hanyeping Company's Joint Stock System in the Late Qing Dynasty," *Journal of Xuchang University* 4 (2009): 101–105.
96 Ibid. Stephen R. Halsey, "Sovereignty, Self-strengthening, and Steamships in Late Imperial China," *Journal of Asian History* 48, no. 1 (2014): 81–111.
97 Covell, *W. A. P. Martin*, 156–157.
98 Ibid.
99 Ibid., 168. Elsewhere, it has been claimed inaccurately that Martin studied for a doctorate at the University of Indiana during this period. Covell's suggestion that Martin studied with Woolsey seems plausible given his whereabouts, connection with Yale, efforts to reach out to leading international jurists, and subsequent decision to translate Woolsey's textbook.
100 Ibid., 172–173.
101 Gustave Rolin-Jaequemyns, "Proposition d'Établir un Collège Americain en Chine," *Revue de Droit International et de Législation Comparée* 4 (1872): 362–363.
102 Ibid.
103 William Alexander Parsons Martin, "Une Université en Chine: Le Présent et l'Avenir de l'Ensiegnement Supérieur International a Peking," *Revue de Droit International et de Législation Comparée* 5 (1873): 8–10.
104 Ibid.
105 Ibid.
106 Ibid.
107 William Alexander Parsons Martin, "Les Vestiges d'un Droit International dans l'Ancienne Chine," *Revue de Droit International et de Législation Comparée* 14 (1882): 227–243.

108 Tsutsumi Koshiji, *Bankoku Kōhō Yakugi* 万国公法訳義 [*A Translation of the Public Law of All States*] (Kyoto: Zeniya Soshirō, 1868).

109 Uryū Mitora, *Kōdō Kigen Ichimei Bankoku Kōhō Zensho* 交道起源一名万国公法全書 [*The Sources of Diplomacy, or the Public Law of All States, Complete Edition*] (Kyoto: Chikuhōrō, 1868).

110 Ibid.

111 See Ōkubo Takeharu, *The Quest for Civilization: Encounters with Dutch Jurisprudence, Political Economy, and Statistics at the Dawn of Modern Japan* (Leiden: Brill, 2014) (David Noble, trans.).

112 Nishi Amane, *Kanban Bankoku Kōhō* 官版万国公法 [*Official Publication of the Public Law of All States*] (Kyoto: Chikuhōrō, 1868); Nishi Amane, *Horan Biserin-shi Bankoku Kōhō* 和蘭畢洒林氏万国公法 [*The Public Law of All States According to the Dutch Scholar Vissering*] (Kyoto: Chikuhōrō, 1868).

113 Tsuda Mamichi, *Taisei Kokuhō Ron* 泰西国法論 [*The State Law of the Far West*] (Edo: Kaiseijo, 1868) (the book was published simultaneously with a number of others in 1868, but had been complete in manuscript form since 1866).

114 Ibid., chapter 3, part 6 ("主権即君権　一切國人此権ニ服従シテ臣民ト稱ス").

115 Ibid., chapter 3, part 5.

116 Alexis Dudden, "Japan's Engagement with International Terms" in Liu (ed.), *Tokens of Exchange*, 169–171; see also, e.g., Gustave Rolin-Jaequemyns, "Rédaction d'un Code civile Japonais," *Revue de Droit International et de Législation Comparée* 4 (1872): 363.

117 See discussion in Cassel, *Grounds of Judgment*, 98–109.

118 Ibid.

119 See Robert Eskildsen, *Transforming Empire in Japan and East Asia: The Taiwan Expedition and the Birth of Japanese Imperialism* (Singapore: Palgrave Macmillan: 2019).

120 Cassel, *Grounds of Judgment*, 98–109.

121 CBYWSM, Tongzhi Era, vol. 82, 66–68; see also Chen Kewei, "Bao Yingshi yu 1871 Nian de Zhong-Ri Tianjin Tiaoyue 应宝时与 1871 年的中日天津修约 [Bao Yingshi and the 1871 China–Japan Treaty of Tianjin]," *Qinghua Daxue Xuebao (Zhexue Shehui Kexue Ban)* 6 (2010): 70–78.

122 QSL, Tongzhi Era, vol. 315.

123 Ibid.

124 CBYWSM, Tongzhi Era, Juan 82.

125 CBYWSM, Tongzhi Era, Juan 89–90.

126 Cassel, *Grounds of Judgment*, 103–105.

127 See Eckhardt Fuchs, Tokushi Kasahara, and Sven Saaler, eds., *A New Modern History of East Asia* (Göttingen: V&R Unipress, 2018), vol. 1, 70–72.

128 Sino-Japanese Treaty of Amity and Commerce, Article 3 ("兩國の政事禁令各異なれは其政事は己國自主の權に任すへし") in *Treaties, Conventions, etc., between China and Foreign States*, vol. 2, 643.

129 Ibid.

130 CBYWSM, Juan 82, Sino-Japanese Treaty of Amity and Commerce, Article 6 ("嗣後兩國往來公文，中國用漢文，日本國用日本文，須副以譯漢文，或只用漢文，亦從其便").

131 Cf. Svarverud, *International Law as World Order in Late Imperial China*, 6–7; Dudden, "Japan's Engagement with International Terms," 168, 171.
132 See, e.g., Tzouvala, *Capitalism as Civilisation*, 56–58.
133 Marshall McLuhan, *Understanding Media: The Extensions of Man* (Toronto: McGraw-Hill, 1964), 3.

Chapter 3

1 Wayne C. McWilliams, "Soejima Taneomi: Statesman of Early Meiji Japan, 1868–1874" (PhD dissertation, University of Kansas, 1973), 226–227; Yasuoka Akio, *Meiji zenki tairiku seisaku shi no kenkyū* [Research on the Meiji Continental Policy] (Tokyo: Hōsei Daigaku Shuppankyoku, 1998), 149–150; Eskildsen, *Transforming Empire*, 43–44, 65.
2 M. Shibata and T. Koyas, eds., *An English and Japanese Dictionary* (Yokohama: Ni-Shu-Sha Printing Office, 1873), 1,094.
3 Mitsukuri Rinsho, *Kokusai Hō Ichimei Bankoku Kōhō* 國際法一名萬國公法 [*Interstate Law, i.e., the Public Law of All States*] (Tokyo: Nishodō, 1873).
4 Eskildsen, *Transforming Empire*, 43–44, 65.
5 Ibid., 78.
6 Ibid., 236.
7 Wang Tseng-Tsai, "The Audience Question: Foreign Representatives and the Emperor of China, 1858–1873," *The Historical Journal* 14, no. 3 (1971): 617–626.
8 Ibid.
9 FRUS 1873, 174.
10 See, e.g., Li, "Wanqing Shiqi Guoti Guan de Bianhua Shitan," 84. The Hanlin scholar Wu Dacheng acknowledged that since the Western powers were now treated as "states equal in form" (*diti pingxing zhi guo* 敵體平行之國), each state's ministers could only be expected to "cling stubbornly to their own *guoti*."
11 FRUS 1873, 176.
12 Ibid.
13 Eskildsen, *Transforming Empire*, 115.
14 The process by which Japan became a recognized "full" member of the Western international law community by the end of the nineteenth century was profoundly shaped by contrasts with the more conservative Qing state. This extended even to aesthetic factors such as the decision, during these 1873 negotiations, for Japanese envoys to wear Western dress in order to blend in with the Western diplomatic corps. It would take another four decades before Qing envoys made this switch.
15 QSL, Tongzhi Era, Juan 90.
16 This term, *yuguo* 與國, dated from ancient times when there were indeed many different states in "China," each of which had equivalent status. See, e.g., Sima Qian, *Shiji Quanben: Shang*史記全本.上 [*Records of the Grand Historian, vol. I*], Juan 7 (Shenyang: Wanjuan Chuban Gongsi, 2016) (originally published circa 94 BCE).

17 Li's positions were in substantial part based on earlier views put forward by Wenxiang as official head of the Zongli Yamen.

18 See Wang, "The Audience Question," 623–625.

19 Gustave Rolin-Jaequemyns, "La Diplomatie Européenne à Péking," *Revue de Droit International et de Législation Comparée* 9 (1877): 401–404.

20 Li Xizhu, "Li Hongzhang Dui Riben de Renshi ji Qi Waijiao Celüe: Yi 1870 Niandai wei Zhongxin 李鸿章对日本的认识及其外交策略 – 以 1870 年代为中心" [Li Hongzhang's Understanding of Japan and Diplomatic Strategy: With Focus on the 1870s], *Jindai Zhongguo Zhengzhi yu Waijiao* 1, no. 204 (2013): 145–159.

21 Wayne C. McWilliams, "East Meets East: The Soejima Mission to China, 1873," *Monumenta Nipponica* 30, no. 3 (1975): 237–275; Mizuno Norihito, "Qing China's Reaction to the 1874 Japanese Expedition to the Taiwanese Aboriginal Territories," *Sino-Japanese Studies* 16 (2009): 100–125; Liu Dan, "1874 Nian Dajiu Baolitong Beijing Tanpan de Dongyin yu Yingxiang 年大久保利通北京谈判的动因与影响" [The Motivations and Effects of Ōkubo's 1874 Negotiations with Beijing], *Waiguo Wenti Yanjiu* 4, no. 9 (2018): 85–92.

22 See, e.g., Ian Nish, *The Iwakura Mission to America and Europe: A New Assessment* (Abingdon: Routledge, 2008).

23 Otto von Bismarck, *Werke in Auswahl: Reichsgestaltung und europäische Friedenswahrung, 1877–1882* (Darmstadt: Wissenschaftliche Buchgesellschaft, 1973), 310–311.

24 See CBYWSM, Tongzhi Era, Juan 97; CBYWSM, *Tongzhi Jiaxu Bing Qin Tai Shimo* 同治甲戌日兵侵台始末, Juan 3 (Taipei: Taiwan Yinhang, 1959).

25 CBYWSM, Tongzhi Era, Juan 97. As we have seen, the section dealing with state acquisition of territory and the nature of territorial dominion/*dominium*/eminent domain in Wheaton's text was not clearly conveyed in Martin's translation.

26 CBYWSM, Tongzhi Era, Juan 97.

27 Emer de Vattel, *Le Droit des Gens, ou Principes de la Loi Naturelle Appliqués a la Conduite et aux Affaires des Nations et des Souverains* (Paris: J. P. Aillaud, 1835) (originally published 1756), 266–267 ("Le Droit des Gens ne reconnoîtra donc la *propriété* & la *souveraineté* d'une nation, que sur les pays vides, qu'elle aura occupés réellement & de fait, dans lesquels elle aura formé un établissement, ou dont elle tirera un usage actuel").

28 In Chinese, the passage is rendered: 一國新佔曠地非實力佔有即就其 地建設館司而獲實益，公法不認其主權. CBYWSM, Tongzhi Era, Juan 97.

29 August Wilhelm Heffter, *Le Droit International Public de l'Europe* (Paris: Cotillon, 1857), 141–142; see also Georg Friedrich von Martens, *Précis du droit des gens moderne de l'Europe* (Paris: Guillaumin et Cie, 1864), vol. 1, 131 ("l'occupation n'est admise que pour les choses qui ne sont pas déjà possédées par un détenteur antérieur et que danns aucun cas elle ne s'applique aux hommes, si ce n'est à ceux qui se soumettent volontairement ou que la guerre a ranges sous la domination d'un vainqueur").

30 Johann Caspar Bluntschli, *Das Modeerne Völkerrecht der civilisirten Staaten als Rechtsbuch dargestellt*, (Nördlingen: C. H. Beck, 1872), 167–168; *Tongzhi Jiaxu Bing Qin Tai Shimo* 同治甲戌日兵侵台始末.

31 Bluntschli, *Das Modeerne Völkerrecht der civilisirten Staaten*, 169–170.

32 See Wilhelm G. Grewe, *Epochen der Völkerrechtsgeschichte* (Baden-Baden: Nomos Verlagsgesellschaft, 1984), 72–82.

33 Li, "Li Hongzhang Dui Riben de Renshi ji Qi Waijiao Celüe." On "balance of power" (*shou pingjun shi zhi li* 守平均勢之例), see the 1874 memorandum of governor-general of Ming-Zhe, Li Henian in Wang Yuanzhi, ed., *Jiaxu Gongdu Chaocun* 甲戌公牘鈔存 [*Public Documents of the Jiaxu Year*] (Taipei: Taiwan Yinhang, 1959).

34 Gao Shulan, "Xiu yu Qichi de Tongzhi Di Siyin 羞于启齿的同治帝死因" [The Unmentionable Cause of Emperor Tongzhi's Death], *Fazhi Bolan* 19 (2011): 30–32.

35 *Xingyao Zhizhang* 星軺指掌 [*A Guide for Emissaries*] (Beijing: Tongwenguan, 1876).

36 Bluntschli, *Das moderne Völkerrecht der civilisirten Staaten*; Johann Caspar Bluntschli, *Gongfa Huitong* 公法会通 (Beijing: Tongwenguan, 1880) (W. A. P. Martin, trans.).

37 Bluntschli, *Gongfa Huitong*. Bluntschli's original passage is rather different in that it refers to the state as a "legal being" (*Rechtswesen*) with a "legal will" (*Rechtswille*), and for which people act as "representative organs" (*repräsentativer Organe*). Bluntschli, *Das moderne Völkerrecht der civilisirten Staaten*, 86–87.

38 Ibid.

39 Bluntschli, *Gongfa Huitong*, 121; Bluntschli, *Das moderne Völkerrecht der civilisirten Staaten*, 96. In addition to *guoti*, the term *mingjie* 名節 is also used in the translation to refer to the state's personality and dignity.

40 See, e.g., Erich Hauer, "Why the Sinologue Should Study Manchu," *Bulletin of the North China Branch of the Royal Asiatic Society* 61 (1930): 156–164, 163 for a discussion of this translation of *Badarangga Doro*.

41 It also seems likely that the Chinese characters for Guangxu 光緒 were chosen as near-homonyms for Guangxu 廣序, which would indeed signify something very close to *Badarangga Doro*/"vast order."

42 Agreement between the Ministers Plenipotentiary of the Governments of Great Britain and China (Chefoo Agreement/Yantai Treaty), Section II(iii), in *Treaties, Conventions, etc., between China and Foreign States*, vol. 1, 495. Cf. Cassel, *Grounds of Judgment*, 77–84.

43 Yantai Treaty, Separate Article, in *Treaties, Conventions, etc., between China and Foreign States*, vol. 1, 498–499.

44 Ibid., Section I, 491–493.

45 See, e.g., Day, *Qing Travelers to the Far West*, 124–131.

46 Ibid.

47 Li Dong, "Yangwu Yundong Shiqqi Xue Fucheng Jiaru Guojifa Da Jiating de Zhuzhang yu Shijian洋务运动时期薛福成加入国际公法大家庭的主张与实践" [Xue Fucheng's Advocacy and Practice of Entering the Great Family of International Law during the Yangwu Movement], *Zhengfa Xuekan* 37, no. 2 (2020): 121–128 ("西人風氣最重條約").

48 Feng Lin, ed., *Xue Fucheng Xuanji* 薛福成选集 [Selected Writings of Xue Fucheng] (Shanghai: Shanghai Renmin Chubanshe, 1987), 81.

49 Guo Songtao, *Lundun yu Bali Riji* 倫敦與巴黎日記 [*London and Paris Diaries*] (Changsha: Yuelu Shushe, 1984), Juan 22; Guo Songtao, *Shixi Jicheng: Guo Songtao Ji* 使西纪程: 郭嵩焘集 [*Record of a Mission to the West: Collected Writings of Guo Songtao*] (Shenyang: Liaoning Renmin Chubanshe, 1994).

50 Guo Songtao, *Lundun yu Bali Riji*, Juan 22. Guo also notes of Grotius that he was the same figure to whom W. A. P. Martin had given the transliterated name of *Hu Ge* 虎哥 (which somewhat comically sounds like "Brother Tiger") in his *Wanguo Gongfa* of 1864.

51 Travers Twiss, *View of the Progress of Political Economy in Europe since the Sixteenth Century* (London: Longman, Brown, Green, and Longmans, 1847). Notably, Twiss's only brief discussions of China in this book on political economy strongly emphasize that its relations with the West demonstrate how "interests of nations [are] reciprocal," given that Western states have an interest in a flourishing Chinese domestic and export market in order to create demand for the import of their own (higher-value) finished goods.

52 Viviane Alleton, "The Migration of Grammars through Languages: The Chinese Case," in Natascha Vittinghoff and Michael Lackner (eds.), *Mapping Meanings: The Field of New Learning in Late Qing China* (Leiden: Brill, 2004), 223–224; see also discussion in Shin Kawashima, "China" in Fassbender, Peters, Peter, and Högger (eds.), *The Oxford Handbook of the History of International Law*, 471.

53 Association for the Reform and Codification of the Law of Nations, *Report of the Sixth Annual Conference Held at Frankfort-on-the-Main, 20–23 August 1878* (London: William Clowes and Sons, 1879), 40–41.

54 Ibid., 38–39.

55 Association for the Reform and Codification of the Law of Nations, *Report of the Seventh Annual Conference Held at the Guildhall, London, 11–16 August 1879* (London: William Clowes and Sons, 1880), 209–219.

56 Ibid. (March 5, 1878).

57 Ibid. (emphasis added).

58 David Dudley Field, "De la Possibilité d'Appliquer le Droit International Européen aux Nations Orientales," *Revue de Droit International et de Législation Comparée* 7 (1875): 659–668.

59 Ibid.

60 Henry M. Field, *The Life of David Dudley Field* (New York: Charles Scribner's Sons, 1898), 96.

61 Ibid., 256–260.

62 Ibid.

63 Ibid., 667.

64 Ibid., 663, 667–668.

65 Institut de Droit International, *Annuaire de l'Institut de Droit International*, vols. 3–4, 1879–1880 (Brussels: C. Muquardt, 1880), 300.

66 Ibid., 298–300.

67 Ibid., 305–307; cf. Joseph Hornung, "Note a Propos de l'Application aux Nations Orientales du Droit des Gens Coutumier de l'Europe," *Revue de Droit International et de Législation Comparée* 11 (1879): 447–449.

68 Ibid.
69 A. Krauel, "Applicabilité du Droit des Gens Européen a la Chine," *Revue de Droit International et de Législation Comparée* 9 (1877): 387–401.
70 See, e.g., Edwin Maxey, "Development of International Law," *American Law Review* 40, no. 188 (1906): 188–195.
71 Fyodor de Martens, *Das Consularwesen und die Consularjurisdiction im Orient* (Berlin: Weidmann, 1874) (H. Skerzt, trans.); cf. Arthur Nussbaum, "Frederic de Martens, Representative Tsarist Writer on International Law," *Nordic Journal of International Law* 22, no. 1 (1952): 51–66; Andreas T. Müller, "Friedrich F. Martens on 'The Office of Consul and Consular Jurisdiction in the East,'" *European Journal of International Law* 25, no. 3 (2014): 871–891.
72 Martens, *Das Consularwesen und die Consularjurisdiction im Orient*, 36–39.
73 Ibid., 501.
74 On the broad contours of this conflict and its diplomatic repercussions, see Hsü, *The Ili Crisis.*
75 Ibid.
76 Fyodor de Martens, *Le Conflit entre la Russie et la Chine, ses Origines, son Développement, et sa Portée Universelle: Étude Politique* (Brussels: C. Muquardt, 1880).
77 Ibid., 6. The incredulous/defensive note "(sic)!" is Martens'.
78 Ibid.
79 Ibid. (italics in original).
80 Johann Caspar Bluntschli, *Denkwürdiges aus meinem Leben* (1861–1881) (Nördlingen: C. H. Beck, 1884), vol. 3, 488.
81 Ibid.
82 WJDA: 02-12-050-01-047; WJDA: 01-27-009-02-060; QSL, Guangxu Era, Juan 63; cf. Elisabeth Kasek, *Bismarcks Missionare: Deutsche Militärinstrukteure in China 1884–1890* (Leipzig: Otto Harrassowitz Verlag, 2002), 38.
83 Bluntschli, *Denkwürdiges aus meinem Leben*, vol. 3, 489.
84 Institut de Droit International, *Annuaire de l'Institut de Droit International*, vol. 6, 1882–1883 (Brussels: Merzbach et Falk, 1883), v–vi, 228–229. The attendees of the relevant session of the "4th Commission" of the *Institut de Droit International* are listed as Bluntschli, Martens, August von Bulmerincq, Travers Twiss, Égide Arntz, Louis Gessner, Ferdinand Perels, and Jacobus Catharinus Cornelis den Beer Poortugael.
85 Ibid.
86 Institut de Droit International, *Annuaire de l'Institut de Droit International*, vol. 6, 229–237, 256–260.
87 W. A. P, Martin, "Les Vestiges d'un Droit International dans l'Ancienne Chine," *Revue de Droit International et de Législation Comparée* 14 (1882): 227–242.
88 Ibid.
89 Ibid., 243.
90 Ibid.
91 Institut de Droit International, *Annuaire de l'Institut de Droit International*, vol. 6, 20, 326–327.
92 Ibid., 256–260.

93 James Lorimer, *The Institutes of the Law of Nations* (Edinburgh: William Blackwood and Sons, 1883), vol. 1, 218.
94 Travers Twiss, *The Law of Nations Considered as Independent Political Communities: On the Rights and Duties of Nations in Time of Peace* (Oxford: Clarendon Press, 1884), 267 (italics in original).
95 Cassel, *Grounds of Judgment*, 65–69.
96 James Lorimer, "Prolegomènes d'un Système Raisonné de Droit International," *Revue de Droit International et de Législation Comparée* 10 (1878): 348.
97 James Dabney McCabe, *A Tour around the World by General Grant: Being a Narrative of the Incidents and Events of His Journey* (Philadelphia: The National Publishing Co., 1879), 696–699.
98 Ibid., 704–705.
99 Li, "Li Hongzhang Dui Riben de Renshi ji Qi Waijiao Celüe," 151.
100 See Wang Yanwei and Wang Liang, eds., *Qing Ji Waijiao Shiliao* 清季外交史料 [*Historical Materials on Qing Diplomacy*] (Beijing: Shumu Wenshu Chubanshe, 1987), vol. 5.
101 Ibid., 60–61, 461–463. (直督李鸿章奏日本议结琉球案牵涉改约暂宜缓允折 ["Governor-general of Zhili Li Hongzhang memorializes that treaty modification should be allowed in order to resolve the Ryūkyū affair with Japan"]).
102 WJDA: 01-21-020-01-002.
103 WJDA: 01-21-020-05-001.
104 Treaty of Saigon, 1874. See also Ministère des Affaires Étrangères, *Documents Diplomatiques: Affaires du Tonkin. Deuxième Partie. Décembre 1882–1883* (Paris: Imprimerie Nationale, 1883), 71.
105 For a discussion of this aspect of the treaty, see Jean Dupuis, *L'ouverture du Fleuve Rouge au Commerce et les Évènements du Tong-kin (1872–1873): Journal de Voyage et d'Expédition* (Paris: Challamel Aîné, 1879), vol. 2.
106 Ministère des Affaires Étrangères, *Affaires du Tonkin*, 92. Significantly, the Chinese versions of such communications did *not* refer to *zhuquan*, only to various other terms such as *zhuguo* – ruling country – etc.
107 WJDA: 01-24-009-01-024.
108 Ministère des Affaires Étrangères, *Affaires du Tonkin*, 144–145. Cf. Anna Irene Baka and Qi Fei, "Lost in Translation in the Sino-French War in Vietnam: From Western International Law to Confucian Semantics: A Comparative-Critical Analysis of the Chinese, French, and American Archives," in Anthony Carty and Janne Nijman (eds.), *Morality and Responsibility of Rulers: European and Chinese Origins of a Rule of Law as Justice for World Order* (Oxford: Oxford University Press, 2018), 389–390 (*souveraineté* in the French was *zhuguo* 主國 in Zeng's original Chinese).
109 Statement of Charles de Freycinet during parliamentary debate of July 7, 1885 in *Journal officiel de la République française. Débats parlementaires. Chambre des députés* (1885), 1332.
110 Ibid.
111 WJDA: 01-24-009-01-024.
112 Ibid.

113 Heinrich Geffcken, "La France en Chine et le Droit International," *Revue de Droit International et de Législation Comparée* 17 (1885): 145–151.
114 Ibid.
115 Lorimer, *The Institutes of the Law of Nations*, 239.
116 Ibid., 218.
117 August Wilhelm Heffter and Friedrich Heinrich Geffcken, eds., *Das europäische Volkerrecht der Gegenwart* (Berlin: Schroeder, 1873) ("Ein überaus vager Begriff, ja beinahe ein Widerspruch in sich").
118 Lorimer, "Prolegomènes d'un Système Raisonné de Droit International," 348.
119 Fyodor de Martens, *Traité de Droit International* (Paris: A. Marescq Ainé, 1883), 286. Earlier, Martens had referred to China and Japan as "non-civilisés ou à demi-barbares." Martens, *Le Conflit entre le Russie et la Chine*, 8.
120 WJDA: 01-17-051-02-004.
121 Eric Schluessel, *Land of Strangers: The Civilizing Project in Qing Central Asia* (New York: Columbia University Press, 2020).
122 William Alexander Parsons Martin, "La Chine et la Droit International," *Revue de Droit International et de Législation Comparée* 17 (1885): 504–509.
123 See, e.g., Hauer, "Why the Sinologue Should Study Manchu," 163.
124 Nowhere in this treaty text, notably, was *shuken/zhuquan*/sovereignty mentioned, despite its central role in Meiji–Qing diplomacy in the previous several years vis-à-vis Taiwan.
125 WJDA: 01-25-015-01-024; WJDA: 01-25-020-01-030; WJDA: 01-25-023-01-025.
126 Jordan Carlyle Winfield, "Buddhism and Insurrection in Burma, 1886–1890," *Journal of the Royal Asiatic Society* 20, no. 3 (2010): 345–367.
127 *Handbook of Treaties, &c., Relating to Commerce and Navigation between Great Britain and Foreign Powers, Wholly or Partially in Force on July 1, 1907* (London: Harrison & Sons, 1908).
128 Ibid., Article 2.
129 Ibid., Article 1.
130 Wang and Wang, *Qing Ji Waijiao*, vol. 5, 14.
131 Michael James Farrelly, "Our New Treaty with Japan," *Macmillan's Magazine*, lxxi, 1895: 69–71.
132 Ibid.
133 See Koskenniemi, *The Gentle Civilizer of Nations*, 129–130; cf., Franz von Liszt, *Das Völkerrecht Systematisch Dargestellt* (Berlin: O. Haering, 1888), 1st ed., 54.
134 David Harvey, *The Condition of Modernity: An Enquiry into the Origins of Cultural Change* (Oxford: Blackwell, 1989), 284–307.

Chapter 4

1 Lin, *Xue Fucheng Xuanji*. *Diqiu* 地球 – literally "the sphere of the Earth" – was a neologism introduced from the West by the Jesuit Matteo Ricci while he served at the imperial court of the Ming Dynasty. In traditional Chinese thought, the Earth was flat and square, while Heaven was round. The new term *diqiu* was seldom used until the broader reception of Western scientific thought beginning

during the period after the Second Opium War. Xue's expression *diqiu gongfa* ("public law of planet Earth") is his own invention, using *diqiu* to replace the standard *wanguo* ("all states" or, more literally, "myriad states") and adopting instead a word redolent of scientific physical geography. The phrase suggests an awareness of Western international law as a rule-set that had expanded from Europe to, now, encompassing most of the globe – while serving as a tool for ordering and ruling physical space.

2 Zheng Guanying, *Sheng Shi Wei Yan* 盛世危言 [*Warnings for a Prosperous Age*] (Shenyang: Liaoning Renmin Chubanshe, 1994).

3 Halsey, *Quest for Power*, 226.

4 Friedrich Engels to Nikolai Danielson in St. Petersburg, September 22, 1892 and Friedrich Engels to Friedrich Adolph Sorge, November 10, 1894, in Karl Marx and Friedrich H. G. Engels, *On Colonialism: Articles from the New York Tribune and Other Writings* (New York: International Publishers, 1972), 345, 347.

5 QSL, Juan 56 (1987), 769. The relevant part of the passage reads: "又諭、電寄李鴻章、連日紛紛章奏。謂台不可棄。幾於萬口交騰。本日又據唐景崧電稱、紳民呈遞血書。內云公法會通第二百八十六章。有云割地須商居民。能順從與否." Bluntschli's §286 reads in relevant part: "Di Rechtsgültigkeit einer derartigen Abtretung setzt voraus ... c) mindestens die Anerkennung von Seite der politisch berechtigten Völkerschaft, welche das abgetretene Gebiet bewohnt und nun in einen neuen Stat übertritt." Bluntschli, *Das moderne Völkerrecht der civilisirten Staten*, 173.

6 Cf. Zhang, "Wanqing Zhongguo Ren de Zhuquan Guannian," 108–112.

7 Zhong-Ri Maguan Tiaoyue 中日馬關條約, Article 2. Available at: www.mofa.gov.tw/cp.aspx?n=B73275F3D7E4D908.

8 Nisshin Ryōkoku Kōwa Jōyaku oyobi Betsuyaku 日清両国媾和条約及別約, Article 2 in *Kanpō* 官報, May 13, 1895.

9 Treaty of Peace between Japan and China, Article 2, in William Frederick Mayers, *Treaties between the Empire of China and Foreign Powers, Together with Regulations for the Conduct of Foreign Trade, Conventions, Agreements, Regulations, etc.* (Shanghai: North China Herald Ltd., 1906), 181–184.

10 Ibid.

11 John Watson Foster, "Results of the Bering Sea Arbitration," *The North American Review* 161, no. 469 (1895): 693–702.

12 John Watson Foster, *Diplomatic Memoirs* (Boston: Houghton Mifflin Company, 1909), vol. 2, 150–192.

13 Ibid.

14 See, e.g., Sarah C. Paine, *The Sino-Japanese War of 1894–1895: Perceptions, Power, and Primacy* (Cambridge: Cambridge University Press, 2005), 290, 305–315.

15 For a representative Late Qing view emphasizing the United States' relative restraint in China compared with the outright imperialist expansionism of European states and Japan, see, e.g., "Memorial of Envoy to Austria-Hungary Shen Ruilin" in QSL, Xuantong Year 3 (1911) ("America has long held to its Monroe Doctrine, and the rights it has acquired in China are far less than those

of England, Japan, Russia, and France. It is thus jealous of these four nation's gains, and will certainly be willing to lend us assistance").

16 Zhonguo Shehui Kexue Yuan Jindaishi Yanjiusuo, *Yang Ru Geng-Xin Cun Gao* 楊儒庚辛存稿 [*Documents on Yang Ru, 1900–1902*] (Beijing: Zhongguo Shehui Xueke Chuban, 1979); Liang Jian, "Yang Ru Jiejue Meiguo Paihua Wenti de Shijian yu Gouxiang Shulun 杨儒解决美国排华问题的实践与构想述论" [Explanation and Commentary on Yang Ru's Perspective and Practice on Solving the Anti-Chinese Sentiment Issue in the United States], *Xinan Jiaotong Daxue Xuebao* (*Shehui Kexue Ban*) 12, no. 2 (2011): 82–86.

17 Ibid.

18 Ibid.

19 See, e.g., Peter Zarrow, *China in War and Revolution, 1895–1949* (Abingdon: Routledge, 2006), 6–7.

20 See Shi Jianguo, *Lu Zhengxiang Zhuan* 陆征祥传 (Shijiazhuang: Hebei Renmin Chubanshe, 1999).

21 Dom Pierre-Célestin Lou Tseng-tsiang [Lu Zhengxiang], *Souvenirs et Pensées* (Bruges: Desclée de Brouwer, 1946).

22 Ibid., 32–35.

23 On the emergence of the language of "*droit publique de l'Europe,*" see Steiger, "Völkerrecht," 123–125.

24 Xiong Xiling, "Wei Xiangsheng Xing Lun Cheng Zhang Zhidong 為湘省行輪呈張之洞" [Memorial to Zhang Zhidong on Allowing Steamboat Travel in Hunan], (1896) in Yi Feizhou (ed.), *Hunan Weixin Yundong Shiliao* 湖南維新運動史料 [*Historical Materials on the Hunan Restoration Movement*] (Changsha: Yuelu Shushe, 2013), 223–230.

25 Ibid.

26 Ibid., 323–328.

27 William Alexander Parsons Martin, *The Siege in Peking: China against the World* (New York: Fleming H. Revell, 1900).

28 Yi, *Hunan Weixin Yundong Shiliao*, 473.

29 See Wang, *Zhongguo Xiandai Sixiang de Xingqi*, vol. 1.

30 Ibid.

31 Yi, *Hunan Weixin Yundong Shiliao*, 490–491.

32 See, e.g., Zarrow, *China in War and Revolution*, 16–19.

33 Zhang, *Quan Xue Pian*.

34 Ibid., 163.

35 See, e.g., Prasenjit Duara, *Sovereignty and Authenticity: Manchukuo and the East Asian Modern* (Lanham, MD: Rowman & Littlefield, 2004).

36 Zhang, *Quan Xue Pian*.

37 See, e.g., Martha Finnemore and Michelle Jurkovich, "Getting a Seat at the Table: The Origins of Universal Participation and Modern Multilateral Conferences," *Global Governance: A Review of Multilateralism and International Organizations* 20, no. 3 (2014): 361–373.

38 See, e.g., Sergei Witte, *The Memoirs of Count Witte* (Sydney Harcave, trans. and ed.) (Armonk, NY: ME Sharpe, 1990), 99–101, 108–109, 135–137. Cf. Martens, *Le Conflit entre le Russie et la Chine*.

39 See Ralph William Huenemann, *The Dragon and the Iron Horse: The Economics of Railroads in China, 1876–1937* (Cambridge, MA: Harvard University Asia Center, 1984), 51–52; G. N. Trubetskoi, *Notes of a Plenipotentiary: Russian Diplomacy and War in the Balkans, 1914–1917* (Ithaca, NY: Cornell University Press, 2016), 11–12.

40 John Albert White, *Transition to Global Rivalry: Alliance Diplomacy and the Quadruple Entente: 1895–1907* (Cambridge: Cambridge University Press, 2002), 64–65.

41 Tian Tao, "Haiya He Hui zai Zhongguo de Fanxiang 海牙和會在中國的反響" [The Impact of the Hague Peace Conferences in China], *Tianjin Shifan Daxue Xuebao (Shehui Kexue Ban)* 3 (2015): 11–16.

42 The Spring and Autumn Era *mibinghui* analogy was nonetheless appealing to many intellectuals, see Tian Tao, "Wan Qing Zhishijie de Mibing Shuo 晚清知识界的弭兵说" [The *Mibing* Theory of the Late Qing Intelligentsia], *Tianjin Shifan Daxue Xuebao (Shehui Kexue Ban)* 1 (2008): 38–43.

43 Ibid.

44 See Bertha von Suttner, *Memoiren von Bertha von Suttner* (Stuttgart: Deutsche Verlags-Anstalt, 1909).

45 See, e.g., Ariga Nagao, *The Red Cross Society of Japan: Its Organization and Activity in Time of Peace and War* (St. Louis, MO: Samuel F. Myerson Printing Company, 1904); Klaus Schlichtmann, "Japan, Germany and the Idea of the Hague Peace Conferences," *Journal of Peace Research* 40, no. 4 (2003): 377–394.

46 See James Brown Scott, *The Reports to the Hague Conferences of 1899 and 1907* (New York: Clarendon Press, 1917), 17; James Brown Scott, *The Proceedings of the Hague Peace Conferences: Translation of the Original Texts* (New York: Oxford University Press, 1920); Arthur Eyffinger, "Caught between Tradition and Modernity: East Asia at the Hague Peace Conferences," *Journal of East Asia and International Law* 1 (2008): 7–46; Maartje Abbenhuis, *The Hague Conferences and International Politics, 1898–1915* (London: Bloomsbury Publishing, 2018).

47 Heinrich Lammasch, "Aus Meinem Leben" in Marga Lammasch and Hans Sperl (eds.), *Heinrich Lammasch: Seine Aufzeichnungen, sein Wirken und seine Politik* (Vienna: Franz Deuticke, 1922), 14–17.

48 Frederick W. Holls, *The Peace Conference at the Hague and Its Bearings on International Law and Policy* (London: Macmillan & Co. Ltd., 1900), 325–326.

49 That the anecdote was conceived in this spirit of mockery rather than neutral reportage is clearly apparent in the brief critical mention of it in Lammasch, "Aus Meinem Leben," 16 ("Yang Yü wurde nachgesagt, er hätte in seinem pidjen English von der Konferenz gesagt too muchee talkee little dooee (sic), und ebenso behaupteten seine bösen Nachbarn, daß der neben ihm sitzende Dr. Kreyer . . . ihn am Zopf rechts oder links ziehe, je nach dem er oui oder non sagen solle").

50 Arthur Eyffinger, *The 1899 Hague Peace Conference: The Parliament of Man, the Federation of the World* (Leiden: Martinus Nijhoff Publishers, 1999), 137.

51 Lammasch, "Aus Meinem Leben," 16.

52 Von Suttner, *Memoiren von Bertha von Suttner*, 419.

53 Ibid.
54 Ibid.
55 William T. Stead, *The Parliament of Peace and Its Members* (London: Review of Reviews, 1899), 6–7.
56 William T. Stead, *The United States of Europe on the Eve of the Parliament of Peace* (Toronto: George N. Morang, 1899), 344.
57 See Robert Kolb, "Origin of the Twin Terms *Jus ad Bellum/Jus in Bello*," *International Review of the Red Cross Archive* 37, no. 320 (1997): 553–562.
58 China had not yet at this point signed the original Geneva Convention of 1864, and so this came up for consideration alongside the Hague Convention.
59 Tang Qihua, "Qingmo Minchu Zhongguo dui 'Haiya Baohehui' zhi Canyu (1899–1917) 清末民初中國對海牙飽和會之參與 (1899–1917)" [China's Participation in the Hague Peace Conferences in the Late Qing and Early Republic Periods], *Guoli Zhengzhi Daxue Lishi Xuebao* 5, no. 23 (2005): 45–49.
60 Ibid.
61 Andrei Mamolea, "Saving Face: The Political Work of the Permanent Court of Arbitration (1902–1914)" in Ignacio de la Rasilla and Jorge E. Viñuales (eds.), *Experiments in International Adjudication: Historical Accounts* (Cambridge: Cambridge University Press, 2019), 193–210.
62 Fu Limin and He Minglun, *Zhongguo Shangye Wenhua Da Cidian* 中国商业文化大辞典 [*Dictionary of Chinese Commercial Culture*] (Beijing: Zhongguo Fazhan Chubanshe, 1994).
63 For receptivity to Yang Ru's discussion of the Red Cross and other humanitarian initiatives as *shanju*, see WJDA: 01-28-001-03-007.
64 Tang, "Qingmo Minchu Zhongguo dui 'Haiya Baohehui' zhi Canyu," 48–49.
65 Ibid.
66 Ibid.
67 Ibid.
68 WJDA: 01-28-001-03-010.
69 Ibid.
70 Tang, "Qingmo Minchu Zhongguo dui 'Haiya Baohehui' zhi Canyu," 48–49. At the same time, China also signed onto the separate conventions regarding banning exploding bullets, the use of balloons in warfare, etc.
71 See, e.g., Robert Bickers and R. Gary Tiedemann, eds., *The Boxers, China, and the World* (Lanham, MD: Rowman & Littlefield Publishers, 2007); Jeffrey N. Wasserstrom, ed., *Twentieth-Century China: New Approaches* (Abingdon: Routledge, 2013), 6–7.
72 On the role of Hart and the MCS in the formulation of the Boxer Protocol's terms, see Hans van de Ven, "Robert Hart and Gustav Detring during the Boxer Rebellion," *Modern Asian Studies* 40, no. 3 (2006): 631–662.
73 International Protocol (1901), Article 6, *Treaties, Conventions, etc., between China and Foreign States*, vol. 1, 301–345.
74 Ibid., Article 5.
75 Ibid., Article 8.
76 Ibid., Article 9.
77 Ibid., Article 10.
78 Ibid., Article 12.

79 On the organization and operation of the "international tribunal," see Benjamin E. Brockman-Hawe, "Accountability for Crimes against the Laws of Humanity in Boxer China: An Experiment with International Justice at Paoting-Fu," *University of Pennsylvania Journal of International Law* 38 (2016): 627–713.

80 Lassa Oppenheim, *International Law: A Treatise* (London: Longmans, Green, and Co., 1905), vol. 1, 199.

81 Franz von Liszt, *Das Völkerrecht systematisch dargestellt*, 2nd ed. (Berlin: Verlag O. Haering, 1902), 283–284.

82 Ibid.

83 Ibid.

84 Martin, *The Siege in Peking*, 45–46.

85 Georg Jellinek, "China und das Völkerrecht," *Deutsche Juristen-Zeitung* 5, no. 19 (1900): 401–403.

86 Ibid.

87 Julius Hirschfeld, "Current Notes on International Law," *Law Magazine and Review: A Quarterly Review of Jurisprudence* 5, no. 26 (1900): 335.

88 FRUS 1900, 216–217, 322–323, 380–381; "The Arbitration Plan," *The New York Times*, October 14, 1900.

89 Frederick W. Holls, "The International Court of Arbitration at the Hague," *American Lawyer* 9 (1901): 160.

90 Fyodor de Martens, "How the Chinese Question Should Be Solved," *The Advocate of Peace* 62, no. 11 (1900): 240–241.

91 Fyodor de Martens, *La Conférence de la Paix á La Haye: Étude d'Histoire Contemporaine* (Paris: Arthur Rousseau, 1900), 18.

92 Bertha von Suttner, *Memoirs of Bertha von Suttner: The Records of an Eventful Life*, vol. 2 (London: International School of Peace, 1910).

93 Ibid.

94 This passage is recorded somewhat differently in Chinese and Western versions of the letter. In the version published in the West, it reads "The Chinese no more desire to be converted to Christianity than the Europeans would wish to embrace the maxims of Confucius." Ibid.

95 Ibid.

96 Ibid.

97 Bertha von Suttner, "Slow Evolution," *The Advocate of Peace* 62, no. 10 (1900): 208–209.

98 See Oppenheim, *International Law*, 1st ed. 111.

99 Lu, *Souvenirs et Pensées*, 39–45.

100 Ibid.

101 Ibid.

102 Ibid.

103 Tyler Dennett, *Americans in Eastern Asia: A Critical Study of the Policy of the United States with Reference to China, Japan and Korea in the 19th Century* (New York: Macmillan, 1922), vii (arguing that "the issue in American policy in Asia was not the open door. That was never a question. The real issue was whether the United States should follow an isolated or a cooperative policy to make sure of the open door").

104 Alfred Thayer Mahan, *The Problem of Asia and Its Effect upon International Policies* (London: Sampson, Low, Marston and Co., 1900), 167.
105 Ibid., 163–167.
106 Agreement relative to Manchuria, in *Treaties, Conventions, etc., between China and Foreign States*, vol. 1, 239–245.
107 WJDA: 02-12-005-01-021.

Chapter 5

1 Mai Menghua, "Paiwai Pingyi 排外平議" [A Critique of Xenophobia], *Qing Yi Bao* (1901): 68.
2 See Li Guilian, *1902: Zhongguo Fa de Zhuanxing* 中国法的转型 [*1902: The Transformation of Chinese Law*] (Guilin: Guangxi Shifan Daxue Chubanshe, 2018).
3 Cf. Tang Qihua, "Qingmo Minchu Zhongguo dui 'Haiya Baohehui' zhi Canyu (1899–1917) 清末民初中國對'海牙飽和會'之參與 (1899–1917)" [China's Late Qing–Early Republican Era Participation in the Hague Peace Conferences], *Guoli Zhengzhi Daxue Lishi Xuebao* 5, no. 23 (2005): 45–90.
4 Cf. Warren F. Kuehl, *Seeking World Order: The United States and International Organization to 1920* (Nashville, TN: Vanderbilt University Press, 1969), 89–90; von Suttner, "Slow Evolution."
5 See Tang, "Qingmo Minchu Zhongguo dui 'Haiya Baohehui' zhi Canyu," 84–86.
6 Svarverud, *International Law as World Order in Late Imperial China*, 108, 177.
7 Qing Dynasty Imperial Examination Collection (via Shu Tong Wen Guji Shujuku).
8 Zhu Chuangyu, ed., *Wang Chonghui Zhuanji Ziliao* 王寵惠傳記資料 [*Biographical Materials on Wang Chonghui*, vols. 1–3 (Taipei: Tian Yi Chubanshe, 1979).
9 Wang Chung Hui [Wang Chonghui], *The German Civil Code: Translated and Annotated with Historical Introduction and Appendices* (London: Stevens and Sons, Ltd., 1907).
10 Wang would later become China's first international judge in 1922, and was well-regarded among his colleagues at the Permanent Court of International Justice. Cf. Ole Spiermann, "Judge Wang Chung-hui at the Permanent Court of International Justice," *Chinese Journal of International Law* 5, no. 1 (2006): 115–128.
11 *Wang Chonghui Zhuan Ji Ziliao*, vol. 1, 55.
12 V. K. Wellington Koo, *The Status of Aliens in China* (New York: Columbia University Press, 1912).
13 See, e.g., Liu Guoming, ed., *Zhonghua Minguo Guomin Zhengfu Jun Zheng Zhiguan Renwu Zhi* 中华民国国民政府军政职官人物誌 [*Almanac of Military and Political Officials of the Republic of China Government*] (Beijing: Chunqiu Chubanshe, 1989), 1167.
14 Ma Do Yün [Ma Derun], "Der Eintritt des chinesischen Reiches in den völkerrechtlichen Verband" (PhD dissertation, University of Berlin, 1907); Tso Tschun Tschou [Zhou Zechun], *Die Reformen des chinesischen Reiches*

in Verfassung, Verwaltung und Rechtsprechung mit Ruecksicht auf die entsprechenden Einrichtungen Europas (Berlin: Druck von Emil Ebering, 1909).

15 Wang Jian, "Modern Legal Periodicals of China," *Frontiers of Law in China* 2, no. 2 (2007): 318–333.

16 Ma Do Yün [Ma Derun], "China im Völkerbunde," *Berliner Tageblatt und Handelszeitung*, July 19, 1907.

17 See, e.g., CNBKSY, Zhou Zechun, *Guoji Gongfa* 國際公法, *Fa Zheng Jiewen* 1–2 (1908) (translating Liszt's international law doctrine and referring to his discussions of *Kultur-* and *Interessengemeinschaft*).

18 von Liszt, *Das Völkerrecht Systematisch Dargestellt*, 1st ed., 72. On the influence of Liszt's textbook, see Florian Herrmann, *Das Standardwerk: Franz von Liszt und das Völkerrecht* (Baden-Baden: Nomos, 2001).

19 Amanda J. Cheney, "Tibet Lost in Translation: Sovereignty, Suzerainty and International Order Transformation, 1904–1906," *Journal of Contemporary China* 26, no. 107 (2017): 769–783.

20 Japanese Foreign Ministry Archives: 5-2-18-0-33_002 (July 31, 1905–September 11, 1905).

21 Theodore Roosevelt, "Annual Message of the President to Congress" in *Papers Relating to the Foreign Relations of the United States*, vol. 1 (Washington, DC: US Government Printing Office, 1904), xlviii.

22 QSL, Guangxu Era, Juan 486.

23 WJDA: 02-21-001-03-009 ("Memorial of Wu Shouquan, June 5, 1907").

24 John Watson Foster, *Diplomatic Memoirs*, vol. 2 (Boston: Houghton Mifflin Company, 1909), 213.

25 Carl Schmitt, *Der Nomos der Erde im Volkerrecht des Jus Publicum Europaeum* (Berlin: Duncker & Humblot, 1950), 204 ("So war eine asiatische Großmacht entstanden und anerkannt.") ("Die Atmosphäre, das 'Ambiente' der ersten Haager Friedenskonferenz von 1899 war noch rein europäisch im Vergleich zu der zweiten Haager Konferenz von 1907... Aber die Füße derer, die sie hinaustragen sollten, standen schon vor der Tür").

26 Lu, *Souvenirs et Pensées*, 51–54.

27 Ibid., 38.

28 WJDA: 02-21-002-01-043 (Diplomatic Cable of Lu Zhengxiang, December 22, 1906).

29 Ibid.

30 Ibid.

31 Wang is not recorded as participating in any of the sessions, but likely conferred with the other Qing delegates.

32 See, e.g., Foster, *Diplomatic Memoirs*, vol. 2, 103–109.

33 Ibid.

34 For a discussion focused mainly on Latin American states' participation in and reaction to the incident, see Becker Lorca, *Mestizo International Law*, 158–168. Cf. Robert A. Klein, *Sovereign Equality among States: The History of an Idea* (Toronto: University of Toronto Press, 1974), 61.

35 James Brown Scott, *The Hague Peace Conferences of 1899 and 1907*, vol. 1 (Baltimore: Johns Hopkins Press, 1909), 428.

36 James Brown Scott, ed., *The Proceedings of the Hague Peace Conferences, The Conference of 1907, Vol. 2, Meetings of the First Commission* (New York: Oxford University Press, 1921), 322 (hereinafter *Proceedings, vol. 2*).
37 Ibid., 321.
38 Ibid., 328.
39 Ibid., 612–613.
40 William T. Stead, "Les juges de la nouvelle cour permanente," *Courrier de la Conférence de la Paix*, August 20, 1907.
41 Scott, *Proceedings, vol. 2*, 605–606.
42 Ibid.
43 Ibid.
44 WJDA: 02-21/10-(1) (Lu Zhengxiang to Waiwubu, September 2, 1907).
45 Departement van Buitenlandsche Zaken, *Deuxième Conférence Internationale de la Paix, Actes et Documents, Vol. 2, Première Commission* (La Haye: Imprimerie Nationale, 1907), 53.
46 Ibid.
47 Scott, *Proceedings, vol. 2*, 622–623.
48 See e.g., discussion in Becker Lorca, *Mestizo International Law*, 160–168.
49 Scott, *Proceedings, vol. 2*, 690–706. See also Becker Lorca, *Mestizo International Law*, 166 (incorrectly listing the date as September 8).
50 "Joseph Choate, of U.S., Beaten at Hague by Brazil Delegate in Hot Word Duel," *Evansville Press*, September 23, 1907.
51 Ruy Barbosa, "Rank among States Not Determined by Their Military Standing," *The Advocate of Peace* 70, no. 36 (1908): 36–38.
52 Scott, *Proceedings, vol. 2*, 817; James Brown Scott, ed., *American Addresses at the Second Hague Peace Conference* (Boston: World Peace Foundation, 1916) (original publication 1910), 210.
53 Alfred Thayer Mahan, *The Influence of Sea Power upon History: 1660–1783* (Boston: Little, Brown, & Co., 1890).
54 Scott, *Proceedings, vol. 2*, 1051–1056.
55 Ibid., 1056–1059.
56 *The Pious Fund of the Californias (United States v Mexico)*, Award of October 14, 1902 [1902] IX Reports of International Arbitral Awards 1.
57 Scott, *Proceedings, vol. 2*, 786 (First Commission, Second Subcommission, meeting of July 4, 1907).
58 Agnes Fry, *A Memoir of the Right Honourable Sir Edward Fry, G.C.B.* (Oxford: Oxford University Press, 1921), 196.
59 Ibid.
60 Ibid.
61 Cf. Cheney, "Tibet Lost in Translation."
62 Fry, *A Memoir of the Right Honourable Sir Edward Fry*, 203.
63 Ibid., 202.
64 Scott, *Proceedings, vol. 2*, 844–845.
65 *II Conferência da Paz Haia 1907: A correspondência telegráfica entre o Barão do Rio Branco e Rui Barbosa* (Rio de Janeiro: Fundação Alexandre de Gusmão, 2014), 97, 152.
66 WJDA: 02-21-004-01-003-046-058 (January 16, 1908).

67 See e.g., James L. Tryon, "International Prize Court and Code," *Yale Law Journal* 20 (1910): 604.

68 Hans Wehberg, *The Problem of an International Court of Justice* (Oxford: Clarendon Press, 1918) (Charles G. Fenwick, trans.) (citing the similar views of the prominent legal scholar Otfried Nippold), 115.

69 Franz von Liszt, *Das Wesen des völkerrechtlichen Staatenverbandes und der international Prisenhof* (Breslau: M. & H. Marcus, 1910), 11.

70 Departement van Buitenlandsche Zaken, *Deuxième Conférence Internationale de la Paix, Actes et Documents, Vol. 1, Séances Plénières de la Conférence* (La Haye: Imprimerie Nationale, 1907), 90–92.

71 Fry, *A Memoir of the Right Honourable Sir Edward Fry*, 222.

72 "The Danger Point at the Hague" *The Times*, September 14, 1907.

73 James Brown Scott, ed., *The Proceedings of the Hague Peace Conferences, The Conference of 1907, vol. 3 Meetings of the Second, Third, and Fourth Commissions* (New York: Oxford University Press, 1921) (hereafter *Proceedings vol. 3*), 167 (meeting of July 12, 1907).

74 Foster, *Diplomatic Memoirs*, vol. 2, 239.

75 Ibid.

76 For an overview of this resolution and its content, see e.g., Adil Ahmad Haque, "The Definition of Aggression and Self-defense," *Just Security* (December 14, 2020). Available at: www.justsecurity.org/73858/the-definition-of-aggression-and-self-defense/.

77 James Brown Scott, *The Hague Peace Conferences of 1899 and 1907*, vol. 2 (Baltimore: Johns Hopkins Press, 1909), 356–367, 415–420.

78 William T. Stead, "Notes," *Courrier de la Conférence de la Paix*, July 7, 1907.

79 Scott, *The Hague Peace Conferences of 1899 and 1907*, vol. 2, 411; *II Conferência da Paz Haia 1907*, 71.

80 Scott, *The Hague Peace Conferences of 1899 and 1907*, vol. 2, 179.

81 William T. Stead, "La Neutralité de la Mer, Discours de M. Foster," *Courrier de la Conférence de la Paix*, July 12, 1907.

82 Ibid.

83 William T. Stead, "Le Défi des Coréens," *Courrier de la Conférence de la Paix*, July 9, 1907.

84 WJDA: 02-19-016-01-012 (September 13, 1907).

85 Ibid.

86 Scott, *Proceedings, vol. 2*, 533.

87 Ibid.

88 Ibid., 115.

89 WJDA: 02-21-002-03-051 (海牙保和會列中國為三等國請修明法律以保主權由 ["The Hague Conference listed China as a third-class state. We request enlightened law reform in order to preserve sovereignty"]).

90 Ibid.

91 WJDA: 02-21-010-01-004 (December 29, 1907).

92 Ibid.

93 Ibid.

94 See Zhongguo Di Er Lishi Dang'an Guan, "Lu Zhengxiang Chuxi Haiya Baohehui Zouzhe Liang Jian 陸徵祥出席海牙保和會奏摺兩件" [Two Memorials of Lu

Zhengxiang Regarding Participation at the Hague Peace Conference], *Minguo Dang'an* 2 (2000): 37–42 (Lu is ambivalent about the notion of cooperation with Japan in such an "Asian faction," noting that China had missed early opportunities for such cooperation before the war of 1894–1895).

95 For critical appraisals of the role of state sovereignty in such (later) discourses of Third World Approaches to International Law (TWAIL), see, e.g., Mohsen al al Attar, "Subverting Eurocentric Epistemology: The Value of Nonsense When Designing Counterfactuals," in Ingo Venzke and Kevin John Heller (eds.), *Contingency in International Law: On the Possibility of Different Legal Histories* (Oxford: Oxford University Press, 2021), 145–161; for a perspective focusing on how the state, like other legal forms, can serve as a site of "relative autonomy" reflecting struggles over agency and distribution between social actors, see Umut Özsu, "The Necessity of Contingency: Method and Marxism in International Law" in ibid., 60–76.

96 Cf. Ingo Venzke "Introduction: Situating Contingency in the Path of International Law" in ibid., 3–19.

97 See e.g., Albert Geouffre de Lapradelle and Ellery C. Stowell, "Latin America at the Hague Conference," *Yale Law Journal* 17 (1907): 270; William I. Hull, "The United States and Latin America at the Hague," *International Conciliation* 1, no. 44 (1911): 12–13; Hayne Davis, "Legal Aspects of the Hague Conference," *American Lawyer* 16, no. 1 (1908): 420–425; Frederick Charles Hicks, "The Equality of States and the Hague Conferences," *American Journal of International Law* 2, no. 3 (1908): 530–561; Alejandro Alvarez, "Latin America and International Law," *American Journal of International Law* 3, no. 2 (1909): 269–353.

98 Max Huber, "Die Gleichheit der Staaten" in *Rechtswissenschaftliche Beiträge: Juristische Festgabe des Auslandes zu Josef Kohlers 60. Geburtstag, 9. März 1909* (Aalen: Scientia Verlag, 1909), 88–118.

99 Thomas Joseph Lawrence, *International Problems and Hague Conferences* (London: J. M. Dent, 1908), 148.

100 Huber, "Die Gleichheit der Staaten," 118.

101 Ibid.

102 Max Huber, "Beiträge zur Kenntnis der soziologischen Grundlagen des Völkerrechts und der Staatengesellschaft" in *Jahrbuch des öffentlichen Rechts der Gegenwart* (Tübingen: J. C. B. Mohr, 1910), 7.

103 Ibid.

104 See e.g., William Dudley Foulke, "Arbitration the Shortest Road to International Justice" in *Report of the Annual Lake Mohonk Conference on International Arbitration* (New York: Lake Mohonk Conference on International Arbitration, 1911), 99–100.

105 Theodore Marburg, "The Significance of the International Court of Arbitral Justice" in *Report of the Annual Lake Mohonk Conference on International Arbitration* (New York: Lake Mohonk Conference on International Arbitration, 1910), 87.

106 Wu Ting-Fang, "China's Attitude towards Arbitration" in *Report of the Annual Lake Mohonk Conference on International Arbitration* (New York: Lake Mohonk Conference on International Arbitration, 1909), 67–71.

107 William H. Taft, *Address of President Taft at the Banquet Given in His Honor by the Americus Club, Pittsburgh, P.A., May 2, 1910* (Washington, DC: Library of Congress, 1910), 18.
108 Ibid., 17.
109 Ibid., 13–15.
110 Elihu Root, "The Basis of Protection to Citizens Residing Abroad," *American Journal of International Law* 4, no. 3 (1910): 517–528, 520.
111 Ibid., 521
112 Ibid.
113 Thomas Barclay, *Problems of International Practice and Diplomacy: With Special Reference to the Hague Conferences and Conventions and Other General International Agreements* (London: Sweet & Maxwell Limited, 1907), 153–156.
114 Ibid.
115 Ibid.
116 See list of appointees in Ole Spiermann, *International Legal Argument in the Permanent Court of International Justice: The Rise of the International Judiciary* (Cambridge: Cambridge University Press, 2005), 134.
117 See e.g., "China Is Not Willing to Be Led by Hand: Is No Longer Interested in Treaty Technicalities, Says Dr. Wang," *The China Press*, November 19, 1925.
118 Arthur Eyffinger, "A Highly Critical Moment: Role and Record of the 1907 Hague Peace Conference," *Netherlands International Law Review* 54, no. 2 (2007): 197–228.
119 *The New York Times*, September 23, 1907 ("To call the meetings at the Hague a fiasco would merely be to repeat the public opinion of the whole of Europe").
120 Walther Schücking, *Die Organisation der Welt* (Leipzig: Kröner, 1909); Walther Schücking, *Das Werk vom Haag, Erster Band: Die Staatenverband der Haager Konferenzen* (Munich: Duncker & Humblot, 1912), 81. See discussion in Koskenniemi, *The Gentle Civilizer of Nations*, 216–218.
121 See Becker Lorca, *Mestizo International Law*, 158, 179.
122 Gerry Simpson, *Great Powers and Outlaw States: Unequal Sovereigns in the International Legal Order* (Cambridge: Cambridge University Press, 2004), 135.
123 Antony Anghie, *Imperialism, Sovereignty, and the Making of International Law* (Cambridge: Cambridge University Press, 2004), 182.

Chapter 6

1 Yuan Shikai, for example, referred to Lu at a 1912 tea reception for senators as "the person with the top reputation out of our country's entire diplomatic community" (外交界上爲吾國第一有聲譽之人). YSQS: 20-502.
2 Julia C. Strauss, *Strong Institutions in Weak Polities: State Building in Republican China, 1927–1940* (Oxford: Clarendon Press, 1998).
3 See, e.g., Lee Lai To and Hock Guan Lee, eds., *Sun Yat-Sen, Nanyang and the 1911 Revolution* (Singapore: Institute of Southeast Asian Studies, 2011).

4 See Dibyesh Anand, "Strategic Hypocrisy: The British Imperial Scripting of Tibet's Geopolitical Identity," *Journal of Asian Studies* 68, no. 1 (2009): 227–252; Cheney, "Tibet Lost in Translation"; Yuan Yi Zhu, "Suzerainty, Semi-sovereignty, and International Legal Hierarchies on China's Borderlands," *Asian Journal of International Law* 10, no. 2 (2020): 293–320. "Suzerainty" in Chinese was originally rendered in various ways, including *shangquan* 上權, but would ultimately be given the Japanese-derived form *zongzhuquan* 宗主權.

5 Anand, "Strategic Hypocrisy."

6 Cf. Zhu, "Suzerainty, Semi-sovereignty, and International Legal Hierarchies on China's Borderlands," 293–294.

7 Oppenheim, *International Law*, 1st ed., 135.

8 "Suzerainty" in *Encyclopaedia Britannica*, vol. 26 (Cambridge: Cambridge University Press, 1911), 173.

9 Ibid., 174.

10 Provisional Constitution of the Republic of China, Article 2 (1912).

11 "Lu Zhengxiang Fa Qi Guoji Fahui 陸徵祥發起國際法會" [Lu Zhengxiang Launches Society for International Law], *Shi Bao*, October 2, 1912.

12 James Brown Scott, "The Chinese Society and Journal of International Law," *American Journal of International Law* 7, no. 1 (1913): 159–161. In Scott's view, Lu hoped to model his society on the *Institut de Droit International*. Ibid., 161.

13 See Edward T. Williams, "The Relations between China, Russia, and Mongolia," *American Journal of International Law* 10, no. 4 (1916): 798–808.

14 Ibid.

15 Chen Lu, "Lun Zhuquan Zongzhuquan Gao Lu Zongzhang 論主權宗主權告陸總長" [Warning to Premier Lu Regarding the Difference between "Suzerainty" and "Sovereignty"], *Shibao*, December 14, 1912.

16 WJDA: 03-32-156-01-004.

17 Ibid.

18 See, e.g., Fang Ke, *Tiexue Gonghe: Tu Shuo Xinhai Geming* 铁血共和: 图说辛亥革命 [*Iron and Blood Republic: A Pictorial Account of the Xinhai Revolution*], (Beijing: Renmin Wenxue Chubanshe, 2011).

19 See, e.g., Zhu, "Suzerainty, Semi-sovereignty, and International Legal Hierarchies on China's Borderlands," 305.

20 WJDA: 03-32-163-01-012 (January 11, 1913).

21 Official French text in Henry G. W. Woodhead and Henry T. Montague Bell, *The China Year Book 1914* (London: George Routledge & Sons, 1914), 633–635. Article 1: "La Russie reconnait que la Mongolie Extérieure se trouve sous la suzeraineté de la Chine."; Article 2: "La Chine reconnait l'autonomie de la Mongolie Extérieure." Chinese version reprinted in "Ben Sheng Sheng Ling: Fu Lu 本省省令 附錄" [Jiangsu Provincial Orders: Appendix], *Jiangsu Sheng Gongbao* 186, December 6, 1913.

22 WJDA: 03-32-162-02-024 (October 8, 1913).

23 WJDA: 03-32-159-01-015 (August 12, 1913).

24 YSQS: 21-1289 (January 24, 1913).

25 WJDA: 03-35-002-01 (*Di San Ci Baohehui Zhunbeihui* 第三次萬國保和會籌備會). On the Preparation Committee's role as an "Organ Appointed by the Special Authority of the President," see ibid., meeting of February 21, 1913.
26 Ibid. meeting of January 18, 1913.
27 Ibid.
28 Ibid. meeting of January 31, 1913.
29 Ibid. meeting of October 31, 1914.
30 Koo, *The Status of Aliens in China*, 356.
31 WJDA: 03-35-002-01, meeting of October 31, 1914.
32 Ibid.
33 See, e.g., Yang Daxin, ed., *Beiyang Zhengfu Zongtong yu Zongli* 北洋政府总统与总理 [*President and Premier of the Beiyang Government*] (Tianjin: Nankai Daxue Chubanshe, 1989), 31.
34 See, e.g., Ma Yong, "From Constitutional Monarchy to Republic: The Trajectory of Yuan Shikai," *Journal of Modern Chinese History* 6, no. 1 (2012): 15–32.
35 See GSG: 116-010101-0003-073; WJDA: 03-12-001-05-036.
36 James Brown Scott, "The Chinese Social and Political Science Association," *American Journal of International Law* 10, no. 2 (1916): 375–378.
37 Franz von Liszt, *Das Völkerrecht Systematisch Dargestellt*, 10th ed. (Berlin: Springer, 1915), 5–6.
38 Ibid.
39 See, e.g., Morikawa Hiroki, "In Pursuit of Peace: Zhou Gengsheng's Internationalism after the World Wars," *ZINBUN* 47 (2017): 177–194.
40 Zhou Gengsheng, "Juwai Zhongli Tiaogui Pingyi 局外中立條规平议" [Commentary on the Neutrality Regulations], *Jiayin Zazhi* 1, no. 8 (1915): 1–16; Zhou Gengsheng, "Zhong-E Jiaoshe Ping 中俄交涉评" [Commentary on the Sino-Russian Negotiations], *Jiayin Zazhi* 1, no. 10 (1915): 1–8; Zhou Gengsheng, "Gonghe Zhengzhi Lun 共和政治论" [The Theory of Republican Politics], *Jiayin Zazhi* 1, no. 10 (1915) 1–17.
41 Zhou Gengsheng, "Zongzhuquan Lun 宗主权论" [The Theory of Suzerainty], *Taipingyang* 1, no. 10 (1918): 1–13.
42 Ibid.
43 See, e.g., Liu Guoming, ed., *Zhonghua Minguo Guomin Zhengfu Jun Zheng Zhiguan Renwu Zhi* 中华民国国民政府军政职官人物誌 [*Almanac of Military and Political Officials of the Republic of China Government*] (Beijing: Chunqiu Chubanshe, 1989), 1,167.
44 Sintchar Tchéou Wei [Zhou Wei], *Essai sur l'organisation juridique de la Société international* (Geneva: Libraire Atar, 1917).
45 See, e.g., Otfried Nippold, *Die Gestaltung des Völkerrechts nach dem Weltkriege* (Zurich: Orell Füssli, 1917) translated as Otfried Nippold, *The Development of International Law after the World War* (Clarke, NJ: The Lawbook Exchange, Ltd., 2004) (original publication 1923) (Amos S. Hershey, trans.), 44 ("the work of the Chinese Tchéou-Weï deserves special attention"); see also Henri Lepert, *Projet de constitution pour la Société des nations: Projet soumis à la Ligue* (Paris: Ligue por une Société des Nations Basée sur une Constitution Internationale, 1917), 24; André Duboscq, Review, CXXXVI *Mercure de*

France, February 1, 1919: 513 ("L'*Essai* . . . est d'une exceptionelle actualité"); Paul Fauchille, *Traité de droit international public* (Paris: Rousseau & Co., 1923), 183.

46 Zhou, *Essai*, 1.

47 Schücking, *Die Organisation der Welt*; Walther Schücking, "L'organisation internationale," *Revue générale de droit international public* 15 (1908): 5–23; cf. Koskenniemi, *The Gentle Civilizer of Nations*, 215–219; Schücking, *Das Werk vom Haag, Erster Band*, 81.

48 See, e.g., Stephen Wertheim, "The League That Wasn't: American Designs for a Legalist-Sanctionist League of Nations and the Intellectual Origins of International Organization, 1914–1920," *Diplomatic History* 35, no. 5 (2011): 797–836.

49 Zhou, *Essai*, 11.

50 See, e.g., ibid., 106.

51 Zhou's conclusion also linked the "general judicial boycott" with the *popular* boycott that is carried out by private consumers refusing to do business with a state whose policies they condemn. Somewhat provocatively, Zhou's main example of the latter was the boycott of American goods that had been carried out in 1905 over the issue of Chinese exclusion, ibid., 141–143.

52 Cf. Oona A. Hathaway and Scott J. Shapiro, "Outcasting: Enforcement in Domestic and International Law," *Yale Law Journal* 121, no. 2 (2011): 252.

53 Institut de Droit International, *Annuaire de l'Institut de Droit International*, vol. 28, 1921 (Brussels: A. Dewit, 1921), xxiv.

54 A full list of China's representatives at Versailles is provided in Thomas F. Millard, *The Shantung Case at the Conference* (Shanghai: Millard's Review of the Far East, 1921), 5.

55 Walter Phillimore, "Appendix: Recent Schemes of Federation" in *The Committee of the League of Nations, Final Report* (Geneva: League of Nations, 1918), 8–24.

56 Ibid.

57 On the role of the commission, see David Hunter Miller, *The Drafting of the Covenant* (New York: Johnson Reprint Corporation, 1969) (original publication 1929).

58 FRUS 1919, vol. 3. Minutes of the Meeting Held by the Representatives of Powers with Special Interests, Paris, January 27, 1919, 3 p.m.

59 Geo A. Finch, "The Peace Conference of Paris, 1919," *American Journal of International Law* 13, no. 2 (1919): 159–186.

60 Miller, *The Drafting of the Covenant*, 125.

61 Ibid., 151–153.

62 Ibid., 152.

63 For a discussion among international jurists while the Versailles Conference was still ongoing of the significance of the Monroe Doctrine and whether it was "legal" or "political," see Institut de Droit International, *Annuaire de l'Institut de Droit International*, vol. 27, 1919 (Brussels: Falk, 1919), 330–331.

64 See Tang Qihua, *Beijing Zhengfu yu Guoji Lianmeng* 北京政府與國際聯盟 [*The Beijing Government and the League of Nations*] (Taipei: Dongda Tushu Gongsi, 1998), 39–45.

65 Miller, *The Drafting of the Covenant*, 450.
66 Millard, *The Shantung Case at the Conference*, 23–24.
67 Wellington Koo, "Bali Hehui Guoji Lianhe Guyiding Mengyue Qingxing Zhaiyao 巴黎和會國際聯合股議定盟約情形摘要" [The Treaty-Signing Situation of the League of Nations Commission at the Paris Peace Conference], *Waijiao Gongbao*, July 1, 1921: 99–109.
68 See Millard, *The Shantung Case at the Conference*, 21–38.
69 Ibid.
70 See, e.g., "Zhuanchang yu Guoji Gongfa de Zhengzhi Xuejia Zhou Gengsheng Xiansheng 专长于国际公法的政治学家周鲠生先生" [The International Law Specialist and Scholar of Politics Zhou Gengsheng], *Tianxia Hunan*, July 19, 2017. Available at: www.txhn.net/index/important/201907/t20190715_787767.htm
71 Ibid.
72 Letter of Lu Zhengxiang to Berthe Bovy, June 29, 1919, quoted in Claire Shu-Chin Chang, *When Confucius Meets Benedictus: The Destiny of Chinese Politician Lou Tseng-tsiang (1871–1949)* (Leuven: Katholieke Universiteit Leuven, 1994), 233.
73 Letter of Carsun Chang to H. J. T. Fisher, July 12, 1919.
74 Eric S. Nelson, "Zhang Junmai's Early Political Philosophy and the Paradoxes of Chinese Modernity," *Asian Studies* 8, no. 1 (2020): 183–208.
75 Mao Zedong, "Zhengming Xieyue Guo de Pingdeng Zhengyi 證明協約國丁平等正義" [Demonstrating the Equality and Justice of the Allied Nations], *Xiangjiang Pinglun*, July 14, 1919, 3.
76 Mao Zedong, "Gaoxing he Shentong 高興和沈痛" [Elation and Suffering], *Xiangjiang Pinglun*, July 21, 1919, 4.
77 Mao Zedong, "Hao Ge Mingzu [sic] Zijue 好個名族自決" [Some National Self-Determination!], *Xiangjiang Pinglun*, July 14, 1919, 3.
78 Zhou Gengsheng, "Zhanqian Zhanhou de Guoji Zhengju 战前战后的国际政局" [The International Situation before and after the War], *Taipingyang* 2, no. 5 (1920): 1–16.
79 Zhou Gengsheng, "Wanguo Tongmeng zhi San Da Yiyi 万国同盟之三大意义" [Three Great Significant Aspects of the League of Nations], *Taipingyang* 2, no. 1 (1919): 43–48.
80 Ibid.
81 Ibid.
82 Zhou Gengsheng, "Wanguo Lianmeng yu Qiangzhi Hejie 万国联盟与强制和解" [The League of Nations and Compulsory Adjudication], *Taipingyang* 2, no. 9 (1920): 1–9.
83 Li Enhan, *Beifa Qianhou de "Geming Waijiao" 1925–1931 北伐前後的'革命外交' 1925–1931 ["Revolutionary Diplomacy" before and after the Warlord Era]* (Taipei: Zhongyang Yanjiuyuan Jindai Shi Yanjiusuo, 1993).
84 Wang Jingwei, ed., *Ouzhou Heyi Hou zhi Shijie yu Zhongguo* 欧洲和议后之世界与中国 [*China and the World after the European Peace Conference*] (Shanghai: Minzhi Shuju, 1926).
85 Zhou Wei, "1919 Nian Hou zhi Guoji Gongfa 一九一九年後之國際公法" [International Law after 1919], *Xu Wu* 35 (1919): 18–21.

86 Lassa Oppenheim, *International Law: A Treatise*, 3rd ed. (London: Longmans, Green and Co., 1920), 191. Elsewhere, Tibet is described as lying under a Chinese "protectorate" – albeit only on the basis of the British–Russian Treaty of St. Petersburg.

87 Ibid.

88 Ibid., 133.

89 *The Consortium: The Official Text of the Four-Power Agreement for a Loan to China and Relevant Documents* (Washington, DC: Carnegie Endowment for International Peace, 1921), 2.

90 Ibid., 30.

91 Henry Wilson Harris, *Geneva, 1921: An Account of the Second Assembly of the League of Nations* (London: Daily News Ltd., 1921), 10; Alison Adcock Kaufman, "In Pursuit of Equality and Respect: China's Diplomacy and the League of Nations," *Modern China* 40,no. 6 (2014): 620.

92 See Ryan Martínez Mitchell, "Monroe's Shadow: League of Nations Covenant Article 21 and the Space of Asia in International Legal Order," *TWAIL Review* 2 (2021): 200–231.

93 Discussed in Kaufman, "In Pursuit of Equality and Respect," 620.

94 Wilson Harris, *An Account of the Second Assembly of the League of Nations*, 10.

95 For discussion of the "Continentalism" initiative, see Tang, *Beijing Zhengfu yu Guoji Lianmeng*, 42–43, 49–51.

96 See ibid., 14–15 for an account of the limited progress of the League on issues of disarmament through 1921.

97 "Fourteenth Session of the Council of the League of Nations Held at Geneva," *League of Nations Official Journal* 2, no. 12. (1921): 1,073.

98 Ishii Kikujirō, *Gaikō Yoroku* 外交余禄 [*Diplomatic Memoirs*] (Tokyo: Iwanami Shoten, 1930), 142.

99 "League Bisects Silesian Triangle," *New York Times*, October 12, 1921.

100 "Die Aufgabe des Völkerbundes," *Freiheit*, August 13, 1921; "Borniertes Unternehmertum," *Freiheit*, October 31, 1921.

101 F. T. Cheng [Zheng Tianxi], *Rules of Private International Law Determining Capacity to Contract* (London: Stevens, 1916).

102 "Limitation of Naval Armament (Five-Power Treaty or Washington Treaty," treaty signed at Washington February 6, 1922. Available at: www.loc.gov/law/help/us-treaties/bevans/m-ust000002-0351.pdf; "Insular Possessions and Dominions in the Pacific (Four-Power Treaty)," treaty and declaration signed at Washington, December 13, 1921. Available at: www.loc.gov/law/help/us-treaties/bevans/m-ust000002-0332.pdf; "Principles and Policies concerning China (Nine-Power Treaty)," treaty signed at Washington February 6, 1922. Available at: www.loc.gov/law/help/us-treaties/bevans/m-ust000002-0375.pdf.

103 Quincy Wright, "The Washington Conference," *American Political Science Review* 16, no. 2 (1922): 285–297.

104 Westel W. Willoughby, *China at the Conference: A Report* (Baltimore: Johns Hopkins Press, 1922), 114–119.

105 Ibid.

106 Charles E. Hughes, Henry Cabot Lodge, Oscar W. Underwood and Elihu Root, "Conference on the Limitation of Armament," *American Journal of International Law* 16, no. 2 (1922): 200.
107 Ibid., 190.
108 British Government Memorandum of November 20, 1919, quoted in Willoughby, *China at the Conference*, 176.
109 Charles de Visscher, "Revues de Langue Anglaise," *Revue de Droit International et de Législation Comparée* 49 (1922): 237–239.
110 Charles G. Fenwick, *International Law*, 3rd ed. (New York: Appleton-Century-Crofts, 1952), 499.
111 Ibid.
112 Ibid.
113 Rudolf Hilferding, "Die nueue Weltpolitik," *Freiheit*, January 1, 1922.
114 *L'Humanité*, December 12, 1921; *L'Humanité*, January 9, 1922.
115 On the process of the Party's founding and role of earlier "Communist Groups" in Beijing, Guangzhou, and Shanghai, as well as liaisons with Soviet and Japanese groups, see Ishikawa Yoshihiro, *The Formation of the Chinese Communist Party* (New York: Columbia University Press, 2013) (Joshua Fogel, trans.), 139, 221, 275, 402 fn 162.
116 Ibid., 366 fn 123.
117 Zhou Enlai, "Huafu Huiyi Hou de Meiguo Diguozhuyizhe 华府会议后的美国帝国主义者" [American Imperialists after the Washington Conference]," *Chiguang* 赤光, February 15, 1924.
118 Jiang Tingfu, *Jiang Tingfu Huyilu* 蒋廷黻回忆录 [Memoirs of Jiang Tingfu] (Changsha: Yuelu Shushe, 2003), 81–82.

Chapter 7

1 Statute for the Permanent Court of International Justice (hereafter PCIJ Statute), *League of Nations Treaty Series* 6 (1921), 391; see also Spiermann, *International Legal Argument in the Permanent Court of International Justice*, 134.
2 PCIJ Statute, Article 9.
3 See generally, *Documents Presented to the Committee Relating to Existing Plans for the Establishment of a Permanent Court of International Justice* (Permanent Court of International Justice, Advisory Committee of Jurists, 1920) (hereafter *Documents Presented to the Committee*).
4 *Procès-verbaux of the Proceedings of the Committee, June 16th–July 24th, 1920, with Annexes* (League of Nations, Advisory Committee of Jurists, 1920), 124.
5 Ibid., 122.
6 Ibid., 123.
7 Simpson, *Great Powers and Outlaw States*, 157–158.
8 See *Annuaire de l'Institut de Droit International*, vol. 28, xvi–xxv.
9 See, e.g., Spiermann, *International Legal Argument in the Permanent Court of International Justice*, 134–139.
10 Ibid., 139.
11 *Documents Presented to the Committee*, 74–76.

12 See, e.g., Ingo Winkelmann, "Regional Groups in the UN" in Helmut Volger (ed.), *A Concise Encyclopedia of the United Nations*, 2nd ed.(Leiden: Martinus Nijhoff Publishers, 2010), 592–596.

13 See Alison Adcock Kaufman, "In Pursuit of Equality and Respect: China's Diplomacy and the League of Nations," *Modern China* 40, no. 6 (2014): 620; Tang, *Beijing Zhengfu yu Guoji Lianmeng*, 39–45.

14 Tang, *Beijing Zhengfu yu Guoji Lianmeng*, 44.

15 Ibid.

16 *Documents Concerning the Action Taken by the Council of the League of Nations under Article 14 of the Covenant and the Adoption by the Assembly of the Statute of the Permanent Court* (Geneva: League of Nations, 1921), 243.

17 Ibid.

18 *The S. S. "Wimbledon," United Kingdom and Others* v. *Germany*, Judgment, (1923) PCIJ Series A no 1; *Status of* Eastern Carelia, Advisory opinion, PCIJ Series B no 5. In the latter affair, the Soviet Union's status as a non-League member and nonsignatory to the Court raised serious questions about the appropriateness of an advisory opinion.

19 Max Huber, *Denkwürdigkeiten, 1907–1924* (Zurich: Orell Füssli, 1974), 277–278; cf. Spiermann, "Judge Wang Chung-hui at the Permanent Court of International Justice," 120.

20 *Questions Relating to Settlers of German Origin in Poland*, Advisory Opinion, (1923) PCIJ Series B no 6.

21 Huber, *Denkwürdigkeiten*, 281.

22 Wang Chung-Hui, "Peaceful Means for Settling International Disputes," *China Law Review* 2 (1926): 336.

23 Shabtai Rosenne, ed., *League of Nations Committee of Experts for the Progressive Codification of International Law (1925–1928): Documents Vol. 1* (New York: Oceana Publications, 1972), 21.

24 Manley O. Hudson, "The Progressive Codification of International Law," *American Journal of International Law* 20, no. 4 (1926): 655–669.

25 A third international lawyer, the Belgian jurist and future ICJ judge Charles de Visscher, was initially part of the subgroup as well, but, in the words of the committee chairman, "was unfortunately prevented from taking any part in the preparation of the report." Questionnaire 4, League of Nations Document C.196.M.70.1927.V (1926), 104. As the subgroup's reporter, Guerrero apparently took the lead role in drafting the resulting report on state responsibility. The exact extent of Wang's involvement in the resulting text requires further investigation. Only Guerrero attended the second committee session in early 1926, at which the report was officially submitted for review and during which some revisions were made. However, a 1930 Chinese summary of the codification process, with Wang's own foreword, suggests that the initial report reflected both his and Guerrero's substantial contributions. *Bianzuan Guojifa Huiyi zhi Jingguo* 编纂国际法会议之经过 [*The Proceedings of the Conference for the Codification of International Law*] (Shanghai: Minzhi Shuju, 1930).

26 See Questionnaire 4.

27 See, e.g., "Wang Chonghui zhi Faquan Tanhua: Shen Dang Qi Chong zhi Kuzhong 王寵惠之法權談話身當其衝之苦衷" [Wang Chonghui Discusses

Jurisdiction: He Is Personally Enduring Attacks and Difficulties], *Yi Shi Bao* (Tianjin), December 4, 1926.

28 See Sun Yat-sen, *China and Japan: Natural Friends, Unnatural Enemies* (Shanghai: China United Press, 1941) (held in Library of Congress); Suzuki Shogo, "Imagining 'Asia': Japan and 'Asian' International Society in Modern History" in Barry Buzan and Yongjin Zhang (eds.), *Contesting International Society in East Asia* (Cambridge: Cambridge University Press, 2014), 51–72. Sun's vague endorsement of the "kingly way" would soon be invoked, just a few years later, as a pretext for Japan's imposition of a neotraditionalist regime in the Manchukuo puppet state.

29 Sun, *China and Japan*.

30 British Embassy to the Department of State, FRUS 1926 vol. 1, 854.

31 See Willoughby, *China at the Conference*, 382.

32 "Wang Chung-hui Scores Austen Chamberlain for Restricting China Tariff Asserts If Peking Agrees to Sign Tariff Treaty under Such Restrictive Lines, Confab Would Sell Sovereignty Cheaply," *The China Press*, September 26, 1925.

33 "Wang Chonghui Zuijin zhi Tanhua 王寵惠最近之談話" [Recent Remarks of Wang Chonghui], *Yishi Bao* (Tianjin), November 11, 1925.

34 "The Special Conference on the Chinese Customs Tariff," FRUS 1925 vol. 1 (Documents 684–724).

35 Ibid.

36 Ibid.

37 "China Is Not Willing to Be Led by Hand: Is No Longer Interested in Treaty Technicalities, Says Dr. Wang," *The China Press*, November 19, 1925.

38 CAB 24/182/24, November 23, 1926.

39 Ibid.

40 CAB 24/181/72, November 8, 1926.

41 Ibid.

42 See, e.g., FRUS 1927 vol. 2, 893.00.

43 See, e.g., Waijiaobu Bianzuan Weiyuanhui, *Zhongguo Huifu Guanshui Zhuquan zhi Jingguo* 中国恢复关税主权之经过 [*The Process of China's Recovery of Tariff Sovereignty*] (Beijing: Waijiaobu Bianzuan Weiyuanhui, 1929).

44 Da Li Yuan, *Chinese Supreme Court Decisions Relating to General Principles of Civil Law, Obligations, and Commercial Law* (Peking: Commission on Extraterritoriality, 1923) (Reprinted Washington, DC: University Publications of America, Inc., 1976); Hungdah Chiu, "The Position of International Law in Chinese Law," *Annals of the Society of International Law* 3 (1966): 94.

45 "Ouverture des travaux de la commission d'extraterritorialité," *L'Europe Nouvelle*, March 6, 1926.

46 Commission on Extraterritoriality in China, *Report of the Commission on Extraterritoriality in China* (London: His Majesty's Stationery Office, 1926), 8, 94, 96.

47 Carl Schmitt, "Die Lage der europäischen Rechtswissenschaft" (1950) in Carl Schmitt (ed.), *Verfassungsrechtliche Aufsätze aus den Jahren 1924–1954. Materialen zu einer Verfassungslehre* (Berlin: Duncker & Humblot 1958), 386–429.

48 FRUS 1926, 855–858; cf. Van de Ven, *Breaking with the Past*, 202.
49 See, e.g., Van de Ven, *Breaking with the Past*, 7–8, 15, 63.
50 Ibid., 210.
51 FRUS 1926, 852.
52 Ibid., 934–935.
53 Van de Ven, *Breaking with the Past*, 211–212.
54 FRUS 1926, 858.
55 Tang Qihua, *Bei "Feichu Bupindeng Tiaoyue" Zhebi de Beiyang Xiuyue Shi (1912–1928)* 被"廢除不平等條約"遮蔽的北洋修約史 (1912–1928) [*Treaty Revision Campaign of the Beijing Government, 1912–1928: Out of the Shadow of the "Abrogation of Unequal Treaties" (1912–1928)*] (Beijing: Shehui Keshue Wenshian Chubanshe, 2010), 367–406.
56 See WJDA: 03-23-074-02; 03-23-077-02-001.
57 FRUS 1926, 996.
58 *Denunciation of the Treaty of November 2nd, 1865, between China and Belgium, Order of 8 January 1927.*
59 "China's Public Finance," *North China Daily News*, January 11, 1927 ("Popularly speaking, the so-called Central Government is bankrupt, and the bailiffs are in possession . . . The victors [i.e., Nationalists] could borrow all the money they will need for the reconstruction of China if they would undertake the present foreign obligations."); Frederic Lee, *Currency, Banking, and Finance in China* (Washington, DC: United States Department of Commerce, 1927).
60 See, e.g., Lin Hai, "Wang Tieya: Guojifa Shengya Qi Shi Er Nian Zai 王铁崖国际法生涯七十二载" [Wang Tieya: An International Law Career of 72 Years], China Law Society, May 19, 2015. Available at: www.chinalaw.org.cn/portal/article/index/id/16096/cid/71.html.
61 Han Tie, *Feng Yu Ban Ji Ming: Wo de Fu Qin Han Depei Zhuan Ji 风雨伴鸡鸣: 我的父亲韩德培传记* [*The Rainstorm and the Rooster's Cry at Dawn: A Biography of My Father, Han Depei*] (Beijing: Zhongguo Fangzheng Chubanshe, 2000), 1–9.
62 Institut de Droit International, *Annuaire de l'Institut de Droit International*, vol. 33, 1927 (Brussels: Goemare, 1927), 515.
63 Ibid.
64 Ibid.
65 Willy van Hille, "Étude sur la Responsabilité Internationale de l'État," *Revue de Droit International et de Législation Comparée* 56, no. 4 (1929): 531–571.
66 Institut de Droit International, *Annuaire de l'Institut de Droit International*, vol. 33, 520–521.
67 Ibid.
68 *Corfu Channel, United Kingdom* v. *Albania* (1949) ICJ Reports 237 (1949).
69 Quincy Wright, "Opinion of the Commission of Jurists in the Janina–Corfu Affair," *American Journal of International Law* 18, no. 3 (1924): 536–544.
70 Ibid.
71 Ibid.
72 See, e.g., Camilo Barcia Trelles, "Francisco de Vitoria et l'école moderne du droit international," *Recueil de Cours de L'Académie de Droit International*

17 (1927): 109–342. Available at: http://dx.doi.org/10.1163/1875-8096_pplrdc_A9789028605428_02 ("reprisals lend themselves to much abuse and serve as a pretext for veritable pillaging"); Yves de la Brière, "Évolution de la doctrine et de la pratique en matière de représailles," *Recueil de Cours de L'Académie de Droit International* 22 (1928): 237–294. Available at: http://dx.doi.org/10.1163/1875-8096_pplrdc_A9789028605923_03 ("it is not necessary to expressly abolish a right so conditional and relative [as reprisal] in order for it to become manifestly defunct, extinguished and non-existent, once there disappears the sole condition that was its *raison d'être* and provided precarious value").

73 John P. Grant and J. Craig Barker, eds., *The Harvard Research in International Law: Original Materials,* vol. 1 (New York: William S. Hein & Co., 2007).

74 Ibid.

75 Frederic L. Kirgis, *The American Society of International Law's First Century, 1906–2006* (Leiden: Brill, 2006), 91.

76 Grant and Barker, eds., *The Harvard Research in International Law*, 217–218.

77 Ibid., 281.

78 Union Interparlementaire, *Compte rendu de la XXVe conférence tenue à Berlin du 23 au 28 août 1928* (Lausanne: Librairie Payot & Co., 1928).

79 Ibid., 72.

80 Ibid.

81 Ibid.

82 Ibid., 79.

83 Ibid., 465.

84 Ibid., 251.

85 Ibid., 252–257.

86 Ibid., 437.

87 Ibid., 522 (emphasis added).

88 Cf. *Corfu Channel* (1949).

89 Walther Schücking, "Die frage der Kündigung des belgisch-Chinesischen handelsverträges von 1865" in Otto Schreiber (ed.), *Die Reichsgerichtspraxis im Deutschen Rechtsleben: Festgabe der juristischen Fakultäten zum 50jährigen Bestehen des Reichsgerichts, vol. 1, Öffentliches Recht* (Berlin: Walter de Gruyter, 1929).

90 James T. Shotwell, *Extraterritoriality in China* (New York: Institute of Pacific Relations, 1929), 20.

91 Ibid.

92 Ibid., 21.

93 Ibid., 22.

94 FRUS 1930, vol. 2, 390.

95 Ibid., 374.

96 Ibid., 379.

97 Zhou Wei, *Xin Guoji Gongfa* 新国际公法 [*The New International Law*] (Shanghai: Shangwu Yinshu Guan, 1930).

98 Ibid.

99 Wang Chonghui, "Preface I" in ibid., 4.

100 GSG: 020-990600-2050.
101 Zhou Gengsheng, *Bupingdeng Tiaoyue Shijiang* 不平等條約十講 [*Ten Lectures on Unequal Treaties*] (Shanghai: Taipingyang Shudian, 1928).
102 Ibid., 170–171.
103 Ibid., 168, 171.
104 Li Shengwu, "Juan Tou Yu 卷頭語 [Foreword]," *Liu Ying Xuebao* 4 (1929): 4–5.
105 For background on Li's Oxford studies, see Li Chen, "Professor James Leslie Brierly and His First Chinese Pupil Li Shengwu at Oxford University Faculty of Law (1927–1930)," *Journal of the History of International Law/Revue d'histoire du droit international* 20, no. 3 (2018): 373–380.
106 Sarvepalli Gopa, *Jawaharlal Nehru: A Biography: Vol. 1, 1889–1947* (Bombay: Oxford University Press, 1976), 103–105.

Chapter 8

1 *League of Nations Official Journal*, Special Suppl. no. 153 (1936): 11.
2 Wang Chonghui, "Jieshao Bijiao Faxue Guoji Huiyi 介绍比较法学国际会议" [Introducing the International Conference on Comparative Law], *Zhonghua Faxue Zazhi* 1, no. 2 (1930): 143–149; cf. Spiermann, "Judge Wang Chung-hui at the Permanent Court of International Justice," 115–128.
3 See Patricia Stranahan, *Underground: The Shanghai Communist Party and the Politics of Survival, 1927–1937* (Lanham, MD: Rowman & Littlefield, 1998); Brian Tsui, *China's Conservative Revolution: The Quest for a New Order, 1927–1949* (Cambridge: Cambridge University Press, 2018).
4 See Edwin M. Borchard, "'Responsibility of States' at the Hague Codification Conference," *American Journal of International Law* 24, no. 3 (1930): 517–540; Arthur K. Kuhn, "The International Conference on the Treatment of Foreigners," *American Journal of International Law* 24, no. 3 (1930): 570–573; see also "United Nations Documents on the Development and Codification of International Law: Supplement," *American Journal of International Law*, 41, no. 4 (1947).
5 *Acts of the Conference for the Codification of International Law, Nos. 14–17* (Geneva: League of Nations, 1930).
6 Ibid., meeting of March 28, 1930.
7 Ibid., meeting of April 4, 1930.
8 See Borchard, "Responsibility of States," 537–538.
9 Ibid.
10 Ibid.
11 The full vote tally was as follows: For: Brazil, Chile, China, Colombia, Czechoslovakia, Free City of Danzig, Egypt, Mexico, Nicaragua, Persia, Poland, Portugal, Romania, El Salvador, Turkey, Uruguay, Yugoslavia. Against: Australia, Austria, Belgium, Canada, Denmark, Estonia, Finland, France, Germany, Great Britain, Greece, Hungary, India, Ireland, Italy, Japan, the Netherlands, Norway, South Africa, Spain, Sweden, Switzerland, the United States. *Acts of the Conference*, meeting of April 4, 1930, 188.
12 Ibid., meeting of March 18, 1930.

13 Ibid.
14 Ibid., meeting of April 11, 1930.
15 Hsü Daulin, "Das Mandschurische Problem," *Sinica* 7, no. 3 (1932): 81–91.
16 Cf. Oona A. Hathaway and Scott J. Shapiro, *The Internationalists: How a Radical Plan to Outlaw War Remade the World* (New York: Simon and Schuster, 2017).
17 Philip A. Reynolds and Edward J. Hughes, *The Historian as Diplomat: Charles Kingsley Webster and the United Nations 1939–1946* (London: Martin Robertson, 1976), 64; for a more positive appraisal of Liang's personality, and particularly his Peking opera singing skills, see Harold Acton, *Memoirs of an Aesthete, 1939–1969* (New York: Viking Press, 1971), 81.
18 Yuen-li Liang, "Le développement et la codification du droit international," *Recueil des Cours* 73 (1948): 407–547.
19 "Terms Tokyo Act Illegal: Chinese Jurist Denounces the Recognition of Manchukuo," *New York Times*, September 18, 1932.
20 Yuen-li Liang, "The Pact of Paris as Envisaged by Mr. Stimson: Its Significance in International Law," *China Law Review* 5 (1932): 198.
21 "Stimson View Held Aid to Peace Pact," *New York Times*, August 14, 1932.
22 Yuen-li Liang, "Women zai Rineiwa de Cuowu 我们在日内瓦的错误" [Our Mistake at Geneva], *Shenbao Yuekan* 2, no. 8 (1933): 17–20.
23 Yuen-li Liang and Wang Feiya, "Li Shengwu Zhu Guoji Gongfa Lun 李聖五著國際公法論" [*Public International Law Theory* by Li Shengwu], *Tushu Pinglun* 2, no. 9 (1934): 35–43.
24 See, e.g., "Liang Yunli Jiangyan Guoji Zuzhi yu Weilai Da Zhan 梁鋆立講演國際組織與未來大戰" [Liang Yunli's Lectures on International Organization and the Future Great War], *Zhongyang Ribao*, April 26, 1934.
25 Liang and Wang, "Li Shengwu Zhu Guoji Gongfa Lun," 38.
26 Liang, "Women zai Rineiwa de Cuowu." 19–20.
27 Ibid.
28 See, e.g., Wu Xiping, "Jiu Guojifa zhi Quedian yu Xin Guojifa zhi Yaoqiu 旧国际法之缺点与新国际法之要求" [The Flaws of the Old International Law and the Requirements of the New International Law], *Zhongfa Daxue Yuekan* 1, no. 4 (1932): 1–14.
29 Zhou Wei, *Xin Guoji Gongfa* 新国际公法 [*The New International Law*] (Shanghai: Shangwu Yinshu Guan, 1930).
30 Liang and Wang, "Li Shengwu Zhu Guoji Gongfa Lun," 41. Wang Tieya, one of China's most important twentieth-century jurists, had a brother named Wang Feiya, with their names distinguished only by the middle character. It is unclear whether this article was actually by Wang's brother (who does not appear to have studied international law or produced other writings on the subject), by someone else with this name, including the relatively rare (for names) 崖 character, or whether Wang Tieya himself (then studying international law under Zhou Gengsheng at Tsinghua) wrote it using his brother's name as a pseudonym. The essay's content is such that it could only have been written by one of the small number of Chinese intellectuals deeply conversant with the most recent international law publications in English, French, and German.

31 Nicolas Politis, *Les Nouvelles Tendances du Droit International* (Paris: Librairie Hachette, 1927).

32 Hans Kelsen, *Das Problem der Souveränität und die Theorie des Völkerrechts: Beitrag zu einer reinen Rechtslehre* (Tübingen: J. C. B. Mohr/P. Siebeck, 1920).

33 Hai Cháo Chiang [Jiang Haichao], "La Chine" in Karl Strupp (ed.), *Bibliographie du Droit des Gens et des Rélations Internationales* (Leiden: A. W. Sijthoff, 1938), 261–267.

34 Qiu Zuming, "Zhuquan yu Lingtu Zhuquan 主权与领土主权" [Sovereignty and Territorial Sovereignty], *Dongfang Zazhi* 25, no. 23 (1928): 77–80.

35 Ibid. The Latin terminology is included in the original – note the use of *dominium* in its signification of territorial ownership, i.e., a reserve property right conditioning subordinate property rights of local or foreign individuals.

36 Li Shengwu, *Guoji Gongfa Lun* 國際公法論 [*Theory of Public International Law*] (Shanghai: Shangwu Yinshuguan, 1935), 71.

37 Ibid.

38 Wen Zhou, "Tan Tan Zhuquan Lun 談談主權論" [Talking about Theories of Sovereignty], *Zhengzhi Hui Kan* 1, no. 2 (1932): 40–57.

39 *Radio Corporation of America* v. *China*, PCA Case No. 1934-01; cf. August Reinisch, "Investors," in Math Noortmann, August Reinisch, and Cedric Ryngaert (eds.), *Non-state Actors in International Law* (London: Bloomsbury Publishing, 2015): 253–272.

40 See, e.g., Zhou Gengsheng, *Guoji Gongfa zhi Xin Fazhan* 國際公法之新發展 [*New Developments in International Law*] (Shanghai: Shangwu Yinshuguan 商务印书馆, 1934); Zhou Gengsheng, "Zhongguo de Guoji Diwei 中国的国际地位" [China's International Status], *Mei Zhou Pinglun* 146 (1934): 18–24; Zhou Gengsheng, "1935 Nian zhi Zhanwang: Guolian de Qiantu 一九三五年之展望:国联的前途" [Prospects for 1935: The Future of the League of Nations], *Dongfang Zazhi* 32, no. 1 (1935): 25–29.

41 Zhou Ziya 周子亚, "Yi Ge Zhuyi Yi Ge Zhengfu Yi Ge Lingxiu 一个主义一个政府一个领袖" [One Ideology, One Government, One Leader], *Minyi* (Hankou) 36 (1938): 11.

42 On the Chiang regime's growing ties with Nazi Germany in the mid 1930s, see William C. Kirby, *Germany and Republican China* (Stanford, CA: Stanford University Press, 1984).

43 See Karl Strupp, *Urkunden zur geschichte des völkerrechts* (Gotha: Friedrich Andreas Perthes, 1911); Karl Strupp, *Documents pour servir à l'histoire du droit des gens* (Berlin: Hermann Sack, 1923); Karl Strupp, *Legal Machinery for Peaceful Change* (London: Constable & Company Limited, 1937); GSG: 129-010000-0033.

44 GSG: 129-010000-0033.

45 Jiang Haichao, "Choushe Guojifa yu Guoji Guanxi Yanjiu Hui Chu Yi 籌設國際法與國際關係研究會芻議" [Modest Proposal for the Establishment of an Association for International Law and International Relations Research], *Yi Shi Bao* (Chongqing), August 6, 1941.

46 See "Shoudu Kaishi Shen Jian Zhou Ni Wei Zuixing Zhenxun Yi Bi Wei Jiangsu Shengzhang Chen Ni Chusi 首都開始審奸周逆緯罪行偵訊已畢僞江蘇省長陳逆處死" [Investigations of Traitors Begin in the Capital; The

Rebel Zhou Wei Has Already Been Interrogated; Execution for Puppet Governor of Jiangsu Chen], *Zhongyang Ribao,* December 15, 1945.

47 Zhou Wei, "Zhou Wei Boshi Yanjiang Su Jilu 周纬博士演讲速记录" [Transcript of Dr. Zhou Wei's Lecture], *Guomin Waijiao Zazhi* (Nanjing) 5 (1934): 57–59.

48 "Zuigao Fayuan Bo Hui Li Shengwu Kang Gao 最高法院駁回李逆聖五抗告" [The Supreme Court Rejects Li Shengwu's Defense], *Zhongyang Ribao*, June 14, 1947.

49 Lin Hai, Wang Tieya: Guojifa Shengya Qi Shi Er Zai 王铁崖 国际法生涯七十二载" [Wang Tieya: A 72-Year-Long International Law Career], *China Law Society*, May 19, 2015. Available at: www.chinalaw.org.cn/portal/article/index/id/16096/cid/71.html.

50 Han, *Feng Yu Ban Ji Ming*, 25–27.

51 Chen Yan, *Kangri Zhanzheng Shiqi Zhongguo Waijiao Zhidu Yanjiu* 抗日战争时期中国外交制度研究 [*Research on the Diplomatic Institutions of China during the War of Resistance against Japan*] (Shanghai: Fudan Daxue Chubanshe, 2002), 48.

52 See, e.g., Wang Chonghui, "Zhan Hou Shijie zhi Jiti Anquan: Zuori Zai Zhongguo Zhengzhixue Hui Nian Hui Jiangyan 戰後世界之集體安全昨日在中國政治學會年會講演" [Postwar Collective Security: Yesterday's Address at the Annual Meeting of the China Political Science Association], *Da Gong Bao* (Chongqing), July 7, 1942.

53 "Soong Says China Wants Asia Freed," *New York Times*, June 10, 1942.

54 HC Deb September 9, 1941 vol. 374 cc. 67–156.

55 Ibid.

56 See Elizabeth Borgwardt, *A New Deal for the World: America's Vision for Human Rights* (Cambridge, MA: Belknap Press, 2007).

57 FRUS 1942, vol. 1, 678 (Mohandas Gandhi to President Roosevelt, July 1, 1942).

58 Gopa, *Jawaharlal Nehru*, 249.

59 GSG: 001-063300-00001-001.

60 Ibid.

61 "Lianheguo Yongjiu Shengli Zai Queli Jiti Anquan Zhengzhi Xuehui Nianhui Zhong Wang ChonghuiYanshuo Yuanwen 聯合國永久勝利 在確立集體安全政治學會年會中王寵惠演說原文" [The Permanent Victory of the United Nations Is in the Establishment of Collective Security; Transcript of Wang Chonghui's Remarks to the Chinese Political Science Association], *Da Gong Bao* (Guilin), November 8, 1942.

62 Zhou Gengsheng, "Zhanhou de Nanyang 战后的南洋" [The South Sea after the War], *Nanyang Yanjiu* 11, no. 1 (1943): 79–82; "Zhou Gengsheng Zhu Wenlun: Taipingyang Yongjiu Zhixu 周鯁生著文論太平洋永久秩序" [Zhou Gengsheng's Essay: A Permanent Order for the Pacific], *Yishibao* (Chongqing), January 8, 1943; "Zhou Gengsheng Lun Taipingyang Yongjiu Zhixu; Bixu Wanquan Jiechu Riben Wuzhuang; Zhuzhang Chengli Taipingyang Lianheguo 周鯁生論太平洋永久秩序必須完全解除日本武裝主張成立太平洋聯合國" [Zhou Gengsheng Writes on a Permanent Order for the

Pacific; Japan Must be Permanently Disarmed; Advocates Setting Up a United Nations of the Pacific], *Zhongyang Ribao Saodang Bao Lianhe Ban*, January 8, 1943.

63 "Soong Asks Set-up of Allied League," *New York Times*, October 11, 1942.

64 Hu Shih, "Speech at Wellesley College, 15 June 1942," *Contemporary China* 2, no. 3(1942): 3–4.

65 FRUS 1943, 472. The next month, the "Executive Committee" was recast as the "Executive Council" in a more fully fleshed out draft "Charter of the United Nations." Ibid., 526.

66 FRUS 1943, Diplomatic Papers, 1943, China, 14–15.

67 Ibid.

68 FRUS 1943, vol. 1, 389.

69 Ibid.

70 FRUS 1943, vol. 7, 1096.

71 FRUS 1945, vol. 7, 331–332.

72 Chiang Kai-shek, *China's Destiny and Chinese Economic Theory* (Leiden: Global Oriental, 2012) (original publication 1943).

73 On ethnic policy, Chiang refuted the Communist claim to represent a more robust form of ethnic autonomy for groups such as China's Hui Muslims, arguing instead the radical position that all of China's "five (main) ethnic groups" – Han, Mongols, Tibetans, Hui, and Manchus – were part of a single race descended from the Yellow Emperor. See Ibid.

74 Ibid.

75 Ibid.

76 "Vast China Credits Forecast by Soong," *New York Times*, October 31, 1942.

77 See, e.g., "Peidu Yi Shenghui Kong Xiangxi Huan Yan Guoji Youren Bing Juxing Gongji Kongzi Dadian 陪都一盛會孔祥熙歡宴國際友人并舉行公祭孔子大典" [A Celebration in the Temporary Capital; Kong Xiangxi Welcomes International Friends and Holds a Great Ceremony to Worship Confucius], *Da Gong Bao* (Hong Kong), August 29, 1941.

78 Ibid.

79 The lend-lease arrangement had allocated US$1.6 billion to China, but much of this was to be conveyed in kind via war materiel and the like. Ensuring that a large sum could be obtained as credit or specie would indeed be crucial for maintaining Chongqing's finances.

80 "Vast China Credits Forecast by Soong," *New York Times*, October 31, 1942.

81 *Proceedings and Documents of the United Nations Monetary and Financial Conference, Bretton Woods, New Hampshire, July 1–22, 1944,* vol. 2 (Washington, DC: US Government Printing Office, 1948), 1165; cf. Kurt Schuler and Andrew Rosenberg, eds., *The Bretton Woods Transcripts* (New York: Center for Financial Stability, 2012).

82 *Proceedings and Documents of the United Nations Monetary and Financial Conference*, 1200.

83 "Faxuejia Choushe Guojifa Xiehui 法學家籌設國際法協會" [Legal Scholars Establish Society of International Law], *Da Gong Bao* (Chongqing), March 3, 1944.

84 "List of Members," *Proceedings of the American Society of International Law at its Annual Meeting* (1921–1969) 38 (1944): 103, 177.
85 "Faxuejia Choushe Guojifa Xiehui," *Da Gong Bao* (Chongqing), March 3, 1944.
86 "'Guojifa zhi Weilai' Guojifa Xuehui Zuo Kai Zuotanhui '國際法之未來'國際法學會昨開座談會" ["The Future of International Law": Seminar Yesterday by the Society of International Law], *Da Gongbao*, January 7, 1945.
87 GSG: 002-020300-00047-040.
88 On the structure of the meetings, see Robert C. Hilderbrand, *Dumbarton Oaks: The Origins of the United Nations and the Search for Postwar Security* (Durham: University of North Carolina Press, 2001).
89 GSG: 002-020300-00047-043.
90 Ibid.
91 Ibid.
92 GSG: 001-063130-00002-007.
93 See Hilderbrand, *Dumbarton Oaks*, 229–244.
94 Cf. Carol L. Thompson, "A History of Disarmament Proposals," *Current History* 36, no. 209 (1959): 38–43.
95 Hilderbrand, *Dumbarton Oaks*, 239–240.
96 Ibid., 238.
97 Ibid., 238–239.
98 Ibid.
99 Ibid., 239.
100 Ibid.
101 GSG: 001-063130-00002-008.
102 *Documents of the United Nations Conference on International Organization, San Francisco, 1945, vol. 14* (New York: United Nations Information Organizations, 1945), 286–287 ("The Report of the Subcommittee on Article 36" [Compulsory Jurisdiction]).
103 Ibid., 146–149.
104 Ibid., 150–151.
105 Ibid., 160.
106 Ibid., 159
107 Ibid., 155.
108 Ibid., 163–165.
109 Ibid.
110 Ibid., 165.
111 Ibid., 286–287.
112 Ibid., 177–179; cf. GSG: 001-063130-00004-010.
113 *Documents of the United Nations Conference*, 159.
114 *Contemporary China* 4, no. 26 (May 14, 1945): 1–4.
115 Cf. Teresa F. Mayr and Jelka Mayr-Singer, "Keep the Wheels Spinning: The Contributions of Advisory Opinions of the International Court of Justice to the Development of International Law," *Zeitschrift für ausländisches öffentliches Recht und Völkerrecht* 76, no. 2 (2016): 425–449.

Chapter 9

1 GSG: 001-063130-00005-015; "China Is First, U.S. Last in Signing of the Charter," *The New York Times*, June 26, 1945; "Nation after Nation Sees Era of Peace in Signing Charter," *The New York Times*, June 26, 1945; Hong Xiaoxia, "Chuxi Jiujinshan Lianheguo Zhixian Huiyi de Zhongguo Daibiaotuan Zucheng Qingkuang Shulüe 出席旧金山联合国制宪会议的中国代表团组成情况述略" [Summary of the Process of Formation of the Chinese Delegation to the San Francisco Conference Drafting the UN Charter], *Wuhan Daxue Xuebao (Renwen Kexue Ban)* 55, no. 3 (2002): 313–319.

2 FRUS 1945, vol. 7, 333.

3 GSG: 002-020400-00003-060.

4 See, e.g., "Heping Jianguo Gangling 和平建國綱領" [Joint Program for Political Administration], *Minguo Ribao*, February 2, 1946 ("遵守大西洋宪章， 開羅会议宣言， 莫斯科四国宣言及联合国宪章， 积极参加联合国组织， 以确保世界和平").

5 "Zhongguo Gongchandang Daibiao Tuan Tichu Heping Jianguo Gangling Cao'an" [Draft Outline for Peaceful National Construction Presented by the Chinese Communist Party Delegation] in Meng Guanghan (ed.), *Zhengzhi Xieshang Huiyi Jilu, Shang Juan* 政治协商会议纪实, 上卷 [*Records of the Political Consultative Conference*, vol. 1] (Chongqing: Chongqing Chubanshe, 1989), 365.

6 GSG: 002-020400-00005-023.

7 Ibid.

8 "Heping Jianguo Gangling 和平建國綱領" [Joint Program for Political Administration]. In the same section of the Joint Program, the parties also committed to "maintaining friendly relations with the USA, Soviet Union, UK, and France as well as other democratic states, adhering to treaties with good faith, and making efforts at economic and cultural cooperation, in order to collectively plan for world prosperity and progress," pursuing trade agreements on a basis of "equality and mutual benefit," and other provisions including "improving the status of members of the Chinese diaspora."

9 See, e.g., Roger B. Jeans, *Democracy and Socialism in Republican China: The Politics of Zhang Junmai (Carsun Chang), 1906–1941* (Lanham, MD: Rowman & Littlefield, 1997); Li Hongxi, *Zhang Junmai Xiansheng de Minzhu Xianfa Sixiang* 張君勱先生的民主憲法思想 [*The Democratic and Constitutional Thought of Dr. Zhang Junmai*] (Taipei: Jinian Zhang Junmai Xiansheng Bai Ling Ming Dan Xueshu Yantaohui [Forum to Celebrate the Centennial of Zhang Junmai's Birth], 1986).

10 Cf. Zhang Zhenguo, "Cong'Wu Wu Xiancao' Dao 'Zhonghua Minguo Xianfa' 从 '五五宪草' 到 '中华民国宪法'" [From the "Double-Five Draft Constitution" to the "Constitution of the Republic of China"] in He Qinhua (ed.), *Quanguo Waiguo Fazhishi Yanjiuhui Xueshu Congshu: 20 Shiji Xifang Xianzheng de Fazhan ji qi Biange* 全国外国法制史研究会学术丛书——20世纪西方宪政的发展及其变革 [*Research Anthology on National and Foreign*

Legal History: The Development and Transformation of Constitutionalism in the Twentieth Century] (Beijing: Falü Chubanshe, 2004).

11 Constitution of the Republic of China (1946), Article 15.

12 "Zhang Junmai Yanjiang Weilai Xianfa Wenti 張君勵演講未來憲法問題" [Address of Zhang Junmai on the Issue of the Future Constitution], *Da Gong Bao*, June 28, 1946; cf. Li Fupeng, "Weima Xianfa Shehuiquan de Zhongguo Zhuanhua 魏玛宪法社会权的中国转化" [The Chinese Adaptation of the Weimar Constitution's Social Rights], *Huanqiu Falü Pinglun* 42, no. 3 (2020): 133–146.

13 Constitution of the Republic of China (1946), Article 141.

14 "Xiancao Zhong Jiben Guoce 憲草中基本國策" [The Fundamental National Policies in the Draft Constitution], *Yi Shi Bao* (Shanghai), December 7, 1946.

15 Zhou Gengsheng, "Xianfa Zhong de Waijiao Yuanze 憲法中的外交原則" [Foreign Policy Principles in the Constitution], *Zhongyang Ribao*, December 28, 1946.

16 Ibid.

17 Han Depei, "Kaiersheng yu Chuncui Faxue 凯尔生与纯粹法学" [Kelsen and the Pure Theory of Law], *Sixiang yu Shidai* 47 (1947): 9–13.

18 See, e.g., Zhou Ziya, "Zenyang Yanjiu Guoji Gongfa 怎样研究国际公法" [How to Research International Law], *Xin Renshi* 9, no. 2 (1944): 13–31; Zhou Ziya and Luo Shipei, "Cong 'Guojia Quanli' Zouxiang 'Shijie Quanli': Gaizao Shijie de Yi Ge Jiben Yuanze 从"国家权利"走向"世界权利":改造世界的一个基本原则" [From "State Rights" to "World Rights": A Basic Principle for the Reconstruction of the World], *Zhongyang Zhoukan* 8, no. 4 (1946): 5.

19 Zhou Ziya, "Xianfa yu Tiaoyue 憲法與條約" [The Constitution and Treaties], *Zhongyang Ribao*, November 28, 1946.

20 Weimar constitution, 1919. Cf. Herbert Kraus, *The Crisis of German Democracy: A Study of the Spirit of the Constitution of Weimar* (Princeton, NJ: Princeton University Press, 1932).

21 "Zhang Junmai Shang Shu Jiang Zhuxi Dui Shiju Ti Si Xiang Jianyi 張君勱上書蔣主席 對時局提四項建議" [Zhang Junmai Submits a Petition to Chairman Jiang, Making Four Suggestions on the Current Situation], *Yi Shi Bao* (Tianjin), November 18, 1946.

22 "Drafting and Implementation of Article 13, Paragraph 1, of the Charter of the United Nations," International Law Commission. Available at: https://legal.un.org/ilc/drafting.shtml; see also Charles G. Fenwick, "Review: Le Développement et la Codification du Droit International. By Yuen-li Liang. Paris: Recueil Sirey, 1949. 126," *American Journal of International Law* 44, no. 4 (1950): 786–787 ("Dr. Yuen-li Liang has written so extensively upon legal questions arising in connection with the activities of the United Nations that he needs no introduction to students of international law").

23 Liang, "Le développement et la codification du droit international."

24 Yuen-Li Liang, "The General Assembly and the Progressive Development and Codification of International Law," *American Journal of International Law* 42, no. 1 (1948): 66–98; Yuen-Li Liang, "Notes on Legal Questions Concerning the United Nations," *American Journal of International Law* 42, no. 1 (1949): 134–144; Yuen-Li Liang, "The Establishment of an International Criminal

Jurisdiction: The First Phase," *American Journal of International Law* 46, no. 1 (1952): 73–88.

25 See, e.g., Kerstin von Lingen, *Transcultural Justice at the Tokyo Tribunal: The Allied Struggle for Justice, 1946–48* (Leiden: Brill, 2018).

26 See *Documents of United Nations Conference on International Organization San Francisco 1945*, vol. 3 (New York: United Nations Information Organizations, 1945), 631–632.

27 Hans Ingvar Roth, *P. C. Chang and the Universal Declaration of Human Rights* (Philadelphia: University of Pennsylvania Press, 2018).

28 Ibid.

29 Ibid.

30 Ibid.

31 Cf. Liu Dasheng, "Shangfang Shi Gongmin de Xianfa Quanli 上访是公民的宪法权利" [Petitioning Is a Constitutional Right of the People], *Hongqi Wengao* 2 (2004): 29–30.

32 Hirad Abtahi and Philippa Webb, eds., T*he Genocide Convention: The Travaux Preparatoires* (Leiden: Martinus Nijhoff Publishers, 2008), 836.

33 See, e.g., ibid., 886–887.

34 Ibid.

35 Charter of the United Nations, Article 76.

36 Ibid., Article 77.

37 Roth, *P. C. Chang and the Universal Declaration of Human Rights*, 142.

38 Wilson Center Digital Archive, "Memorandum of Conversation between Anastas Mikoyan and Mao Zedong," February 4, 1949.

39 Ibid.

40 "Hanjian Zhou Wei Tu Zisha Wei Sui 漢奸周緯圖自殺未遂" [The Traitor Zhou Wei Failed in a Suicide Attempt], *Minguo Ribao*, February 13, 1946.

41 See An Zuozhang, ed., *Shandong Tongshi* 山东通史 [*History of Shandong*], vol. 8, part 2 (Jinan: Shandong Renmin Chubanshe, 1994), 984.

42 Wei-man Huanggong Bowuguan and Jilinnsheng Fangzhiguan, *Wei-Manzhouguo Zhimin Tongzhi Jigou Tuzhi* 伪满洲国殖民统治机构图志 [*Diagram of the Colonial Administration of False Manchukuo*] (Jilin: Jilin Renmin Chubanshe 吉林人民出版社, 2010).

43 Han Depei, "Women Suo Xuyao de 'Fazhi' 我们所需要的'法治" [The "Rule of Law" That We Need], *Guancha* 1, no. 10 (1946): 1–2.

44 See, e.g., Li Bingnan, Zeng Jianyuan, and Lin Zixuan, "'Dongyuan Kanluan Shiqi Linshi Tiaokuan' zhi Zhidu Jingyan ji qi Yingxiang '動員戡亂時期臨時條款' 之制度經驗及其影響" [The Institutional Experience and Effects of the "Temporary Measures Effective during the Period of Communist Rebellion"] *Taiwan Minzhu Jikan* 1, no. 2 (2004): 95–129.

45 GSG: 002-060100-00221-022.

46 See Suzanne Pepper, *Civil War in China: The Political Struggle 1945–1949* (Berkeley: University of California Press, 1978), 64–66.

47 "Guo Da Bu Ying Xiugai Xianfa Zhou Gengsheng Deng de Yijian 國大不應修改憲法周鯁生等的意見" [The National Assembly Should Not Revise the Constitution: Views of Zhou Gengsheng and Others], *Heping Ribao*, April 11, 1948.

48 Ibid.

49 Ti-Chiang Chen (L. C. Green, ed.), *The International Law of Recognition* (London: Stevens & Sons., 1951); cf. Chen Li, "Tracing Chinese Scholar Chen Tiqiang's Pursuit of International Law Education and His Major Contribution to the Doctrine of Recognition," *Asian Journal of International Law* 10, no. 1 (2020): 68–93.

50 See, e.g., Li Dade, "Guanyu Zhou Gengsheng Hu Shi zhi de Lunzhan: Tongyi Zhou Gengsheng Kanfa, Hu Shi zhi You 'Kong Su Bing' 關於周鯁生胡適之的論戰 同意周鯁生看法，胡適之有'恐蘇病" [On the War of Words between Zhou Gengsheng and Hu Shi: Agreeing with Zhou Gengsheng that Hu Shi Has "Sovietphobia"], *Zhongyang Zhoukan* 10, no. 9 (1948): 355; cf. Vincent Y. C. Shih, "A Talk with Hu Shih," *China Quarterly* 10 (1962): 149–165.

51 Zhou Ziya, "Cong Guojifa Lichang Lun Meijun Baoxing zhi Xingzhi ji Waiguo Jundui zhi Xingshi Guanxia Wenti 從國際法立場論美軍暴行之性質及外國軍隊之刑事管轄問題" [Discussing the Nature of the American Troops' Atrocity and the Issue of Criminal Jurisdiction over Foreign Troops from the Standpoint of International Law], *Guancha* 1, no. 23 (1947): 4–7.

52 Wang Tieya, "Dulumenzhuyi yu Menluozhuyi 杜鲁门主义与门罗主义" [The Truman Doctrine and the Monroe Doctrine], *Minzhu Luntan* 1, no. 9 (1947): 3–6.

53 Zhou Ziya, *Meiguo Meizhou yu Shijie* 美国美洲与世界 [*America, the Americas, and the World*] (Shanghai: Shangwu Yinshuguan, 1946); Chen Tiqiang, "Shei Shi Guojifa de Pohuaizhe? 谁是国际法的破坏者?" [Who Is Undermining International Law?], *Shijie Zhishi* 8 (1950): 7–8.

54 Han Depei and Zhu Xingqian, "Wei Le Shijie Heping, Women Yao Gei Su-Mei Liang Guo Jian Zuo Yi Ge Meipo, Shi Qi Chong Hao 為了世界和平，我們要給蘇美兩國間作一個媒婆，使其重好" [For the Sake of World Peace, We Must Act as a Matchmaker for the Soviet Union and America, Helping Them to Restore Their Relations], *Chang Qing Zhou Bao* 13, nos. 2–3 (1948): 2–3.

55 Jiang Haichao, "Gaizao Guojifa de Lilun ji Jianshe Shijie Heping de Wenti 改造國際法的理論及建設世界和平的問題" [The Theory of Reconstructing International Law and the Problem of Establishing World Peace], *Yi Shi Bao* (Shanghai), February 16–17, 1948.

56 Han Depei, "Ping Kai'erxun 'Fa he Guojia de Yiban Lilun' 评凯尔逊'法和国家的一半理论'" [On Kelsen's "General Theory of Law and State"] in Huang Jin (ed.), *Han Depei Wenxuan* 韩德培文选 [*Collected Writings of Han Depei*] (Wuhan: Wuhan University Press, 1996), 602–606.

57 Albert Blaustein, ed., *Fundamental Legal Documents of Communist China* (South Hackensack, NJ: Fred B. Rothman & Co., 1962), 53.

58 Cf. Zhang Xiruo, "Xin Zhongguo de Heping Waijiao Zhengce 新中國的和平外交政策" [The Peaceful Diplomatic Policy of the New China], *Shijie Zhishi* 40 (1952): 5–6.

59 See Zhu, *Wang Chonghui Zhuan Ziliao*, vol. 1.

60 Bin Cheng, *General Principles of Law as Applied by International Courts and Tribunals* (London: Stevens & Sons Ltd., 1953).

61 Bin Cheng, "United Nations Resolutions on Outer Space: 'Instant' International Customary Law?," *Indian Journal of International Law* 5 (1965): 35–40.
62 See *Barcelona Traction, Light and Power Company, Limited* (*Belgium* v. *Spain*), Separate Opinion of Vice-President Wellington Koo, July 24, 1964; *South West Africa* (*Liberia* v. *South Africa* and *Ethiopia* v. *South Africa*), Dissenting Opinion of Vice-President Wellington Koo, July 18, 1966.
63 Wilson Center Digital Archive, "Record of Conversation between I.V. Stalin and Chairman of the Central People's Government of the People's Republic of China Mao Zedong on 16 December 1949."
64 Hans Kelsen, *The Law of the United Nations: A Critical Analysis of Its Fundamental Problems: With Supplement* (Clark, NJ: The Lawbook Exchange, Ltd., 2000) (1951), 934.
65 Ibid. (emphasis added).
66 Ibid., 912.
67 Chen Tiqiang, "Wei Shenme Bixu Queding Qinlüe Dingyi? 为什么必须确定侵略定义?" [Why Is It Necessary to Determine the Definition of Aggression?], *Shijie Zhishi* 2, no. 9 (1953): 9–10 (arguing that clearly defining prohibited forms of aggression was "very unfavorable for the imperialists. The more things are muddled and right and wrong are confused, the easier it is for the imperialists to snatch fish out of the muddy waters").
68 Josef L. Kunz, "The Chaotic Status of the Laws of War and the Urgent Necessity for Their Revision," *American Journal of International Law* 45, no. 1 (1951): 37–61. Josef L. Kunz, "Legality of the Security Council Resolutions of June 25 and 27, 1950," *American Journal of International Law* 45, no. 1 (1951): 137–142. At the same time, Kunz lamented the "chaotic status of the laws of war." As Quincy Wright summarized international law doctrine on Korea at the end of the conflict: "to some the Korean 'war' and United Nations reaction to it demonstrate the effectiveness of the outlawry of war, and to others precisely the reverse." Quincy Wright, "The Outlawry of War and the Law of War," *American Journal of International Law* 47, no. 3 (1953): 365–376.
69 S. Myres McDougal, "International Law, Power, and Policy: A Contemporary Conception," *Recueil des Cours* 82 (1953): 133–259.
70 Hersch Lauterpacht, *Recognition in International Law* (Cambridge: Cambridge University Press, 2012) (original publication 1947); Hersch Lauterpacht, "Recognition of Governments," *The Times*, January 6, 1950.
71 See, e.g., Yuen-Li Liang, "The General Assembly and the Progressive Development and Codification of International Law," *American Journal of International Law* 42, no. 1 (1948): 66–97; C. G. Fenwick, "Draft Code of Offenses against the Peace and Security of Mankind," *American Journal of International Law* 46, no. 1 (1952): 98–100; David H. N. Johnson, "The Draft Code of Offences against the Peace and Security of Mankind," *International and Comparative Law Quarterly* 4, no. 3 (1955): 445–468.
72 See, e.g., 14th meeting, May 3, 1949, *Yearbook of the International Law Commission 1949* (Geneva: United Nations, 1956), 105. Liang's suggested formula was also decades later incorporated into the Rome Statute.
73 61st meeting, July 5, 1950 UNDOC: A/CN.4/R.1, 158.

74 See Zhai Qiang, "China and the Geneva Conference of 1954," *China Quarterly* 129 (1992): 103–122.

75 Ibid.

76 Ibid.

77 Ibid.

78 Wilson Center Digital Archive, "Agreement between the Republic of India and the People's Republic of China on Trade and Intercourse between the Tibet Region of China and India," April 29, 1954.

79 Wilson Center Digital Archive, "Minutes of Chairman Mao Zedong's Second Meeting with Nehru," October 23, 1954.

80 See Luis Eslava, Michael Fakhri, and Vasuki Nesiah, eds., *Bandung, Global History, and International Law: Critical Pasts and Pending Futures* (Cambridge: Cambridge University Press, 2017); see also Christopher J. Lee, ed., *Making a World after Empire: The Bandung Moment and Its Political Afterlives* (Athens: Ohio University Press, 2010); Adom Getachew, *Worldmaking after Empire: The Rise and Fall of Self-determination* (Princeton, NJ: Princeton University Press, 2019).

81 Ministry of Foreign Affairs, Republic of Indonesia, *Asian–African Conference Bulletin*, April 20, 1955: 17.

82 Ibid., 6–7.

83 Richard Wright, *The Color Curtain: A Report on the Bandung Conference* (New York: World Publishing, 1956), 164.

84 Charles N. Li, *The Bitter Sea: Coming of Age in a China before Mao* (New York: Harper Collins, 2009), 184.

85 See, e.g., Zhu Liru, "Bo Chen Tiqiang Guanyu Guojifa de Miulun 驳陈体强关于国际法的谬论" [Refuting Chen Tiqiang's International Law Fallacies], *People's Daily*, September 18, 1957.

86 Chen Tiqiang, "Guojifa Xiehui Di Sishiqi Jie Da Hui 国际法协会第四十七届大会" [The Fourty-seventh Meeting of the International Law Association], *Faxue Yanjiu* 3, no. 49 (1957): 5.

87 Ibid. See also Jerome Alan Cohen and Hungdah Chiu, *People's China and International Law: A Documentary Study* (Princeton, NJ: Princeton University Press, 1974), 33–64.

88 Zhou Ziya, "Aobenhai Guojifa Pingjia 奥本海国际法评介" [Critical Review of *Oppenheim's International Law*], *Faxue* 1 (1957): 3.

89 Zhou Gengsheng, *Xiandai Guojifa de Sixiang Dongxiang* 现代英美国际法的思想动向 [*The Intellectual Tendencies of Modern International Law*] (Beijing: Shijie Zhishi Chubanshe, 1963).

90 Ibid., 9.

91 Ibid., 25.

92 Zhou Ziya, "Chuncui Fa Xueshuo Zhong de 'Falü', 'Guojia', he 'Zhengyi' 纯粹法学说中的'法律'、'国家'和'正义'" ["Law," "State," and "Justice" in the Pure Theory of Law], *Xiandai Waguo Zhexue Shehui Kexue Wenzhai* 8 (1961): 37–38.

93 "Lianheguo Wuquan Pai Guanchayuan Dao Xiongyali Qu 联合国无权派观察员到匈牙利去" [The UN Has No Authority to Dispatch Observers to Hungary], *People's Daily*, December 10, 1956; "Zhongguo zai Lianheguo de

Hefa Quanli Bixu Huifu 中国在联合国的合法权利必须恢复" [China's Legitimate Rights in the UN Must be Restored], *People's Daily*, December 5, 1961.

94 "'Chuncui Faxue' de Fandong Shizhi '纯粹法学'的反动实质" [The Reactionary Essence of the "Pure Theory of Law"], *People's Daily*, February 27, 1962; "Meiguo Faxue Zhong de 'Shijie Zhuyi' Fandong Sichao 美国法学中的'世界主义'反动思潮" [The Reactionary Trend of "Cosmopolitanism" in American Legal Scholarship], *People's Daily*, December 17, 1963.

95 Wilhelm Röpke, *International Order and Economic Integration* (Dordrecht: D. Reidel Publishing Company, 1959), 79. Röpke also claimed that "the programme of action of the Communist Manifesto anticipated many features of the later national socialist policy in Germany after 1933." Wilhelm Röpke, "Economic Order and International Law," *Recueil des Cours* 86 (1954): 203–273.

96 FO 371/120935, May 5, 1956.

97 Ibid.

98 "Risk of Nuclear War over Taiwan in 1958 Said to Be Greater Than Publicly Known," *The New York Times*, May 22, 2021.

99 UNDOC, A/CONF.13/38 1–3 (1958).

100 Ibid.

101 Cohen and Chiu, *People's China and International Law*, 1308.

102 See, e.g., Ronald St. John MacDonald, ed., *Essays in Honour of Wang Tieya* (Leiden: Martinus Nijhoff Publishers, 1994), 5; cf. Mei Ju-ao, *The Tokyo Trial and War Crimes in Asia*, 2nd ed. (Singapore: Springer Nature, 2016), xix.

103 Zhou Gengsheng, *Guojifa* 国际法 [*International Law*] (Beijing: Shangwu Yinshuguan, 1983).

104 Memcon, Kissinger and Zhou, July 11, 1971, 10:35 a.m.–11:55 a.m.; box 1033, China HAK Memcons July 1971. Available at: https://nsarchive2.gwu.edu/NSAEBB/NSAEBB66/#docs.

105 Ling Qing, *Cong Yan'an Dao Lianheguo: Ling Qing de Waijiao Shengya* 从延安到联合国:凌青外交生涯 [*From Yan'an to the United Nations: The Diplomatic Career of Ling Qing*] (Fujian: Fujian Renmin Chubanshe, 2008), 161–165.

106 UNDOC, A/CONF.62/SR.112.

107 UNDP, *Our 40 Year Journey, 1979–2019: United Nations Development Programme in China* (Geneva: UNDP, 2019).

108 Kerstin Leitner, *When Only the Sky Is the Limit: Memoirs of a Nomadic International Civil Servant Working for Global Peace and Development, 1975–2005* (Berlin: lulu.com, 2013), 49.

109 Ibid., 233–236.

110 Harold Karan Jacobson and Michel Oksenberg, *China's Participation in the IMF, the World Bank, and GATT: Toward a Global Economic Order* (Ann Arbor: University of Michigan Press, 1990), 136–137.

111 See Isabella M. Weber, *How China Escaped Shock Therapy: The Market Reform Debate* (Abingdon: Routledge, 2021), 193–200.

112 Among the major human rights instruments China would join in the Reform Era were: The Convention on the Elimination of All Forms of Discrimination

against Women (CEDAW) (1979; 1980); International Convention on the Elimination of All Forms of Racial Discrimination (CERD) (1969; 1981); Convention against Torture and Other Cruel, Inhuman or Degrading Treatment or Punishment (CAT) (1985; 1988); Convention on the Rights of the Child (CRC) (1989; 1992); International Covenant on Economic, Social, and Cultural Rights (ICESCR) (1966; signed 1997, ratified 2001); and International Covenant on Civil and Political Rights (ICCPR) (1966; signed 1998, not yet ratified).

113 Han Tie, *Feng Yu Ban Jiming: Wo de Fu Qin Han depei Zhuan Ji* (Beijing: Zhongguo Fangzheng Chubanshe, 2000), 92–95.

114 He Shi, "Li Shuangyuan: Zai Guoji Sifa Daolu Shang Zhizhuo Qianxing 李双元 在国际私法道路上执着前行" [Li Shuangyuan: Committed to Progress on the Road of Private International Law], Hunan Zuojia Wang, April 20, 2017. Available at: www.frguo.com/Info.aspx?ModelId=1&Id=31212.

115 Zhu Xueshan, "Cong 'Yi Wen Hui You' Tan Qi: Xiao Yi Zhongguo Guoji Jingjifa Xuehui Zishen Jianshe Wenti 从"以文会友"谈起: 小议中国国际经济法学会自身建设问题" [On "Literary Camaraderie": A Brief Comment on the Self-construction of the CSIEL], *Guoji Jingji Fa Xue Kan* 4 (2004): 417–422.

116 Zhou Ziya, "Ping Chuncui Fa Xueshuo He Ta de Chuangshiren Kaierxun 评纯粹法学说和它的创始人凯尔逊" [Assessing the Pure Theory of Law and Its Creator Kelsen], *Shehui Kexue* 1 (1979): 111–114.

117 "China – BITs," Investment Policy Hub, UNCTAD. Available at: https://investmentpolicy.unctad.org/international-investment-agreements/countries/42/china?type=bits.

118 Han Depei, "Ping 'Taiwan Zijue' Lun 评'台湾自觉'论" [On the Theory of "Taiwan Self-determination"], in *Han Depei Wenxuan*, 610–613.

119 Ling, *Cong Yan'an Dao Lianheguo*, 208–209. Ni was one of the few international lawyers who had been sufficiently sensitive to shifting political winds to avoid serious persecution during both the Antirightist Movement and the Cultural Revolution.

120 Ni Zhengyu, *Danbo Congrong Li Haiya* 淡泊从容莅海牙 [*Prudent and Serene, Presiding at the Hague*], expanded edition (Beijing: Peking University Press, 2015), 255–256.

121 *Nicaragua* v. *United States*, Separate Opinion of Judge Ni Zhengyu, June 27, 1986.

122 Ling, *Cong Yan'an Dao Lianheguo*, 109.

123 Han Chengdong and Pan Baocun, eds., *Guojifa Jiaocheng* 国际法教程 [*Course in International Law*] (Nanjing: Nanjing University Press, 1988).

124 Wang Huning, "Lun Xian-Dangdai Zhuquan Lilun de Xin Fazhan 论现当代主权理论的新发展" [On New Developments in Modern and Contemporary Theories of Sovereignty], *Zhengzhixue Yanjiu* 1 (1985): 39–45; Wang Huning, *Guojia Zhuquan* 國家主權 [*State Sovereignty*] (Beijing: Renmin Chubanshe, 1987), 98–101, 110–117.

125 For a discussion of the economic dimension of the growing unease over uncritical acceptance of foreign prescriptions, such as the "shock therapy"

of sweeping privatization and elimination of price controls, see Weber, *How China Escaped Shock Therapy*, 130–146, 255–258.

126 William Alford, *To Steal a Book Is an Elegant Offense: Intellectual Property Law in Chinese Civilization* (Palo Alto, CA: Stanford University Press, 1995), 112–114; see also Ho-Fung Hung, "The US–China Rivalry Is About Capitalist Competition," *Jacobin*, July 11, 2020. Available at: https://jacobinmag.com/2020/07/us-china-competition-capitalism-rivalry.

127 Cf. George T. Crane, "Imagining the Economic Nation: Globalisation in China," *New Political Economy* 4, no. 2 (1999): 215–232.

128 Haig Patapan and Yi Wang, "The Hidden Ruler: Wang Huning and the Making of Contemporary China," *Journal of Contemporary China* 27, no. 109 (2018): 47–60.

129 UN Division for Ocean Affairs and the Law of the Sea, Declarations and Statements (1996). Available at: www.un.org/depts/los/convention_agreements/convention_declarations.htm#China.

130 Cf. Nicolas Becquelin, "Xinjiang in the Nineties," *The China Journal* 44 (2000): 65–90.

131 "Former Judges," ICTY. Available at: www.icty.org/en/sid/10572.

132 See, e.g., Rao Geping, "Wang Tieya Xiansheng he Bei Da Guojifa Yanjiusuo 王铁崖先生和北大国际法研究所" [Wang Tieya and the International Law Research Centre of Peking University], *Zhongguo Guojifa Xuehui* [*Chinese Society of International Law*], May 6, 2015. Available at: www.csil.cn/Director/Detail.aspx?AId=12.

133 UNDOC, UN Diplomatic Conference of Plenipotentiaries on the Establishment of an International Criminal Court, June 15–July 17, 1998, A/CONF.183/C.1/SR.42.

134 Liu Daqun, *Lianheguo Xianzhang Quanshi* 聯合國憲章詮釋 [*A Commentary on the Charter of the United Nations*] (Shanxi: Shanxi Jiaoyu Chubanshe, 1999).

135 For the evolutions in China's increasingly skeptical approach to doctrines of humanitarian intervention under the "Responsibility to Protect" (R2P) doctrine since its articulation in the year 2000, see Courtney J. Fung, *China and Intervention at the UN Security Council: Reconciling Status* (Oxford: Oxford University Press, 2019); on China's active but strictly delimited engagement with international human rights bodies and authorities, see Bjorn Ahl, "The Rise of China and International Human Rights Law," *Human Rights Quarterly* 37 (2015): 637.

136 Cf. Ryan Martinez Mitchell, "Chinese Receptions of Carl Schmitt since 1929," *Penn State Journal of Law and International Affairs* 8, no. 1 (2020): 181–245.

137 Shen Minrong, "Zhengfu, Shichang yu Jingjifa de Dingwei 政府, 市场与经济法的定位" [Government, Markets, and Determination of the Position of Economic Law] (PhD dissertation, Central Party School of the Chinese Communist Party, 2000).

138 Yuan Yuan, "Looking back 14 Years after Accession: Case of China," Third China Round Table on WTO Accessions, June 2, 2015. Available at: www.wto.org/english/thewto_e/acc_e/session2yuanyuanpostaccessionlookingback14yearafter.pdf.

139 Heng Wang, "Selective Reshaping: China's Paradigm Shift in International Economic Governance." *Journal of International Economic Law* 23, no. 3 (2020): 583–606.

140 CPC Leadership Group of the Ministry of Commerce, "Understanding the Great Trend of Economic Globalization and Expanding Opening Up on All Fronts," *Qiu Shi*, March 18, 2021. Available at: http://en.qstheory.cn/2021-03/18/c_603462.htm.

141 G. John Ikenberry and Darren J. Lim, "China's Emerging Institutional Statecraft: The Asian Infrastructure Investment Bank and the Prospects for Counter-Hegemony" (April 2017), 2. Available at: www.brookings.edu/wp-content/uploads/2017/04/chinas-emerging-institutional-statecraft.pdf.

142 Xi Jinping, "Zashi Tuidong Gongtong Fuyu 扎实推动共同富裕" [Firmly Advancing towards Common Prosperity], *Qiu Shi*, October 15, 2021. Available at: www.qstheory.cn/dukan/qs/2021-10/15/c_1127959365.htm.

143 Wang, *Guojia Zhuquan*, 117.

Conclusion

1 Cf. "Global Law: Ruling the British Empire," in Koskenniemi, *To the Uttermost Parts of the Earth*, 699–794.

2 Xue Hanqin, "China and International Law: 60 Years in Review," Chatham House, March 8, 2013. Available at: www.chathamhouse.org/sites/default/files/public/Research/International%20Law/080313summary.pdf.

3 Evgeny Pashukanis, *The General Theory of Law and Marxism* (Abingdon: Routledge, 2017).

4 Bhupinder Singh Chimni, *International Law and World Order: A Critique of Contemporary Approaches* (Cambridge: Cambridge University Press, 2017).

5 Ibid.

6 Abi-Saab, "The Newly Independent States and the Rules of International Law: An Outline," 98.

7 [Zhou] Gengsheng, "Zhan Qian Zhan Hou de Guoji Zhengju," 1–16.

8 A/C.3/34/SR.25 (October 23, 1979).

9 Cf. Daniel J. Whelan, "'Under the Aegis of Man': The Right to Development and the Origins of the New International Economic Order," *Humanity* 6, no. 1 (2015): 93–108.

10 Quinn Slobodian, *Globalists: The End of Empire and the Birth of Neoliberalism* (Cambridge, MA: Harvard University Press, 2018). Slobodian describes "[t]he core [aim] of ordoglobalism" as a form of "re-embedding the market ... to prevent state projects of egalitarian redistribution and secure competition, alternatively defined as the optimal functioning of the price-signaling system"). Ibid., 19. To these ends, transnational rules and institutions are enshrined as "apparatuses of juridical power to encase markets beyond democratic accountability [while also seeking] to create legitimacy through offering direct private rights to citizens beyond the nation." Ibid., 266.

11 Cf. Julien Chaisse and Mitsuo Matsushita, "China's 'Belt and Road' Initiative: Mapping the World Trade Normative and Strategic Implications," *Journal of World Trade* 52, no. 1 (2018): 163, 167; Gregory Shaffer and Henry Gao, "A

New Chinese Economic Order?," *Journal of International Economic Law* 23, no. 3 (2020): 607–635.

12 See Ryan Martínez Mitchell, "The Human Community of Fate: A Conceptual History of China's Ordoglobal Idea" *Humanity* 13, no. 3 (forthcoming, 2022).

13 Cf. Gilbert Guillaume, "Rocks in the Law of the Sea: Some Comments on the South China Sea Arbitration Award," *EJIL: Talk*, February 25, 2021. Available at: www.ejiltalk.org/ricks-in-the-law-of-the-sea-some-comments-on-the-south-china-sea-arbitration-award/.

14 David A. Welch and Kobi Logendrarajah. "Is China Still an Outlaw in the South China Sea?," *Open Canada*, July 29, 2019. Available at: https://opencanada.org/china-still-outlaw-south-china-sea/.

15 For similar cases of nonparticipation in or nonrecognition of international tribunals by the United States, United Kingdom, France, and Russia, respectively, see *Military and Paramilitary Activities in and against Nicaragua (Nicaragua* v. *United States*), 1984. I.C.J. 392; *Legal Consequences of the Separation of the Chagos Archipelago from Mauritius in 1965* (ICJ Advisory Opinion, February 25, 2019); *Nuclear Tests Case* (*Australia* v. *France*), 1974 I.C.J. 253; *Arctic Sunrise Arbitration* (*Netherlands* v. *Russia*) PCA case 2014-02.

16 Cf. Kenneth Anderson, *Russia–China Joint Declaration on the Promotion and Principles of International Law*, Law Fare Blog (July 7, 2016, 7:18 a.m.). Available at: www.lawfareblog.com/text-russia-china-joint-declaration-promotion-and-principles-international-law.

17 On the harmony of Party rule with sovereigntist forms of expanded international engagement and economic integration, cf. Tom Ginsburg, "The BRI, Non-interference, and Democracy," *Harvard International Law Journal* 62, special issue (2021): 40–65.

18 Cf. Samuel Moyn "From Situated Freedom to Plausible Worlds," in Venzke and Heller (eds.), *Contingency in International Law*, 532–541.

19 "About the Commission," International Law Commission. Available at: https://legal.un.org/ilc/ilcintro.shtml (given that Liang participated in the ILC's work not as a member of the body itself, but as its main liaison with the UN Secretariat, he is not included under the list of former ILC members – neither is he mentioned in the site's brief overview of institutional history).

20 "All Members," International Court of Justice. Available at: www.icj-cij.org/en/all-members (listing "Vi Kuiyuin Wellington Koo," which adds a superfluous syllable to Koo's two-syllable given name, Vi Kyuin = Wei Jun 維鈞).

21 Eyffinger, *The 1899 Hague Peace Conference*, 137.

22 Immanuel Wallerstein, *European Universalism: The Rhetoric of Power* (New York: The New Press, 2006), 84.

Bibliography

Abbenhuis, Maartje. *The Hague Conferences and International Politics, 1898–1915*. London: Bloomsbury Publishing, 2018.

Abi-Saab, Georges M. "The Newly Independent States and the Rules of International Law: An Outline." *Howard Law Journal* 8, no. 2 (1962): 97–121.

Abtahi, Hirad, and Philippa Webb, eds. *The Genocide Convention: The Travaux Preparatoires*. Leiden: Martinus Nijhoff Publishers, 2008.

Acton, Harold. *Memoirs of an Aesthete, 1939–1969*. New York: Viking Press, 1971.

Afinogenov, Gregory. *Spies and Scholars: Chinese Secrets and Imperial Russia's Quest for World Power*. Cambridge, MA: Belknap Press, 2020.

Ahl, Bjorn. "The Rise of China and International Human Rights Law." *Human Rights Quarterly* 37 (2015): 637.

Alexandrowicz, Charles Henry. "Some Problems in the History of the Law of Nations in Asia" [1963]. In *The Law of Nations in Global History*, David Armitage and Jennifer Pitts, eds. Oxford: Oxford University Press, 2017: 76–82.

Alford, William. *To Steal a Book Is an Elegant Offense: Intellectual Property Law in Chinese Civilization*. Palo Alto, CA: Stanford University Press, 1995.

Alleton, Viviane. "The Migration of Grammars through Languages: The Chinese Case." In *Mapping Meanings: The Field of New Learning in Late Qing China*, Natascha Vittinghoff and Michael Lackner, eds. Leiden: Brill, 2004: 223–224.

Althusser, Louis, and Etienne Balibar. *Reading Capital*. New York: Verso, 1970.

Alvarez, Alejandro. "Latin America and International Law." *American Journal of International Law* 3, no. 2 (1909): 269–353.

American Free-Trade League. *Some Account of the American Free-Trade League and of Its Purposes*. New York: American Free-Trade League, 1869.

An Zuozhang, ed. *Shandong Tongshi*, vol. 8, part 2. Jinan: Shandong Renmin Chubanshe, 1994.

Anand, Dibyesh. "Strategic Hypocrisy: The British Imperial Scripting of Tibet's Geopolitical Identity." *Journal of Asian Studies* 68, no. 1 (2009): 227–252.

Anghie, Antony. *Imperialism, Sovereignty, and the Making of International Law*. Cambridge: Cambridge University Press, 2004.

Anonymous. "The Life and Work of the Late Dr. W. A. P. Martin." *The Chinese Recorder* 48, no. 2 (1917): 116–123.

Association for the Reform and Codification of the Law of Nations. *Report of the Sixth Annual Conference Held at Frankfort-on-the-Main, 20–23 August 1878*. London: William Clowes and Sons, 1879.

Report of the Seventh Annual Conference Held at the Guildhall, London, 11–16 August 1879. London: William Clowes and Sons, 1880.

Attar, Mohsen al. "Subverting Eurocentric Epistemology: The Value of Nonsense When Designing Counterfactuals." In *Contingency in International Law: On the Possibility of Different Legal Histories*, Ingo Venzke and Kevin John Heller, eds. Oxford: Oxford University Press, 2021: 145–161.

Baka, Anna Irene, and Qi Fei. "Lost in Translation in the Sino-French War in Vietnam: From Western International Law to Confucian Semantics: A Comparative-Critical Analysis of the Chinese, French, and American Archives." In *Morality and Responsibility of Rulers: European and Chinese Origins of a Rule of Law as Justice for World Order*, Anthony Carty and Janne Nijman, eds. Oxford: Oxford University Press, 2018: 389–390.

Banquet to His Excellency Anson Burlingame and His Associates of the Chinese Embassy by the Citizens of New York, on Tuesday, June 23, 1868. New York: Sun Book and Job Printing House, 1868.

Barbosa, Ruy. "Rank among States Not Determined by Their Military Standing." *The Advocate of Peace* 70, no. 36 (1908): 36–38.

Barclay, Thomas. *Problems of International Practice and Diplomacy: With Special Reference to the Hague Conferences and Conventions and Other General International Agreements.* London: Sweet & Maxwell Limited, 1907.

Barcia Trelles, Camilo. "Francisco de Vitoria et l'école moderne du droit international." *Recueil de Cours de L'Académie de Droit International* 17 (1927): 109–342.

Bassin, Mark. *Imperial Visions: Nationalist Imagination and Geographical Expansion in the Russian Far East, 1840–1865.* Cambridge: Cambridge University Press, 1999.

Becquelin, Nicolas. "Xinjiang in the Nineties." *The China Journal* 44 (2000): 65–90.

Bickers, Robert, and R. Gary Tiedemann, eds. *The Boxers, China, and the World.* Lanham, MD: Rowman & Littlefield Publishers, 2007.

Bin Cheng. *General Principles of Law as Applied by International Courts and Tribunals.* London: Stevens & Sons Ltd., 1953.

"United Nations Resolutions on Outer Space: 'Instant' International Customary Law?" *Indian Journal of International Law* 5 (1965): 23–48.

Bismarck, Otto von. *Werke in Auswahl: Reichsgestaltung und europäische Friedenswahrung, 1877–1882.* Darmstadt: Wissenschaftliche Buchgesellschaft, 1973.

Blaustein, Albert, ed. *Fundamental Legal Documents of Communist China.* South Hackensack, NJ: Fred B. Rothman & Co., 1962.

Bloch, Ernst. "Nonsynchronism and the Obligation to Its Dialectics," trans Mark Ritter. *New German Critique* 11 (1977) [original publication 1935]: 22–38.

Bluntschli, Johann Caspar. *Alt-asiatische Gottes- und Weltideen in ihren Wirkungen auf das Gemeinleben der Menschen.* Nördlingen: C. H. Beck, 1866.

Das moderne Völkerrecht der civilisirten Staten: als Rechtsbuch dargestellt, 1st ed. Nördlingen: C. H. Beck, 1872.

Das moderne Völkerrecht der civilisirten Staten: als Rechtsbuch dargestellt, 2nd ed. Nördlingen: C. H. Beck, 1878.

"Arische Völker und arische Rechte." In *Gesammelte kleine Schriften*, vol. 1. Nördlingen: C. H. Beck, 1879.

Gongfa Huitong, trans. W. A. P. Martin. Beijing: Tongwenguan, 1880.

Denkwürdiges aus meinem Leben, vol. 3 (1861–1881). Nördlingen: C. H. Beck, 1884.
Allgemeine Staatslehre. Stuttgart: G. Cotta, 1886.

Boecking, Felix. "Tariffs, Powers, Nationalism, and Modernity: Fiscal Policy in Guomindang-Controlled China, 1927–1945." PhD dissertation, University of Cambridge, 2008.

Borchard, Edwin M. "'Responsibility of States' at the Hague Codification Conference." *American Journal of International Law* 24, no. 3 (1930): 517–540.

Borgwardt, Elizabeth. *A New Deal for the World: America's Vision for Human Rights*. Cambridge, MA: Belknap Press, 2007.

Brière, Yves de la. "Évolution de la doctrine et de la pratique en matière de représailles." *Recueil de Cours de L'Académie de Droit International* 22 (1928): 237–294.

Brockman-Hawe, Benjamin E. "Accountability for Crimes against the Laws of Humanity in Boxer China: An Experiment with International Justice at Paoting-Fu." *University of Pennsylvania Journal of International Law* 38 (2016): 627–713.

Cain, Peter J. "Character and Imperialism: The British Financial Administration of Egypt, 1878–1914." *Journal of Imperial and Commonwealth History* 34, no. 2 (2006): 177–200.

Carrai, Maria Adele. *Sovereignty in China: A Genealogy of a Concept since 1840*. Cambridge: Cambridge University Press, 2019.

Cassel, Pär Kristoffer. *Grounds of Judgment: Extraterritoriality and Imperial Power in Nineteenth-Century China and Japan*. Oxford: Oxford University Press, 2011.

Chaisse, Julien, and Mitsuo Matsushita. "China's 'Belt and Road' Initiative: Mapping the World Trade Normative and Strategic Implications." *Journal of World Trade* 52, no. 1 (2018): 163–186.

Chang, Claire Shu-Chin. *When Confucius Meets Benedictus: The Destiny of a Chinese Politician Lou Tseng-tsiang (1871–1949)*. Leuven: Katholieke Universiteit Leuven, 1994.

Chen Kaike. "Qiying Yu Di Er Ci Yapian Zhanzheng Zhong De Zhong E Jiaoshe." *Jindaishi Yanjiu* 4 (2009): 60–76.

Chen Kewei. "Bao Yingshi yu 1871 Nian de Zhong-Ri Tianjin Tiaoyue." *Qinghua Daxue Xuebao (Zhexue Shehui Kexue Ban)* 6 (2010): 70–78.

Chen, Li. *Chinese Law in Imperial Eyes: Sovereignty, Justice, and Transcultural Politics*. New York: Columbia University Press, 2015.
"Professor James Leslie Brierly and His First Chinese Pupil Li Shengwu at Oxford University Faculty of Law (1927–1930)." *Journal of the History of International Law/Revue d'histoire du droit international* 20, no. 3 (2018): 373–380.
"Tracing Chinese Scholar Chen Tiqiang's Pursuit of International Law Education and His Major Contribution to the Doctrine of Recognition." *Asian Journal of International Law* 10, no. 1 (2020): 68–93.

Chen, Ti-Chiang, *The International Law of Recognition*, Leslie Claude Green, ed. London: Stevens & Sons. 1951.

Chen Tiqiang. "Shei Shi Guojifa de Pohuaizhe?" *Shijie Zhishi* 8 (1950): 7–8.
"Wei Shenme Bixu Queding Qinlüe Dingyi?" *Shijie Zhishi* 2, no. 9 (1953): 9–10.
"Guojifa Xiehui Di Sishiqi Jie Da Hui." *Faxue Yanjiu* 3, no. 49 (1957): 5.

Chen Yan. *Kangri Zhanzheng Shiqi Zhongguo Waijiao Zhidu Yanjiu*. Shanghai: Fudan Daxue Chubanshe, 2002.

Cheney, Amanda J. "Tibet Lost in Translation: Sovereignty, Suzerainty and International Order Transformation, 1904–1906." *Journal of Contemporary China* 26, no. 107 (2017): 769–783.

Cheng, F. T. [Zheng Tianxi]. *Rules of Private International Law Determining Capacity to Contract*. London: Stevens, 1916.

Chiang, Hai Cháo [Jiang Haichao]. "La Chine." In *Bibliographie du Droit des Gens et des Rélations Internationales*, Karl Strupp, ed. Leiden: A. W. Sijthoff, 1938: 261–267.

Chiang Kai-shek. *China's Destiny and Chinese Economic Theory*. Leiden: Global Oriental, 2012.

Chiu, Hungdah. "The Position of International Law in Chinese Law." *Annals of the Chinese Society of International Law* 3 (1966): 88–97.

Chun Yu. "Wei Yuan, Lin Zexu yu 'Haiguo Tuzhi.'" *Wenshi Zazhi* 4 (2006): 26–30.

Clark, Martin. "Ambivalence, Anxieties/Adaptations, Advances: Conceptual History and International Law." *Leiden Journal of International Law* 31, no. 4 (2018): 747–771.

Cohen, Jerome Alan, and Hungdah Chiu. *People's China and International Law: A Documentary Study*. Princeton, NJ: Princeton University Press, 1974.

Commission on Extraterritoriality in China. *Report of the Commission on Extra-territoriality in China*. London: His Majesty's Stationery Office, 1926.

Cosmo, Nicola di. "Nurhaci's Gambit: Sovereignty as Concept and Praxis in the Rise of the Manchus." In *The Scaffolding of Sovereignty: Global and Aesthetic Perspectives on the History of a Concept*, Zvi Ben-Dor Benite, Stefanos Geroulanos, and Nicole Jerr, eds. New York: Columbia University Press 2017: 102–123.

Covell, Ralph. *W. A. P. Martin: Pioneer of Progress in China*. Washington, DC: Christian University Press, 1978.

Crane, George T. "Imagining the Economic Nation: Globalisation in China." *New Political Economy* 4, no. 2 (1999): 215–232.

Craven, Matthew. "Introduction: International Law and Its Histories." In *Time, History and International Law*, Matthew Craven, Fitzmaurice Malgosia, and Maria Vogiatzi, eds. Leiden: Martinus Nijhoff Publishers, 2007: 1–26.

"Between Law and History: The Berlin Conference of 1884–1885 and the Logic of Free Trade." *London Review of International Law* 3, no. 1 (2015): 49–59.

"Theorizing the Turn to History in International Law." In *The Oxford Handbook of the Theory of International Law*, Anne Orford and Florian Hoffmann, eds. Oxford: Oxford University Press 2016.

Da Li Yuan. *Chinese Supreme Court Decisions Relating to General Principles of Civil Law, Obligations, and Commercial Law*. Peking: Commission of Extraterritoriality, 1923.

Davis, Hayne. "Legal Aspects of the Hague Conference." *American Lawyer* 16, no. 1 (1908): 420–425.

Day, Jenny Huangfu. *Qing Travelers to the Far West: Diplomacy and the Information Order in Late Imperial China*. Cambridge: Cambridge University Press, 2018.

Dennett, Tyler. *Americans in Eastern Asia: A Critical Study of the Policy of the United States with Reference to China, Japan and Korea in the 19th Century*. New York: Macmillan, 1922.

Departement van Buitenlandsche Zaken. *Deuxième Conférence Internationale de la Paix, Actes et Documents, Vol. 1, Séances Plénières de la Conférence*. La Haye: Imprimerie Nationale, 1907.

Deuxième Conférence Internationale de la Paix, Actes et Documents, Vol. 2, Première Commission. La Haye: Imprimerie Nationale, 1907.

Documents of United Nations Conference on International Organization San Francisco 1945, vol. 3. New York: United Nations Information Organizations, 1945.

Dom Pierre-Célestin Lou Tseng-tsiang [Lu Zhengxiang]. *Souvenirs et Pensées*. Paris: Desclée de Brouwer, 1946.

Duara, Prasenjit. *Sovereignty and Authenticity: Manchukuo and the East Asian Modern*. Lanham, MD: Rowman & Littlefield, 2004.

Dudden, Alexis. "Japan's Engagement with International Terms." In *Tokens of Exchange: The Problem of Translation in Global Circulations*, Lydia He Liu, ed. Durham, NC: Duke University Press, 1999: 165–191.

Dupuis, Jean. *L'ouverture du Fleuve Rouge au Commerce et les Évènements du Tong-kin (1872–1873): Journal de Voyage et d'Expédition*, vol. 2. Paris: Challamel Aîné, 1879.

Encyclopaedia Britannica, vol. 26. Cambridge: Cambridge University Press, 1911.

Eskildsen, Robert. *Transforming Empire in Japan and East Asia: The Taiwan Expedition and the Birth of Japanese Imperialism*. Singapore: Palgrave Macmillan: 2019.

Eslava, Luis, Michael Fakhri, and Vasuki Nesiah, eds. *Bandung, Global History, and International Law: Critical Pasts and Pending Futures*. Cambridge: Cambridge University Press, 2017.

Eyffinger, Arthur. *The 1899 Hague Peace Conference: The Parliament of Man, the Federation of the World*. Leiden: Martinus Nijhoff Publishers, 1999.

"A Highly Critical Moment: Role and Record of the 1907 Hague Peace Conference." *Netherlands International Law Review* 54, no. 2 (2007): 197–228.

"Caught between Tradition and Modernity: East Asia at the Hague Peace Conferences." *Journal of East Asia and International Law* 1 (2008): 7–46.

Fairbank, John King. "Synarchy under the Treaties." In *Chinese Thought and Institutions*, John King Fairbank, ed. Chicago: University of Chicago Press, 1957: 204–234.

ed. *The Chinese World Order: Traditional China's Foreign Relations*. Cambridge, MA: Harvard University Press, 1968.

Fan Xianzheng. "'Guoti' yu 'Zhengti' Zai Jindai Zhongguo de Yanbian yu Fenhua." *Xueshu Yanjiu* 3 (2014): 40–45.

Fang Ke. *Tiexue Gonghe: Tu Shuo Xinhai Geming*. Beijing: Renmin Wenxue Chubanshe, 2011.

Fauchille, Paul. *Traité de droit international public*. Paris: Rousseau & Co., 1923.

Feng Lin, ed. *Xue Fucheng Xuanji*. Shanghai: Shanghai Renmin Chubanshe, 1987.

Fenwick, Charles G. *International Law*, 3rd ed. New York: Appleton-Century-Crofts, 1952.

"Review: Le Développement et la Codification du Droit International. By Yuen-li Liang. Paris: Recueil Sirey, 1949. 126." *American Journal of International Law* 44, no. 4 (1950): 786–787.

"Draft Code of Offenses against the Peace and Security of Mankind.' *American Journal of International Law* 46, no. 1 (1952): 98–100.

Fenwick, Charles G., and Westel W. Willoughby. *Types of Restricted Sovereignty and of Colonial Autonomy*. Washington, DC: Government Printing Office, 1919: 99–112.

Field, David Dudley. "De la Possibilité d'Appliquer le Droit International Européen aux Nations Orientales." *Revue de Droit International et de Législation Comparée* 7 (1875): 659–668.

Field, Henry M. *The Life of David Dudley Field*. New York: Charles Scribner's Sons, 1898.

Finch, Geo A. "The Peace Conference of Paris, 1919." *American Journal of International Law* 13, no. 2 (1919): 159–186.

Finnemore, Martha, and Michelle Jurkovich. "Getting a Seat at the Table: The Origins of Universal Participation and Modern Multilateral Conferences." *Global Governance: A Review of Multilateralism and International Organizations* 20, no. 3 (2014): 361–373.

Flynn, Dennis O., and Arturo Giráldez. "Cycles of Silver: Global Economic Unity through the Mid-Eighteenth Century." *Journal of World History* 13, no. 2 (2002): 391–427.

China and the Birth of Globalization in the 16th Century. Farnham: Ashgate Variorum, 2010.

Foster, John Watson. "Results of the Bering Sea Arbitration." *The North American Review* 161, no. 469 (1895): 693–702.

Diplomatic Memoirs, vol. 2. Boston: Houghton Mifflin Company, 1909.

Foulke, William Dudley. "Arbitration the Shortest Road to International Justice." In *Report of the Annual Lake Mohonk Conference on International Arbitration*. New York: Lake Mohonk Conference on International Arbitration, 1911: 99–100.

Fry, Agnes. *A Memoir of the Right Honourable Sir Edward Fry, G. C. B.* Oxford: Oxford University Press, 1921.

Fu Limin and He Minglun. *Zhongguo Shangye Wenhua Da Cidian*. Beijing: Zhongguo Fazhan Chubanshe, 1994.

Fuches, Walter. "Der Russisch–Chinesische Vertrag Von Nertschinsk Vom Jahre 1689: Eine Textkrische Betrachtung." *Monumenta Serica* 4, no. 2 (1940): 546–593.

Fuchs, Eckhardt, Tokushi Kasahara, and Sven Saaler, eds. *A New Modern History of East Asia*. Göttingen: V&R Unipress, 2018.

Fung, Courtney J. *China and Intervention at the UN Security Council: Reconciling Status*. Oxford: Oxford University Press, 2019.

Gao Quanxi, Zhang Wei, and Tian Feilong. *Xiandai Zhongguo Zou Xiang Fazhi zhi Lu*. Beijing: Social Sciences Academic Press China, 2012.

Gao Shulan. "Xiu yu Qichi de Tongzhi Di Siyin." *Fazhi Bolan* 19 (2011): 30–32.

Geertz, Clifford. *Negara: The Theatre-State in Nineteenth-Century Bali*. Princeton, NJ: Princeton University Press, 1980.

Geffcken, Heinrich. "La France en Chine et le Droit International." *Revue de Droit International et de Législation Comparée* 17 (1885):145–151.

Getachew, Adom. *Worldmaking after Empire: The Rise and Fall of Self-determination*. Princeton, NJ: Princeton University Press, 2019.

Ginsburg, Tom. "The BRI, Non-interference, and Democracy." *Harvard International Law Journal* 62, Special Issue (2021): 40–65.

Gobineau, Arthur. *Essai sur l'inégalité des races humaines*. Paris: Didot Frères, 1853.

Goetzmann, William N., Andrey D. Ukhov, and Ning Zhu. "China and the World Financial Markets 1870–1939: Modern Lessons from Historical Globalization." *Economic History Review* 60, no. 2 (2007): 267–312.

Gong, Gerrit W. *The Standard of "Civilization" in International Society*. New York: Oxford University Press, 1984.

Gopa, Sarvepalli. *Jawaharlal Nehru: A Biography, Vol. 1: 1889–1947*. Bombay: Oxford University Press, 1976.

Grant, John P., and J. Craig Barker, eds. *The Harvard Research in International Law: Original Materials*. Vol. 1. New York: William S. Hein & Co., Inc., 2007.

Grewe, Wilhelm G. *Epochen der Völkerrechtsgeschichte*. Baden-Baden: Nomos Verlagsgesellschaft, 1984.

Guo Songtao. *Shixi Jicheng: Guo Songtao Ji* 使西纪程: 郭嵩焘集 [Record of a Mission to the West: Collected Writings of Guo Songtao]. Shenyang: Liaoning Renmin Chubanshe, 1994.

Lundun yu Bali Riji. Changsha: Yuelu Shushe, 1984.

Gützlaff, Karl Friedrich August. *China Opened*. Cambridge: Cambridge University Press, 2015.

Halsey, Stephen R. *Quest for Power: European Imperialism and the Making of Chinese Statecraft*. Cambridge, MA: Harvard University Press, 2015.

"Sovereignty, Self-strengthening, and Steamships in Late Imperial China." *Journal of Asian History* 48, no. 1 (2014): 81–111.

Han Chengdong, and Pan Baocun, eds. *Guojifa Jiaocheng*. Nanjing: Nanjing University Press, 1988.

Han Depei. "Women Suo Xuyao de 'Fazhi.'" *Guancha* 1, no. 10 (1946): 1–2.

"Kaiersheng yu Chuncui Faxue." *Sixiang yu Shidai* 47 (1947): 9–13.

"Ping Kai'erxun 'Fa he Guojia de Yiban Lilun.'" In *Han Depei Wenxuan*, Huang Jin, ed. Wuhan: Wuhan University Press, 1996: 602–606.

"Ping 'Taiwan Zijue' Lun." In *Han Depei Wenxuan*, Huang Jin, ed. Wuhan: Wuhan University Press, 1996: 610–613.

Han Depei and Zhu Xingqian. "Wei Le Shijie Heping, Women Yao Gei Su-Mei Liang Guo Jian Zuo Yi Ge Meipo, Shi Qi Chong Hao." *Chang Qing Zhou Bao* 13, nos. 2–3 (1948): 2–3.

Han Tie. *Feng Yu Ban Jiming: Wo de Fu Qin Han Depei Zhuan Ji*. Beijing: Zhongguo Fangzheng Chubanshe, 2000.

Hanes, W. Travis, and Frank Sanello. *The Opium Wars: The Addiction of One Empire and the Corruption of Another*. Naperville, IL: Sourcebooks Inc., 2002.

Harris, Henry Wilson. *Geneva, 1921: An Account of the Second Assembly of the League of Nations*. London: Daily News Ltd., 1921.

Harvey, David. *The Condition of Modernity: An Enquiry into the Origins of Cultural Change*. Oxford: Blackwell, 1989.

Hathaway, Oona A., and Scott J. Shapiro. "Outcasting: Enforcement in Domestic and International Law." *Yale Law Journal* 121, no. 2 (2011): 252–349.

The Internationalists: How a Radical Plan to Outlaw War Remade the World. New York: Simon and Schuster, 2017.

Hauer, Erich. "Why the Sinologue Should Study Manchu." *Bulletin of the North China Branch of the Royal Asiatic Society* 61 (1930): 156–164.

Haushofer, Karl. "Gesamtasiatische Fragen." In *Wörterbuch des Völkerrechts und der Diplomatie*, vol. 1, Karl Strupp, ed. Berlin: Walter de Gruyter, 1924: 390–394.

He Qinhua. "Wanguo Gongfa' yu Qingmo Guojifa." *Faxue Yanjiu* 23, no. 5 (2001): 137–148.

Heffter, August Wilhelm. *Le Droit International Public de l'Europe*. Paris: Cotillon, 1857.

Heffter, August Wilhelm, and Friedrich Heinrich Geffcken, eds. *Das europäische Volkerrecht der Gegenwart*. Berlin: Schroeder, 1873.

Herrmann, Florian. *Das Standardwerk: Franz von Liszt und das Völkerrecht*. Baden-Baden: Nomos, 2001.

Hevia, James L. *Cherishing Men from Afar: Qing Guest Ritual and the Macartney Embassy of 1793*. Durham, NC: Duke University Press, 1995.

English Lessons: The Pedagogy of Imperialism in Nineteenth-Century China. Durham, NC: Duke University Press, 2003.

Hicks, Frederick Charles. "The Equality of States and the Hague Conferences." *American Journal of International Law* 2, no. 3 (1908): 530–561.

Hilderbrand, Robert C. *Dumbarton Oaks: The Origins of the United Nations and the Search for Postwar Security*. Durham: University of North Carolina Press, 1990.

Hille, Willy van. "Étude sur la Responsabilité Internationale de l'État." *Revue de Droit International et de Législation Comparée* 56, no. 4 (1929): 531–571.

Hirohiko, Otsuka. "Japan's Early Encounter with the Concept of the 'Law of Nations.'" *Japanese Annual of International Law* 13, no. 35 (1969): 35–65.

Hirschfeld, Julius. "Current Notes on International Law." *Law Magazine and Review: A Quarterly Review of Jurisprudence* 5, no. 26 (1900): 335.

Holls, Frederick W. *The Peace Conference at the Hague and Its Bearings on International Law and Policy*. London: Macmillan & Co. Ltd., 1900.

"The International Court of Arbitration at the Hague." *American Lawyer* 9 (1901): 160.

Hong Xiaoxia. "Chuxi Jiujinshan Lianheguo Zhixian Huiyi de Zhongguo Daibiaotuan Zucheng Qingkuang Shulüe." *Wuhan Daxue Xuebao (Renwen Kexue Ban)* 55, no. 3 (2002): 313–319.

Hornung, Joseph. "Note a Propos de l'Application aux Nations Orientales du Droit des Gens Coutumier de l'Europe." *Revue de Droit International et de Législation Comparée* 11 (1879): 447–449.

Hsü Daulin. "Das Mandschurische Problem." *Sinica* 7, no. 3 (1932): 81–91.

Hsü, Immanuel C. Y. *China's Entrance into the Family of Nations: The Diplomatic Phase, 1858–1880*. Cambridge, MA: Harvard University Press, 2013.

The Ili Crisis: A Study of Sino-Russian Diplomacy 1871–1881. Oxford: Clarendon Press, 1965.

Hu Shih. "Speech at Wellesley College, 15 June 1942." *Contemporary China* 2, no. 3 (1942): 3–4.

Hu Zengyi. *Xin Man-Han Cidian*, 2nd ed. Shanghai: Shangwu Yinshuguan, 2020.

Huber, Max. "Die Gleichheit der Staaten." In *Rechtswissenschaftliche Beiträge: Juristische Festgabe des Auslandes zu Josef Kohlers 60. Geburtstag, 9. März 1909*. Aalen: Scientia Verlag, 1909: 88–118.

"Beiträge zur Kenntnis der soziologischen Grundlagen des Völkerrechts und der Staatengesellschaft." In *Jahrbuch des öffentlichen Rechts der Gegenwart*, vol. 4. Tübingen: J. C. B. Mohr, 1910: 56–134.

Denkwürdigkeiten, 1907–1924. Zurich: Orell Füssli, 1974.

Hudson, Manley O. "The Progressive Codification of International Law." *American Journal of International Law* 20, no. 4 (1926): 655–669.

Huenemann, Ralph William. *The Dragon and the Iron Horse: The Economics of Railroads in China, 1876–1937*. Cambridge, MA: Harvard University Asia Center, 1984.

Hughes, Charles E., Henry Cabot Lodge, Oscar W. Underwood and Elihu Root, "Conference on the Limitation of Armament." *American Journal of International Law* 16, no. 2 (1922): 159–233.

Hull, William I. "The United States and Latin America at the Hague." *International Conciliation* 1, no. 44 (1911): 12–13.

II Conferência da Paz Haia 1907: A correspondência telegráfica entre o Barão do Rio Branco e Rui Barbosa. Rio de Janeiro: Fundação Alexandre de Gusmão, 2014.

Institut de Droit International. *Annuaire de l'Institut de Droit International*, vols. 3–4, 1879–1880. Brussels: C. Muquardt, 1880.

Annuaire de l'Institut de Droit International, vol. 6, 1882–1883. Brussels: Merzbach et Falk, 1883.

Annuaire de l'Institut de Droit International, vol. 27, 1919. Brussels: Falk, 1919.

Annuaire de l'Institut de Droit International, vol. 28, 1921. Brussels: A. Dewit, 1921.

Annuaire de l"institut de Droit International, vol. 33, 1927. Brussels: Goemare, 1927.

Ishii Kikujirō. *Gaikō Yoroku*. Tokyo: Iwanami Shoten, 1930.

Ishikawa Yoshihiro. *The Formation of the Chinese Communist Party*, trans. Joshua Fogel. New York: Columbia University Press, 2013.

Jacobson, Harold Karan, and Michel Oksenberg. *China's Participation in the IMF, the World Bank, and GATT: Toward a Global Economic Order*. Ann Arbor: University of Michigan Press, 1990.

Jameson, Fredric. *Postmodernism, or the Cultural Logic of Late Capitalism*. Durham, NC: Duke University Press, 1991.

Jeans, Roger B. *Democracy and Socialism in Republican China: The Politics of Zhang Junmai (Carsun Chang), 1906–1941*. Lanham, MD: Rowman & Littlefield, 1997.

Jellinek, Georg. "China und das Völkerrecht." *Deutsche Juristen-Zeitung* 5, no. 19 (1900): 401–403.

Jiang Tingfu. *Jiang Tingfu Huyilu*. Changsha: Yuelu Shushe, 2003.

Jin, Guantao, Liu Qingfeng, and Qiu Weiyun. "Zhongguo Xiandai Zhuquan Guannian Xingcheng de Shuwei Renwen Yanjiu." *Ershiyi Shiji Shuangyuekan* 172 (2019): 49–67.

Johnson, David H. N. "The Draft Code of Offences against the Peace and Security of Mankind." *International & Comparative Law Quarterly* 4, no. 3 (1955): 445–468.

Kahn, Paul W. *The Origins of Order: Project and System in the American Legal Imagination*. New Haven, CT: Yale University Press, 2019.

Kasek, Elisabeth. *Bismarcks Missionare: Deutsche Militärinstrukteure in China 1884–1890*. Leipzig: Otto Harrassowitz Verlag, 2002.

Kaufman, Alison Adcock. "In Pursuit of Equality and Respect: China's Diplomacy and the League of Nations." *Modern China* 40, no. 6 (2014): 605–638.

Kawashima, Shin. "China." In *The Oxford Handbook of the History of International Law*, Bardo Fassbender, Anne Peters, Simone Peter, and Daniel Högger, eds. Oxford: Oxford University Press, 2012: 451–474.

Keene, Edward. *Beyond the Anarchical Society: Grotius, Colonialism and Order in World Politics*. Cambridge: Cambridge University Press, 2002.

Kelsen, Hans. *Das Problem der Souveränität und die Theorie des Völkerrechts: Beitrag zu einer reinen Rechtslehre*. Tübingen: J. C. B. Mohr/P. Siebeck, 1920.

The Law of the United Nations: A Critical Analysis of Its Fundamental Problems: With Supplement. Clark, NJ: The Lawbook Exchange, Ltd., 2000.

Kirby, William C. *Germany and Republican China*. Stanford, CA: Stanford University Press, 1984.

Kirgis, Frederic L. *The American Society of International Law's First Century, 1906–2006*. Leiden: Brill, 2006.

Klein, Robert A. *Sovereign Equality among States: The History of an Idea*. Toronto: University of Toronto Press, 1974.

Kolb, Robert. "Origin of the Twin Terms *Jus ad Bellum/Jus in Bello*." *International Review of the Red Cross Archive* 37, no. 320 (1997): 553–562.

Koo, V. K. Wellington. *The Status of Aliens in China*. New York: Columbia University Press, 1912.

"Bali hehui guoji lianhe guyiding mengyue qingxing zhaiyao." *Waijiao gongbao* 1 (1921): 3–5.

Koselleck, Reinhart. "Staat und Souveränität." In *Geschichtliche Grundbegriffe: Historisches Lexicon zur Politisch-Sozialen Sprache in Deutschland*, vol. 6. Otto Brunner, Werner Conze, and Reinhart Koselleck, eds. Stuttgart: Klett-Cotta, 1972–1990: 1–54.

Koskenniemi, Martti. *The Gentle Civilizer of Nations: The Rise and Fall of International Law 1870–1960*. Cambridge: Cambridge University Press, 2001.

"A History of International Law Histories." In *The Oxford Handbook of the History of International Law*, Bardo Fassbender, Anne Peters, Simone Peter, and Daniel Högger, eds. Oxford: Oxford University Press, 2012.

To the Uttermost Parts of the Earth: Legal Imagination and International Power 1300–1870. Cambridge: Cambridge University Press, 2021.

Krauel, A. "Applicabilite du Droit des Gens Européen a la Chine." *Revue de Droit International et de Législation Comparée* 9 (1877): 387–401.

Kraus, Herbert. *The Crisis of German Democracy; A Study of the Spirit of the Constitution of Weimar*. Princeton, NJ: Princeton University Press, 1932.

Kroll, Stefan. *Normgenese durch Re-interpretation: China und das europäische Völkerrecht im 19. und 20. Jahrhundert*. Baden-Baden: Nomos, 2012.

Kuehl, Warren F. *Seeking World Order: The United States and International Organization to 1920*. Nashville, TN: Vanderbilt University Press, 1969.

Kuhn, Arthur K. "The International Conference on the Treatment of Foreigners." *American Journal of International Law* 24, no. 3 (1930): 570–573.

Kunz, Josef L. "The Chaotic Status of the Laws of War and the Urgent Necessity for Their Revision." *American Journal of International Law* 45, no. 1 (1951): 37–61.

"Legality of the Security Council Resolutions of June 25 and 27, 1950." *American Journal of International Law* 45, no. 1 (1951): 137–142.

Lai Xinxia. *Lin Zexu Nianpu Chang Pian*, vol. 1. Shanghai: Shanghai Jiatong Daxue Chubanshe, 2011.

Lammasch, Heinrich. "Aus Meinem Leben." In *Heinrich Lammasch: Seine Aufzeichnungen, sein Wirken und seine Politik*, Marga Lammasch and Hans Sperl, eds. Vienna: Franz Deuticke, 1922: 14–17.

Lapradelle, Albert Geouffre de, and Ellery C. Stowell. "Latin America at the Hague Conference." *Yale Law Journal* 17 (1907): 270–280.

Lauterpacht, Hersch. *Recognition in International Law*. Cambridge: Cambridge University Press, 2012 [original publication 1947].

Lavelle, Peter B. *The Profits of Nature: Colonial Development and the Quest for Resources in Nineteenth-Century China*. New York: Columbia University Press, 2020.

Lawrence, Thomas Joseph. *International Problems and Hague Conferences*. London: J. M. Dent, 1908.

Lee, Christopher J., ed. *Making a World after Empire: The Bandung Moment and Its Political Afterlives*. Athens: Ohio University Press, 2010.

Lee, Daniel. "Sources of Sovereignty: Roman Imperium and Dominium in Civilian Theories of Sovereignty." *Politica Antica* 2, no. 1 (2012): 79–94.

"'Office Is a Thing Borrowed': Jean Bodin on Offices and Seigneurial Government." *Political Theory* 41, no. 3 (2013): 409–440.

Lee, Frederic. *Currency, Banking, and Finance in China*. Washington, DC: United States Department of Commerce, 1927.

Lee Lai To and Hock Guan Lee, eds. *Sun Yat-Sen, Nanyang and the 1911 Revolution*. Singapore: Institute of Southeast Asian Studies, 2011.

Leitner, Kerstin. *When Only the Sky Is the Limit: Memoirs of a Nomadic International Civil Servant Working for Global Peace and Development, 1975–2005*. Berlin: lulu.com, 2013.

Lepert, Henri. *Projet de constitution pour la Société des nations: Projet soumis à la Ligue*. Paris: Ligue por une Société des Nations Basée sur une Constitution Internationale, 1917.

Li Bingnan, Zeng Jianyuan, and Lin Zixuan. "'Dongyuan Kanluan Shiqi Linshi Tiaokuan' zhi Zhidu Jingyan ji qi Yingxiang." *Taiwan Minzhu Jikan* 1, no. 2 (2004): 95–129.

Li, Charles N. *The Bitter Sea: Coming of Age in a China before Mao*. New York: Harper Collins, 2009.

Li Dade. "Guanyu Zhou Gengsheng Hu Shi zhi de Lunzhan: Tongyi Zhou Gengsheng Kanfa, Hu Shi zhi You 'Kong Su Bing.'" *Zhongyang Zhoukan* 10, no. 9 (1948): 355.

Li Dong. "Yangwu Yundong Shiqqi Xue Fucheng Jiaru Guojifa Da Jiating de Zhuzhang yu Shijian." *Zhengfa Xuekan* 37, no. 2 (2020): 121–128.

Li Enhan. *Beifa Qianhou de "Geming Waijiao" 1925–1931*. Taipei: Zhongyang Yanjiuyuan Jindai Shi Yanjiusuo, 1993.

Li Fupeng. "Weima Xianfa Shehuiquan de Zhongguo Zhuanhua." *Huanqiu Falü Pinglun* 42, no. 3 (2020): 133–146.

Li Guanghe. "Yapian Zhanzheng Qianhou Qiying Dui Wai Jiaoshe Lunshu." *Huabei Meishiyuan Xuebao (Zhexue Shehui Kexue Ban)* 2 (1999): 3–5.

Li Guilian. *1902: Zhongguo Fa de Zhuanxing*. Guilin: Guangxi Shifan Daxue Chubanshe, 2018.

Li Hongxi. *Zhang Junmai Xiansheng de Minzhu Xianfa Sixiang*. Taipei: Jinian Zhang Junmai Xiansheng Bai Ling Ming Dan Xueshu Yantaohui [Forum to Celebrate the Centennial of Zhang Junmai's Birth], 1986.

Li Shengwu. "Juan Tou Yu." *Liu Ying Xuebao* 4 (1929): 4–5.

Guoji Gongfa Lun. Shanghai: Shangwu Yinshuguan, 1935.

Li Xizhu. "Li Hongzhang Dui Riben de Renshi ji Qi Waijiao Celüe: Yi 1870 Niandai wei Zhongxin." *Jindai Zhongguo Zhengzhi yu Waijiao* 1, no. 204 (2013): 145–159.

Li Yumin. "Wanqing Shiqi Guotiguan de Bianhua Shitan." *Renwen Zazhi* 6 (2013): 71–90.

Li, Yu-qin. "Analysis of the Establishment and Operation of Hanyeping Company's Joint Stock System in the Late Qing Dynasty." *Journal of XuChang University* 4 (2009): 101–105.

Liang Jian. "Yang Ru Jiejue Meiguo Paihua Wenti de Shijian yu Gouxiang Shulun." *Xinan Jiaotong Daxue Xuebao (Shehui Kexue Ban)* 12, no. 2 (2011): 82–86.

Liang, Yuen-li. "The Pact of Paris as Envisaged by Mr. Stimson: Its Significance in International Law." *China Law Review* 5 (1932): 198–227.

"Le développement et la codification du droit international." *Recueil des Cours* 73 (1948): 407–532.

"The General Assembly and the Progressive Development and Codification of International Law." *American Journal of International Law* 42, no. 1 (1948): 66–97.

"Notes on Legal Questions Concerning the United Nations." *American Journal of International Law* 43, no. 1 (1949): 134–144.

"The Establishment of an International Criminal Jurisdiction: The First Phase." *American Journal of International Law* 46, no. 1 (1952): 73–88.

"Women zai Rineiwa de Cuowu." *Shenbao Yuekan* 2, no. 8 (1933): 17–20.

Liang, Yuen-li, and Wang Feiya "Li Shengwu Zhu Guoji Gongfa Lun." *Tushu Pinglun* 2, no. 9 (1934): 35–43.

Lieber, Francis. *Fragments of Political Science on Nationalism and Internationalism*. New York: Charles Scribner & Co., 1868.

Notes on Fallacies Peculiar to American Protectionists, or Chiefly Resorted to in America. New York: American Free-Trade League, 1869.

Ling Qing. *Cong Yan'an Dao Lianheguo: Ling Qing de Waijiao Shengya*. Fujian: Fujian Renmin Chubanshe, 2008.

Liszt, Franz von. *Das Völkerrecht systematisch dargestellt*, 1st ed. Berlin: O. Haering, 1888.

Das Völkerrecht systematisch dargestellt, 2nd ed. Berlin: Verlag O. Haering, 1902.

Das Wesen des völkerrechtlichen Staatenverbandes und der international Prisenhof. Breslau: M. & H. Marcus, 1910.

Das Völkerrecht Systematisch Dargestellt. 10th ed. Berlin: Springer, 1915.

Liu, Andrew B. *Tea War: A History of Capitalism in China and India*. New Haven, CT: Yale University Press, 2020.

Liu Dan. "1874 Nian Dajiu Baolitong Beijing Tanpan de Dongyin yu Yingxiang." *Waiguo Wenti Yanjiu* 4, no. 9 (2018): 85–92.

Liu Daqun. *Lianheguo Xianzhang Quanshi*. Shanxi: Shanxi Jiaoyu Chubanshe, 1999.

Liu Dasheng. "Shangfang Shi Gongmin de Xianfa Quanli." *Hongqi Wengao* 2 (2004): 29–30.

Liu Gengsheng. "Yixin yu Zongli Yamen de Jianli Shuping." *Lishi Dangan* 3 (1990): 93–98.

Liu Guoming, ed., *Zhonghua Minguo Guomin Zhengfu Jun Zheng Zhiguan Renwu Zhi.* Beijing: Chunqiu Chubanshe, 1989.

Liu, Lydia He. *The Clash of Empires.* Cambridge, MA: Harvard University Press, 2004.

"Legislating the Universal: The Circulation of International Law in the Nineteenth Century." In *Tokens of Exchange: The Problem of Translation in Global Circulations*, ed. Lydia He Liu. Durham, NC: Duke University Press, 2000.

Liu Yi. "Lun Zongli Yamen de Jianli Ji Qi Lishi Diwei." *Suzhou Daxue Xuebao* 3 (1991): 112–120.

Lin Laifan. "Guoti Gainianshi: Kuaguo Yizhi yu Yanbian." *Zhongguo Shehui Kexue* 3 (2013): 65–84.

Lin Zexu. *Lin Zexu Quanji: Riji Juan.* Fuzhou: Haixia Wenyi Chubanshe, 2002.

Ling, Qing. *Cong yan'an dao lianheguo: Ling Qing de waijiao shengya.* Fujian: Fujian Renmin Chubanshe, 2008.

Lingen, Kerstin von. *Transcultural Justice at the Tokyo Tribunal: The Allied Struggle for Justice, 1946–48.* Leiden: Brill, 2018.

Long Xiaofei. "Qiying Waijiao Lilun Chu Tan." *Shoudu Bowuguan Congkan* 0 (1995): 30–36.

Lorca, Arnulf Becker. *Mestizo International Law.* Cambridge: Cambridge University Press, 2014.

Lorimer, James. "Prolegomènes d'un Système Raisonné de Droit International." *Revue de Droit International et de Législation Comparée* 10 (1878): 348.

The Institutes of the Law of Nations, vol 1. Edinburgh: William Blackwood and Sons, 1883.

Lou, Dom Pierre-Célestin Tseng-tsiang [Lu Zhengxiang]. *Souvenirs et Pensées.* Bruges: Desclée de Brouwer, 1946.

Loughlin, Martin. *Foundations of Modern Public Law.* Oxford: Oxford University Press, 2010.

Luo Zhufeng. *Hanyu Dacidian.* Shanghai: Shanghai Cishu, 1990.

Lutz, Jessie Gregory. *Opening China: Karl F. A. Gützlaff and Sino-Western Relations, 1827–1852.* Cambridge: Wm. B. Eerdmans Publishing, 2008.

Ma Do Yün [Ma Derun]. "Der Eintritt des chinesischen Reiches in den völkerrechtlichen Verband." PhD dissertation, University of Berlin, 1907.

Ma Yong. "From Constitutional Monarchy to Republic: The Trajectory of Yuan Shikai." *Journal of Modern Chinese History* 6, no. 1 (2012): 15–32.

Ma Ziyi. "Cong 'Tianxia' Dao 'Zhuquan': Cong Tiaoyue, Chuanjiao Kan Qingmo Shehui Guannian de Bianhua." *Shilin* 6 (2004): 15–22.

MacDonald, Ronald St. John, ed. *Essays in Honour of Wang Tieya.* Leiden: Martinus Nijhoff Publishers, 1994.

Mahan, Alfred Thayer. *The Influence of Sea Power upon History: 1660–1783.* Boston: Little, Brown, & Co., 1890.

The Problem of Asia and Its Effect upon International Policies. London: Sampson, Low, Marston and Co., 1900.

Mamolea, Andrei. "Saving Face: The Political Work of the Permanent Court of Arbitration (1902–1914)." In *Experiments in International Adjudication:*

Historical Accounts, Ignacio de la Rasilla and Jorge E. Viñuales, eds. Cambridge: Cambridge University Press, 2019: 193–210.

Marburg, Theodore. "The Significance of the International Court of Arbitral Justice." In *Report of the Annual Lake Mohonk Conference on International Arbitration*. New York: Lake Mohonk Conference on International Arbitration, 1910: 85–89.

Martens, Charles de (Karl von). *Xingyao Zhizhang*. Beijing: Tongwenguan, 1876.

Martens, Fyodor de. *Das Consularwesen und die Consularjurisdiction im Orient*, trans. H. Skerzt. Berlin: Weidmann, 1874.

Le Conflit entre la Russie et la Chine, ses Origines, son Développement, et sa Portée Universelle: Étude Politique. Brussels: C. Muquardt, 1880.

Traité de Droit International. Paris: A. Marescq Ainé, 1883.

"How the Chinese Question Should Be Solved." *The Advocate of Peace* 62, no. 11 (1900): 240–241

La Conférence de la Paix á La Haye: Étude d'Histoire Contemporaine. Paris: Arthur Rousseau, 1900.

Martens, Georg Friedrich von. *Précis du droit des gens moderne de l'Europe*, vol. 1. Paris: Guillaumin et Cie, 1864.

Martin, William Alexander Parsons. *A Cycle of Cathay: Or, China, South and North, with Personal Reminiscences*. New York: Fleming H. Revell, 1896.

"La Chine et la Droit International." *Revue de Droit International et de Législation Comparée* 17 (1885): 504–509.

"Les Vestiges d'un Droit International dans l'Ancienne Chine." *Revue de Droit International et de Législation Comparée* 14 (1882): 227–242.

The Siege in Peking: China against the World. New York: Fleming H. Revell, 1900.

"Une Université en Chine: Le Présent et l'Avenir de l'Ensiegnement Supérieur International a Peking." *Revue de Droit International et de Législation Comparée* 5 (1873): 8–10.

Marx, Karl. *Grundrisse: Foundations of the Critique of Political Economy*. New York: Penguin Books in association with the New Left Review, 1973.

Marx, Karl, and Friedrich H. G. Engels. *Karl Marx Friedrich Engels Gesamtausgabe* (MEGA), Part 3, *Briefwechsel*, vol. 9, Januar 1858 bis August 1859. Berlin: Akademie Verlag, 2003.

On Colonialism: Articles from the New York Tribune and Other Writings. New York: International Publishers, 1972.

Maxey, Edwin. "Development of International Law." *American Law Review* 40, no. 188 (1906): 188–195.

Mayers, William Frederick. *Treaties between the Empire of China and Foreign Powers, Together with Regulations for the Conduct of Foreign Trade, Conventions, Agreements, Regulations, etc.* Shanghai: North China Herald Ltd., 1906.

Mayr, Teresa F., and Jelka Mayr-Singer. "Keep the Wheels Spinning: The Contributions of Advisory Opinions of the International Court of Justice to the Development of International Law." *Zeitschrift für ausländisches öffentliches Recht und Völkerrecht* 76, no. 2 (2016): 425–449.

McCabe, James Dabney. *A Tour around the World by General Grant: Being a Narrative of the Incidents and Events of His Journey*. Philadelphia: The National Publishing Co., 1879.

McDougal, S. Myres. "International Law, Power, and Policy: A Contemporary Conception." *Recueil des Cours* 82 (1954): 133–259.

McLuhan, Marshall. *Understanding Media: The Extensions of Man*. Toronto: McGraw-Hill, 1964.

McWilliams, Wayne C. "Soejima Taneomi: Statesman of Early Meiji Japan, 1868–1874." PhD dissertation, University of Kansas, 1973.

"East Meets East: The Soejima Mission to China, 1873." *Monumenta Nipponica* 30, no. 3 (1975): 237–275.

Mei Ju-ao. *The Tokyo Trial and War Crimes in Asia*, 2nd ed. Singapore: Springer Nature, 2016.

Meng Guanghan, ed. *Zhengzhi Xieshang Huiyi Jilu, Shang Juan*. Chongqing: Chongqing Chubanshe, 1989.

Merlin, Philippe-Antoine. *Répertoire universel et raisonné de jurisprudence*, vol. 17. Paris: Garnery, 1827–1828.

Millard, Thomas F. *The Shantung Case at the Conference*. Shanghai: Millard's Review of the Far East, 1921.

Miller, David Hunter. *The Drafting of the Covenant*. New York: Johnson Reprint Corporation, 1969.

Ministère des Affaires Étrangères. *Documents Diplomatiques: Affaires du Tonkin. Deuxième Partie. Décembre 1882–1883*. Paris: Imprimerie Nationale, 1883.

Minzhi Shuju. *Bianzuan Guojifa Huiyi zhi Jingguo*. Shanghai: Minzhi Shuju, 1930.

Mitchell, Ryan Martínez. "International Law as Project or System?" *Georgetown Journal of International Law* 51, no. 3 (2019): 623–689.

"Chinese Receptions of Carl Schmitt since 1929." *Penn State Journal of Law and International Affairs* 8, no. 1 (2020): 181–245.

"Monroe's Shadow: League of Nations Covenant Article 21 and the Space of Asia in International Legal Order." *TWAIL Review* 2 (2021): 200–231.

"The Human Community of Fate: A Conceptual History of China's Ordoglobal Idea." *Humanity* 13, no. 3 (forthcoming 2022).

Mitsukuri Rinsho. *Kokusai Hō Ichimei Bankoku Kōhō*. Tokyo: Nishodō, 1873.

Mizuno, Norihito. "Qing China's Reaction to the 1874 Japanese Expedition to the Taiwanese Aboriginal Territories." *Sino-Japanese Studies* 16 (2009): 100–125.

Morikawa Hiroki. "In Pursuit of Peace: Zhou Gengsheng's Internationalism after the World Wars." *ZINBUN* 47 (2017): 177–194.

Morse, Hosea Ballou. *The International Relations of the Chinese Empire*, vols. 1–3. London: Longmans, Green, and Company, 1918.

Mowat, Robert Case. "From Liberalism to Imperialism: The case of Egypt 1875–1887." *The Historical Journal* 16, no. 1 (1973): 109–124.

Moyn, Samuel. "From Situated Freedom to Plausible Worlds." In *Contingency in International Law: On the Possibility of Different Legal Histories*, Ingo Venzke and Kevin John Heller, eds. Oxford: Oxford University Press, 2021: 532–541.

Müller, Andreas T. "Friedrich F. Martens on 'The Office of Consul and Consular Jurisdiction in the East.'" *European Journal of International Law* 25, no. 3 (2014): 871–891.

Nagao, Ariga. *The Red Cross Society of Japan: Its Organization and Activity in Time of Peace and War*. St. Louis, MO: Samuel F. Myerson Printing Company, 1904.

Nayar, Pramod, ed. *The Trial of Bahadur Shah Zafar*. Hyderabad: Orient Longman, 2007.

Nelson, Eric S. "Zhang Junmai's Early Political Philosophy and the Paradoxes of Chinese Modernity." *Asian Studies* 8, no. 1 (2020): 183–208.

Ni Zhengyu. *Danbo Congrong Li Haiya*. Beijing: Peking University Press, 2015.

Nippold, Otfried. *Die Gestaltung des Völkerrechts nach dem Weltkriege*. Zurich: Orell Füssli, 1917.

Nish, Ian. *The Iwakura Mission to America and Europe: A New Assessment*. Abingdon: Routledge, 2008.

Nishi Amane. *Kanban Bankoku Kōhō*. Kyoto: Chikuhōrō, 1868.

Horan Biserin-shi Bankoku Kōhō. Kyoto: Chikuhōrō, 1868.

Norman, Jerry. *A Comprehensive Manchu-English Dictionary*. Leiden: Brill, 2020.

Nussbaum, Arthur. "Frederic de Martens, Representative Tsarist Writer on International Law." *Nordic Journal of International Law* 22, no. 1 (1952): 51–66.

Ōhara Shigemi to Iwakura Tomomi, January 12, 1873. In *Iwakura Tomomi kankei monjo*, vol. 5. Tokyo: Tokyo Daigaku Shuppankai, 1968: 216–220.

Onuma Yasuaki. "When Was the Law of International Society Born?: An Inquiry of the History of International Law from an Intercivilizational Perspective." *Journal of the History of International Law* 2, no. 1 (2000): 1–66.

A Transcivilizational Perspective on International Law: Questioning Prevalent Cognitive Frameworks in the Emerging Multi-polar and Multi-civilizational World of the Twenty-First Century. Leiden: Martinus Nijhoff Publishers, 2010.

Oppenheim, Lassa. *International Law: A Treatise*, vol. 1. London: Longmans, Green, and Co., 1905.

International Law: A Treatise, 3rd ed. London: Longmans, Green, and Co., 1920.

Özsu, Umut. "Ottoman Empire." In *The Oxford Handbook of the History of International Law*, Bardo Fassbender, Anne Peters, Simone Peter, and Daniel Högger, eds. Oxford: Oxford University Press, 2012: 429–446.

"The Ottoman Empire, the Origins of Extraterritoriality, and International Legal Theory." In *The Oxford Handbook of the Theory of International Law*, Anne Orford and Florian Hoffmann, eds. Oxford: Oxford University Press, 2016: 123–137.

"The Necessity of Contingency: Method and Marxism in International Law." In *Contingency in International Law: On the Possibility of Different Legal Histories*, Ingo Venzke and Kevin John Heller, eds. Oxford: Oxford University Press, 2021: 60–76.

Paine, Sarah C. *The Sino-Japanese War of 1894–1895: Perceptions, Power, and Primacy*. Cambridge: Cambridge University Press, 2005.

Pashukanis, Evgeny. *The General Theory of Law and Marxism*. Abingdon: Routledge, 2017.

Patapan, Haig, and Yi Wang. "The Hidden Ruler: Wang Huning and the Making of Contemporary China." *Journal of Contemporary China* 27, no. 109 (2018): 47–60.

Peng Jianying. "Zhongguo Chuantong Jimi Zhengce Lüelun." *Xibe Daxue Xuebao: Zhexue (Shehui Kexue Ban)* 34, no. 1 (2004): 104–108.

Pepper, Suzanne. *Civil War in China: The Political Struggle 1945–1949*. Berkeley: University of California Press, 1978.

Perdue, Peter C. *China Marches West: The Qing Conquest of Central Eurasia*. Cambridge, MA: Harvard University Press, 2009.

Phillimore, Walter. "Appendix: Recent Schemes of Federation." In *The Committee of the League of Nations, Final Report*. Geneva: League of Nations: 1918: 8–24.

Pitts, Jennifer. *Boundaries of the International: Law and Empire*. Cambridge, MA: Harvard University Press, 2018.

Platt, Stephen R. *Imperial Twilight: The Opium War and the End of China's Last Golden Age*. New York: Alfred A. Knopf, 2018.

Politis, Nicolas. *Les Nouvelles Tendances du Droit International*. Paris: Librairie Hachette, 1927.

Proceedings and Documents of the United Nations Monetary and Financial Conference, Bretton Woods, New Hampshire, July 1–22, 1944, 2 vols. Washington, DC: United States Government Printing Office, 1948.

Qingdai Wai Zhai Shi Ziliao. Beijing: Zhonghua Renmin Gongheguo Caizheng Bu: 1988.

Qiu Zuming. "Zhuquan yu Lingtu Zhuquan." *Dongfang Zazhi* 25, no. 23 (1928): 77–80.

Rao Geping. "Wang Tieya Xiansheng he Bei Da Guojifa Yanjiusuo." *Zhongguo Guojifa Xuehui*, May 6, 2015. Available at: www.csil.cn/Director/Detail.aspx?AId=12.

Reimann, Mathias. "The Historical School against Codification: Savigny, Carter, and the Defeat of the New York Civil Code." *The American Journal of Comparative Law* 37, no. 1 (1989): 95–119.

Reinisch, August. "Investors." In *Non-state Actors in International Law*, Math Noortmann, August Reinisch, and Cedric Ryngaert, eds. London: Bloomsbury Publishing, 2015: 253–272.

Reynolds, Philip A., and Edward J. Hughes. *The Historian as Diplomat: Charles Kingsley Webster and the United Nations 1939–1946*. London: Martin Robertson, 1976.

Rolin-Jaequemyns, Gustave. "*Notes on Fallacies Peculiar to American Protectionists, or Chiefly Resorted to in America*, by Francis Lieber." *Revue de Droit International et de Léglisation Comparée* 2 (1870): 354–356.

"Proposition d'Établir un Collège Americain en Chine." *Revue de Droit International et de Législation Comparée* 4 (1872): 362–363.

"Rédaction d'un Code civile Japonais." *Revue de Droit International et de Législation Comparée* 4 (1872): 363.

"La Diplomatie Européenne à Péking." *Revue de Droit International et de Législation Comparée* 9 (1877): 401–404.

Roosevelt, Theodore. "Annual Message of the President to Congress." In *Papers Relating to the Foreign Relations of the United States*, vol. 1. Washington, DC: US Government Printing Office, 1904: xlviii.

Root, Elihu. "Basis of Protection to Citizens Residing Abroad." *American Journal of International Law* 4, no. 3 (1910): 517–528.

Röpke, Wilhelm. "Economic Order and International Law." *Receuil des Cours* 86 (1954): 207–273.

International Order and Economic Integration. Dordrecht: D. Reidel Publishing Company, 1959.

Rosenne, Shabtai, ed. *League of Nations Committee of Experts for the Progressive Codification of International Law (1925–1928): Documents Vol. 1*. New York: Oceana Publications, 1972.

Roth, Hans Ingvar. *P. C. Chang and the Universal Declaration of Human Rights*. Philadelphia: University of Pennsylvania Press, 2018.

Ruskola, Teemu. *Legal Orientalism*. Cambridge, MA: Harvard University Press, 2013.

Schlichtmann, Klaus. "Japan, Germany and the Idea of the Hague Peace Conferences." *Journal of Peace Research* 40. no. 4 (2003): 377–394.

Schluessel, Eric. *Land of Strangers: The Civilizing Project in Qing Central Asia*. New York: Columbia University Press, 2020.

Schmitt, Carl. *Der Nomos der Erde im Volkerrecht des Jus Publicum Europaeum*. Berlin: Duncker & Humblot, 1950.

"Die Lage der europäischen Rechtswissenschaft" (1950). In *Verfassungsrechtliche Aufsätze aus den Jahren 1924–1954. Materialen zu einer Verfassungslehre*, Carl Schmitt, ed. Berlin: Duncker & Humblot, 1958: 386–429.

The Nomos of the Earth in the International Law of the Jus Publicum Europaeum, trans. G. L. Ulmen. New York: Telos Press, 2003.

Schücking, Walther. "L'organisation international." *Revue générale de droit international public* 15 (1908): 5–23.

Die Organisation der Welt. Leipzig: Kröner, 1909.

Das Werk vom Haag, Erster Band: Die Staatenverband der Haager Konferenzen. Munich: Duncker & Humblot, 1912.

"Die frage der Kündigung des belgisch-Chinesischen handelsverträges von 1865." In *Die Reichsgerichtspraxis im Deutschen Rechtsleben: Festgabe der juristischen Fakultäten zum 50jährigen Bestehen des Reichsgerichts, vol. 1, Öffentliches Recht*, Otto Schreiber, ed. Berlin: Walter de Gruyter, 1929.

Schuler, Kurt, and Andrew Rosenberg, eds. *The Bretton Woods Transcripts*. New York: Center for Financial Stability, 2012.

Scott, James Brown. *The Hague Peace Conferences of 1899 and 1907*, vol. 1. Baltimore: Johns Hopkins Press, 1909.

The Hague Peace Conferences of 1899 and 1907, vol. 2. Baltimore: Johns Hopkins Press, 1909.

"The Chinese Society and Journal of International Law." *American Journal of International Law* 7, no. 1 (1913): 159–161.

ed. *American Addresses at the Second Hague Peace Conference*. Boston: World Peace Foundation, 1916.

"The Chinese Social and Political Science Association." *American Journal of International Law* 10, no. 2 (1916): 375–378.

The Reports to the Hague Conferences of 1899 and 1907. New York: Clarendon Press, 1917.

The Proceedings of the Hague Peace Conferences: Translation of the Original Texts. New York: Oxford University Press, 1920.

ed. *The Proceedings of the Hague Peace Conferences, The Conference of 1907, Vol. 2, Meetings of the First Commission*. New York: Oxford University Press, 1921.

ed., *The Proceedings of the Hague Peace Conferences, The Conference of 1907, vol. 3, Meetings of the Second, Third, and Fourth Commissions*. New York: Oxford University Press, 1921.

Sebes, Joseph. *The Jesuits and the Sino-Russian Treaty of Nerchinsk (1689): The Diary of Thomas Pereira, S. J.* Rome: Institutum Historicum, 1962.

Shaffer, Gregory, and Henry Gao, "A New Chinese Economic Order?" *Journal of International Economic Law* 23, no. 3 (2020): 607–635.

Shen Minrong. "Zhengfu, Shichang yu Jingjifa de Dingwei." PhD dissertation, Central Party School of the Chinese Communist Party, 2000.

Shi Jianguo. *Lu Zhengxiang Zhuan*. Shijiazhuang: Hebei Renmin Chubanshe, 1999.

Shibata, M., and T. Koyas, eds. *An English and Japanese Dictionary*. Yokohama: Ni-Shu-Sha Printing Office, 1873.

Shih, Vincent Y. C. "A Talk with Hu Shih." *China Quarterly* 10 (1962): 149–165.

Shotwell, James T. *Extraterritoriality in China*. New York: Institute of Pacific Relations, 1929.

Sima Qian. *Shiji quanben: Shang*. Shenyang: Wanjuan Chuban Gongsi, 2016.

Simpson, Gerry. *Great Powers and Outlaw States: Unequal Sovereigns in the International Legal Order*. Cambridge: Cambridge University Press, 2004.

Singh Chimni, Bhupinder. *International Law and World Order: A Critique of Contemporary Approaches*. Cambridge: Cambridge University Press, 2017.

Skinner, Quentin. "Meaning and Understanding in the History of Ideas." *History and Theory* 8, no. 1 (1969): 3–53.

"Meaning and Understanding in the History of Ideas." In *Meaning and Context: Quentin Skinner and His Critics*, James Tully, ed. Princeton, NJ: Princeton University Press, 1988: 29–67.

Skouteris, Thomas. "Engaging History in International Law." In *New Approaches to International Law*, José María Beneyto and David Kennedy, eds. The Hague: T. M. C. Asser Press, 2012: 99–121.

Slobodian, Quinn. *Globalists: The End of Empire and the Birth of Neoliberalism*. Cambridge, MA: Harvard University Press, 2018.

Smith, Adam. *An Inquiry into the Nature and Causes of the Wealth of Nations*, vol. 1. London: Printed for W. Strahan; and T. Cadell in the Strand, 1776.

Speranskii, Mikhail M. *Polnoe Sobranie: Zakonov Rossiiskoi Imperii s 1649 Goda, Vol. 3, 1689–1699*. St. Petersburg: Tipografiya Ego Imperatorskogo Velichestva Kantselyarii, 1830.

Spiermann, Ole. *International Legal Argument in the Permanent Court of International Justice: The Rise of the International Judiciary*. Cambridge: Cambridge University Press, 2005.

"Judge Wang Chung-hui at the Permanent Court of International Justice." *Chinese Journal of International Law* 5, no. 1 (2006): 115–128.

Stead, William T. *The Parliament of Peace and Its Members*. London: Review of Reviews, 1899.

The United States of Europe on the Eve of the Parliament of Peace. Toronto: George N. Morang, 1899.

Steiger, Heinhard. "Völkerrecht." In *Geschichtliche Grundbegriffe*, vol. 7, Otto Brunner, Werner Conze, and Reinhart Koselleck, eds. Stuttgart: Klett-Cotta, 1972–1990: 97–140.

Stranahan, Patricia. *Underground: The Shanghai Communist Party and the Politics of Survival, 1927–1937*. Lanham, MD: Rowman & Littlefield, 1998.

Strauss, Julia C. *Strong Institutions in Weak Polities: State Building in Republican China, 1927–1940*. Oxford: Clarendon Press, 1998.

Strupp, Karl. *Urkunden zur geschichte des völkerrechts*. Gotha: Friedrich Andreas Perthes, 1911.

Ausgewählte diplomatische Aktenstücke zur orientalischen Frage. Gotha: Friedrich Andreas Perthes, 1916.

Documents pour servir à l'histoire du droit des gens. Berlin: Hermann Sack, 1923.

Legal Machinery for Peaceful Change. London: Constable & Company Limited, 1937.

Sun Yat-sen. *China and Japan: Natural Friends, Unnatural Enemies*. Shanghai: China United Press, 1941.

Suttner, Bertha von. "Slow Evolution." *The Advocate of Peace* 62, no. 10 (1900): 208–209.

Memoiren von Bertha von Suttner. Stuttgart: Deutsche Verlags-Anstalt, 1909.

Memoirs of Bertha von Suttner: The Records of an Eventful Life, vol. 2. London: International School of Peace, 1910.

Suzuki Shogo. "Imagining 'Asia': Japan and 'Asian' International Society in Modern History." In *Contesting International Society in East Asia*, Barry Buzan and Yongjin Zhang, eds. Cambridge: Cambridge University Press, 2014: 51–72.

Svarverud, Rune. *International Law as a World Order in Late Imperial China: Translation, Reception and Discourse; 1847–1911*. Leiden: Brill, 2007.

Taft, William H. *Address of President Taft at the Banquet Given in His Honor by the Americus Club, Pittsburgh, P.A., May 2, 1910*. Washington, DC: Library of Congress, 1910.

Takeharu, Ōkubo. *The Quest for Civilization: Encounters with Dutch Jurisprudence, Political Economy, and Statistics at the Dawn of Modern Japan*, trans. David Noble. Leiden: Brill, 2014.

Tang Qihua. *Beijing Zhengfu yu Guoji Lianmeng*. Taipei: Dongda Tushu Gongsi, 1998.

"Qingmo Minchu Zhongguo dui 'Haiya Baohehui' zhi Canyu (1899–1917)." *Guoli Zhengzhi Daxue Lishi Xuebao* 5, no. 23 (2005): 45–49.

Bei "Feichu Bupindeng Tiaoyue" Zhebi de Beiyang Xiuyue Shi (1912–1928). Beijing: Shehui Keshue Wenxian Chubanshe, 2010.

Tchéou-Wei, Sintchar [Zhou Wei]. *Essai sur l'organisation juridique de la Société international*. Geneva: Libraire Atar, 1917.

The International Law Association. *Reports of the First Conference Held at Brussels, 1873, and of the Second Conference Held at Geneva, 1874*. London: West, Newman & Co., 1903.

Thompson, Carol L. "A History of Disarmament Proposals." *Current History* 36, no. 209 (1959): 38–43.

Tian Tao. "Wan Qing Zhishijie de Mibing Shuo." *Tianjin Shifan Daxue Xuebao (Shehui Kexue Ban)* 1 (2008): 38–43.

"Haiya He Hui zai Zhongguo de Fanxiang." *Tianjin Shifan Daxue Xuebao (Shehui Kexue Ban)* 3 (2015): 11–16.

Tomlins, Christopher. "After Critical Legal History: Scope, Scale, Structure." *Annual Review of Law and Social Science* 8, no. 1 (2012): 31–68.

Trubetskoi, G. N. *Notes of a Plenipotentiary: Russian Diplomacy and War in the Balkans, 1914–1917*. Ithaca, NY: Cornell University Press, 2016.

Tryon, James L. "International Prize Court and Code." *Yale Law Journal* 20 (1910): 604–619.

Tso Tschun Tschou [Zhou Zechun]. *Die Reformen des chinesischen Reiches in Verfassung, Verwaltung und Rechtsprechung mit Ruecksicht auf die entsprechenden Einrichtungen Europas*. Berlin: Druck von Emil Ebering, 1909.

Tsuda Mamichi. *Taisei Kokuhō Ron*. Edo: Kaiseijo, 1868.

Tsutsumi Koshiji. *Bankoku Kōhō Yakugi*. Kyoto: Zeniya Soshirō, 1868.

Tsui, Brian. *China's Conservative Revolution: The Quest for a New Order, 1927–1949*. Cambridge: Cambridge University Press, 2018.

Tuck, Richard. *The Rights of War and Peace: Political Thought and the International Order from Grotius to Kant*. Oxford: Oxford University Press, 1999.

Twiss, Travers. *Two Introductory Lectures on the Science of International Law*. London: Longman, 1856.

The Law of Nations Considered as Independent Political Communities: On the Rights and Duties of Nations in Time of Peace. Oxford: Clarendon Press, 1884.

View of the Progress of Political Economy in Europe since the Sixteenth Century. London: Longman, Brown, Green, and Longmans, 1847.

Tzouvala, Ntina. *Capitalism as Civilisation: A History of International Law*. Cambridge: Cambridge University Press, 2020.

UNDP. *Our 40 Year Journey, 1979–2019: United Nations Development Programme in China*. Geneva: UNDP, 2019.

Union Interparlementaire. *Compte rendu de la XXVe conférence tenue à Berlin du 23 au 28 août 1928*. Lausanne: Librairie Payot & Co., 1928.

Uryū Mitora. *Kōdō Kigen Ichimei Bankoku Kōhō Zensho*. Kyoto: Chikuhōrō, 1868.

Vattel, Emer de. *The Law of Nations*, trans. Joseph Chitty. London: S. Sweet and A. Maxwell, 1834.

Le Droit des Gens, ou Principes de la Loi Naturelle Appliqués a la Conduite et aux Affaires des Nations et des Souverains. Paris: J. P. Aillaud, 1835.

Vec, Miloš. "Sources in the 19th Century European Tradition: The Myth of Positivism." *European Journal of International Law* 16 (2005): 539–559.

Ven, Hans van de. "Robert Hart and Gustav Detring during the Boxer Rebellion." *Modern Asian Studies* 40, no. 3 (2006): 631–662.

Breaking with the Past: The Maritime Customs Service and the Global Origins of Modernity in China. New York: Columbia University Press, 2014.

Venzke, Ingo. "Introduction: Situating Contingency in the Path of International Law." In *Contingency in International Law: On the Possibility of Different Legal Histories*, Ingo Venzke and Kevin John Heller, eds. Oxford: Oxford University Press, 2021: 3–19.

Visscher, Charles de. "Revues de Langue Anglaise." *Revue de Droit International et de Législation Comparée* 49 (1922): 237–239.

Wade, Thomas Francis. *Note upon the Condition and Government of the Chinese Empire in 1849*. Hong Kong: China Mail Office, 1850.

Waijiaobu Bianzuan Weiyuanhui. *Zhongguo Huifu Guanshui Zhuquan zhi Jingguo* 中国恢复关税主权之经过. Beijing: Waijiaobu Bianzuan Weiyuanhui, 1929.

Wallerstein, Immanuel. *European Universalism: The Rhetoric of Power*. New York: The New Press, 2006.

The Modern World System II: Mercantilism and the Consolidation of the European World-Economy, 1600–1750. New York: Academic Press, 1980.

Wang Chung Hui [Wang Chonghui]. *The German Civil Code: Translated and Annotated with Historical Introduction and Appendices*. London: Stevens and Sons, Ltd., 1907.

"Peaceful Means for Settling International Disputes." *China Law Review* 2 (1926): 336.

"Jieshao Bijiao Faxue Guoji Huiyi." *Zhonghua Faxue Zazhi* 1, no. 2 (1930): 143–149.

Wang Ding'an. *Xiang Jun Ji*, vol. 1. Shanghai: Jiangnan Shuju, 1889.

Wang, Heng. "Selective Reshaping: China's Paradigm Shift in International Economic Governance." *Journal of International Economic Law* 23, no. 3 (2020): 583–606.

Wang Hui. *Zhongguo xiandai Sixiang de Xingqi*, 4 vols. Beijing: Sanlian Shudian, 2004.

Wang Huning "Lun Xian-Dangdai Zhuquan Lilun de Xin Fazhan." *Zhengzhixue Yanjiu* 1 (1985): 39–45.

Guojia Zhuquan. Beijing: Renmin Chubanshe, 1987.

Wang Jian "Modern Legal Periodicals of China." *Frontiers of Law in China* 2, no. 2 (2007): 318–333.

Wang Jingwei, ed. *Ouzhou Heyi Hou zhi Shijie yu Zhongguo*. Shanghai: Minzhi Shuju, 1926.

Wang Ruicheng. "The 'Outward Flow of Power' and the Evolution of the Late Qing Power Structure, 1855–1875." *Modern Chinese History Studies* 2 (2012): 28–46.

Wang Tieya. "Dulumenzhuyi yu Menluozhuyi." *Minzhu Luntan* 1, no. 9 (1947): 3–6.

"International Law in China: Historical and Contemporary Perspectives," *Recueil de Cours de L'Académie de Droit International* 221 (1990): 195–369.

Wang Tseng-Tsai, "The Audience Question: Foreign Representatives and the Emperor of China, 1858–1873." *The Historical Journal* 14, no. 3 (1971): 617–626.

Wang Yanwei and Wang Liang, eds. *Qing Ji Waijiao Shiliao*. Beijing: Shumu Wenshu Chubanshe, 1987.

Wang Yuanshen. *Sheng Dao Dong Lai Kao*. Hong Kong, self-published, 1899.

Wang Yuanchong. "Defining Chosŏn: Qing China's Depiction of Chosŏn's Status, 1862–76." In *Remaking the Chinese Empire: Manchu-Korean Relations, 1616–1911*. Ithaca, NY: Cornell University Press, 2018: 121–143.

Wang Yuanzhi, ed. *Jiaxu Gongdu Chaocun*. Taipei: Taiwan Yinhang, 1959.

Wasserstrom, Jeffrey N., ed. *Twentieth-Century China: New Approaches*. Abingdon: Routledge, 2013.

Weber, Isabella M. *How China Escaped Shock Therapy: The Market Reform Debate*. Abingdon: Routledge, 2021.

Wehberg, Hans. *The Problem of an International Court of Justice*, trans. Charles G. Fenwick. Oxford: Clarendon Press, 1918.

Wei Yuan. *Wei Yuan Quanji*, vol. 7. Changsha: Yuelu Shushe, 2004.

Wei-man Huanggong Bowuguan and Jilinnsheng Fangzhiguan. *Wei-Manzhouguo Zhimin Tongzhi Jigou Tuzhi*. Jilin: Jilin Renmin Chubanshe, 2010.

Wen Zhou. "Tan Tan Zhuquan Lun." *Zhengzhi Hui Kan* 1, no. 2 (1932): 40–57.

Wertheim, Stephen. "The League That Wasn't: American Designs for a Legalist-Sanctionist League of Nations and the Intellectual Origins of International Organization, 1914–1920." *Diplomatic History* 35, no. 5 (2011): 797–836.

Witte, Sergei. *The Memoirs of Count Witte*. Sydney Harcave, trans. and ed. Armonk, NY: ME Sharpe, 1990.

Wheaton, Henry. *Elements of International Law*, 6th ed. William Beach Lawrence, ed. Boston: Little, Brown, & Co., 1855.

Wanguo Gongfa, trans. W. A. P. Martin. Beijing: Tongwenguan, 1864.

Whelan, Daniel J. "'Under the Aegis of Man': The Right to Development and the Origins of the New International Economic Order." *Humanity* 6, no. 1 (2015): 93–108.

White, Hayden. "Foreword." In Reinhart Koselleck. *The Practice of Conceptual History: Timing History, Spacing Concepts*, trans. Todd Samuel Presner. Stanford, CA: Stanford University Press, 2002: 13–23.

Metahistory: The Historical Imagination in Nineteenth-Century Europe. Baltimore: Johns Hopkins University Press, 2014.

White, John Albert. *Transition to Global Rivalry: Alliance Diplomacy and the Quadruple Entente: 1895–1907*. Cambridge: Cambridge University Press, 2002.

Williams, Edward T. "The Relations between China, Russia, and Mongolia." *American Journal of International Law* 10, no. 4 (1916): 798–808.

Williams, S. Wells. "Christian Missions among the Chinese." In *The Middle Kingdom*, vol. 2. Leiden: Global Oriental, 2007: 275.

Willoughby, Westel W. *China at the Conference: A Report*. Baltimore: Johns Hopkins Press, 1922.

Winfield, Jordan Carlyle. "Buddhism and Insurrection in Burma, 1886–1890." *Journal of the Royal Asiatic Society* 20, no. 3 (2010): 345–367.

Winkelmann, Ingo. "Regional Groups in the UN." In *A Concise Encyclopedia of the United Nations*, 2nd ed. Helmut Volger, ed. Leiden: Martinus Nijhoff Publishers, 2010.

Wong, John Yue-wo. *Deadly Dreams: Opium and the Arrow War (1856–1860) in China*. Cambridge: Cambridge University Press, 2002.

Woodhead, Henry G. W., and Henry T. Montague Bell, *The China Year Book 1914*. London: George Routledge & Sons, 1914.

Wright, Quincy. "The Washington Conference." *American Political Science Review* 16, no. 2 (1922): 285–297.

"Opinion of the Commission of Jurists in the Janina–Corfu Affair." *American Journal of International Law* 18, no. 3 (1924): 536–544.

"The Outlawry of War and the Law of War." *American Journal of International Law* 47, no. 3 (1953): 365–376.

Wright, Richard. *The Color Curtain: A Report on the Bandung Conference*. New York: World Publishing, 1956.

Wu Ting-Fang "China's Attitude towards Arbitration." In *Report of the Annual Lake Mohonk Conference on International Arbitration*. New York: Lake Mohonk Conference on International Arbitration, 1909: 67–71.

Wu Xiping. "Jiu Guojifa zhi Quedian yu Xin Guojifa zhi Yaoqiu." *Zhongfa Daxue Yuekan* 1, no. 4 (1932): 1–14.

Xing Zhiyu. "Cong 'Shuize Tanpan' Kan He Guiqing yu Zhongyang Zhengce de Boyi." *Xue Lilun* 7 (2019): 135–138.

Xiong Xiling. "Wei Xiangsheng Xing Lun Cheng Zhang Zhidong." In *Hunan Weixin Yundong Shiliao*, Yi Feizhou, ed. Chansha: Yuelu Shushe, 2013: 223–230.

Yang Daxin, ed. *Beiyang Zhengfu Zongtong yu Zongli*. Tianjin: Nankai Daxue Chubanshe, 1989.

Yasuoka Akio. *Meiji zenki tairiku seisaku shi no kenkyū*. Tokyo: Hōsei Daigaku Shuppankyoku, 1998.

Yu Zhong. "Suowei Guoti: Xianfa Shike yu Liang Qichao de Gonghe Zaizao Shike." *Faxuejia* 4 (2015): 158–175.

Zarrow, Peter. *China in War and Revolution, 1895–1949*. Abingdon: Routledge, 2006.

After Empire: The Conceptual Transformation of the Chinese State, 1885–1924. Stanford, CA: Stanford University Press, 2012.

Zhai Qiang. "China and the Geneva Conference of 1954." *China Quarterly* 129 (1992): 103–122.

Zhang Xiruo. "Xin Zhongguo de Heping Waijiao Zhengce." *Shijie Zhishi* 40 (1952): 5–6.

Zhang Yongle. *Jiu Bang Xin Zao: 1911–1917*. Beijing: Peking University Press, 2016.

Zhang Yongxin. "Wanqing Zhongguoren de Zhuquan Guannian: Guojifa Shijiao." *Beijing Shixue* 10 (2004): 102–134.

Zhang Zhenguo. "Cong 'Wu Wu Xiancao' Dao 'Zhonghua Minguo Xianfa.'" In *Quanguo Waiguo Fazhishi Yanjiuhui Xueshu Congshu: 20 Shiji Xifang Xianzheng de Fazhan ji qi Biange*, He Qinhua, ed. Beijing: Falü Chubanshe, 2004.

Zhang Zhidong. *Quan Xue Pian*. Changsha: Liang Hu Shu Yuan, 1898.

Zheng Guanying. *Sheng Shi Wei Yan*. Shenyang: Liaoning Renmin Chubanshe, 1994.

Zhongguo Di Er Lishi Dang'an Guan. "Lu Zhengxiang Chuxi Haiya Baohehui Zouzhe Liang Jian." *Minguo Dang'an* 2 (2000): 37–42.

Zhonguo Shehui Kexue Yuan Jindaishi Yanjiusuo. *Yang Ru Geng-Xin Cun Gao*. Beijing: Zhongguo Shehui Kexue Chuban, 1979.

Zhou Gengsheng. "Juwai Zhongli Tiaogui Pingyi." *Jiayin Zazhi* 1, no. 8 (1915): 1–16.

"Zhong-E Jiaoshe Ping." *Jiayin Zazhi* 1, no. 10 (1915): 1–8.

"Gonghe Zhengzhi Lun." *Jiayin Zazhi* 1, no. 10 (1915): 1–17.

"Zongzhuquan Lun." *Taipingyang* 1, no. 10 (1918): 1–13.

"Wanguo Tongmeng zhi San Da Yiyi." *Taipingyang* 2, no. 1 (1919): 43–48.

"Zhanqian Zhanhou de Guoji Zhengju." *Taipingyang* 2, no. 5 (1920): 1–16.

"Wanguo Lianmeng yu Qiangzhi Hejie." *Taipingyang* 2, no. 9 (1920): 1–9.

Bupingdeng Tiaoyue Shijiang. Shanghai: Taipingyang Shudian, 1928.

Guoji Gongfa zhi Xin Fazhan. Shanghai: Shangwu Yinshuguan, 1934.

"Zhongguo de Guoji Diwei." *Mei Zhou Pinglun* 146 (1934): 18–24.

"1935 Nian zhi Zhanwang: Guolian de Qiantu." *Dongfang Zazhi* 32, no. 1 (1935): 25–29.

"Zhanhou de Nanyang." *Nanyang Yanjiu* 11, no. 1 (1943): 79–82.

Xiandai Guojifa de Sixiang Dongxiang. Beijing: Shijie Zhishi Chubanshe, 1963.

Guojifa. Beijing: Shangwu Yinshuguan, 1983.

Zhou Wei. "1919 Nian Hou zhi Guoji Gongfa." *Xu Wu* 35 (1919): 18–21.

Xin Guoji Gongfa. Shanghai: Shangwu yinshu guan, 1930.

Zhou Ziya. "Yi Ge Zhuyi Yi Ge Zhengfu Yi Ge Lingxiu." *Minyi* (Hankou) 36 (1938): 11.

"Zenyang Yanjiu Guoji Gongfa." *Xin Renshi* 9, no. 2 (1944): 13–31.

Meiguo Meizhou yu Shijie. Shanghai: Shangwu Yinshuguan, 1946.

"Cong Guojifa Lichang Lun Meijun Baoxing zhi Xingzhi ji Waiguo Jundui zhi Xingshi Guanxia Wenti." *Guancha* 1, no. 23 (1947): 4–7.

"Aobenhai Guojifa Pingjia." *Faxue* 1 (1957): 3.

"Chuncui Fa Xueshuo Zhong de 'Falü', 'Guojia', he 'Zhengyi'." *Xiandai Waiguo Zhexue Shehui Kexue Wenzhai* 8 (1961): 37–38.

"Ping Chuncui Fa Xueshuo He Ta de Chuangshiren Kaierxun." *Shehui Kexue* 1 (1979): 111–114.

Zhou Ziya and Luo Shipei. "Cong 'Guojia Quanli' Zouxiang 'Shijie Quanli': Gaizao Shijie de Yi Ge Jiben Yuanze." *Zhongyang Zhoukan* 8, no. 4 (1946): 5.

Zhu Chuangyu, ed. *Wang Chonghui Zhuanji Ziliao*, vols. 1–3. Taipei: Tian Yi Chubanshe, 1979.

Zhu Xueshan. "Cong 'Yi Wen Hui You' Tan Qi: Xiao Yi Zhongguo Guoji Jingjifa Xuehui Zishen Jianshe Wenti." *Guoji Jingji Fa Xue Kan* 4 (2004): 417–422.

Zhu, Yuan Yi. "Suzerainty, Semi-sovereignty, and International Legal Hierarchies on China's Borderlands." *Asian Journal of International Law* 10, no. 2 (2020): 293–320.

Zuo Zongtang. "Preface." In *Lin Wen Zhong Gong Zheng Shu*. Shanghai: Shangwu Yinshuguan, 1935.

Index

Printed in the USA
CPSIA information can be obtained
at www.ICGtesting.com
LVHW071915170224
772113LV00005B/131

9 781108 498968